2011

"Anthony Le Donne's *Historical Jesus* is among the most remarkable of recent efforts to comprehend Jesus historically. Engaging, informative, and provocative, the book is at once a brilliant portrait of the historical Jesus and a valuable contribution to social memory scholarship. Le Donne's 'postmodern paradigm,' which includes an astute analysis of perception and memory, transcends postmodernism itself. . . . No one can read Le Donne's book and fail to think in new ways about the historical Jesus."

— Barry Schwartz
University of Georgia

"Some philosophers of history have underscored how closely interwoven are history as a narrative and the meaning attached to that history by those who tell it. History is not just the record of events but is inherently a matter of perspective. Anthony Le Donne here sets out in clear and accessible terms how this critical view of history has begun to exert a dramatic impact on our assessments of Jesus."

— Bruce Chilton
Bard College

"As a rule postmodernism means historical skepticism. . . . Le Donne opens the door to the past again, not by refusing postmodern historiography but by applying its insights. If all reality is interpretive reality — perception, memory, and history — it is possible to make responsible statements on the past and on the historical Jesus. His book is a convincing plea against historical resignation — written with lucidity, esprit, and common sense."

— Gerd Theissen
University of Heidelberg

D0050500

HISTORICAL JESUS

What Can We Know and
How Can We Know It?

Anthony Le Donne

William B. Eerdmans Publishing Company
Grand Rapids, Michigan / Cambridge, U.K.

Published 2011 by
Wm. B. Eerdmans Publishing Co.
2140 Oak Industrial Drive N.E., Grand Rapids, Michigan 49505 /
P.O. Box 163, Cambridge CB3 9PU U.K.

Printed in the United States of America

16 15 14 13 12 11   7 6 5 4 3 2 1

Library of Congress Cataloging-in-Publication Data

Le Donne, Anthony, 1975-
Historical Jesus: what can we know and how can we know it? /
Anthony Le Donne.
p.   cm.
Includes bibliographical references.
ISBN 978-0-8028-6526-7 (pbk.: alk. paper)
1. Jesus Christ — Historicity.   I. Title.

BT303.2.L38   2011
232.9′08 — dc22
                                        2010049780

www.eerdmans.com

to the Habibis,
for ten years of decadence

Contents

CONTENTS

PART THREE

Foreword

I am happy to commend this volume, whose significance is greater than its slim size might intimate. Le Donne has much to teach us.

Perhaps the chief virtue of *Historical Jesus* is that its author fully recognizes the complexity of historical reconstruction. For far too long, New Testament scholars have operated with simplistic antitheses, such as event vs. interpretation, memory vs. legend, fact vs. fiction. They have also been overly and vainly confident in their own abilities to strip away the supposed secondary interpretations in the gospels so as to reveal the historical events beneath. But, as Origen shrewdly observed long ago, it has always been exceedingly difficult to show that a recorded event took place, even if it did take place. No less importantly, and as Le Donne patiently explains at length, recent study of human perception puts the lie to our convenient, traditional dichotomies. So too does postmodern historiography, which undoes so many of our old methods and presuppositions. It is time to rethink much.

Le Donne helps us to do this, as he explains that memories of Jesus were memories of perceptions of him, and then elucidates how all perception is — in part because it is always social — inevitably distorted and shot through with interpretation from beginning to end. One important implication is that the gospels cannot be what so many Christians have naively assumed them to be, namely, something like courtroom transcripts. At the same time, it turns out that skepticism which justifies itself by appeal to the undeniable fact that the gospels overflow with interpretation is also naive. Interpretation may always distort, but without interpretation there is no memory and so no past, no possibility of doing history at all. Le Donne effectively makes this point throughout the book, stressing that "the more significant a memory is, the more interpreted it will become."

He also unveils for us the nature of history by contemplating what its custodians, that is, critical historians, really do. Although they preserve perceptions from and of the past, they do this by discussing what seems relevant to them, by imposing their own categories upon their materials, and by ignoring what they find of little or no value. So as they focus their eyes on what has gone before, they also, at least implicitly, engage the present — which is, upon reflection, not so far from what the original tradents of the Jesus tradition did. Furthermore, and again like those tradents, historians of Jesus interpret and reinterpret previous interpretations and reinterpretations.

This last point is especially important for the study of Jesus. Contemporary historians recognize that the gospel writers theologize events, that they construe Jesus typologically, and that they interpret the events in his life in terms of this scriptural text or that Jewish theologoumenon. None of this, however, entails that we cannot learn about Jesus of Nazareth from them. Within an ancient Jewish context, memories of Jesus had to be theologized, construed typologically, and interpreted in the light of religious tradition. Otherwise he would have been forgotten. Thus typology is not just a literary device but a strategy of memory. Beyond that, Jesus and those who knew him must also, while he was yet alive, have construed his ministry within a religious narrative framework, which surely ups the odds that many of the interpretive strategies of the post-Easter period go back to the pre-Easter period. Indeed,

Le Donne plausibly contends that, "by appealing to and mimicking Scripture, Jesus himself often defined the pattern by which . . . memories would be refracted." The implications of this are considerable.

Likewise significant, although it may prove troubling for some, is the homage Le Donne pays to imagination in historical reconstruction. The central role that our subjectivity plays means that Cartesian certainty is out the window, that objectivity is a mirage, and that our imaginations are inexorably involved in finding Jesus. Our vocation is not to emulate Sergeant Joe Friday, whose watchword was, "Just the facts, ma'am" — although we certainly cannot do without facts. We should rather aspire to be the best storytellers we can be; that is, our goal is to construct narratives that plausibly account for the various and sometimes conflicting interpretations in our sources. It is precisely when we come to understand and try to account for the competing agendas of the evangelists and their predecessors that we can find our way with assurance to the historical Jesus.

It follows that we do not proceed by peeling away early Christian interpretations of Jesus. Rather, we seek to gain our "approximate image of the past" by, first, scouring the extant interpretations for large memory patterns and then, second, trying to account for their existence. In other words, we do not construct the historical Jesus by discarding editorial agendas and theological reflections but instead by explaining those agendas and reflections.

All of this may sound a bit abstract, but Le Donne brings his points home by tackling several interesting problems having to do with Jesus. For instance, he considers John 2:1-11, where Jesus rebukes his mother after she asks him for more wine; Mark 3:21, 31-35, where Jesus insults his family, including his mother; and Luke 11:27-28, where Jesus, upon hearing someone say, "Blessed is the womb that bore you and the breasts that nursed you!," responds with this: "Blessed rather are those who hear the word of God and obey it!"

(cf. Gospel of Thomas 79). Le Donne finds a memory pattern embedded in these three seemingly independent texts. That pattern may be elaborated differently in each text, but all three presuppose that Jesus was at odds with his family, especially his mother. Le Donne then argues that whereas, on the one hand, this memory pattern would not have come into being without real mnemonic warrant, on the other hand Christians remembered the awkward circumstance precisely because it brought comfort to individuals whose faith commitments had alienated them from their families.

Now all of this makes good sense to me, but Le Donne goes a step further. He asks, Why did Jesus not get along with his immediate family? His answer is: Mary had high hopes for Jesus. She believed that her son was destined for great things. She accordingly projected her aspirations onto him: he was to be her means to social status. Jesus, however, had other things in mind.

All this could be correct. But one can tell another story, too. Mary's husband and Jesus' father, Joseph, never shows up during the ministry. Nor does he, unlike his wife in Acts, put in an appearance as a member of the early church. It is a very good guess, then, that he died before his son became a public figure. This matters because, if Jesus was Mary's first-born, as the gospels assume, his family would surely have expected him to stay at home and take his father's place, to become the new, surrogate *paterfamilias*. If he instead chose, because of a religious calling, to hit the road, to become an itinerant preacher, his mother and siblings might well have been displeased. And maybe this was the source of their conflict.

I do not see how to decide such an issue as this with much confidence. One story may be true, the other false. Or both stories may be false. Or perhaps both have some truth in them. Yet this only brings home one of Le Donne's major points, which is that we have to give up old-fashioned certainty. "Historians make decisions that essentially create stories"; and often different historians are going to come up with different stories to explain the same memory pattern; and sometimes we are going to be hard put to judge which story among the competitors is the best. From which it follows that humility seems to be in order — but then that is exactly one of the lessons we otherwise learn from Le Donne's exposition of postmodern historiography.

I have thus far commended the content of this book. But I cannot sign off without saying a word about its style. *Historical Jesus* is a pleasure to read. The writing is clear, the phrases well-turned. Beyond that, the whole is enlivened by engaging, instructive, and often personal illustrations. Plainly the author has not just labored over what he has to say: he has equally worked hard on how to say it. The result is that this volume, again and again, turns the obscure into the obvious. Would that more in the guild were as self-conscious about communicating and felt the imperative to write so well.

Le Donne has given us a good book. Let us hope it is a good book at the right time, so that it gains appreciative readers, among them historians of early Christianity, who will go and do likewise.

DALE C. ALLISON JR.

In Gratitude

This book is a very narrow slice of what others have invested in me. I offer my deepest thanks

to Sarah, who has the best laugh in the history of laughs,
to the Big Nasty and his lovely wife,
to Chad Carmichael, Kevin Foster, Chris Keith, Tara Le Donne, Ed Peacock, Christopher Simpson, and Tim Stafford; their generous critique shaped this book in helpful ways,
to the academic midwifery of James Dunn and John Barclay; I promise to pretend to be erudite in my next book,
to Dale Allison for adding considerable clout to this project,
to Michael Thomson and the fine folks at Eerdmans,
and
to Andy Almlie, Mark Almlie, Stephen Ausburne, Matthew Curtis, Nathan Strong, Jason Swain, and one good hoof, to whom this book is dedicated.

Mr. Isaac Newton tested everything
Poked and prodded, then said
"Solid things are as real as they seem"
Mr. Albert Einstein pondered light and speed
And with his mind's eye, declared "oh my,
This is a world of dreams"

Peter Mayer, "World of Dreams"

Beginnings

Enveloping the earliest antiquity, so remote from ourselves, there shines the eternal and never failing light of a truth beyond all question: that the world of civil society has certainly been made by men, and that its principles are therefore to be found within the modifications of our own mind.

Giambattista Vico

Beginning with the historical Jesus would be the most entertaining way to start this book. After all, if Jesus isn't the most important figure in history, he's at least the most interesting. Jesus' face still covers more magazines than any contemporary political leader, rock star, or social pariah. Following the adage that controversy sells, I could launch right into Jesus' sexual identity, his politics, or his tortured psyche. Starting with something like his dysfunctional relationship with his mother might catch a few more casual readers.

These topics interest me and will be explored in this book. But if I led off with any of these, you wouldn't trust me. You wouldn't trust me because you'd be suspicious that this book was just one more attempt to shock you — and your suspicion would be warranted. Writers who try to shock their readers are usually more interested in attention seeking than they are with the integrity of their task. That is why this book won't begin with a telling of Jesus' life. I, of course, do want your attention, but not at the expense of your trust. So rather than beginning with a historical portrait of Jesus, this book will begin with the philosophical questions that guide the postmodern historian.

This book is called "Historical Jesus." These two words set together represent my two goals: (1) The *how* and *why* of historical theory and method and (2) the *what* of Jesus. So before I tell you *what* happened in the life of Jesus, I will explain *how* and *why* the historian can make these claims with any degree of confidence. I want you, the reader, to know why I approach history the way I do so that when I speak about Jesus, you can trace my steps.

Studying ancient history, especially religious history, is a very difficult task. It's often hard to tell which stories originated from human perception and which stories originated from legend. Indeed, sometimes it's a combination of both! In order to wade through all of the agendas and motives of the storytellers (both past and present), the conscientious historian must begin with a philosophical framework. The historian must have some working theory of the nature of history — what it is, what it isn't, what we bring to the task, and what to expect from it. In order to do justice to the "Jesus of history," I have to know *what* it is that I'm looking for, *how* to go about looking for it, and *why*. Unless some philosophical groundwork is laid, the historian will unwittingly create a history without the appropriate historical context. We call this philosophical groundwork "the philosophy of history" or "historiography."[1]

This book uses a philosophy that takes seriously the concerns of postmodern thought. In doing so I will make Jesus' life accessible to those who have abandoned the notion of historical certainty. The historical Jesus, once obscured by modern philosophy of history, is now a live subject of historical research from a postmodern perspective.

At this point, you may want to choose your own adventure. If

4

you have no interest in academic delimitation, please do yourself a favor and skip the rest of this introduction. The rest of this chapter will be about defining terms and answering the common questions of specialists. It's only a few pages, but you may prefer to use that time smelling flowers. I recommend freesias. When you're finished, Part One awaits you on page 11.

What Makes It Postmodern?

The word "postmodern" is often maligned and even more often misunderstood. Having used this term several times already, I risk being maligned and misunderstood — of this I am well aware. If the word is evil, I am convinced it is necessary nonetheless. I prefer to use this word as an adjective because the nouns "postmodernity" and "postmodernism" tend to confuse people.[2] It can be confusing because most "isms" refer to an established system of propositions or beliefs. This is not the case with postmodernism.[3] There is no unified system of propositions or beliefs that can define "postmodernism" clearly. To understand what makes something "postmodern" requires an understanding of what made the forerunner of that thing "modern."

Consider the following examples: modern medicine, modern architecture, and modern dance. Is there a philosophical umbrella big enough to cover these examples? What makes each of these an example of "modernism" is dramatically different. It might be said that each of these examples represents a "minimalist" approach. But what makes modern medicine minimal is much different than what makes modern architecture minimal.[4] A building reduced to its most primary shapes looks much different than a medical patient reduced from a human to a mere subject. As such, the consequences of reduction are much different. And minimalism is only one concept associated with "modernism." My point here is that "modernism" has so many diverse expressions that it is difficult to find a common philosophical system to connect them all adequately.

This makes "postmodernism" even more elusive. For something to be considered *post*modern, it must have reacted in some way against a modern approach. So what that thing has reacted against will determine what makes it postmodern.

What I am specifically interested in is postmodern philosophy of history — that is, the ways in which contemporary philosophers of history have reacted against previously "modern" presuppositions, theories, and methods of doing history. More than that, I will emphasize certain aspects of postmodern thought that I consider most helpful for doing historical Jesus research. In short, you will be getting my take on the key issues of the philosophy of history.

Admittedly, I will be standing on the shoulders of important philosophers and using their work to achieve my own aims — and, in some cases, I will be using their work in ways that they may not approve (or wouldn't have). But, as students of philosophy and biblical studies will already know, this kind of unsolicited departure from former ideas is nothing new. I want to make this clear from the start, as I will be leaning heavily on a few philosophers that were thoroughly modern in their outlook, yet their work remains relevant and useful to postmodern thought.

Applying Postmodern Ideas to a Pre-modern Jesus

There is another issue that deserves mention before moving forward. There will be those who question the validity of applying a contemporary philosophy (in this case, postmodern historiography) to ancient history. This may seem anachronistic to some. I need to make it clear that I am not trying to say that Jesus or his followers had a postmodern vision of the world.[5] The society in which Jesus was raised had a "pre-modern" outlook. This fact does not hinder us from applying new insights into human perception, interpretation, memory, etcetera to previous time periods. Presumably, Socrates[6] didn't know the anatomy of the human eye. This doesn't mean that the anatomy of Socrates' eyes was different than what we know of the human eye today. In this limited way, we now know more of how he viewed the world than he did.[7]

In this book I will examine the natures of human perception, memory, and history. I will be asking questions like *to what extent do we perceive what we expect to perceive?* And *how much creativity is required to remember what we've perceived?* When I ask such questions (and work toward answers), I am attempting to analyze something common to the human experience. Surely, to some extent, Italian philosopher Giambattista Vico (1668-1744) was correct to suggest that the best link we have to ancient history is through the examination of the human mind.[8] If it is safe to assume some continuity of human experience between the ancients and ourselves, we are justified in applying new theories to previous eras. And even more so with Jesus and his contemporaries, since they stand midway between ourselves and what we might call "pre-history."

Why Even Try?

Some parts of this book may trouble readers with a strongly conservative faith. Some might cringe at the notion of Jesus' psyche or his sexuality because they believe in Jesus' divine nature in a way that ignores his humanity. To shock is not my intention. I would gently remind readers that an "orthodox" understanding of Jesus has always asserted that he was *fully* human, however paradoxical this might seem. As a historian, I agree with this position of orthodoxy: Jesus *was* fully human and therefore can be analyzed as a historical figure.

The subject of the historical Jesus also risks alienating those hostile to traditional Christianity. This reader might find Jesus objectionable from the start, and hope that the emphasis on his humanity will debunk his place in Christian theology. I would remind this reader that the study of Jesus' sexuality, inner conflicts, or the limits of his knowledge will not offend the vast majority of Christians. I hope that this book might be a good place to bracket hostilities and find some common ground. After all, history is the property of all people regardless of bias.

The very fact that you're reading this book suggests that you're interested in Jesus as a historical figure. So perhaps I'm preaching to the choir. But there is need to answer two challenges often voiced against the enterprise of historical Jesus research. The first challenge (or series of challenges) goes something like this:

> What is the point of trying to study Jesus as a historical figure? Jesus' relevance to society is that he can be personally known through religious experience. And those who do not approach Jesus via faith will be blocked by the fact that our best historical documents are *faith* texts. So either you accept Jesus by faith or you end up dismantling the historical sources by removing all of the faith elements from them. There is simply no point in trying to study a pre-Christian Jesus. We only know of Jesus through the witness of early Christians or those reacting against early Christians. Therefore, the Jesus of history is largely unknowable, but "Jesus Christ" is knowable and it is Jesus *as Christ* that matters.[9]

In response, it must be said that there is no need to draw a line between the text as a document of faith and the same text as a document of history. Those who attempt to arrive at a non-religious historical Jesus do not follow the advice of any contemporary philosophy of history. These interpreters do not strip away religious elements from the gospels because they are hostile to Christianity; they do so because they are poor historians.

Also, I must remind Christians that Jesus is not the property of Christianity. Nor are the "faith texts" of Christianity only the property of the Christian church. Such a stance excludes all voices outside Christianity from the historical dialogue. To the contrary, the topic of the historical Jesus actually provides a good meeting place for those otherwise divided by faith. This topic continues to attract interest from those of many faiths and of no faith at all. Christians who wish to understand their faith within the context of their culture ought to take the historical Jesus more seriously.

The second challenge goes something like this:

What is the point of trying to look at the history *behind* the gospels? The gospels need to be studied from a *literary* perspective. Treating the gospels as historical sources only deconstructs their literary integrity.

In response to the second challenge, I must argue that studying the history behind the gospels does not necessarily undermine their literary integrity. I most often hear this challenge from scholars who have become discontented with 300 years of "historical criticism." This group has rightly seen that a historical-critical approach[10] to the gospels has often been more concerned with the recognition of sources and has tended to neglect the books as holistic compositions. I could not agree more. However, I think that the pendulum toward literary criticism[11] has swung a bit too far. We can study Mathew, Mark, Luke, and John as literary units and also use these books as sources for the historical Jesus. One does not preclude the other.

Perhaps more importantly, I think it is important for a literary approach to acknowledge that the gospel writers are collectors of tradition. Because of this, they often neglect to develop fully the details introduced by their predecessors (those who passed on the stories of Jesus to them). Many of the subjects mentioned in the gospels are underdeveloped. Unless there is some acknowledgment of this, the reader will be frustrated by the text's tendency to introduce certain subjects without further explanation.[12] For this reason, I think it unwise to throw out historical criticism in favor of literary criticism. Both are needed in biblical studies.

One last comment to both of the above challenges: Jesus' historical context is important because it is the only anchor that resists the misuse of his name and words (and the authority that comes with these). For example, I wish there had been more attention to Jesus' Jewishness among German scholars in the 1930s.[13] Nazi anti-Semitism and the Lutheran Church might not have been as easily married if Jesus had not become supra-historical.

What This Book Will Not Do

There is no doubt that Jesus is much more than just a historical figure. He is perhaps the most culturally diverse icon in the world. He is a psychological archetype. To many he represents a corrupt religious/political establishment. To many others he is Lord. For better or worse, he is much more now than he was when he walked among the people of Judea.

This book does not attempt to survey all the things that Jesus *is now* — I am concerned primarily with Jesus as he was remembered by his contemporaries. Surely there must be some overlap, some continuity between his historical presence and his historical impact. This will be discussed in due course, but first we start at the beginning: *What does it mean that Jesus was a "historical" figure?*

It may take a while to answer this question fully, but I think that a good preliminary answer might be something like this: *Jesus was perceived in time and space and was remembered.* What follows will attempt to unpack this.

Part One

When we investigate the highest heavens
They seem to race away faster than we can follow
And when we penetrate the heart of atoms
We find there something strangely resembling
Nothing at all

Peter Mayer

Totally Mental?

To speak of studying the mind of Jesus from within may seem presumptuous; but no other method is of the slightest value.

R. G. Collingwood

Was Jesus ever married? Did he ever have sex? Did he have sexual thoughts? He wasn't genderless, was he? Sexuality is a prerequisite of gender, isn't it? Did Jesus have a sexual identity?

How self-aware was Jesus anyway? Did Jesus think he was a messiah? Did he think he was more than a messiah? Did he have a divinity complex? Did Jesus' mother think he was *from* God? Did she tell him this? What kind of person would do that to a kid?! Was Jesus a psychological mess? Did people think that he was crazy?

Wasn't Jesus' family life just a big cover-up? Didn't his followers try to keep embarrassing details about Jesus a secret? Aren't the stories about Jesus just fictions? Weren't they invented to illustrate disputes between early Christians? If there did happen to be "historical" stories in the Bible, how would we know? Wouldn't it be impossible to separate the memory-stories from the made-up-stories?

Does the Bible provide us with any historical data that tells of Jesus' personal goals? Did he really aspire to be an exorcist? Did Jesus' contemporaries believe that he could bring about acts of God? The supernatural? What could lead somebody to such a belief? What would it take to convince you that you just saw a supernatural event? Is it even a matter of convincing? Or is it something more primary — some primary conception of reality embedded in the mind of the perceiver?

Thinking from the Outside In

Science is nothing but perception.

Plato

The question that kicks off this discussion goes like this: *How does a person gain access to her thoughts?* Or, put another way, *how does a person relate to his mental content?* As questions go, this is one of the most foundational. Our relationship to the world around us — people, things, ideas — is all filtered through our thoughts. We relate to the rest of the world based on our thoughts, whether they are conscious or subconscious. So in order to relate to people, things, and ideas we must relate in some way to our own mental content.[1] The question is *how?*

I start with this question because, once upon a time, Jesus made a historical impact that was *perceived* by his contemporaries. Indeed, even before Jesus became a historical figure, he was the object of people's perceptions. In other words, people saw his actions, heard his words, felt his touch. Therefore it will be necessary to have some understanding of how perception functions. It is perception that shapes the nature of Jesus' impact from the very beginning.

In order to provide a postmodern perspective to this discussion, we must first dialogue with the quintessential herald of modern philosophy, René Descartes (1596-1650). I must briefly qualify my comments by saying that these few paragraphs will not sum up the key points of Descartes' legacy. Those unfamiliar with Descartes will need to go elsewhere to learn more about his most influential ideas.[2] I will not introduce his general impact. I begin instead with just one concept that Descartes championed: the mind's eye.

Like most philosophers (both ancient and contemporary), Descartes measured his own ideas first and foremost with the ideas of Socrates, and Plato (c. 427-348 BCE). Plato taught that the content of a person's mind (knowledge/science) was remembered by the "preservation of perception."[3] Plato's mentor, Socrates (c. 469-399 BCE), described this in visual terms, "Just as we make impressions from seal rings; and whatever is imprinted we remember and know as long as its image lasts."[4] This concept of *seeing* mental *images* the way the eye sees physical objects was passed on for generations. Descartes inherited this model at the dawn of the modern world.

Now, there can be no doubt that visualization is an important function of the human mind; I have no problem with the *metaphor* of "seeing" our thoughts. But we run into trouble when this process is oversimplified. Our minds are complex beyond any single metaphor. I think that an oversimplification on this point is where Descartes went wrong.

Descartes believed that people have a rather simple (or direct) relationship with their thoughts. He argued that people have the capacity to gain access to their thoughts in the same way that they can perceive by seeing (seeing was considered to be a direct, simple, and immediate sensation).[5] Descartes held that a person's ability to relate to his own thoughts is without error. He *did* allow for errors due to lapses in judgment like prejudice or an overdependence on physical sensation, but for Descartes, these were considered exceptions to the rule. His "rule" was that you have a front-row seat to what is going on inside your mind and that you can "see" this content simply and clearly.

Philosopher Bertrand Russell (1872-1970), for the most part, agreed with Descartes and took this idea a step further. He argued that a person's relationship to his/her thoughts is direct, without error and *non-perspectival,* meaning that there is no barrier, filter, or lens between you and your thoughts. In other words, no perspective is needed to be introspective.

Russell also suggested that a person is able to "suppose" or "judge" without any influence from the outside world. You might recognize the problems with this model straight away. But before we dismiss Descartes and Russell too hastily, let us consider if there might be good reasons for describing mental content like they do.

Take, for example, the experience of pain. When you experience pain, you don't say, "I *think* this hurts!" No, you say, "This hurts!" Seemingly, people do not need to *think about* whether or not they hurt — they just hurt. Whatever thoughts are involved in the experience of pain are (so it seems) immediate and without the need of "perspective."

This line of reasoning may seem intuitive, but it cannot be taken too far before it becomes problematic. Because in order to deal with pain, people must *interpret* their pain. Perhaps a more specific example of pain will be helpful:

Imagine that a person, we'll call him Jason, is in a nasty car accident. He bought a red convertible during his midlife crisis and flipped it. Imagine that Jason's toes are crushed in the accident and that he is knocked unconscious. He is rushed to the hospital and the surgeon is forced to amputate the better part of both his feet. Jason eventually regains consciousness and declares, "Good grief, I feel horrible! I have a stomachache, my jaw is sore, and my toes hurt!"

Now, if Jason had not mentioned his "toes," there would be no reason to correct him. No doctor with any bedside manner would say, "I'm sorry, my dear fellow, you only *think* that your jaw hurts." No doctor I wish to know would *ever* say, "You poor confused man! It would be more correct to say that your relationship with your mental content has caused you to *interpret* a stomachache." We just don't casually think of our mental content (in this case, pain) like this. And even if we did, it would be a boorish thing to say. Nobody appreciates overcomplication! And yet, the doctor is forced to say something remarkably similar to this in response to Jason's relationship to his "toe pain."

The doctor must tell Jason that he is actually feeling what amputees refer to as "ghost pain." Since Jason no longer has toes, he cannot be experiencing pain in his toes. And yet his severed nerve endings are still transmitting signals of pain that his brain interprets as toe pain. So the doctor has to explain, "You only *think* that your toes hurt. . . ." The doctor has to *teach* Jason something about human anatomy for him to properly interpret his pain. Jason's experience of his pain is now guided by his relationship to a doctor who is "external," a member of the world outside his mind. In reality, Jason's thought-world was guided by the outside world from the beginning, but he had not considered this before he needed help interpreting his sense of touch. While most thought processes seem intuitive, Jason's situation shows that there is a much more complicated reality behind every perception.

. . . there is no thought, no feeling, no conception of mental content that presents itself to the person without interpretation.

My point is not that people shouldn't trust their thoughts. *My point is that every thought, conscious or subconscious, is the result of interpretation and has some relationship with the external world —*

other people, things, ideas. It's not that Jason's nerves were lying to his brain. Generally speaking, his brain was interacting with his nervous signals in the same way in each case of pain. He had no reason to mistrust his jaw pain or his stomachache. It just so happened that, in the case of his toes, Jason had no previous frame of reference from which to judge the kind of pain that he was experiencing. His mental content was therefore categorized as "toe pain" — the brain's closest frame of reference.

Contrary to Descartes and Russell, there is no thought, no feeling, no conception of mental content that presents itself to the person without interpretation. Even our most "direct" and "immediate" thoughts must be categorized in order to make sense of them. And the fact is, much of this interpretation (via category recognition) happens on a subconscious level.

Culture Focus A: Jesus Was a Jew

Most of our stories about Jesus come from what Christians call the *New Testament*. The NT is a collection of narratives, letters, and visions that constitutes the final one-fourth of most Bibles. Some of these books were written as early as fifteen years after Jesus died. Some of this material was written as late as 100 years after.

What is often overlooked is the fact that the NT was composed, for the most part, by deeply religious Jews. There are a few exceptions, but most of the books in the NT were composed by Jews, for Jews, about matters of Jewish theology. This is because Jesus' first followers, his first audiences, his first adversaries, and his first believers and skeptics were Jewish folk. So in order to understand Jesus' words, we must try to hear him as his contemporaries heard him. We must try to understand Jesus as he intended to be understood in that context. No doubt, each member of Jesus' audience saw and heard him differently, but what they all had in common was a particular culture. And in Jesus' context, culture and religion were not often separated.

For example, before Jesus was well known, he was baptized by a popular teacher named John. Now, in our context, baptism is an act of conversion. But in that context, baptism was a purification ritual. It was meant to prepare people to worship the God of Israel. Jesus was a Jew, and he never converted.

Philosopher Tyler Burge has argued that mental content is dependent upon the relationship between individual persons and the external world. We get our categories from the things, people, and ideas in our environment. Burge's position is known as *Externalism,* or *Anti-Individualism,* as he argues against the overly individualistic stance of Descartes. Burge's position has become the dominant position on this matter among analytic philosophers.

I did my doctoral work in England. This required two educations, one having to do with theology and the other with British culture. And perhaps the most important thing to learn about any culture is what to call dessert. In Britain, dessert is called "pudding." It doesn't matter if it's cake, pie, truffles, or chocolate goo. "Pudding" is a general word that denotes the sweet part of the meal that arrives after the main course. This is relevant to my discussion of mental content because of the interesting problem created by this cultural category.

To an American, "pudding" is a much narrower category. Pudding is gelatinous. It is generally eaten with a spoon. It is most often chocolate, vanilla, butterscotch, or tapioca. It is the stuff that Bill

Cosby advertises. Chocolate cheesecake with blackberry topping is *not* pudding. When I order chocolate cheesecake with blackberry topping from an American menu, I don't *think* that I am going to get pudding. On the other hand, if the Queen orders chocolate cheesecake with blackberry topping, she thinks that she's going to get "pudding." Because, for her, chocolate cheesecake with blackberry topping *is* "pudding." The point is that the nature of your thought is dependent upon your relationship to your external environment. As mentioned already, this is what philosophers call *Externalism* or *Anti-Individualism*.

When you think about an individual thing (e.g., pudding) you have to separate that individual thing from other mental categories. This is what philosophers call *Individuation*. When in the USA, I individuate pie from pudding upon recognition. But when I am in the UK, I recognize pie as "pudding." Those that argue for Anti-Individualism are not merely saying that words have different meanings in different contexts. Anti-Individualism is the idea that people's *thoughts* are dependent on their relationships with the outside world (that is, the world external to the mind).

So far, I have tried to emphasize the necessary relationship between thought and interpretation. It must be said in no uncertain terms that the very act of thinking requires interpretation. Every perception is necessarily interpreted by other familiar thought categories.

. . . the very act of thinking requires interpretation.

The illustration of Jason's pain provides an example of perception by touch. Let's look at another example of perception, this time by sight recognition. A while back, my mother sent me a "thought experiment" by email. It took the form of a mass email forward (which I would normally delete immediately — happily, I read this one). It went like this:

> Aoccdrnig to a rscheearch at Cmabirgde Uinervtisy, it deo'snt mttaer in waht oredr the ltteers in a wrod are, the olny iprmoetnt tihng is taht the frist and lsat ltteer be at the rghit pclae. The rset can be a toatl mses and you can sitll raed it wouthit porbelm. Tihs is bcuseae the huamn mnid deos not raed ervey lteter by istlef, but the wrod as a wlohe.

This paragraph aptly illustrates the essential function of thought categories. In this case, we're dealing with thought categories exemplified in language. If you were able to read this paragraph with any success it is because you were able to project an interpretation onto each word. More than that, you were able to project an interpretation that deviated from what was originally typed. The word "porbelm" has no intrinsic meaning. However, in the given context the word "problem" seems to fit best. Therefore, the fluent English-reader projects this familiar word onto the nonsensical word to make sense of it.

This illustration only works if the words represent familiar thought categories. For example, the paragraph above credits this study to "Cmabirgde Uinervtisy." In fact, this study was first done at the "Uinervtisy of Ntgahintom."[6] Now, if you're not from the United Kingdom, you may have more trouble with the word "Ntgahintom." This is because the University of Nottingham is not as well known an institution outside of the UK.[7] But because almost everyone has heard of Cambridge, the word "Cmabirgde" is able to evoke this familiar thought category. Simply, Cambridge is a more familiar thought category than is Nottingham for most people.

One wonders if the person who sent this email consciously changed Nottingham to Cambridge for this very reason. Whatever the case, this caveat further illustrates my point: *Perception is fil-*

tered through familiar thought categories. Indeed, interpretation requires that certain patterns of mental categorization are in place.

Perception is not a simple act of data-input.[8] What you perceive is (at least in part) shaped by your perception of previous experiences — what we would commonly call "memory." My next chapter will discuss memory, what it is, how it functions, and why that matters for historical Jesus research.

Before going forward, I must make one point as clearly as possible. If, as I have argued here, perception requires interpretation, this guides the historian between two absurd extremes. On one side, there are many folks who expect from the gospels something similar to a courtroom transcript. For these people the historical Jesus is simply the biblical Jesus. The less interpretation, the better. On the other side, there are many folks who recognize fictive elements in the gospels and conclude that the gospels are wholesale invention. For these people, the gospels are *not* like courtroom transcripts and therefore *must* be fiction. Both views assume that remembering one's perceptions is a simple, straightforward act. However, a modest grasp of the nature of perception makes either extreme absurd. The first perceptions of Jesus were shaped by the external spurs and constraints unique to his historical context.

Suggestions for Further Reading

Tyler Burge. *Externalism and Self-Knowledge.* Edited by Peter Ludlow and Norah Martin. Center for the Study of Language and Information, 1998.

Michael O'Shea. *The Brain: A Very Short Introduction.* Oxford: Oxford University Press, 2005.

Family Matters

Forgetfulness is suspended in certain cases.

Friedrich Nietzsche

I am convinced that many people misunderstand the nature of history because they do not quite appreciate how memory works. Those interested in asking the question *What is history?* must make some account for how individuals and groups remember the past. So those interested in the historical Jesus must first ask, "How was Jesus remembered?" With this in mind, I will take some time to explore the nature of human memory.

I suppose the first thing that must be appreciated about memory is that it is, in itself, the exception to the rule. As Nietzsche (1844-1900) points out, our tendency is to forget. We forget much, much more than we remember. Most stories, names, facts, truths, and details simply float down the river of time into oblivion.

But every now and again, a bit of someone's story is snatched up out of this current and remembered. Like water, it is impossible to hold the past in our fingers. What we "save" from the current is not the past, but something else; the past cannot be preserved. What is left in the wetness of our palms is an impression of what was once there. Memory is the impression left by the past, not the preservation of it. In memory, we do not re-experience the past. What we experience is the impact left by the past.

It is absolutely crucial that this point is firmly grasped because, if something is to be remembered at all, it must have left some kind of impression or impact. In other words, there must be some reason why it wasn't forgotten. If a story, detail, fact, etcetera doesn't make an impact upon our perception, it will simply be lost to an unknowable past. This point will be revisited below.

Now, if you've followed my argument leading to this chapter, you will recall my claim that perception requires interpretation. So, if perception requires interpretation and memory requires perception, then memory is an interpretive process. Or if you prefer a more logical layout:

Premise 1: Memory requires perception.
Premise 2: Perception requires interpretation.
Conclusion: Therefore, memory requires interpretation.

Remembering is not a simple retrieval of data. Our minds do not passively preserve information about the past. If something is to be remembered, it must be interpreted and reinterpreted by the ever-changing now. The first and most important priority of your mind is the present. This means that your memories are always in active service to the needs of the present. Every memory brought to mind is colored by these needs. Memory is what is happening in our minds *now*. We remember stories, details, facts, etcetera according to the needs of our present state of mind.

Memory does not preserve the past — it can only perceive how the past has impacted the present.

Consider the late great actor, Paul Newman. We do not hold the essence of Newman in our minds when we remember him. His person, his presence, is not available for any sort of observation. When we rewatch *Cool Hand Luke* or see his face on a salad dressing label, it does not evoke his person, only an impression of his person. It is his impact on the present that we feel when we remember him. Again, memory does not preserve the past — it can only perceive how the past has impacted the present.

The third thing that must be appreciated about memory is that its interpretation (at least in part) is determined by the outside world. In the previous chapter, I gave an illustration involving "pudding" to describe a particular topic in the philosophy of mind (Anti-Individualism). As you will recall, "pudding" is the name for all kinds of dessert in England. This stands in contrast to how Americans think of pudding — as gelatinous, sweet goo that is eaten with a spoon. In England, "pudding" is synonymous with dessert in general.

This is not to say that Britons do not have gelatinous, sweet goo that is eaten with a spoon. They do and it is quite tasty. In fact, they even call it "pudding." We are now in a position to examine a thought experiment well known to Anti-Individualists:

Culture Focus B: Mamzer

Mamzer is an ancient derogatory term that now survives in Yiddish. The English equivalent is "bastard." In modern America, where a baby is just as likely to be conceived out of wedlock as it is within, the concept of illegitimacy isn't all that scandalous. But to be called a mamzer in Jesus' day was a serious charge and might have had dire implications. Many of Jesus' contemporaries were suspicious of his conception.[1] In John 8:41, Jesus' adversaries imply that he was "born of fornication." Later Jewish sources suggest that Mary was raped by a Roman soldier. This kind of thing is not uncommon in places of military occupation. Moreover, there is quite a bit of evidence that Jesus was accused of being a foreigner — that he was overly sympathetic to the concerns of non-Jewish folk.

Matthew begins his story of Jesus by tracing his patriarchal lineage. But Matthew also inserts the names of four women into Jesus' family tree. The one thing that all of these women had in common was that they were attached to scandalous stories (e.g., adultery and prostitution). Matthew seems to be providing a precedent for Mary's poor reputation and Jesus' questionable conception. Matthew's genealogy was meant to remind his fellow messianic-minded Jews that great things can come from scandalous beginnings. Ironically, it probably didn't help matters that Matthew — in the very same chapter — was repeating a story attributing Jesus' conception to the Spirit of God. While Matthew's intention was to offset the ill-repute of Mary, such a story might have been counterproductive. To many, a divine appeal would have made Jesus' status as mamzer seem even more likely.

Imagine that a young boy, let's call him Mark, spends most of his childhood in California. On occasion, Mark's mother takes him out after their evening meal to get a chocolate-peanut butter milkshake. At no point in Mark's childhood does he ever consider calling this treat "pudding." To think of a chocolate-peanut butter milkshake as "pudding" in this context would be incorrect. Indeed, nobody where he lives would understand this label if he did call it "pudding." According to Mark's external context, milkshakes are simply not classified as "pudding." Thus Mark's perception of chocolate-peanut butter milkshakes conforms to his social environment.

Young Mark grows up, meets a girl on the Internet, and decides to move to England to be near her. Mark marries her and they grow old together. During this time, Mark becomes fluent in British nomenclature. He learns to say "*hire* a car" (not "*rent* a car"); he learns to say "*ring* me on my *mobile*" (not "*call* me on my *cell phone*"). And of course, Mark learns to say "pudding" (not "dessert").

One evening, Mark and his spouse are enjoying a lovely "supper" over at a friend's house. After supper, this friend brings out "pudding" and to Mark's surprise, it happens to be the makings for chocolate-peanut butter milkshakes (a treat incomprehensible to most Britons). Mark takes a taste and remarks, "I haven't had pudding like this since I was a boy!" The taste of this treat reminds Mark of all of those times as a boy when his mother took him out after supper for "pudding." *And Mark thinks nothing of the fact that he has casually remembered his boyhood treat as "pudding."* It has become so natural for him to think of the after-supper-sweet-food as pudding that he simply remembers it that way.[2]

If you've ever lived in another culture for an extended period of time, this scenario is not hard to imagine. It is our external environs that shape our memories. Most often we are completely unaware of such subtle shifts. This is a good thing, for if our memories make dramatic shifts, it can be disorienting. If I wake up one morning and forget the word for doorknob, it would be frustrating. This was a common occurrence for my grandfather late in his life. He would stop mid-sentence and search in vain for a word he had known all his life. It is important to understand that this is not the kind of memory shift that we saw in the case of Mark's pudding. In Mark's case, and as is most often the case, memory categories shift subtly (notice that the essence of the memory is the same, but the way that it is categorized has shifted). These subtle category shifts happen so that our minds can remain relevant to our ever-shifting external environment. But subtle or not, my point is that our memories must remain in tune to our external environment because it is often the external that prompts our memories. Our memories are prompted by familiar tastes, smells, and sights. They are prompted by social settings as well, like conversations, stories, and questions.

The social aspect of memory was first given full voice by French thinker Maurice Halbwachs (1877-1945). Sixty years before Burge argued for Anti-Individualism from a philosophical perspective, Halbwachs made a similar argument from a sociological perspective.[3] He argued that, most often, our memories are spurred by external social and environmental cues. External environments prompt the memories required to operate within them.

Examples are manifold. Consider the most common manifestation of "social memory": family memories. Have you ever been corrected by a sibling as you recalled a childhood event? Have you ever heard a husband and wife finish each other's sentences when telling a story? Or have you heard an elderly couple tell a story in tandem — one supplies the main plot points while the other inserts pertinent details? Several wonderful examples of this can be seen in Rob Reiner's film *When Harry Met Sally*.[4] The fictional story is punctuated throughout by real-life interviews. Consider the following excerpt from the screenplay involving an old married couple:

> (New old couple again)
> (They "cross-talk" all the time, they kind of overlap each other's speech.)

> **Man:** We were both born in the same hospital.
> **Woman:** Nineteen twenty-one.

Man: Seven days apart.

Woman: In the same hospital.

Man: We both grew up one block away from each other.

Woman: We both lived in tenements.

Man: On the lower east side.

Woman: On Delancey Street.

Man: My family moved to the Bronx when I was ten.

Woman: He lived on Fordham Road.

Man: Hers moved when she was eleven.

Woman: I lived on a hundred and eighty-third Street.

Man: For six years she worked on the fifteenth floor as a nurse where I had a practice on the fourteenth floor in the very same building.

Woman: I worked for a very prominent neurologist, Dr. (someone or other). We never met.

Man: Never met.

Woman: Can you imagine that?

Man: You know where we met? In an elevator. In the Ambassador Hotel in Chicago, Illinois.

Woman: I was visiting family. He was on the third floor. I was on the twelfth.

Man: I rode up nine extra floors just to keep talking to her.

Woman: Nine extra floors.

Significant details have been emphasized and their proper interpretation has been made clear.

Social memory is also the foundation of larger social institutions, those which extend beyond family. I recently attended the wedding of my friend Andy. The church was perched on a cliff over the Pacific Ocean. The bride was a vision. She sang a song she'd written for the occasion. The groom wore traditional Norwegian attire. The event was memorable. But, most importantly, the core of that event was the exchange of traditional wedding vows. They were a variation on the same vows ritualized by every married person in the sanctuary. In that moment, the event wasn't just memorable, it was identity shaping. As I heard those vows, I remembered my own vows to my wife. I relived my memory and reaffirmed my identity as the husband to my wife. As an audience, we felt the collective identity of the institution of marriage was reinforced. Oddly, I remember very little of that crucial moment in my own wedding. I was anxious, overjoyed, and shot through with adrenaline. Needless to say that my memory of that moment — the most important moment of my life — is vague. But I remember that moment better with every new wedding I attend. The social institution of marriage is built on collective remembering.

Or consider a different kind of social memory. One of my longest friendships began with a pellet-gun fight in an apple orchard. The summer of my eighth-grade year, my friends were playing a very painful game involving very little wisdom. A boy I hadn't met before, Steve, aimed at my face from five feet away. Acting out the *fight* part of my fight-or-flight instinct, I tackled Steve to wrestle away the pellet gun. Fortunately, neither of us was hurt. We didn't meet again for several years. When we were reacquainted, we became great friends and remain so. Here is where the social memory enters.

A few years ago, I reminded Steve of how we first met and he had no recollection of the event whatsoever. He had forgotten the incident completely. Since then, the story has been told and retold to our friends and family. It took four or five tellings, but Steve now claims to remember the incident. He is one of the most honest fellows I know, so I believe him. Steve is now convinced that he has some recollection of the event. What had been completely forgotten previously has been socially reinforced in his memory. However, Steve is unable to determine how much he actually remembers of the event and how much has been imagined by my telling of the story.

I have made the claim that in order to understand the nature of history, we must first rethink our understanding of human memory. As illustrated here, memory is an ongoing process of imaginative reinforcement. I will continue to make this case over the course of this book. I hope to convince you that because human memory is such a fluid process, we most often rely on our external environment to both spur and constrain our interpretation(s) of the past. I am not saying that our memories are unreliable. I am saying that our memories are reliable because they rely upon external (including social) frameworks.

As the quote from Nietzsche indicates, the human default position is forgetfulness. It takes an active effort to remember. We are active participants in the shaping of our memories.

SUGGESTIONS FOR FURTHER READING

Henri Bergson. *Matter and Memory.* Authorized translation by Nacy Margaret Paul and W. Scott Palmer. London: Allen, 1912.

James Fentress and Chris Wickham. *Social Memory.* Oxford: Blackwell, 1992.

Patrick Hutton. *History as an Art of Memory.* Hanover, NH: University Press of New England, 1993.

Barbara A. Miztal. *Theories of Social Memory.* Philadelphia: Open University Press, 2003.

A Type of Now

True science investigates and brings to human perception such truths and such knowledge as the people of a given time and society consider most important.

Leo Tolstoy

As I aim toward a definition of history, an immediate problem surfaces. The problem is that there are two (both very popular) definitions of history. Hopefully, I can address this problem now and avoid confusion as we go forth. I will make a distinction here that must be kept in mind throughout the reading of this book.

Any decent dictionary will provide both definitions of history. The first definition understands history as something synonymous with *the past*. This definition understands history to be everything that ever happened over the course of time. Merriam-Webster offers this definition as follows:

> events that form the subject matter of a history . . . events of the past . . . one that is finished or done for ‹the winning streak was *history*› . . .

Mark Twain (1835-1910) paraphrases this understanding of history in his famous quip, "History is just one damned thing after another." In other words, history is just a sequence of things that happen in time. This definition is not what interests the postmodern historian. It is not what I mean when I refer to "history."

The second definition of history is what I'll build upon in this book. This definition understands history as a discipline that analyzes accounts, artifacts, and theories *associated* with past events. Consider now Merriam-Webster's second definition:

> a chronological record of significant events (as affecting a nation or institution) often including an explanation of their causes . . . a branch of knowledge that records and explains past events . . .

The difference between these two definitions might seem subtle, but there is an enormous consequence if they are confused. The first definition of history can be seen as a synonym for the word "past"; the second definition cannot. History, *as a discipline of knowledge,* is not what happened in the past, it is an accounting of how the past was remembered and why. To confuse these is to confuse the very nature of the historian's task.

Here is why:

The second definition acknowledges that the vast majority of "the past" has not been remembered and therefore *is not history.* History includes only the past that has been interpreted through memory.[1] That which has not been remembered is not history. This is why it is so important for the philosopher of history (the historiographer) to understand what memory is, how it functions, and why.

In the previous chapter, I argued that memory does not preserve the past — it perceives how the past has impacted the present. The same is true of history. Historians tell the stories of history from a particular contemporary perspective. They ask and answer historical questions by using the methods of interpretation that are acceptable in their contexts. Because of this, history telling is as much about the teller and his/her audience as it is about the subject. Documentarian Ken Burns (1953-) explains that "history isn't really about the past — settling old scores. It's about defining the present and who we are."

History, as a discipline of knowledge, is not what happened in the past, it is an accounting of how the past was remembered and why.

Perhaps Burns overstates his case, but not by much. History is indeed *about* the past inasmuch as the past has been emphasized through memory. But, in order for this statement to be true, it must be granted that memory functions to assimilate impressions of the past with our present contexts. Similarly, historians (acting as "remembrancers") take what seems relevant about historical memories and make them intelligible to their contemporary audiences.

Notice here the relationship between historian, as remembrancer, and the historian's audience, as remembering community. As remembrancer, the historian conveys to his audience what he believes is important for them to remember. In turn, the remembering community (the family, society, subculture, religious group, partisans, etc.) responds to the historical memory by accepting, rejecting, or ignoring it.

If you look at any standard American history text before 1950, you'll see very little mention of the role that Black soldiers played in the Civil War. In texts published in the 1960s you might find incidental commentary about "Afro-American" soldiery. However, after the American Civil Rights movement, this story is told much differently. It is not uncommon for texts published in the 1990s to claim that the

Union Army could not have won the Civil War without Black participation. More recent texts have tempered this historical claim.

My point is that, as the interests of society change, the stories we tell of our past change also. Americans have become a more racially conscious people since the 1950s. As a result, we have *revised* our memories to perceive our history more correctly. I emphasize the conception of revision to show the affinity of this example with what many would call "revisionist history."

The more significant a memory is, the more interpreted it will become.

This example shows how the interests and values of a society force historians to reevaluate historical evidence to re-forge its national memory. Yet it is also important to point out that my example is only one kind of reevaluation. With Black American history, we see a shift from little interest to much interest. Or, more accurately, White America had very little interest in Black history until after the Civil Rights movement. Before this time the historical data on this subject went largely undeveloped by most institutional historians. In this case, a devil's advocate might argue that the historian is not so much "revising" as "filling in the gaps" of what we know about a particular time frame. Perhaps there is merit to this charge, but consider the example of Abraham Lincoln.

Lincoln was a public figure for much of his life. Because of this, his historical significance was open to public scrutiny. Historians were already assessing his legacy as an American president during his lifetime and shortly after his death. In contrast to anonymous and under-represented soldiers, Abraham Lincoln was never an obscurity. Yet since his death, each generation has reshaped his legacy. Because Lincoln is one of America's most significant figures, his story must be reshaped to be made relevant to each new generation. In doing so, each new remembering community re-forges a collective identity for themselves (of course, always in relationship to previous identities).[2]

I bring this to the fore to articulate an absolutely crucial aspect of my overarching thesis: The more significant a memory is, the more interpreted it will become. The great figures, moments, movements, and shifts of history will ever be shaped and reshaped by new interpretative contexts. History makes new impact with every telling. With every telling history is impacted.

In keeping with the example of Lincoln, this chapter was written during the 2008 United States presidential election. This year of media culture was a fascinating sociological experiment on several levels, and absolutely spellbinding for folks interested in social memory. Being the first African American candidate for president to win the nomination of one of the major political parties, Senator Barack Obama and his story give us a fantastic window into the politics of memory, how national memories shift as they are retold.

In an article written on January 17th, 2007 (*before* Obama formalized his candidacy), journalist Lynn Sweet anticipated Obama's story by measuring his significance with the memory of Abraham Lincoln:

> A kickoff in the Illinois capital will serve to marry the Obama political narrative with that of Springfield's Abraham Lincoln. Lincoln, like Obama, was a member of the Illinois General Assembly, before his election to Congress and then the White House. Like Obama, Lincoln didn't have much experience before becoming president and leading the nation through a turbulent era. Obama, the son of a Kenyan father, will kick off his quest at or near the home of the man who freed the African slaves.[3]

Notice the language that Sweet uses here, "will serve to *marry* the Obama political narrative" to Lincoln. *What is being claimed here?*

And what is the logical result of this claim? As the metaphor of "marriage" indicates, we should expect two complementary results.

(1) Sweet is claiming that in order to understand the significance of Obama's story, we should begin with Abraham Lincoln. Obama is thus an extension of Lincoln's legacy.

(2) Sweet is claiming that the significance of Lincoln's story is aptly remembered through the lens of Obama's story. Lincoln, according to Sweet, is a precursor to Barack Obama. This is no small claim!

This is a clear incidence of "typology." Typology is the study of types. In this case, Sweet is saying that Obama is a type of Lincoln. Now, be advised, Sweet's interpretation is still on trial. Her audience will accept, reject, or ignore her telling of the Lincoln story depending on how future generations interpret Obama's legacy.

Culture Focus C: One of the Prophets

According to Mark's story, Jesus began to build his own reputation shortly after John the Baptist was executed. Jesus starts to wonder what people are saying about him and so he asks his disciples to tell him what rumors are circulating. According to Mark, the disciples tell Jesus that people think he is John the Baptist come back from the dead. Others think that Jesus is the second coming of one of the ancient prophets of old: "And they told him, 'John the Baptist,' others say 'Elijah,' still others say 'one of the prophets'" (Mark 8:28).

Many historians consider this saying to have been invented. In other words, Jesus didn't really ask the question, and his disciples didn't really give this answer. Rather this was a liturgical confession invented by the second generation of Christianity. I am less certain that this saying was invented. But either way, it demonstrates well how Jesus' contemporaries thought. In that context, if someone achieved greatness, they were often compared with ancient heroes.

There was a Jewish historian named Josephus who wrote 50 to 75 years after Jesus died. Aside from briefly mentioning Jesus (*Antiquities* 18.3.3), Josephus helpfully told of several popular leaders of this period who mimicked ancient heroes like Moses and Joshua and prophets like Jeremiah. Josephus wrote for a non-Jewish audience, so he didn't explicitly appeal to these ancient heroes by name. But he provided enough details to show that Jewish folk considered these latter-day prophets to be recycled versions of the old prophets. The disciples' answer in Mark 8 shows a similar interpretation of Jesus. Jesus' significance was often measured against the ancient heroes of Israel's history.

This sort of historical typology is often politically advantageous. The Kennedys were often called "Camelot." It is traditional for a new pope to take the name of a previous (fondly remembered) pope. Saddam Hussein commissioned statues of the Babylonian king, Nebuchadnezzar, but with his own likeness carved onto the face of the statue. In each of these cases, the historical (and/or legendary) stories of the past have been reframed to serve political agendas. And more importantly, these agendas are apparent in the lifetime of the historical figures in question. This must be kept in mind as we read how Jesus was remembered in conjunction with the narratives and characters of the Hebrew Bible.

From here I will make two additional points that will be fleshed out more fully over the course of this book.

First, history often takes the form and/or function of story. The uninterrupted past does not have beginnings, ends, transitional motifs, plot twists, and climaxes. These are elements that the historian projects and imposes upon the past to form a narrative worth telling.

Second, the historian is not the first person to impose meaning onto the past. The vast majority of historical data is only available to the historian by way of surviving memory. The historian is essentially an interpreter of memories. Because memory is interpretation from the start, historians are interpreters of previous interpretations. Previous postmodern theorists have underemphasized this point.

Both points must be acknowledged as we focus on the historical Jesus:

1. The storytellers behind the gospels are interpreters by discipline. In telling the Jesus story they interpret, revise, metaphorize, theologize, apply typologies, highlight character developments and plot movements. These are not things that they do because they had such little care for history. This is what telling history looks like — what it *ought* to look like!

2. We should expect that the very first memories of Jesus by his family, followers, and adversaries were creatively constructed by way of interpretation. When the gospels demonstrate revision, metaphor, theology, typology, character development, and plot movement, this is not necessarily evidence of invention or fiction. We should not think that the writers of the gospels were the first to interpret Jesus' significance. Such interpretive devices are common to human perception and memory. People perceive themselves and the world around them within narrative frameworks. Many of these interpretations *must have* begun during Jesus' lifetime. If Jesus had not been interpreted by his contemporaries, he would not have been remembered at all.

Now, let us look more directly at the memories about Jesus.

SUGGESTIONS FOR FURTHER READING

Leonhard Goppelt. *Typos: The Typological Interpretation of the Old Testament in the New.* Translated by D. H. Madvig. Grand Rapids: Eerdmans, 1982.

Anthony Le Donne. *The Historiographical Jesus: Memory, Typology, and the Son of David.* Waco, TX: Baylor University Press, 2008.

Barry Schwartz. *Abraham Lincoln in the Post Heroic Era: History and Memory in Late Twentieth-Century America.* Chicago: The University of Chicago Press, 2008.

Dysfunctional Family

Jesus never let me down
You know Jesus used to show me the score
Then they put Jesus in show business
Now it's hard to get in the door.

Bono

It is not uncommon to stretch the canvas for a historical portrait with some preliminary observations about the person's family. Why is this? Why do we find it relevant that St. Francis was the son of a wealthy merchant? Or, why do we find it interesting that Gandhi was obsessed with the story of Harishchandra as a child?[1] These observations are relevant and interesting because they open the windows to possible motivations. Such details are interesting inasmuch as they allow us to juxtapose details about the person's family with the characteristics of their careers.

Previous discussions of Jesus' family, both in academic and popular dialogue, have proved controversial. There are several reasons for this, but one of the central reasons is that family presupposes sexuality. In order to say something of Jesus' family life we must presuppose certain claims about the sexuality of Jesus and/or his parents. This is an interesting question in the case of Jesus because tradition tells us that Mary conceived by divine intervention. Tradition tells us very little about Jesus' sexuality, but it has been generally assumed that Jesus never married.

One of the central themes of Nikos Kazantzakis's *The Last Temptation of Christ* is Jesus' sexuality. Both the book and the film take seriously an important tension created by the doctrine of the Incarnation.[2] Specifically, the question that Kazantzakis asks is this: *Given that Jesus was fully human* (the orthodox position of church doctrine), *did he ever consider settling down and starting a family?* Because Kazantzakis took this question seriously, he created a vivid portrait of Jesus' *possible* struggle with sexual temptation. Without a doubt, this question is a valid one both for the historian and the world of literature/film. However, the historian does not have the same freedom that the writer of a historical fiction has. Mere possibility is not enough; the historian must tell a story on the basis of historical plausibility.

Allow me to take a moment to show the difference between historical possibility and plausibility. If a story is historically *possible* it cannot be reasonably disproved. If a story is historically *plausible* it seems likely, has a ring of authenticity to it. A historical argument aims toward the most likely explanation given the historical context and the events that followed by way of impact.

Even though they may have tried, the early Christians had very little success in suppressing embarrassing details about Jesus' life. This is especially true with his family life.

Historically speaking, it is "possible" that Judas looked like Harvey Keitel wearing a Little Orphan Annie wig. In contrast, it is *not* possible that Judas spoke with a Brooklyn accent. Both of these elements of the film are highly unlikely, but only the latter can be definitely ruled out (on grounds of anachronism). In similar terms, it is completely "possible" that Jesus was married at some point. It is possible that he had several wives. Perhaps he was a wealthy husband with a dozen children. There is nothing in the evidence for Jesus that definitively rules out this possibility.

But while it is possible that Jesus was a happy husband and father, there is no way of telling this story without it reeking of implausibility. The lack of evidence simply doesn't allow for a plausible telling of this story. Those who attempt to do so are forced to appeal to conspiracy theories and grand cover-up jobs due to lack of evidence.

There is a simple historical fact that keeps the serious historian from "inventing" revisions of Jesus' life on the basis of early church conspiracy. This simple fact is assumed by all judicious historians whether orthodox or not, whether religious or not, whether mainstream or not. The simple fact is this: Even though they may have tried, the early Christians had very little success in suppressing embarrassing details about Jesus' life. This is especially true with his family life.

The canonical gospels[3] contain several stories about Jesus that are awkward to say the least. Jesus was remembered for publicly rebuking his mother (who was later highly revered by the church). Jesus was remembered for refusing to speak to his mother and brothers (tantamount to disowning them)! He was remembered for disparaging the role of (what we would now call) traditional family values. His family, in turn, was remembered for accusing Jesus of insanity!

The canonical gospels betray his reputation for being a partying hedonist and his often socially inappropriate associations with women. Jesus seems to have kept regular company with hookers and vamps. Add to this a rather "queer" saying concerning gender and it is hard to believe that anything about Jesus' family or sexuality was suppressed due to embarrassment.[4] More to the point, later rabbinic traditions may also attest the widespread belief that Jesus was a bastard (compare John 8), the result of the rape of Mary by a Roman centurion. If there *was* some massive effort to cover up embarrassing details about Jesus' family life, it failed massively.

The most plausible explanation for the complete lack of information about Jesus' wife is that he did not have one or that she died before Jesus began his public career. While it is difficult to say why, his bachelor status may have allowed him more freedom to have casual relationships. Historians agree that women played a major role in the early church and Jesus' friendships with women (many rather than one) might explain this. Though it might sell more books to say otherwise (unfortunately for me), Jesus was most likely single during his career as a preacher. But if it's scandal that you're looking for, there are enough *plausible* scandals in the historical evidence without resorting to the *possible* scandals of historical fiction.

For the historian studying Jesus, embarrassing details about Jesus aren't only interesting, they are valuable windows into plausible historical memories of Jesus. In fact, such details are examples of a well-known criterion for determining whether a story is the product of memory or fiction. Historical Jesus scholars call this the "Criterion of Embarrassment."[5] The logic behind the Criterion of Embarrassment goes like this: *If a story contains details about Jesus, his family, or his disciples that would have proved embarrassing to the early church, this story was probably not invented by the early church.*

Consider the story told about Jesus and his mother in John 2:1-11. In this story, Jesus arrives at a party that has gotten out of hand. The guests at this party have drained the wine supply. Considering that this was a wedding celebration, the host had probably provided a great deal of alcohol at no little expense. The way that John tells the story, we get the impression that Jesus' mother had arrived before Jesus and his disciples. Mary, upset by the lack of wine, informs Jesus that "they have no wine."

If a story contains details about Jesus, his family, or his disciples that would have proved embarrassing to the early church, this story was probably not invented by the early church.

Mary's statement seems factual enough. At most, the statement seems to imply a request. Yet Jesus' response is so harsh we are led to assume that the story provides a small window into their relationship. Perhaps there was something in the intonation of her voice. Perhaps we witness a glimpse of a larger and ongoing argument between the two. Whatever the case, Jesus rebukes Mary sharply. He says, *"Ti emoi kai soi, gunai?"* This is a Greek gloss of an Aramaic saying.[6] Greek, like English, has a difficult time translating this figure of speech. Literally translated, it would say, "How to you and to me, woman?"

A dynamic translation of this idiom (one that captures the sense of the phrase) would read something like this: "What does my business have to do with you? — Mind your own business, woman!"

If this translation seems overly harsh, keep in mind that this exact idiom is used by "demon-possessed" people to rebuke Jesus in Mark 1:24 and 5:7. It is the hostile rebuke of someone who is about to be tormented or forcibly made to do something against his will. Jesus' strong rebuke of his mother suggests that their relationship was less than cordial.

Would the church have invented rumors of the Son of God's overbearing mother? Would they have invented stories that portrayed Jesus as disrespectful, talking to his mother the way a demon talks to an exorcist? Probably not. The Criterion of Embarrassment suggests that this is a memory-story and not an invented story.

Yet this is only one bit of historical evidence. The Jesus historian requires more than mere suggestion to tell a plausible story. With this in mind, let's look at two other stories that might lend support to this interpretation.

Culture Focus D: Demons

The belief in demons is extremely hard to find in the Hebrew Bible (what Christians usually call the Old Testament). But in Matthew, Mark, and Luke, much of Jesus' story involves demon-possessed folk and healing exorcisms. So when did Jews like Jesus start telling stories about demons? One of our earliest stories about demons comes from a book called *Jubilees* (now found in the *Pseudepigrapha*[7]).

Jubilees was written about 100 years before Jesus was born. This book is a historical fiction based on Genesis 6. *Jubilees* retells the story of Noah and the Ark. In this retelling, divine creatures (Genesis calls them "sons of God") have sex with human women. The women give birth to evil giants who teach humans naughty things and generally wreak havoc on earth. According to this popular mythology of Jesus' day, God sent the flood to wipe out these giants.

Unfortunately, though the flood killed the bodies of the giants, their souls lived on. Many Jews of Jesus' day believed that this was the origin of demons — they originated from the disembodied souls of the evil giants of Genesis 6. According to *Jubilees*, the leader of these spirits was named "Mastema," or Satan.

While virtually every Jesus historian agrees that Jesus and many of his contemporaries believed in demons, there is some evidence that there were varying perspectives on this issue. The Gospel of John shows very little evidence of this belief. So perhaps from the earliest stages of Christianity, Jesus' followers did not share the same understanding of the spiritual realm. Contemporary Christianity continues to reflect this conceptual plurality.

Mark (3:31-35) windows Jesus' teaching career. We are given the impression that Jesus was so popular that he packed rooms and blocked doorways with anxious listeners. On this occasion, the room is so full that those outside are denied entry. As Jesus teaches, Mary and her other sons approach the building to find that they can't get in to see him. Perhaps implying a feeling of entitlement, they send word that they have arrived and expect to see him.

Or maybe we can read this another way. Perhaps Mary simply requests to talk with Jesus. Perhaps it's a modest request from a woman who doesn't want to barge in. In either case, Jesus' answer is undoubtedly pointed. "Who are my mother and brothers?" Jesus asks. The question implies that the right answer, the one that Jesus will soon make clear, doesn't presume bloodlines. Jesus makes it clear that his true family is already inside of the room as opposed to those outside asking for him. "My mother and my brothers are those who do the will of God."

It might not be difficult to imagine the first Christians redefining traditional family bonds — many were disowned for their new religious beliefs. However, it is highly unlikely that the first Christians would invent a story that disrespects James the brother of Jesus. James was an important leader in early Jewish Christianity. This story betrays a clear belittling (if not overt disrespect) of Jesus' mother and brothers. Add to this picture the detail from Mark 3:21: Jesus' kin thought he had gone insane. Such details are so embarrassing, they are most likely not fiction.

Furthermore, these details betray a tension between Jesus and his biological family that "coheres" with other memory-stories concerning the life of Jesus. In this case, I am adapting what historians studying Jesus call the "Criterion of Coherence." If a story or saying seems to cohere with other historically plausible evidence, we may suggest that it was derived from memory and not invention.[8]

Coherence is among the less reliable criteria for locating early memories about Jesus. It requires confidence in the historical value of other stories or sayings that may or may not prove convincing. However, when used to lend further support to other evidence, the historian can paint a more plausible portrait by appealing to coherence. The Criterion of Coherence is especially helpful when several stories and sayings support a single claim of historical plausibility.

With this in mind, consider Luke 11:27-28:

And it came about while he said these things, one of the women in the crowd raised her voice, and said to him, "Blessed is the womb that bore you, and the breasts at which you nursed." But he said, "On the contrary, blessed are those who hear the word of God, and observe it."

This saying coheres with the previous example in Mark 3:31-35. Again, Jesus suggests that his mother shouldn't be revered simply because she is a blood relative. The simple coherence of these two sayings is not enough to argue that this is an example of memory instead of invention.[9] After all, Mark might have invented it and Luke (following Mark) might have reinvented it. Again, the Criterion of Coherence is not compelling by itself. But compare these examples with a similar saying in the Gospel of Thomas:[10]

A woman in the crowd said to him, "Blessed is the womb that bore you and the breasts that fed you." He said to her, "Blessed are those who have heard the word of the Father and have truly kept it. For there will be days when you will say, 'Blessed are the womb that has not conceived and the breasts that have not given milk'" (Thom. 79).

Because the sayings recorded in Thomas were relatively independent from the other gospels, we may also appeal to the "Criterion of Multiple Attestation." I consider this criterion to be among the most compelling. The logic behind this criterion goes like this: *If a saying or story is attested by multiple sources, it is more likely to have been early and widespread.*

When taken together, these briefly surveyed texts compellingly suggest that the historical Jesus was at odds with his immediate family and his mother in particular. The most plausible treatment of the evidence is that these stories and sayings are the product of historical memories. It is highly unlikely that they were invented by the early church.

So far, I have said nothing very postmodern in this chapter. Authenticity criteria have been used (and overused) by modern historical Jesus scholars for a long time. Allow me to make two qualifications.

(1) For the postmodern historian, the simple appeal to criteria falls fatally short of the historian's task. It is not enough simply to establish historical facts. These facts must be interpreted again (and again) through the telling of the story.

(2) Many previous generations of "modern" historians tended to look at these criteria as a way of locating an authentic past reality — as if a core of past events could be stripped of all interpretive agendas and treated like bedrock artifact. If these criteria are to be useful, historians must realize that history always must be about explaining how memory emerges and evolves. These criteria cannot

uncover historical facts that are devoid of perception and memory. What they offer is a window into the dynamic give and take between memory and counter-memory in social discourse. As such, these criteria can give a better way to navigate between memory and invention.

We are now in a position to ask a critical historical question: *Why was Jesus' poor relationship with his mother remembered?* This is an important question because the postmodern historian cannot adequately tell the *what* of the history without explaining the *why* of the history. This is what philosopher and historian R. G. Collingwood (1889-1943) had in mind in the quote that led off this section.[11] Collingwood was adamant that, as the historian retold the story, both questions would be asked and answered simultaneously. Thus on to the telling:

The story of Jesus' adult life must be told without a father in the picture. Perhaps the best explanation for Joseph's absence is that Mary married an older man and was widowed by the time Jesus was in his thirties. In that time and place, being a female without a breadwinner could be fatal. Jewish law instructed the care for people in her situation, but social taboos made it very difficult for women of ill-repute. And the rumors of her youthful promiscuity persisted.

Mary knew that her own survival depended upon her ability to climb the social ladder, and she was shrewd enough to do it. More importantly, she actually believed that her son was destined for great things. It is only natural for a mother to project high aspirations onto her oldest son. But if you asked her, Jesus' path to the top was divinely preordained.

Jesus had never known life without absurd expectations. His mother was convinced that he would be a leader like Moses. Like Moses! The expectations could hardly be higher or more unreasonable. Moses was the archetypal liberator, lawgiver — mediator of the very acts of God! Did she really want him to do miracles, divine signs?

Mary knew that her son just needed a nudge. Moses provided

water from a dry rock in the wilderness, so why couldn't her son turn water into wine? Mind her own business? This *was* her business!

Jesus did his best to distance himself from his mother and brothers. Whatever other hopes they might have for his career, he saw himself as an exorcist.

Jesus did his best to distance himself from his mother and brothers. Whatever other hopes they might have for his career, he saw himself as an exorcist and a spiritual healer. This was something he could do; people were flocking to him for help. Some people thought him crazy, or that he was casting out demons with the help of foreign gods (Mark 3:20-27). His family didn't understand and started to believe the rumors.

After Jesus was gone, his followers remembered Jesus' strained relationship and took solace in this memory. As followers of Jesus, they were disowned by their families and hometowns. Their very livelihoods were jeopardized because they associated with other disciples of Jesus. It was comforting to remember Jesus' teaching about family: Your family is all around you — people that listen to God and obey. They remembered that God's call for collective repentance supersedes blood relations.

Suggestions for Further Reading

J. P. Meier. *A Marginal Jew: Rethinking the Historical Jesus,* vol. 1. New York: Doubleday, 1991.

Loren T. Stuckenbruck. "Satan and Demons." Chapter 7 in *Jesus among Friends and Enemies.* Edited by Chris Keith and Larry W. Hurtado. Grand Rapids: Baker Academic, 2011.

Gerd Theissen and Annette Merz. *The Historical Jesus: A Comprehensive Guide.* Minneapolis: Fortress Press, 1998.

Part Two

In the smallest measure of anything at hand
Entities of energy are alive in a whirling dance
Even our own bodies are not as we perceive
But made of the same stuff our thoughts are made
In this world of dreams

Peter Mayer

Could It Be . . . Satan?

What does it mean to accept an historical proposition as true? to believe an historical truth? Does it mean anything other than this: to accept this proposition, this truth as valid? To accept that there is no objection to be brought against it? To accept that one historical proposition is built on one thing, another on another, that from one historical truth another follows? to reserve to oneself the right to estimate other historical things accordingly? Does it mean anything other than this?

Gotthold Lessing

Do the biblical authors really expect us to believe in the spirit world? Did Jesus really believe in demons? Did he believe that people could be possessed by Satan? The Devil? *Seriously?* Did Jesus talk to demons? Did he think he could cast them out by talking to them?

Was Jesus out to change the world? Or was he just a teacher of wisdom? If he was just a teacher, what made him so unique? What made him any different from other teachers and prophets? Did Jesus teach that the end of the world was near? Where did he get this idea? Wasn't he wrong?

Understanding Is Construing

People only see what they are prepared to see.

Ralph Waldo Emerson

I was recently interviewed for a documentary on exorcism. Before they scheduled my interview, the filmmakers traveled to Africa, South America, and all over North America to film the rituals of exorcists. Before and after my official interview, I got to do a bit of interviewing myself. What I learned was that "perceiving" an exorcism is tricky. The modern mindset (where scientific reason is king) tends to see psychology where other cultures see demons. After witnessing several rituals, these filmmakers weren't so sure anymore. When I talked with them, they were still processing their experiences.

I argued previously that the very act of perception requires interpretation. My argument stems from the philosophy of Friedrich Schleiermacher (1768-1834). Schleiermacher said that interpretation is a circular process. He imagined the model of a "hermeneutical circle."[1] Most often, this model has been used in literary criticism. The circle was originally used to explain the relationship between text (i.e., supposed author) and reader. Schleiermacher argued that the reader of a book must interpret in a circular movement from the "part" to the "whole" of the text.[2] The argument can be summarized like this:

(A) no single concept can be understood outside of its context;
(B) no context can be understood without an understanding of the smaller concepts of which it is made.

You might see the circular nature of these two propositions immediately. But allow me to unpack this a bit.

The value of the hermeneutical circle for this book has less to do with literary theory and more to do with social-psychology. Schleiermacher extended his model beyond literary interpretation to what he called "psychological" hermeneutics. He was concerned with how people tended to interpret the world around them. Schleiermacher suggested that there is a fundamental interconnectedness between thought and language. This circle is especially helpful as he discusses "pre-understanding" or "fore-comprehension" (in German: *Vorverständnis*).

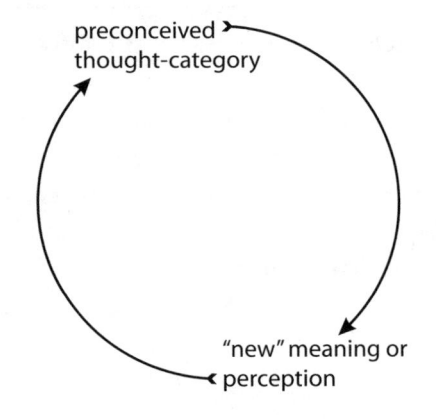

He argued that when something is understood, it must be compared with a previously known category. Schleiermacher gives the example of a child learning a new word through the process of comparison. Children are able to understand new words by relating new word-meanings with a previously established category of meaning.

One of my nephew's first words was "ball." He would speak this label upon anything that was round. He'd point to a baseball and say "ball." He'd do the same for basketballs, tennis balls, and beach balls. Indeed, almost everything that was circular in his life was a ball. One night we were outside under a clear sky, and he pointed to the moon and said, "Ball!" We realized then that my nephew's concept of "ball" meant something more like "circle." But he rarely ever heard us call any of the other round things in his world "circles"; we called most of those things balls. My nephew was labeling the world around him through category association. Schleiermacher argued that this kind of association is a natural way of relating new parts of our environment to our previous understanding of how things ought to be categorized.

Culture Focus E: Hellenistic Rome

For centuries before Jesus was born, Israel was a political pawn. Larger empires like Assyria and Babylon occupied Israel, leaving her very little autonomy. When larger nations vied for power, Israel was caught in the middle. This cycle continued as Alexander the Great extended the borders of the Greek-speaking world. We call this period of common Greek language and culture "Hellenism."

The Roman Empire arose in the wake of the decline of Greece. But the Romans fashioned much of their own culture after their immediate predecessor. Certain democratic ideals carried over, alongside the worship of several Greek gods. Of course, these gods were given decidedly Roman identities. Eventually, Roman "democracy" (or more accurately democratic oligarchy) gave way to tyranny and Caesar-worship. This would have been repugnant and oppressive to observant Jews.

Much of the New Testament was written by Jews in reaction to this culture. (1) It was written in Greek. (2) A very early argument among Christian leaders involved the place of Kosher law (i.e., Jewish diet) among non-Jewish believers in Jesus. (3) Another argument hinged on the role of ritual circumcision.

When reading about the life of Jesus, keep in mind that Roman political and religious imperialism was a chief concern. Not only was Jesus from an "inferior" class in Rome, his religious beliefs were compromised at every turn by the presence of an invader in the so-called "Promised Land." Jewish religious identity was built on the notion of political autonomy and religious freedom; without these, there could be no true peace.

When learning a new word, a person must fit a complex perception into a language-category. An orb, dimpled with texture, grooved and stitched in various materials, catching and reflecting light, weighted in your hand with memories is called, casually, a "ball." Most of us cannot remember when we first learned to associate this kind of object with the word "ball." But, as seen with my nephew's budding language-category, "ball" can be associated with any number of objects — it is quite a useful word, even if it has a limited range of meaning. To apply a simple label to something is to guide the way we perceive that thing.

My nephew's original category, "ball," had to change as he encountered new objects. As he encountered rugby balls, he learned that some objects labeled by that name are less round than others. As he encountered Frisbees, he learned that not all round projectiles can be classified as balls. Eventually he learned categories like "sphere" and "game" by association. *Thus his conception of the word "ball" is different now than it once was.* This language-category has a different significance than it originally had.

It is absolutely crucial that this point be understood. It implies that interpretation is ever changing and fluid. More importantly, it shows that reinterpretation is essential to the process of perception. Consider the trouble that my nephew might run into if he continued to call the moon a "ball" as he got older. This is what Schleiermacher termed the "grammatical" aspect of hermeneutics.

Schleiermacher expanded on this to relate hermeneutics to general categories of perception. He wrote that nothing can be understood that a person "cannot perceive and construct as necessary. In accordance with this maxim, understanding is an unending task."[3] Like a circle in constant motion, interpretation and perception dance together — each leading the other — to form our thoughts. This leads us to Schleiermacher's second definition of understanding: "Nothing is understood that is not construed."[4] This idea of the *construal* of perception/interpretation is very close to my own theory of memory, which I will discuss later in this book.

The hermeneutical circle was picked up and given definition by Wilhelm Dilthey (1833-1911).[5] For Dilthey, the hermeneutical circle meant that "all understanding always remains relative."[6] Dilthey lamented this because it meant that every conclusion was always only provisional. In his mind, the circular process of interpretation made scientific certainty impossible. It was a "vicious circle" — there was no getting off the hamster wheel.

This was a problem for Dilthey because philosophers of his era were preoccupied with the prospect of attaining human perfection through scientific knowledge. Modernity had (and has) a very linear approach to knowledge: The scientist gathered facts, interpreted them without bias, and then attempted to solve the problems presented to him. One of the key ideas of modernity was (and is) that humanity would eventually gain enough knowledge to be able to solve all the world's problems: Salvation by science. But, as Dilthey saw it, if knowledge was always only incomplete, scientists would always be forced to return to their drawing boards and problems could never be solved with finality. In his mind, perpetual interpretation meant that scientists would always be chasing their tails.

But what is a problem for the "modern" philosopher is not a problem at all for postmodern philosophy. An important forerunner to postmodern thought (including the philosophy of history) is existentialist philosopher Martin Heidegger (1889-1976).[7] Heidegger addressed the "problem" of circularity.[8] His philosophy of knowledge latched onto the hermeneutical circle as he discussed the concepts of "fore-having, fore-sight and fore-conception."[9] As with almost everything Heidegger wrote, simplifying his ideas is a tall order. I will attempt to take a small slice of his complexity with the example of anticipation.

Consider an aspect of anticipation common to the human experience: tickling. When my daughter was five, she would lie on the couch where I was sitting and ask for a "tickle test." Parents everywhere know that this request is unique to five-year-olds. It is highly uncertain whether the tickle test will survive the sixth birthday and so this opportunity must not be taken for granted. The rules of the tickle test vary from family to family, but in my house the five-year-old is required to lie still and close her eyes. Then comes my favorite part. Without lifting a hand, I inform the child that the test will commence forthwith beginning with the neck. She, of course, recoils in laughter, shielding her neck in anticipation. Never once did my daughter pass a tickle test in her fifth year; never once did I lift a finger. With five-year-olds, it is entirely possible to tickle them with words alone. If you tell them that their little neck is in jeopardy, they will be tickled by anticipation alone. This is a reality rife with Heideggerian complexity: *The anticipation of a perception determines the perception itself.* At the same time, if my daughter's neck had never been tickled, she would have no frame of reference by which to anticipate the experience.

Consider the example that led off this chapter. The filmmakers that witnessed several exorcism rituals had a notion of what they might see beforehand. They used whatever scientific training and pop-psychology they could remember to process what they saw. But upon gaining the new experience, they had to reassess the ideas they previously held. They formed new thoughts, came to new conclusions. Perhaps their worldviews expanded. That is not for me to say. I can, however, speak to their long-term interpretation of their initial perceptions.

The interpretation of new perceptions naturally involves the recycling of previously known interpretations.

In the initial moments of perception, these filmmakers witnessed something that caused them to rethink their presuppositions. If nothing else, they learned something new about human psychology. In the process of making the documentary and reviewing the film, they questioned the reality of demons (this was the point where I got to talk with them). After a bit of healthy distance and immersion in modern American culture, they eventually came to a conclusion very near to their original presuppositions. They will think back to their experiences of "exorcism" and interpret them in purely psychological terms. Social contexts shape perception and new social contexts reshape them.

It is often the case that new perceptions conform to preconceived thought-categories and that thought-categories remain in constant flux to accommodate new perceptions. Put more simply, you understand what you already understand. At the same time, understanding is possible only if previously held notions are flexible enough to add new information. If this sounds circular, it is because it is. According to Heidegger, "Any interpretation which is to contribute to understanding must already have understood what is to be interpreted."[10] Heidegger is careful to qualify this circularity:

> But if interpretation must in any case already operate in that which is understood, and if it must draw its nurture from this, how is it to bring any scientific results to maturity without moving in a circle, especially if, moreover, the understanding which is presupposed still operates within our common information about man and the world? . . .
>
> *But if we see this circle as a vicious one and look out for ways of avoiding it, even if we just "sense" it as an inevitable imperfection, then the act of understanding has been misunderstood from the ground up.*[11]

Heidegger therefore moved away from the idea that knowledge (here historical knowledge) is dubious because of the subjectivity of perception. As long as we embrace our anticipations and projections while remaining judicious, analyzing historical knowledge can be as rigorous as "the most exact sciences" (by which he means mathematics). He argued that the historian should not attempt to get out of the circle but "come into it in the right way," because the "circle of understanding is not an orbit in which any random kind of knowledge may move."[12] On the contrary, the circle does not distort reality for those who are self-aware; it makes new perceptions meaningful by using previous thought-categories, anticipations, and projections.

Here Heidegger clarifies two key points: (1) The inherent subjectivity of perception is not to be lamented or circumvented by the historian; (2) The interpretation of new perceptions naturally involves the recycling of previous experiences.[13]

As we saw with my nephew's experience, the idea of a "ball" was projected onto several objects in an attempt to classify them. He attempted several language associations until this process stretched and clarified that category. *Category projection shapes perception and perception reshapes categories.* As seen with my daughter's experience, the anticipation of tickling determined the sensation of tickling. Conversely, her anticipation was determined by previous experiences. *Anticipation shapes perception and perception reshapes anticipation.*

As we move this discussion to the postmodern arena, questions surface about the nature of reality. Do we really have direct perceptions of the world around us or do we create our reality based on the projection of our thought-categories? Is our perception of reality limited by our worldview? The implications of the hermeneutical circle suggest that our view of reality is shaped by our expectations of what we might perceive.

Suggestions for Further Reading

Hans-Georg Gadamer. *Philosophical Hermeneutics.* Translated by David E. Linge. Berkeley: University of California Press, 1976.

Martin Heidegger. *Being and Time.* Translated by John Macquarrie and Edward Robinson. London: SCM, 1962.

Variation and Stability

Take care of all your memories. For you cannot relive them.

Bob Dylan

Take care of your memories for you shall not relive them.

Bob Dylan

In the midst of writing this chapter I attended a Bob Dylan concert. Now, as any good Dylan fan will tell you, his concerts are equal parts profound and incoherent. He is the most influential lyricist of the twentieth century, but it is difficult to hear his lyrics when he sings them. His voice is raspy and garbled and he slurs his lyrics together. Still, he's Bob Dylan.

When he sang the songs off his new albums, I didn't understand a word. But when he sang the songs he'd recorded in the 1960s and '70s, I understood every word. I even sang along. I can honestly say that this was not because he enunciated any better with the earlier songs. The opposite might actually be true. The reason that I could understand certain lyrics and not others is because I had heard some of the songs hundreds of times from the radio, records, CDs, and live performances. I knew them by heart and therefore I "heard" them more clearly. I even recognized when Dylan departed from the recorded versions of the songs because I was familiar with the general context, meter, and rhyme. Perhaps most importantly, the songs carried meaning for me. The lyrics of my memory were not memorized by rote; I never set out to memorize them. They just seeped into my consciousness over time. Therefore I just naturally perceived a reflection of these lyrics at the concert.

This concert reinforced for me two of the key claims of this book: (1) Memory helps to interpret the perception of reality and vice versa; and (2) interpretation is both foundational and paramount. With this in mind, I propose that the study of memory patterns (what I will later call memory refraction) fills out the model of the hermeneutical circle. As Schleiermacher and others have argued, interpretation is an ongoing cyclical process. I propose that memory functions as the momentum required for this constant to and fro motion. As I have suggested elsewhere,[1] recent memory theory advances the discussion of hermeneutics in helpful ways. As this diagram indicates, memory moves forward in particular patterns. These patterns help to localize "new" meanings and "new" perceptions within previous thought-categories. My perceptions at the Bob Dylan concert were localized within my previous memorization of his lyrics. In this way, I was able to project meaning upon my "new" perception of these lyrics.

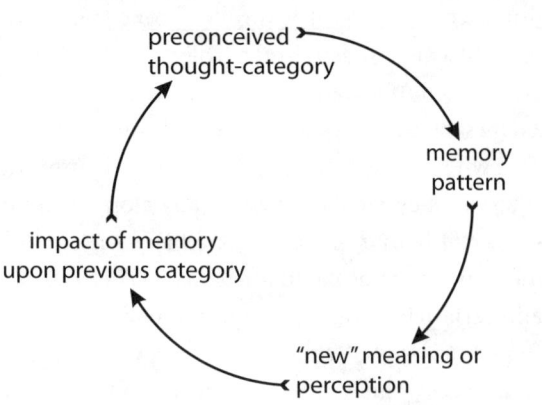

Also indicated by this diagram, once "new" perceptions have been localized within previous categories the old categories are impacted (and therefore changed) in the process. Now, whenever I hear the old recordings of Dylan's music, I frame this hearing within my memories of the concert. These old songs have new meaning for me. Most importantly, I must make it clear that the changes I impose upon my memories function to make them intelligible in the present. It is memory's fluidity that makes it seem constant and reliable.

RELATEDLY, MY concert illustration also provides help in understanding the nature of "orality." Orality is a term used in contrast to literacy. It simply draws a distinction between the act of writing and the act of speaking. An "oral culture" is one where the spoken word is the default for communication, memory, and tradition. Cultures that are largely illiterate are, by default, oral cultures. While modern American culture is highly literate, my experience at the Dylan concert provided me a small window into what oral cultures know instinctively: *Orality is a balance of variation and stability.*

Allow me to explain what I mean by this. Students of orality will tell you that every act of oral performance is dynamic and fluid. Performers will inevitably vary their performances, both intentionally and subconsciously. According to the mutual needs of the performer and audience, details shift, emphases change, lines are omitted, backgrounds are explained. This is what I mean by the "variation" part.

Bob Dylan began his career by learning a repertoire of traditional folk and country songs. For this reason, the young Dylan sought out the aging folk musician Woody Guthrie. Musician Pete Seeger talks about learning from Guthrie and alongside Dylan:

> The moment I became acquainted with old songs, I realized that people were always changing them. Think of it as an age-old

process that's been going on for thousands of years. People take old songs, change them a little, add to them, adapt them for new people. It happens in every other field: lawyers take old laws to fit new citizens. So I'm one in this long chain and so are millions of other musicians. And Woody stepped right into that. He was always making up new verses. Songs about real life, real people, real events. . . . I look upon us all as Woody's children.[2]

The oral transmitting of traditional songs and folklore is marked by a process of variation. Not surprisingly, Bob Dylan's songs took on this character as well. His music is covered by countless singers and bands. His "Along the Watchtower" is a perfect example. After Dylan, Jimi Hendrix gave the song new life. U2 did the same in the 1980s. The Dave Matthews Band covered it in the 1990s. With each rendering, the song took on a new shape. Still, each time it was recognizable as the same song. This is what I mean by stability. There are enough core elements retained to keep the identity and genius of the song stable.

When I heard Dylan perform "All Along the Watchtower" in the present decade, it was certainly the same song I remembered. Simultaneously, it was a new creation. Thus "variance and stability." Bob Dylan borrowed this key feature of folk music and folklore and infused his music with it.[3]

Culture Focus F: Preaching Politics

One of the most commonly held opinions about Jesus was that he was a "teacher." I have often wondered whether this statement is true enough to be helpful. It most certainly is factual. Jesus taught publicly. He had students who sat at his feet to learn from him. Nobody really doubts that he was in the business of teaching. But this description of Jesus might also be profoundly misleading. To modern Western ears, teaching sounds secular. This is to say that the word "preaching" sounds religious, even confrontational, while the word "teaching" sounds less so. To call Jesus a teacher, in my cultural context, defangs him. On the contrary, not only was Jesus a religious preacher, his most common sermon had to do with politics.

According to Matthew, "Jesus went throughout all Galilee, teaching in their synagogues and preaching the good news of the kingdom . . ." (4:23). Notice that the categories "teaching" and "preaching" overlap in this summary. Here Matthew summarizes Jesus' central message: the good news about the kingdom.

The word "kingdom" doesn't sound quite as political to people in a democracy, but it was certainly a political category to Jesus' hearers. Jesus was preaching about theocracy to an oppressed people. In Roman-occupied Galilee, this was a dangerous sermon. In a land where Caesar was considered divine, the "good news" of God's kingdom meant "bad news" for Caesar. Not only did Jesus "preach," he chose a topic that made it impossible to remain neutral. In order to honestly maintain the claim that "Jesus was a teacher," we must first shake the notions of passivity and impartiality that this implies.

Understanding the difference between literate culture and oral culture is important for us because Jesus was first remembered by a largely oral culture. His words and deeds were not initially recorded, nor were they archived. Jesus' words and deeds were *re-*

membered by an oral community. Every time Jesus told a parable worth remembering it was remembered by several witnesses with degrees of variance and stability. Every public debate that Jesus won was remembered several times over.

The stories we read now in the gospels existed in the collective memory of his disciples for over two decades before they were committed to parchment. The importance of this point will be shown in my next chapter. For now, I simply must emphasize that Jesus' words and deeds were remembered with variance and stability from the outset. When dealing with sources for the life of Jesus, there are no "original" documents to be found; there never were.

I MUST make one more point with this chapter. For those of us in a literate culture — if you're reading this book, this includes you — the game of telephone may come to mind. It's a party game where a group of mischievous folks sit in a circle and whisper a phrase into the ear of the person next to them. Without stating the phrase loudly or clearly, the phrase is only shared one whisper at a time. What begins as an "original" statement is slowly altered with each whisper. After the phrase is sent person by person to the last person in the circle, that person repeats the phrase loudly and everybody laughs at how the phrase has changed.[4]

It must be said that this is *not* a controlled exercise in orality. It is an exercise in variation without stability. The vast majority of human civilization operated with largely illiterate cultures. Are we to imagine that all these civilizations were the equivalent of giggling children? That the golden ages of Egypt, Rome, Britain, the Maya, etcetera had no confidence in the reliability of social communication?[5] No. Oral cultures have been capable of tremendous competence. The human mind can remember vast amounts of information with great accuracy when it remains active and fluid. The oral culture in which Jesus was reared trained their brightest children to remember entire libraries of story, law, poetry, song, etcetera.

In Jesus' culture, there were different kinds of memory with different functions. Important stories, important sayings were not remembered casually. When a rabbi imparted something important to his disciples, the memory was expected to maintain a high degree of stability.

Ironically, it was often the case that the most stable memories were those that were also the most flexible and malleable. The more important a memory is to a community, the more interpreted it will be. In Memory III, I will unpack this statement in my discussion of memory refraction.

SUGGESTIONS FOR FURTHER READING

James D. G. Dunn. *Jesus Remembered.* Cambridge and Grand Rapids: Eerdmans, 2003.

W. Kelber. *The Oral and the Written Gospel: The Hermeneutics of Speaking and Writing in the Synoptic Tradition, Mark, Paul, and Q.* Philadelphia: Fortress, 1983.

Between Certainty and History

Historical sense and poetic sense should not, in the end, be contradictory, for if poetry is the little myth we make, history is the big myth we live, and in our living, constantly remake.

Robert Penn Warren

There is no history, only fictions of varying degrees of plausibility.

Voltaire

Historical Jesus research is a discipline that is about four hundred years old. For all of that time, there has been a contingent of historians that voiced angst or frustration with their inability to get back to the "real" Jesus. According to these scholars, the Jesus of history was veiled by uncertainty due to the legendary character of the gospels.

Early Jesus historian Gotthold Lessing (1729-81) openly wished that he could believe the many supernatural reports about Jesus.[1] These stories just led to uncertainty because they didn't square with the reality in which he lived. He lamented that historical uncertainty "is the wide ugly ditch, over which I cannot come, however often and earnestly I have tried to make the leap." He pleaded, "If anyone can help me over, please do it. I ask, I implore him."[2]

Lessing's short essay is like a charged landmine from a previous generation's war. Reading it reminds me that many of my default thought-categories are still at home in modern thought. Lessing's angst is far too relatable to my own for me to claim otherwise. Lend your attention to Lessing's notion of human perception.

> The problem is that *reports of* fulfilled prophecies are not fulfilled prophecies; that *reports of* miracles are not miracles. These, the prophecies fulfilled before my eyes, the miracles that occur before my eyes, are immediate in their effect. But those — the reports of fulfilled prophecies and miracles, have to work through a medium which takes away all their force.[3]

Here Lessing makes a distinction between actual reality (what really happened) and the "reports" of reality (what people said happened). For Lessing, all the power of the miraculous was robbed by the fact that the only proof of these happenings "has sunk to the level of human testimonies."

Notice that Lessing, a child of the enlightenment, maintained a firm distinction between *what really happened* and the perceptions, memories, and reports of human testimony. He doubted that a historical witness could be trusted with certainty — and he needed certainty. He concludes:

> If no historical truth can be demonstrated, then nothing can be demonstrated by means of historical truths. That is: *accidental truths of history can never become the proof of necessary truths of reason.*[4]

This is Lessing's most famous saying, and it cannot be fully unpacked here. My intention is to measure Lessing's need for certainty against what I have claimed of perception and memory over the course of this book.

Many historians have doubted historical reports because they needed certainty. The postmodern historian knows that uncertainty looms behind every perception of reality. Certainty is not attained simply because we've seen something with our own eyes. The best we can hope for is a higher degree of certainty along the spectrum of reliable perception. We rely on such "uncertainties" all of the time. This is why New Testament scholars Gerd Theissen and Dagmar Winter suggest the application of a "Criterion of Plausibility" to better measure historical accounts. At the end of the day, it is *plausibility* that compels us to rely on received information, whether it is seen firsthand or otherwise.[5]

Scholars determined to attain historical certainty will always be frustrated by the limits of modern presuppositions. Modern presuppositions have made skeptics out of a small (but boisterous) contingent of Jesus historians in every generation since Lessing. But the larger portion of historians have been no less guilty of a hunger for certainty. Historians who are more optimistic about historical certainty have tried to attain it through something akin to textual archaeology.

The physical evidence of the New Testament is manifested in several ancient documents and fragmented scraps of parchment. Each "version" of these texts is unique in some way. Almost every "manuscript" is slightly different in the way that it words the accounts and letters about Jesus. Very rarely does a manuscript have dramatic variance, but a handful of texts insert or omit entire paragraphs and/or alter the theological impact significantly. The academic discipline that analyzes the relationship of these versions is called textual criticism.

One of the central presuppositions of textual criticism is that priority should be given to the best reconstruction of the "original manuscripts" of the New Testament. Furthermore, textual criticism was founded on the notion that the closer we get to the original manuscripts, the closer we get to the original Jesus.

The most likely solution is that there were no "original manuscripts" of the gospels . . . rather, there were several remembered compositions.

If you recall my discussion of "orality" in the previous chapter, you might see the fatal flaw of this presupposition: Where the gospels are concerned, *there were no original manuscripts.* To suppose that there were "originals" is to impose a literary anachronism onto a largely oral culture. Since no one doubts that the words and deeds of Jesus were actively remembered by a community for over a decade,[6] one must conclude that there were several versions of these memories from the start. With this in mind, the best explanation of many textual variants is that there was no one original story. In fact, many recent studies of the gospels conclude that the variation and stability we see in the gospels are exactly what you'd expect from the variation and stability in any oral tradition.[7]

Keep in mind that in the earliest decades of Christianity there was not one but four (or five) "books" about Jesus' life. Keep in mind that Luke begins his story about Jesus by referring to several other "accounts" which he has used to form his story (Luke 1:1-3). Keep in mind that at the height of Jesus' public career he sent out several disciples to share his message and story *orally* to other regions (Matt. 10:7). Keep in mind that we have no physical evidence of any "original" documents of the New Testament.

The most likely solution is that there were no "original manuscripts" of the gospels (i.e., handwritten documents); rather, there were several remembered compositions. Moreover, we should expect that in an oral culture there would be no call to write down these compositions until the first generation of living memory began to die. Once that first generation began to die off, there would be a greater call for written accounts.[8] Upon the realization of such a "crisis" of collective memory, one should expect several varying compositions to emerge both independently and in relationship to other similar accounts. This is exactly what we see with the emergence of the gospels.

Any hope to reconstruct a single life of Jesus must navigate multiple variations — none of which are "original."[9] The postmodern historian is not concerned with solidifying a single account of the original story.

Another key deficiency in the quest for certainty is the mirage of objectivity. Consider the following assessment by the great theologian Rudolf Bultmann:

> No sane person can doubt that Jesus stands as founder behind the historical movement whose first distinct stage is represented by the oldest Palestinian community. But how far that community preserved an objectively true picture of him and his message is another question.[10]

The historian who continues to look for a "preserved" Jesus has no other recourse but skepticism. The historian who is intent to find "an objectively true picture" of Jesus has simply misunderstood the historian's task to account for varying and evolving social memories and explain their most plausible relationship.

Bultmann's brilliance was that he encouraged the modern historian to "encounter" Jesus existentially. He insisted that the modern historian should enter an intimate dialogue with history by way of its impact. Ironically, while Bultmann encouraged the modern mind to dispatch with objectivity, he faulted the ancient mind for not being objective enough. There is an unfortunate inconsistency here.

As odd as it might sound, historians do not work with the events as they actually happened, nor should they suppose that any single account will provide a picture of this with certainty or objectivity. Rather, the historian's task is to account plausibly for the multiple memories represented by those who interpreted past events.

Once this task is properly defined, the fact of uncertainty does not concern the historian. It should not concern the historian any more than it concerns the person who cannot "prove" the reality of any past occurrence. You don't have to "prove" the reality of your memories to believe earnestly that they represent reality. Since the past cannot be conjured up to verify a memory, we don't try to analyze the past. We simply analyze the memory itself as something that represents the past. Historians, like everybody else, are in the business of relying on memories that cannot be verified in absolutes.[11]

I say again: *The unremembered and uninterpreted past is not history.*

I will give another example of how modern presuppositions mislead historians. There are some historians who are concerned only with hard facts. Facts are hard to come by for the Jesus historian because the gospels look very much like other legendary stories. Some historians are of the mind that when an ancient story mirrors other well-known stories it must be bracketed out as fiction. Those who are less apt to label entire stories as "myth" try to peel away the layers of mythology to get to a historical core.

For instance, there are several indications that John the Baptist mimicked the prophets Elijah and Elisha (in dress, geography, message, and ministry[12]). Historians with minimalist tendencies see these imitations as literary invention. In other words, they think that the storytellers invented these details to retell the legends of Elijah and Elisha. Many modern historians think that such interpretive "embellishments" are of little value to the historian.

On the other hand, the postmodern historian is keenly interested in all interpretations, whether they are "factual" or not. After all, the true job of the historian is to measure and compare interpretations in order to explain the most plausible interpretation of the story. The postmodern mind doesn't attempt to peel away interpretation in order to find facts. The postmodern mind knows that no facts are available for analysis that have not been preceded, followed, and mediated by interpretation.

In the case of John the Baptist, we would do well to remember that many first-century Jews believed that Elijah would return someday to judge Israel's corrupt priesthood.[13] If people expected the coming of Elijah in the last days, might this have colored their interpretation of John? More to the point, many Jews eagerly *wanted* to believe that they were living in the last days. Might this have motivated their perceptions of John? The historian's true task is to tell the story of John the Baptist in a way that illuminates this memory category. John was remembered as a type of Elijah. But why?

Those who are only interested in the "facts" devoid of interpretation are doomed to miss the crucial why-questions. Sometimes it is the embellishments of a story that serve to answer these why-questions. Indeed, sometimes the historical figures themselves invite such embellishments.

As argued, the interpretive process of perception and memory moves like a circle. But, I have suggested, this cycle implies that memories are in a state of constant change. This is just as true for historical memories. Historical memories are in continual flux. This continuous fluctuation is what makes memories intelligible in the present. So instead of talking of a single hermeneutical circle, we should really be thinking of several turns around a spiraling trajectory.

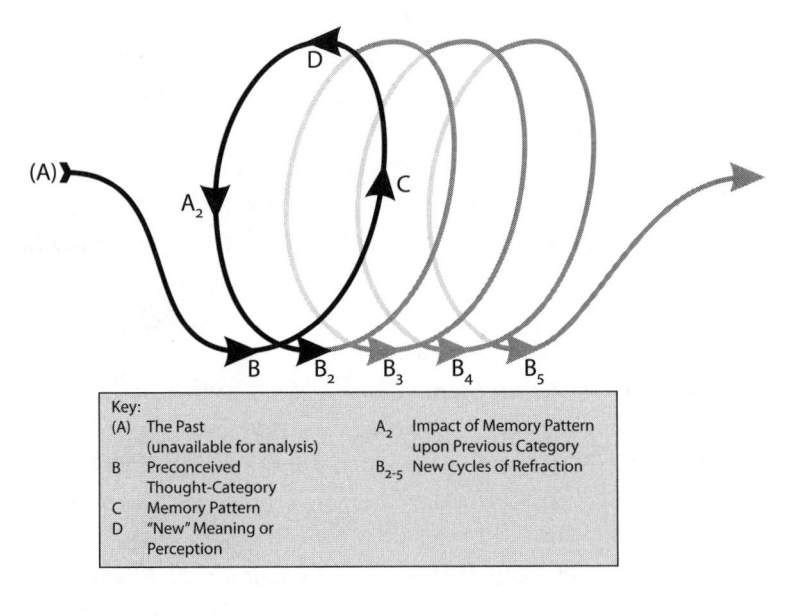

Key:
(A)	The Past (unavailable for analysis)	A₂	Impact of Memory Pattern upon Previous Category
B	Preconceived Thought-Category	B₂₋₅	New Cycles of Refraction
C	Memory Pattern		
D	"New" Meaning or Perception		

Each new cycle of the memory process reinterprets historical memory. In most cases, several cycles of memory have occurred before "history" gets written down. What this diagram illustrates is that history is an interpretive trajectory that is interpreted and reinterpreted with each new remembering. What this diagram does not show is that history is a combination of several memory trajectories, each with its own pattern of interpretation. The historian's task is to account for these interpretive trajectories, to tell the story of what set these memories in motion.

Previously (in History I), I quoted political columnist Lynn Sweet, who "married" the legacy of (then) Senator Barack Obama to the legend of Abraham Lincoln. According to Sweet, Obama and his campaign staff intentionally sought out venues and dates that recalled Lincoln's legacy. This is remarkably similar to what the first interpreters of John the Baptist did with the legacy of Elijah. In both cases, it is the whirling movement from old category to new meaning that moves these memories forward. When the "new" meaning of John the Baptist is localized within the previous category of Elijah, both are altered in the process. Both move forward in memory according to this new pattern.

Telling the stories of history requires much more than fact finding. Telling history requires analysis of how the facts have been mediated. The historian cannot separate the facts from the interpretations, nor should he/she try.

SUGGESTIONS FOR FURTHER READING

Dale, Allison. *Constructing Jesus: Memory, Imagination, and History.* Grand Rapids: Baker Academic Press, 2010.

Alan Kirk and Tom Thatcher. *Memory, Tradition, and Text: Uses of the Past in Early Christianity.* Semeia Studies 52. Leiden: Brill, 2005.

Gerd Theissen and Dagmar Winter. *The Quest for the Plausible Jesus: The Question of Criteria.* Louisville: Westminster/John Knox Press, 2002. Originally titled *Die Kriterienfrage in der Jesusforschung.* Fribourg: Universitätsverlag, 1997.

Talking Politics

I think the first reason that we should love our enemies, and I think this was at the very center of Jesus' thinking, is this: that hate for hate only intensifies the existence of hate and evil in the universe.

Martin Luther King Jr.

Many people in Jesus' culture believed that there were dramatic events unfolding in Heaven and Hell, and that this divine drama was mirrored on Earth. Great events on Earth were reflections of gods, angels, and demons warring and vying for power. In fact, one does not need to look far to find a similar worldview in modern Western culture. Look, for example, at the lyrics of the metal band, Demon Hunter. Their imagery is rife with supernatural predators and brute maulers who wreak havoc on personal spiritual realities.

In the Jewish version of this worldview, victories and losses by God's angelic armies had direct implications for Israel's political reality. Because politics were indelibly linked to religious belief, Jews believed that national repentance and righteousness were prerequisites for political autonomy. If Israel was unfaithful, many Jews believed that God would refuse to protect them on the battlefield. Even worse, Israel had a long history of seeing their God's hand

against them, manifested in the soldiers and swords of their enemies.

This is the historical and theological backdrop necessary to understand John the Baptist and Jesus. Many believed that the Baptizer was a medium between Heaven and Earth — that is to say, he
was a prophet who spoke for God. But, according to some, John
was "more than a prophet." The Gospel of Matthew addresses this
belief:

> Jesus began to speak to the crowds about John, "What did you go
> out into the wilderness to see? A reed shaken by the wind? But
> what did you go out to see? A man dressed in softness? Those
> who wear soft clothing are in kings' palaces! But what did you go
> out to see? A prophet? Yes, I tell you, and one who is more than a
> prophet. This is the one about whom it is written, *'Behold, I send
> my messenger ahead of you, who will prepare your way before
> you.'"* (Matt. 11:7-10; cf. Luke 7)[1]

Here Jesus claims that John is not merely a prophet but the "mes-
senger" (this is the same word for angel) expected to come in the
last days. At the end of Malachi, we learn that this angelic figure is
the legendary Elijah (4:5). Following the lead of Malachi, Jesus
claims that "John himself is Elijah who was to come" (Matt. 11:14).

In Jewish lore, Elijah was an especially mysterious prophet because the story of his death is never told. Rather, the biblical story
tells of Elijah riding a chariot of fire skyward and beyond the realm
of mortals. According to the prophet Malachi, Elijah would return
someday to judge the corruption in Israel's leadership.

In the worldview of Jesus and his contemporaries, human
events were perceived through the lens of ancient characters and
biblical prophecies. Texts like Malachi guided people's expectations
and perceptions. Figures like John the Baptist were perceived and
remembered from this vantage point. In several key ways, this way

of perceiving the world is alien to us. But we don't have to look far to find analogous thought-categories.

As I write this chapter, my email inbox flashes. My father has forwarded me the following Major League Baseball blog post. Pay special attention to the language used in the last paragraph:

Sunday, July 13, 2008
Giants sign 16-year-old Rodriguez

It's a beautiful day at Wrigley. The wind is blowing out, so maybe the Giants will get their first homer of the trip today.

Anyway, the Giants announced the anticipated signing of 16-year-old outfielder Rafael Rodriguez from the Dominican. Here is part of the notebook I am writing for tomorrow:

. . . The deal was announced on Rodriguez's 16th birthday, the first day he was eligible to sign. The Dominican hype machine has labeled Rodriguez the second coming of Vladimir Guerrero. Giants special assistant John Barr, the team's scouting director, said he dislikes such comparisons, but he described a Vlad-type player. . . .

Posted By: Henry Schulman

In the late 1990s, Montreal Expo Vladimir Guerrero became the archetypal "five-tool" player. This is shorthand for saying that Guerrero had all the talent necessary for excelling in every aspect of baseball. The player of interest here (Rodriguez) isn't just reminiscent of Vladimir Guerrero, he is "the second coming." The blogger attempts to temper the "hype" by simply saying that the youngster is a "Vlad-type player." This is the language of typology. It is not dissimilar to the contemporary political examples I gave previously in History I.

In Jesus' day, John the Baptist was seen as the second coming of Elijah. John was an Elijah-type. One of the key differences between this typology and ours is that the return of Elijah was linked to God's final judgment, apocalypse, and a new world order. Contemporary Western perspectives tend to use typology differently, but we are not strangers to "end of the world" talk. Those growing up under the shadow of the atomic bomb know this all too well.

It was only a generation ago when children practiced bomb safety rituals and parents dug underground bomb shelters. Such expectations stand behind the lyrics of Bob Marley's "Redemption Song." After singing of historical slavery to begin the song, his second stanza warns of metaphorical slavery:

> Emancipate yourselves from mental slavery;
> None but ourselves can free our minds.
> Have no fear for atomic energy,
> cause none of them can stop the time.
>
> How long shall they kill our prophets,
> While we stand aside and look? ooh!
> Some say it's just a part of it:
> We've got to fulfill de book.

Notice the presumption of biblical prophecy in the last two lines. Marley presupposes that many of his contemporaries read themselves into "de book" when it speaks of the last days. Indeed, there are those in every generation who interpret the violence they see around them as signs of the last days. Our contemporaries have this in common with the contemporaries of Jesus. When people start believing in the end of the world, many turn to the biblical prophets.

John the Baptist wasn't the first or the last prophetic voice to preach that God's judgment was imminent. But in Jesus' day, the Baptizer might have been the most popular. John the Baptist was known all over Judea. His words were heard by the power elite in Jerusalem. He had gained such popularity among the masses that politicians dared not criticize him publicly. For a while, John was considered untouchable. But his condemnation of the power elite eventually got him beheaded.

It is important to point out that, at the height of his career, John was much more well known than Jesus. John was a revolutionary who preached that the political reign of God was about to be established on Earth — this was good news for the repentant and bad news for those corrupted by power. This is exactly the message that Jesus adopted after John was hauled off and arrested.

In one of the most dramatic ideological shifts in human history, Jesus took on John's massive following and began to preach nonviolence.

Jesus' primary theological/political platform was that God's reign would be "good news" (this is the same word as "gospel") for the repentant (Mark 1:14-15). God's final judgment was on the way, and a new world order was close enough to touch. This was a shrewd political move by Jesus considering John's popularity. After John was arrested, many of his following dispersed, but a few faithful transferred their allegiance to Jesus.

When this theological/political platform is referred to in the gospels, it is given a pithy slogan: "the kingdom of God."[2] In Matthew, Mark, and Luke, talk of "the kingdom" is all over the place. It is mentioned in sayings, parables, and narrative. This is a good reason to think that there were early and widespread memories of Jesus' politics. Jesus historians appeal to this as the "Criterion of Multiple Forms." This criterion says that if a common topic or theme is seen in multiple genres within the gospels, it can be plausibly connected to historical memory rather than later invention. The scholarly consensus is that Jesus' career was hinged on "the kingdom of God."

For this reason, it is very likely that Jesus' early career was an extension of the message and ministry of John the Baptist. In fact, Jesus asks some of his followers about what the general public was saying about him: "Who do people say that I am?" The disciples tell Jesus that people think he is "John the Baptist; and others say 'Elijah'; but others say 'one of the prophets'" (in Mark 8:27-28). Early memories of Jesus typologically linked him to the legacies of both John and Elijah.

But it was not long before Jesus' concept of the kingdom departed from John's. Initially, John happily endorsed Jesus as God's chosen revolutionary. However, once John was imprisoned, Jesus didn't do much in the way of revolution. John preached of the kingdom coming by way of axes and fire (Luke 3:9). He used violent metaphors for the coming of a literal judgment. Most people who heard this message would think of a military uprising. John passed this mantle to Jesus, but was soon disappointed.

In one of the most dramatic ideological shifts in human history, Jesus took on John's massive following and began to preach nonviolence:

> Truly I say to you, among those born of women there has not arisen anyone greater than John the Baptist! Yet the one who is least in the Kingdom of Heaven is greater than he. From the days of John the Baptist until now the Kingdom of Heaven suffers violence, and violent men take it by force (Matt. 11:11-12).

What is Jesus saying here? Is he holding John in reverence? Or is he saying that the humble and the meek are to be held in higher esteem? Jesus seems to be condemning violent men. Was he associating John with men who attempted to advance God's politics by force?

This kind of preaching must have alienated many of John's supporters. Talk of humility and nonviolence throws a wet blanket onto hopes for revolution. Jesus must have lost a large portion of his following after this speech. Even Jesus' inner circle of disciples were confused. The sons of Zebedee asked Jesus if they should "call fire down from Heaven" onto their enemies (Luke 9:54). This is an unmistakable appeal to Elijah typology. In 2 Kings 1:10, the prophet prays down fire upon the oppressors of Israel. The request of his zealous disciples seems to have earned them the mocking nickname "Sons of Thunder" — i.e., the boys of loud noises, but not very bright. Jesus continued to preach nonsense to the ears of zealous men:

> . . . love your enemies, do good to those who hate you, bless those who curse you, pray for those who mistreat you. Whoever hits you on the cheek, offer him the other also; and whoever takes away your coat, do not withhold your shirt from him either. Give to everyone who asks of you, and whoever takes away what is yours, do not demand it back. (Luke 6:27-30)

Jesus continued to preach about judgment, but he was convinced that God would do his own judging and that Israel shouldn't attempt to literalize the violent metaphors of Scripture.

According to Jesus, if someone takes your outer garment, you are obligated to give them your undershirt as well. Keep in mind that this implies nakedness in a two-garment culture.[3] New Testament scholar Walter Wink suggests that this kind of action is a form of passive resistance rather than simple passivity. Wink points out that, in this culture, when a man is seen nude by another, the clothed man is shamed in the seeing. Therefore, Jesus was teaching his followers how to shame their oppressors. If so, Jesus' politics were revolutionary in a quite ironic way.

Shortly before John's death, he sent word to Jesus from jail.

John had started to doubt whether Jesus was Israel's next great leader. John asked of him, "Are you the 'Expected One' or should we look for somebody else?" (Luke 7:21). John had hoped to see city walls felled like trees, and corruption burnt away like grass. As he neared the end of his life, John must have wondered if Jesus had any intention of marching toward "kingdom come."

WHY? WHY did Jesus depart so dramatically from John's initial message?

The answer to this question is found in Jesus' perception of the spiritual realm. When Jesus looked into the eyes of his oppressors, he didn't just see evil men with evil motives, he saw the demonic. Jesus believed that the "real" war was between Heaven and Hell. He honestly believed that the real enemy was Satan and his demonic armies.

Jesus, like many in his culture, believed that demons could cause illness and death. In the perception of Jesus, demons stood between Israel and God's kingdom. Physical aggression wouldn't solve the fundamental problems that plagued humankind. If Satan could be defeated, the promises of Isaiah 11 could be fulfilled:

> And the wolf will dwell with the lamb, and the leopard will lie down with the young goat, and the calf and the young lion and the fatling together; and a little boy will lead them. Also the cow and the bear will graze, their young will lie down together, and the lion will eat straw like the ox. The nursing child will play by the hole of the cobra, and the weaned child will put his hand on the viper's den. They will not hurt or destroy in all my holy mountain, for the earth will be full of the knowledge of the LORD as the waters cover the sea. . . . And he will lift up a standard for the nations and assemble the banished ones of Israel, and will gather the dispersed of Judah from the four corners of the earth. (Isa. 11:6-12)

According to Isaiah, the leader who would usher in this peaceful kingdom would be a "Prince of Peace" (Isa. 9:6). This leader wouldn't have need of handheld weapons because he would win his battles with his wisdom and the spoken word: "The Spirit of the LORD will rest on him, the Spirit of wisdom and understanding. . . . With the breath of his lips he will slay the wicked" (Isa. 11:2-4).

Jesus believed that, by the Spirit of God, he could slay the *source* of evil by casting out demons with his words. He claimed that "if I cast out demons by the Spirit of God, then the kingdom of God has come upon you" (Matt. 12:28). God's kingdom could be achieved, not with physical violence, but with the "Spirit of wisdom." Once the spiritual power behind Rome was bound, God's peaceable kingdom would become a reality.

. . . lest we judge too quickly, we ought to remember that Jesus' career as an exorcist went hand in hand with his nonviolent gospel.

To the sensibilities of contemporary Western culture, this kind of thing is perceived as pre-modern naiveté. To some, Jesus' marriage of spiritual and political realities bordered the insane. Both then and now many question whether Jesus' demon hunting is really evidence of a "Spirit of wisdom." But lest we judge too quickly, we ought to remember that Jesus' career as an exorcist went hand in hand with his nonviolent gospel. Perhaps our enlightened, violent culture is just as problematic. According to Jesus, "Wisdom is vindicated by her deeds" (Matt. 11:19).

THIS WINDOW into the Jesus tradition allows me to make three observations.

(1) The memories of Jesus weren't shared orally merely because

his culture lacked pens and paper. The spoken word defined his political movement. Orality was Jesus' weapon of choice. He believed that his words held the very power of God. By his oratory, the very Spirit of God was assailing the gates of hell.

With his words, Jesus made a memorable impact upon each of his hearers. Some believed that his words healed them. Others were impacted by his redefinition of the kingdom. Still others were offended by his subversive message and saw him as an affront to Israel's proper political aspirations. In each case, the impact of his message varied from interpreter to interpreter. At the same time, the Jesus tradition maintained a stable core of memory. The message of God's kingdom was at the heart of this core.

(2) As the memories of Jesus took shape in story-form (we might think of the gospels first as dramatic performances and subsequently as written "books"), certain typologies acted as interpretive frameworks. The author of Luke-Acts seems especially interested in portraying Jesus as an Elijah-type.

Typology is both a memory-shaping filter and a literary device. When historical texts appeal to typology, they naturally mimic historical memories that were shaped by typology. Consider the story of Jesus' ascension:

In the first chapter of Acts, Jesus simply flies away. He leaves Earth in grand fashion, through the clouds, and is gone.[4] Now, as a historian, I simply have a hard time imagining Jesus flying into outer space like Superman. I readily admit that my post-enlightenment, modern biases shape my skepticism. As a postmodern, I will not rule out a story's origin in memory simply because of these biases. However, I think that the most plausible explanation is that Luke has been impacted by the Elijah typology present in the tradition he has collected and has allowed this to color his interpretation of Mark 16:19.

Just like Elijah, Jesus was taken into Heaven alive and ready to return someday. This also allows Luke to postpone the literal realization of the kingdom. Just before he ascends, his disciples ask him, "Lord, is it at this time you are restoring the kingdom to Israel?" (Acts 1:6). Jesus tells them that only the Father can answer this question. But because Jesus was taken as Elijah was, the reader expects him to return at the end of days. In this way, Jesus now occupies the place formerly occupied by Elijah's legend.[5]

But this story is still of historical value, as it allows us to see Luke's literary agenda clearly. While modern historians have tended to bracket "legendary" material, I suggest that this story can serve as a measuring stick by which to assess other stories included in Luke.

If Luke's motives were to portray Jesus as an Elijah-type, why would he include Jesus' claim that *John was Elijah?* This seems to undermine the author's literary agenda. The best answer to this is that the author included sayings and stories in his gospel simply because they were well remembered. As indicated in Luke's prologue, the author saw himself as a collector of stories. Luke held the memories of Jesus in such high regard that he chose to include them even when they did not suit his literary aims.[6]

Jesus historians call this the "Criterion of Contrary Tendency" or "Divergent Traditions." The idea here is that if a story or saying contains details that promote an agenda that runs contrary to editorial tendencies, these details are not as easily explained as fiction. The Baptizer's affinity to Elijah seems to be a product of memory because Luke had no motive to invent this detail.

(3) Finally, there is a small contingent of Jesus historians who are inclined to label the gospels as historical fiction on the basis of typology and scriptural frameworks. They argue that most of the stories about Jesus were *invented* to mirror precedents and prophecies of the Hebrew Bible.

It must be said that while typology is a prominent literary device, it is first a device of memory. The impact that narratives and types have on perception cannot be understated. The climactic moments of our lives are measured against and interpreted by the climactic moments of great stories and indeed history itself. The political message of Jesus was memorable precisely because he was able to tap into (and reshape) the interpretive categories already present in his culture.

Suggestions for Further Reading

Richard Horsley. *Jesus and the Spiral of Violence: Popular Jewish Resistance in Roman Palestine.* San Francisco: Harper & Row, 1987.

Walter Wink. *Jesus and Nonviolence: A Third Way.* Minneapolis: Fortress Press, 2003.

PART THREE

So do we live and move amidst illusions?
Has what we're seeing fooled us
And only exists in our minds?
And what are we to do with such conclusions?
For what cannot come true in a world of a
Mystical kind?

Peter Mayer

Do You Think You're What They Say You Are?

Lieutenant Daniel Taylor: Have you found Jesus yet, Gump?
Forrest Gump: I didn't know I was supposed to be looking for
him, sir.

Eric Roth

Did Jesus have royal aspirations? Did he fancy himself as Israel's king? How did he expect to deal with the power structures of Jerusalem and Rome? Wasn't he terribly mistaken about God's coming kingdom? Isn't this what got him killed?

What can we really expect from a pre-enlightenment peasant like Jesus? What could he have to offer historical memory besides quaint folk wisdom? If he wasn't equipped with a modern understanding of the universe, wasn't his perception of reality inherently flawed?

Isn't the Bible's portrayal of Jesus historically flawed? Given the many contradictions in the gospels, how is a historical portrait even possible? Aren't we better off reading the gospels as stories? Are we in any position to suggest a relationship between ancient story and ancient history? How can the historian speak of the historical Jesus with any degree of confidence?

Believing Is Seeing

As a Christian I have no duty to allow myself to be cheated,
but I have the duty to be a fighter for truth and justice.

Martin Luther King Jr.

The genius of Martin Luther King was his ability to manipulate public perception. Like Gandhi before him, King knew that the perpetrators of an oppressive system could be embarrassed. Otherwise apathetic bystanders were won over by what they saw on television. White America was given a front-row seat to the injustice they had enabled. But, in order to gain the public's sympathy, King needed the TV cameras in the right places at the right times.

Much of what America saw on television was intentionally choreographed. King's "passive" demonstrations were planned to provoke violent responses from the police. When he suspected that dogs or fire hoses would be used, King would tip the press. His protestors were taught to play the victim dramatically rather than fight or flee. Masterfully, Martin Luther King shaped public opinion by "scripting" reality for the cameras. It was at the same time contrived and real. The ability to manipulate perception can be a powerful tool.

But I have a confession to make. I led this chapter with a quote that read:

As a Christian I have no duty to allow myself to be cheated, but I have the duty to be a fighter for truth and justice.

Martin Luther King Jr.

Would you view this saying differently if this was said, not by King, but by Adolf Hitler? In fact, it *is* a quote from Hitler. It may well describe the theology of King, but (as far as I know) he never said these words. If this changes your perception of the quote, I would encourage you to ask yourself why. *Why does it matter who said it? Does the source change the truth of what is said?*

When you give source information for a quotation, you make an appeal to authority. By providing the name of a historical figure, you frame the quote by the historical memory of that person. I first (falsely) framed the above quotation with the memory of the archetypal "fighter for truth and justice." In doing so, I subversively coerced you to read the word "fighter" metaphorically. If King were to have used this phrase, "fighter" would invoke his legacy of *passive* resistance.

Most of the time, our interpretive frameworks are unknown to us. It often takes a dramatic shift to reveal them. But, and I must emphasize this strongly, the reframing of interpretive frameworks is not so dramatic.

But the word becomes denotative on the lips of the archetypal fascist. In other words, by invoking Hitler's legacy of violence, the word "fighter" is less likely to be read metaphorically. To modern sensibilities, this word means something entirely different when framed with the memory of Adolf Hitler. In this way, I manipulated your perception by reframing the context of those words.

This demonstrates much more than simple semantics. I intentionally chose to use historical archetypes that represent opposites. The name King represents much more than the historical figure; it is an embodiment of a complex group of hopes, ideals, and opinions. The name is a cipher for several cultural thought-categories. In the same way, the name Hitler is also an archetype. By falsely appealing to King and then shifting the spotlight to Hitler, I set an entirely different interpretive framework in place.

Most of the time, our interpretive frameworks are unknown to us. It often takes a dramatic shift to reveal them. But, and I must emphasize this strongly, the reframing of interpretive frameworks is not so dramatic.

This kind of subtle reframing happens all the time. Have you ever heard an old married couple argue over the color of a piece of clothing? One is convinced that it's black. The other is equally convinced that it's navy blue. Have you ever been asked to help solve such a debate? I have to admit that I've taken part in such disputes. Inevitably, someone in the room will appeal to a similar color and compare by contrast.

Wife: "Look! *This* is black, *that* is navy blue!"
Husband: "No it's just faded. Compare it to your Levis. How can you say it's not black?"

Both husband and wife think that if they change the surrounding context, the other person will recognize the color correctly. It is a simple reframing of interpretive frameworks. An annoying reframing to be sure; I highly recommend avoiding these if you can.

Once a framework is entrenched, it is hard to reframe. Consider the prayer of St. Francis:

Lord, make me an instrument of your peace,
Where there is hatred, let me sow love;

where there is injury, pardon;
where there is doubt, faith;
where there is despair, hope;
where there is darkness, light;
where there is sadness, joy;

O Divine Master, grant that I may not so much seek to be
consoled as to console;
to be understood as to understand;
to be loved as to love.

For it is in giving that we receive;
it is in pardoning that we are pardoned;
and it is in dying that we are born to eternal life.

Historically speaking, these words have no connection to St. Francis. The prayer was written anonymously for a French magazine called *La Clochette* (1912) and then printed on the back of a picture of St. Francis in 1920. Yet, even for those of us who know the true origin, it is very difficult to shake the association of St. Francis. Sometimes I wonder whether my perception of the prayer is helped or hurt by the association.

Perceptions are constantly being manipulated like this, both by design and by accident. For many beneficiaries of democratic capitalism, the ideas of Marx have been reframed in the legacies of Lenin, Stalin, and Castro. The phrase "Helter Skelter" was given new meaning by the Beatles, then reframed by Charles Manson, and then reframed again by U2. The words of St. Paul have been reframed by misogynists and feminists alike.

A similar manipulation of perception can be seen in storytelling. A good storyteller has the power to reveal crucial details at the end of a story that force you to see earlier plot points in a new light. Consider M. Night Shyamalan's *The Sixth Sense*. In this ghost story, the main character investigates the possibility of paranormal activity. Bruce Willis plays a skeptical psychiatrist with a client who talks to dead people. As the story concludes *(if you haven't seen the film, I'm about to ruin it for you)*, the audience learns that the psychiatrist is, himself, a ghost.

When this plot twist is revealed, the audience is forced to rethink the entire story from a new perspective. In 1999, this film was so successful that many viewers chose to see it a second time to reframe their initial perception of the plot. When perceived a second time, the audience recognized hints of the eventual plot twist throughout the film. These details held very little meaning for the audience during their first viewing. While these details were easily overlooked in the first viewing, they were of great interest in the second.

What this demonstrates is that the manipulation of perception is not necessarily underhanded. People enjoyed this film precisely because it manipulated them so well! It is the same reason why magicians attract a crowd. Illusions are interesting.

UNTIL NOW this chapter has given examples of intentional and strategic perception manipulation. But it is important to realize that *all* perception is malleable to some extent. Building on the model of a circle (Perception II), perception can be thought of as a continuous cycle of impressions and projections, projections and impressions. We project onto the world what we expect to perceive. Therefore familiar categories shape what we are likely to perceive. Yet with every new perception, our thought-categories are slightly altered. The more impressive the perception, the more it will alter our categories.

Philosopher Hans-Georg Gadamer (1900-2002) argued that this ebb and flow between projection and impression is largely subconscious.

The prejudices and fore-meanings that occupy the interpreter's consciousness are not at his disposal. He cannot separate in advance the productive prejudices that enable understanding from the prejudices that hinder it and lead to misunderstandings.[1]

With this in mind, perception always presents the likelihood of misunderstanding. In a way, because we are always refining our understanding of the world, every perception is (however slightly) a misunderstanding. What is learning if it isn't the reframing of naïve thought-categories?

Here is what I am *not* saying: I am not saying that the objects around us are hopelessly relative. Our senses must be trusted if we are to survive. Still, there is always room to improve our perceptions. This kind of relativism isn't hopeless; it gives us hope that we can train our senses to perceive better.

Any new parent listening to a baby monitor will tell you that it takes a while before you trust your senses. When my daughter was new, I would hear a sound over the monitor and ask my wife, "Was that her?" This question is always followed by an attentive silence — both parents waiting to get a better listen. Both know that it is possible to think you heard something that you didn't really hear. We must trust our senses and, therefore, they must be honed.

Depending on your environment and occupation, it is possible to hone your senses beyond what is normal to other people. Mothers can often identify their babies from other children (blindfolded) based on smell alone. An accomplished sailor can see wind before he feels it by recognizing the texture and color of the water. Baseball great Buck O'Neill was able to recognize batters by the sound of their swing.

On the other hand, when our senses dull, we trust them less; we become needier and must learn to trust others. My father takes medication that has dulled his sense of smell (making him an interesting cook). If he suspects that the oven pilot is out, he knows that he must ask someone else if it "smells like gas." The older we get, the more obvious it is how very precarious our perceptions are.

FINALLY, IT'S necessary to move from a nuanced discussion to the extreme. In this chapter, I have tried to give examples of the subtle manipulations, misunderstandings, and trainings of perception. I've done this to show how very prevalent and mundane "category projection" is when we perceive. The malleable nature of our perception isn't an outlandish philosophical construct; it is common sense in everyday life.

But, in order to show how powerful category projection can be, an extreme (and utterly tragic) example is helpful. This final example is a true story that was reported by every major news outlet in 2008:

A van carrying Taylor University students crashed, killing three students and a member of the university's staff. In the aftermath of the crash, two girls were misidentified. Whitney Cerak was identified as Laura Van Ryn and Laura Van Ryn was identified as Whitney Cerak. Cerak survived; Van Ryn did not. It was a tragically simple mistake made by public servants who meant well. Whitney Cerak's family was told that she was dead and they grieved her loss. Meanwhile, Van Ryn's family nursed the woman they thought was Laura Van Ryn back to health.

For five full weeks, Laura Van Ryn's family and boyfriend took care of Whitney Cerak and perceived her as Laura. It took five weeks of sitting by her bedside, twenty-four hours a day, before they realized that they were calling a stranger by a familiar name.[2] The two girls have similar characteristics, but also many distinct differences. The families of both girls were interviewed by Matt Lauer of *Dateline*.[3] Lauer editorializes:

> It's true that Whitney and Laura shared a superficial resemblance. Both were young, blonde, attractive. But there were key differences, too. The teeth, the eyes, the piercing. And Whitney is about four inches taller than Laura. How could they [the family and friends of Laura] not see those differences?

After a severe crash, one might expect a familiar face to be swollen or disfigured. It is also understandable that without facial expressions (Whitney was unconscious after the crash), a face is more difficult to identify. But what makes this story remarkable is that Whitney Cerak was misperceived for over a month. This month included group therapy, face-to-face conversations, and physical interaction. How could a boyfriend, a sister, or a parent be fooled for so long?

The transcript of Matt Lauer's interview with the Van Ryn family addresses this key question:[4]

Matt Lauer: Let's just try and handle the one question that so many viewers are going to ask once and for all. They're going to say, "They were right up against the bed 24 hours a day. There were these little moments of eye color and teeth and the belly button." And they're going to say, "How could this have gone on so long?" How do you explain it to people?

Don Van Ryn [father of the deceased]: Well, first I say you're right. It's an amazing thing, isn't it? How could it have gone on so long? But as we've tried to describe, you have to try and put yourself in our shoes at the time. . . . It just goes back to what we were told on the way down. That our daughter had been, you know, in a bad accident. Expect to see her altered. And we walked in, we saw that. And with the tubes hanging out. And we — she looked like Laura. And there were a lot of similarities, definitely. As I look at the two now, no, I don't think she looks like Laura. But again, you have to realize too that at least 100 other people, other friends were in that room and saw her.

Matt Lauer: Is that perhaps it? That when people face a trauma like this and a world turned upside down that in some ways you see what you're told to see and believe what you hope to believe?

Don Van Ryn: It's quite possible. And all our energy was focused on making her well. Healing her. And it became her identity. We talk about . . . it's like you say, it —

Lisa Van Ryn [sister of the deceased]: Her altered state became her identity.

Don Van Ryn: Yeah. And you say, "well, it's just — " None of these things we were looking for. I mean we weren't looking to establish the fact that this wasn't our daughter.

Lisa Van Ryn: Viewers are all saying, "Why didn't you notice the teeth or the shoes or the whatever?" It's like those are pieces to a puzzle that we didn't even know existed.

Susie Van Ryn [mother of the deceased]: We didn't know there was a puzzle.

Lisa Van Ryn: We didn't know we were supposed to be putting together a puzzle.

For the purposes of this book, Don Van Ryn's explanation is quite important. He said, "It just goes back to what we were told on the way down. That our daughter had been, you know, in a bad accident. Expect to see her altered. And we walked in, we saw that."

The family was *told* what to *expect* to perceive. When given these expectations, they perceived according to their expectations.

Expectation is a large part of perception.

OVER THE course of this book, I've provided examples of perception that show its essential interpretive nature. I've argued that the act of perceiving *requires* interpretation. This is true for the little things, like color association. It is also true of the big things, like identifying your own child in your darkest moment. It is true of every act of perception in between.

Perception is interpretation. Your environment, family, culture, emotional state, and prejudices color everything. The human mind perceives according to its continually shifting thought-categories.

SUGGESTIONS FOR FURTHER READING

S. J. Ceci. "False Beliefs." Pages 91-125 in *Memory Distortion.* Edited by D. Schachter. Cambridge, MA: Harvard University Press, 1995.

Judith C. S. Redman. "How Accurate Are Eyewitnesses? Bauckham and the Eyewitnesses in the Light of Psychological Research." *Journal of Biblical Literature* 129, no. 1 (2010): 177-97.

D. J. Simons. "Inattentional_blindness," *Scholarpedia* 2, no. 5 (2007): 3244. Available from www.scholarpedia.org/article/Inattentional_blindness.

Through a Glass Darkly

Get your facts first, then you can distort them as you please.

Mark Twain

This will be a short chapter. I offer you here my foundational conception of memory. Because I do not want this concept to be lost in
a barrage of illustrations and examples, I will only use one: I will
use the analogy of a telescope to introduce what I think is the essence of memory: refraction.

Professional memory theorists use a technical term that has
gotten me into trouble. The term is "distortion," or "memory distortion." The basic concept here is that all memories are filtered,
colored, emphasized, utilized, made vague over time, etcetera. It's
a term intended to shock readers out of the "memory bank"
model of memory. Many theorists like the word "distortion" to
emphasize the utter deficiency of the notion that the mind acts
like a simple storage unit for memories. Memory is not "passively
preserved," they argue, it is shaped and reshaped with each new
interpretation. Therefore the act of remembering is always an act
of distortion.

I am largely sympathetic to this description of memory. I
have previously diagrammed the process of remembering in

terms of memory "patterns." We are now in a position to see that memory is actually distorted by these patterns. However, whenever I refer to "memory distortion," people cringe with distaste. The word "distortion" has negative connotations that distract readers from an otherwise compelling argument. When memory theorists refer to memory distortion, most often they are not talking about "false memory." To many people, "distortion" evokes ideas of brainwashing or revisionist history. But in order to explain memory distortion, I must emphasize its necessary and beneficial function. It is crucially important to point out that distortion is, most commonly, *a natural, necessary, and benign function of memory selection.*

Perspective and interpretation are the very basis for memory's existence. In order to remember anything, it must be selected as relevant and distinguished from all irrelevant details. It is simply impossible to know every detail about any object; most details must be forgotten for others to be emphasized. It is impossible to recollect an object without emphasizing certain details, or to recall an object without perspective or interpretation. We distort our perceptions when we select them for memory.

The fact that we do not "see" the past as it exists in time is the very reason that we must rely on our memories. What we see is a bent, or refracted, version of the past.

So, really, *memory is distortion.* This does not mean that our memories are not true. If the criteria for truth were defined by a given memory's *lack of distortion,* all discussion about our perceptions of the past would be rendered futile. Memory theorist Michael Schudson describes the confusion: "The notion that memory can be 'distorted' assumes that there is a standard by which we can judge or measure what a [truthful] memory must be."[1] Similarly memory theorist Jan Assmann says that the "notion 'distorted memory' seems to presuppose that there is something like 'undistorted memory.'"[2] Schudson argues that such a standard is nonexistent since "[d]istortion is inevitable. Memory is distortion since memory is invariably and inevitably selective."[3]

Still, no matter how clearly or often I say that *all memory is memory distortion* and that this claim in no way denigrates the reliability of memory, the negativity of the word "distortion" distracts people.[4] As the above quote of Twain illustrates, the distortion of facts seems anything but benign. So, instead of distortion, I've chosen a different model that allows me to use different language. I use the model of the telescope lens and speak in terms of "memory refraction."

The telescope allows us to see things that are not visible to the naked eye. This is so because a telescope has a series of lenses that bend light. By bending the light between the not-visible object and your eye, these lenses make the object seem larger than it is. Thus the image available to sight is a "distorted" version of the object. Therefore, we do not see the object as it exists in reality, but a "distorted" (in this case, enlarged) image of that object by way of refracted light.

This is exactly what memory does for us. We are unable to see the past. It is not visible. However, we have a tool called "memory" that focuses our attention onto present cognitive states associated with the past. Through the process of memory, we are able to see an approximate image of the past. Therefore memory distorts the distance between the not-visible past and the present. Memory acts like a series of lenses that, by their design, bend light. The fact that we do not "see" the past as it exists in time is the very reason that we must rely on our memories. What we see is a bent, or refracted, version of the past. *Memory is memory refraction.*

There are different sizes and shapes of lenses that refract memory in different ways. Schudson suggests four categories of memory distortion (what I call "refraction"):[5]

(1) distanciation: the tendency for memories to become vague or for details to be forgotten;[6]
(2) instrumentalization: the tendency for memories to be reinterpreted to serve the present better;
(3) conventionalization: the tendency for memories to conform to socio-typical experiences; and
(4) narrativization: the tendency for memories to be conventionalized through the constraints of storytelling.[7]

As we move again from memory to history, each of these areas has a place in our discussion. The next chapter will focus on the fourth category: the refractive lens of story.

One additional point: In order for a series of refractions to be trustworthy, they must seem plausible. If they are distorted in a way that makes them look like a kaleidoscope, we will be confused and we will not trust our memories. Memory is a series of slight refractions along a trajectory. It is this continuity of slight refractions that renders memory intelligible. If there are dramatic shifts or large gaps in this continuity, we will notice a problem. Most often we don't — memory is simply taken for granted.

Most often, memory is refracted in familiar patterns. This is helpful to historians because these patterns can be charted.

SUGGESTIONS FOR FURTHER READING

A. Le Donne, "Theological Memory Distortion in the Jesus Tradition." In *Memory and Remembrance in the Bible and Antiquity,* edited by L. T. Stuckenbruck, S. C. Barton, and B. G. Wold. Tübingen: Mohr Siebeck, 2007.
Judith C. S. Redman. "How Accurate Are Eyewitnesses? Bauckham

and the Eyewitnesses in the Light of Psychological Research."
Journal of Biblical Literature 129, no. 1 (2010): 177-97.

D. Schacter. *Memory Distortion: How Minds, Brains, and Societies Reconstruct the Past.* Cambridge, MA: Harvard University Press, 1995.

If Memory Serves

Let the science and research of the historian find the fact and let his imagination and art make clear its significance.

George Trevelyan

To look back upon history is inevitably to distort it.

Norman Pearson

My favorite film is Steven Spielberg's *Schindler's List*. It is a magnificent study in irony, darkness, and grace. Amon Göth is perhaps the most despicable character ever to touch the silver screen. Oskar Schindler is the most complex protagonist on whom you'll ever project empathy. I have yet to find a better story of collective exile and ultimate belonging in the space of three hours. This film also happens to fall into the category of "true," by which moviegoers associate the phrase "based on a true story." This phrase tends to mean "historical" in some sense of that word.

Telling a historical story is slippery business. In the case of *Schindler's List*, the medium dramatically shapes the story itself. Anyone who has read the preface of the book *Schindler's Ark* will be aware of the changes that happen to a history as it moves from memory to novel to film. Still, the story continues to be "true."

I have often wondered whether the truth of this story transcends the telling of it, or if it is mediated through the telling.

Some would say that the truth of a story depends on how well the storyteller has reflected the events *as they actually happened.* I am happy to grant that this is a valid concern as long as I am allowed to rephrase it: The truth of the story depends on how well the storyteller has reflected the events *as they have been collectively remembered.* This conceptual shift demonstrates one of my central interests in postmodern philosophy of history. Still, this perspective only reveals part of the picture.

Others would say that the truth of this story depends on how well the story has been told. Has it drawn the audience toward the memory? Has it used this momentum to push them toward a compelling interpretation of the events? Has it made the memory relevant enough to be retold? If the storyteller fails in these ways, the historical truths of the story will be forgotten. If the storyteller succeeds, historical truth has been upheld.

I hope that both of the above descriptions of truth make sense to you. However, you might find yourself uncomfortable with the second description of historical truth. If so, I won't begrudge your misgivings. This is perhaps the most contentious issue in philosophy of history: *Do historians "uncover" their stories or do they "create" their stories?*

Musician Paul Simon (1941-) explores the logical consequences of describing historians as storytellers:

Tell us all a story 'bout how it used to be;
Make it up and then write it down, just like history.
'Bout Goldilocks and the three bears,
Angels in the crosshairs;
About how we all descended from the deep green sea.[1]

Here Simon sings of history as something that is told or written down. This description juxtaposes several kinds of stories: fairy tale, myth, and natural history. Natural historians might protest that this is an unhelpful collapsing of genres. But the point is clear: storytelling looks much the same regardless of sub-genre. Once they are set alongside writers, filmmakers, and poets, the expectation of historians increases significantly. Unless history is told artfully, it risks becoming irrelevant and unremembered.

The name that is most often associated with postmodern philosophy of history is Hayden White. White emphasizes the essentially creative nature of the historian's task. He writes:

> It is sometimes said that the aim of the historian is to explain the past by "finding," "identifying," or "uncovering" the "stories" that lie buried in the chronicles; and that the difference between "history" and "fiction" resides in the fact that the historian "finds" his stories, whereas the fiction writer "invents" his. This conception of the historian's task, however, obscures the extent to which "invention" also plays a part in the historian's operations.[2]

If White is to be correctly understood, we must grant that he writes here of emphasis. This is to say that his objection to modern tendencies is the underemphasis of the "extent to which" the historian is also an inventor. Some may say that White overemphasizes the creative aspect of the historian's task. I have said as much elsewhere.[3] However, I now wonder whether my previous criticism of White was a bit too hasty. I still must depart from White in one important way, which I will address in due course. But I agree with him that historians make decisions that essentially create stories.

Consider the difference between history and time: As far as human memory can tell, time has no beginning. As far as we can see, time has no end. Time has the look of infinity in both directions. The discipline of history, on the other hand, deals in beginnings, middles, and ends. So in order to tell the history of a particular person, people, concept, etcetera, I must determine where to begin, what comes next, and where to stop.

> History must be told in a way that interprets how the elements of the plot fit together. This process requires the historian to determine which details are most important to this plot.

Should the history of baseball begin in New Jersey or Massachusetts? Or perhaps this history ought to begin with the European game "rounders," which was its predecessor. In the determination of a starting point, a particular geographical bias is at work. Do I have motives to explain baseball as a distinctly American invention? Should I react against these motives or embrace them?

Where does the history of John F. Kennedy end? Should I continue telling the events that took place after 1963? Should I conclude with the findings of the Warren Commission? Does this suggest that I think that these findings were conclusive? Choosing where to begin and end greatly shapes the story and betrays the motives of the historian.

White suggests that by imposing a beginning, middle, and end upon events in time, we historians actually *create* a story in the same way that a writer of fiction creates. Historians must use literary devices like "inaugural motifs" and "terminating motifs" (methods of beginning and ending), just like storytellers. In the end, according to White, historians are storytellers. This idea of imposing a story onto a selection of time-sequences is what he calls "emplotment." History must be told in a way that interprets how the elements of the plot fit together. This process requires the historian to determine which details are most important to this plot.

Culture Focus G: The Dead Sea Scrolls

In 1947, some Bedouin goatherds were walking through the Qumran desert. One of them threw a stone into a nearby cave. Instead of hearing a thud, they heard a crack. The stone had hit a clay jar containing ancient scrolls. The series of caves in that location turned out to be an extremely valuable archaeological find for Jesus historians. While none of the Dead Sea Scrolls mention Jesus, this library provides a unique window into a particular Jewish political-theology of Jesus' day.

For example, one fragmentary text is a commentary on the Hebrew Bible's Habakkuk (1QpHab). The Dead Sea author quotes Habakkuk 2: "Surely the stone will cry out from the wall, and the rafter will answer it from the framework. 'Woe to him who builds a city with bloodshed and founds a town with violence!'" This Dead Sea author then claims that this passage from Habakkuk condemns the "wicked priest" of the Jerusalem temple. According to the Dead Sea author, the Jerusalem temple of Jesus' day was built by a false priesthood and was corrupted by greed and Roman influence. This author claims that the temple's "stones were laid by tyranny and the wooden rafters by robbery" (1QpHab 10.1). The idea here is that even the stones of the temple disapprove of Jerusalem's corrupt priesthood.

Even though Jesus is not mentioned in the Dead Sea Scrolls, there are several texts like this that show a common disapproval of the Jerusalem priesthood and Roman occupation among Jesus' contemporaries. Scrolls like this provide a backdrop for Jesus' dispute with the Jerusalem religious leaders concerning the temple.

In the previous chapter I suggested that narrativization is an important feature of memory refraction. I will tell you an autobiographical story that illustrates how pervasive narrative is on multiple layers of memory refraction. This illustration will not negate White's argument, but it will point out a particular deficiency.

I was twenty years old and in a dark place. A series of close relationships had broken before me. My loss of faith in institution, friendship, and vocation was depressing both me and the unfortunate people who had to put up with me. Although I'd had a religious upbringing, I had no intention of returning to religion for answers. At about the same time, a good friend of mine had become a rather zealous Christian. Matt had always been a bit countercultural, but now he was a vow-of-poverty sort of dude. He knocked on my door around eight p.m.

I invited him inside; he invited me outside. There was a plastic blue tub filled with water sitting on my porch. He asked me to take my shoes off. I knew immediately that Matt was inviting me to re-enact a particular story. I had heard the story of Jesus' foot-washing enough times to recognize it when I saw it. I also knew that resisting the story would only play me into Matt's plan. I'd just be acting like Peter who refused to let Jesus wash his feet. Matt had trapped me in that narrative. He proceeded to wash my feet and pray for me.

Matt used to carry around a Gideon's Bible in his back pocket. But he didn't need to pull it out and read it for me to understand what had just taken place. We both knew the story well enough that neither of us needed to say it out loud. Ever since, whenever I hear that part of the Passion Narrative, I can't help but project my own experience onto it.

Notice the narrative refraction on four levels:

(1) Matt had obvious intentions to evoke a narrative before he arrived. The guy brought a plastic tub for this very purpose. The narrative was in place in his mind before and during the event.

(2) I recognized the story in which I was going to participate. I knew my cues and knew their significance without needing a verbal explanation.

(3) Subsequent tellings of Jesus' act of service continue to cause me to juxtapose my own story alongside the original narrative.

(4) As I write of Matt's Christlike act, I am presently retelling the story with a particular agenda. I have included details that serve to illustrate my point.

My point is that cultural narratives influence actions and interpretations long before the historian sits down to tell the story. What Hayden White underemphasizes is that the narrative process precedes even the initial perceptions of the historical events. The historian exploits the narrative elements already embedded in the memories of events.

My memories of zealous Matt and his blue tub are forever framed within the story of Jesus in John 13. And, as the hermeneutical circle demands, I have since reframed the story of John 13 within my memory of zealous Matt and his blue tub. These stories are now mutually informative within my mind. It is a form of memory refraction that was set in motion along a particular trajectory from the very start. *Narratives shape intentions, perceptions, memories, and histories.*

Matt chose the pattern along which my memory would be refracted. As an active participant, I have propelled this refraction trajectory forward along the pattern we had (nonverbally) agreed upon.

I have another friend who is an accomplished musician and songwriter. Nathan is also a gadget addict. He is constantly collecting technological doodads and electronic widgets. He has a garage filled with devices designed to streamline his life — but he has so many that navigating between technologies and the real world has become complicated. Realizing that his proclivity for technology is often counterproductive, he wrote a song called "I Want to Be Simple."[4] Nathan wrote himself into a verse to project himself in a new direction. Both Matt and Nate are examples of intentionally choreographed memory refractions. But narrativization is not always intentional. It is also a subconscious lens by which we see the world. Fentress and Wickham write:

> [A] plot functions as a complex memory image, and learning a repertoire of plots is equivalent to learning a large-scale "mnemotechnique"[5] that permits the ordering, retention, and subsequent transmission of a vast amount of information. Remembering in visual images, syntactically linked and articulated in a causal and logical relation, we make up little stories. This is a "mnemotechnique" we constantly use without being aware of it. . . . To be remembered and transmitted at all, the facts must be transformed into images, arranged in stories. Internal contexts, such as narrative genres, exist as the typical patterns in which we experience and interpret events of all kinds. Accommodating remembered facts into predisposed internal contexts may impose a radical reordering of that memory at the outset.[6]

So narratives actually shape our perceptions of the world and bend our memories to make them intelligible.

This a crucially important point to remember when we're reading the stories about Jesus in the gospels. As we saw with Elijah typology, Jesus' story mirrors many stories of Hebrew Scripture. There can be no doubt that both perceptions and memories of Jesus were cast along narrative patterns in order to measure his historical significance and project meaning onto his legacy. This is true of how the gospels pattern his larger narrative, but it is also true of how the first perceivers of Jesus interpreted his mission and identity. Indeed, by appealing to and mimicking Scripture, Jesus himself often defined the pattern by which these memories would be refracted.

SUGGESTIONS FOR FURTHER READING

David Lowenthal. *The Past Is a Foreign Country.* Cambridge: Cambridge University Press, 1985.

Hayden White. *Figural Realism: Studies in the Mimesis Effect.* Baltimore: Johns Hopkins University Press, 1999.

The Big Stage

I am an historian, I am not a believer, but I must confess as an historian that this penniless preacher from Nazareth is irrevocably the very center of history. Jesus Christ is easily the most dominant figure in all history.

H. G. Wells

With great power comes great responsibility.

Spiderman

Walking from Nazareth to Jerusalem was like walking from Ukiah to San Francisco. Chances are good that you've never heard of the tiny Californian town of Ukiah and that you've heard lots of San Francisco. Jesus was from northern Galilee. His hands were callused and his accent was thick. Jesus was a backwater country bumpkin from nowhere.

Jerusalem was the center of the Jewish universe. Jerusalem featured prominently in almost every story Jesus heard around the campfire. It's where Jacob rested his head on that famous rock and where David snuck through the water duct. For the Jews of Jesus' day, Jerusalem was literally where Heaven and Earth met. According to the Hebrew Scriptures, God's very presence resided in the Jerusalem temple (or was supposed to). This kind of religious currency also meant power. The power elite of Jesus' people were walking the temple precincts, presiding over God's chosen land and people.

It was festival time in Jerusalem. This meant that Jews from all over would flock to the city to remember by ritual the story of their exodus from Egypt. The festival of Passover celebrated national liberation and looked forward to a new liberation and a new Moses to lead it. Some thought that the messiah (the anointed king) would arrive in grand fashion in Jerusalem. The messiah would establish a relationship with the temple powerbrokers and declare independence from Roman occupation.

Jesus projected his own story onto the national narrative of Israel. Jesus' arrival in Jerusalem invited messianic interpretation by way of his chosen geography (the Mount of Olives) and time of year (Passover). His small following attempted to choreograph a royal procession to mimic Solomon's historic coronation (1 Kings 1:32-40 and Zech. 9:9). But, compared to the grand Roman processions, Jesus' little spectacle on the back of a donkey must have seemed embarrassing. It ended at the temple steps, and nobody of importance was there to greet him. He, the popular faith healer and teacher from the north, was just another pilgrim in Jerusalem.

The Jerusalem priesthood had no need for a revolutionary messiah. They were comfortably wealthy with Rome in charge. They had no intention of siding with a country faith healer against the Roman Empire.

Jesus' following had waned. Maybe it was his talk of nonviolence or maybe it was his choice to walk through Samaria. Many patriotic and xenophobic Jews would have been suspicious of any leader who made friends with Samaritans. By the time Jesus got to the city he looked more like Balaam than Moses. He would have to do something dramatic to get his movement noticed.

One of the best ways to muster sympathy among the poor is to criticize the power elite. To this end, the Jerusalem temple establishment was a particularly large target for many voices within Judaism. Many Jews believed that the temple priesthood had been corrupted by impurity, greed, and foreign influence. There was a longstanding tension between religious "purists" and the Jerusalem priesthood. Ezekiel 8–10 describes God's presence leaving and forsaking the temple. Other texts (like the Targum[1] of Isa. 53:5) describe the future return of God's presence on Earth in the form of a heavenly temple. As seen previously, Malachi predicted the return of Elijah who would level a curse because of the priesthood's corruption.

With this backdrop in place, think of what Jerusalem must have looked like to religious pilgrims. Year after year, Jews traveled to (what was supposed to be) the holiest place on earth to worship the one true God. They brought their best gifts to sacrifice on the altar. It was this experience that provided them with a sense of worth, a cultural identity, and the hope that God would someday provide a final exodus from brokenness to a new world order. Now imagine a scenario where the priests had exploited this hope and partnered with Rome for money and power. Many were disillusioned.[2]

Culture Focus H: Christian Scripture

Most first-time readers of the New Testament start with the gospels. This is a logical place to start because they are placed at the very front. What isn't apparent, however, is that these were not the first books written. Letters like Thessalonians and Galatians were written within twenty years of the crucifixion. Surprisingly, these texts show that Christians worshiped Jesus as the "Son of God" very early on. During this time, the stories of Jesus' life were still being circulated and dramatized orally.

Most of the letters (called "epistles") were written by a Jewish Christian named Paul. These letters are characterized by persuasive arguments. Paul often defended himself, his theology, and his mission to the leaders of other churches. For Paul, it was crucially important that followers of Jesus were not divided by race and ritual. This theme is pervasive in his letters. Other letters were written in Paul's name, the names of other prominent disciples, or anonymously.

The book of Revelation (like Daniel) is a political commentary written in dream language. Revelation was probably written by the same group responsible for John's gospel. While it is the last book of the Bible, it was actually written down before the gospel.

The temple of Jesus' day had become a taxing station for the Roman Empire. The official religion of Rome was Caesar worship. There were temples all over the empire where faithful citizens worshiped their king. However, while the Caesars fancied their own divinity, they also allowed religious pluralism for occupied nations who were willing to live in peace within the empire. In Jerusalem, "peace" meant that Caesar received a hefty percentage of every gift given to Israel's God. Rome had selected Jewish priests who were willing to line the pockets of the Caesar. Even worse, in order to stay in the good graces of their overlords, this puppet priesthood was known to bleed every last cent from traveling peasants.

The Jerusalem priesthood had no need for a revolutionary messiah. They were comfortably wealthy with Rome in charge. They had no intention of siding with a country faith healer against the Roman Empire. Besides, Jerusalem had seen would-be messiahs come and go frequently. Each new pretender arrived with big promises, mimicking Joshua or Moses or Jeremiah. Each was dispatched in turn by the Roman military. Jesus was just one more troublemaker in a long string of purists and naïve idealists.

Ironically, Jesus didn't arrive with any army except his band of fishermen, widows, and reformed prostitutes. He had no sword other than the wit and wisdom of his tongue. Jesus walked up those steps to the temple as a complete unknown. It is no surprise that Jesus appealed to the memory of John the Baptist when asked to defend himself. John the Baptist's name carried authority even in Jerusalem. In contrast, Jesus was nobody of consequence. Who would have guessed that, *by the end of the week(!),* Jesus would be perceived as a threat by the mightiest political force on earth?

When Jesus arrived in Jerusalem to an insulting (lack of) reception, he decided to play the role of prophet. To the chagrin of many, Jesus was simply not going to secure a throne in Jerusalem. Rather, he would be a prophetic voice, speaking truth to power. Jesus' shift from messianic type to prophetic type was not a whimsical concession. He was acting out an "apocalyptic motif." This is quite an important point, so I'll take a moment to explain what I mean.

Jewish apocalyptic literature (e.g., Daniel 7–12) is political commentary rendered in dream language. Angels, beasts, dragons, and heavenly battlefields color apocalyptic literature. It often reads like ancient fantasy or science fiction. One apocalyptic image is the "Day of Visitation." This is a recurring apocalyptic motif that is also found in other genres like historical narrative and prophetic literature. The Day of Visitation is a day of divine judgment. It is when the God of the Bible *visits* his creation to take a closer look at world happenings to decide whether to bless or curse the behavior of humankind. In general, when the Bible describes this day, Israel's enemies and corrupt leadership are judged wrathfully. Conversely, a righteous remnant of humankind is blessed. Oftentimes, this judgment is tied to the care of the poor and the oppressed or lack thereof.

As Mark tells the story of Jesus and the temple, Jesus is portrayed in apocalyptic terms. Mark 13 is often called the "little apocalypse" because Jesus teaches in language that sounds much like Daniel, Ezekiel, and Revelation. As Mark paints this picture, Jesus stands on a hill opposite the temple so that the temple is in view. Mark writes:

> As [Jesus] was going out of the Temple, one of his disciples said to him, "Teacher, behold what wonderful stones and what wonderful buildings!" And Jesus said to him, "Do you see these great buildings? Not one stone will be left upon another which will not be torn down." (Mark 13:1-2)

Here Mark paints Jesus as an apocalyptic prophet who stands in judgment against the temple establishment. This sets the stage for Jesus' trial scene, which is also laden with apocalyptic language. Mark's story is about to climax in a final war of words between Jesus and the high priest. Jesus will reveal himself as the apocalyptic kingdom luminary of Daniel 7:13 called the "Son of Man." While many question the historical plausibility of Mark's trial narrative (and so too must I) there can be little doubt that Jesus was commonly remembered by this title. Jesus most often calls himself the Son of Man.[3]

This must be kept in mind as we read about Jesus' first entry into the temple. As Mark tells it, Jesus goes marching up to the temple and is simply "looking around at everything" (Mark 11:11). After his visitation, he leaves. The next time Jesus enters the temple he comes in judgment. He throws over commerce tables and pronounces judgment on those who are handling money. Keep in mind that it is the exchange of money that represents Rome's relationship to the temple priesthood. Jesus is specifically targeting the institution that keeps the elite in power and the poor powerless. In Mark's story, Jesus is the divine visitor who judges corruption and power abuse. As already seen, Mark 13:1-2 suggests that Jesus intended to see this temple fall.

> If Jesus did view his mission through an apocalyptic worldview, it is the historian's responsibility to plausibly interpret Jesus' aspirations and motives with this in mind. Jesus' apocalyptic teaching likely evoked thought-categories (in this case, narratives) by which his identity was perceived.

It is entirely possible that Jesus' prediction of the temple's destruction was invented by Christian storytellers after the historical temple fell in 70 CE. Even so, there is good reason to believe that the historical Jesus did, in fact, make such a claim and that he viewed the temple in apocalyptic categories. If Jesus did view his mission through an apocalyptic worldview, it is the historian's responsibility to interpret plausibly Jesus' aspirations and motives with this in mind. Jesus' apocalyptic teaching likely evoked thought-categories (in this case, narratives) by which his identity was perceived.

But how does the historian responsibly move from Mark's story to the plausible origins of this story in memory or fiction?[4] I will answer this question by demonstrating "historical triangulation." In this section I have described memory refraction as the way in which memories are altered to make them intelligible to the present. I am convinced that by analyzing conflicting interpretations in the gospels, the historian can plausibly suggest the historical memory that shaped these interpretations. Here is how this works:

In order to triangulate historical memory, two points (traditions) must be located that are along separate lines (of interpretation). This means that we're looking for two separate passages in separate sources that disagree on a similar topic.

With this in mind, consider this excerpt of Jesus' trial narrative in Mark:

> For many were giving false testimony against [Jesus], but their testimony was not consistent. Some stood up and began to give false testimony against him, saying, "We heard him say, 'I will destroy this Temple made with hands, and in three days I will build another made without hands.'" Not even in this respect was their testimony consistent. (Mark 14:56-59)

Notice that in Mark's narrative these "false" witnesses accuse Jesus of claiming the ability to destroy the temple. Mark does not call them liars; he only states that they were "inconsistent." Given what Jesus says in Mark 13:1-2, the author would have a difficult time denying the accusation outright. However, Mark does aim to distance Jesus from this accusation. Now compare Mark to the Gospel of John. Immediately after Jesus overturns the money tables in the temple, John writes:

> The Jews then said to him, "What sign do you show us as your authority for doing these things?" Jesus answered them, "Destroy this Temple, and in three days I will raise it up." The Jews then said, "It took forty-six years to build this Temple, and you will raise it up in three days?" But he was speaking of the Temple of his body. (John 2:18-21)[5]

Here John places this saying directly on the lips of Jesus. But the narrator interprets the saying metaphorically. According to John, Jesus didn't predict the destruction and rebuilding of the *literal* temple. Biblical scholar Raymond Brown suggested that Jesus' prediction was an embarrassment to the early church because it wasn't literally fulfilled.[6] So Mark attempts to distance the saying from Jesus, and John attempts to render it as a metaphor for Jesus' resurrection.

In both texts, Jesus' temple saying has been framed within a particular editorial interpretation. In memory terms, we could say that the memory has been reframed according to the needs of the new narrative context. Presumably, each gospel represents a faith community that has remembered the stories of Jesus in particular ways. Many scholars argue that each faith community created stories about Jesus to inform their own theological interests. This school of thought argues that many of Jesus' sayings were invented and placed on his lips.

Considering what John has done with this saying, there is no better example in the gospels of a discrepancy between a saying by Jesus and the later interpretation of the saying. John's reframing of this saying plainly illustrates the memory refraction that has occurred between Jesus' original preaching and later preaching about Jesus. *And yet, even though the saying proved embarrassing, John 2:19 includes Jesus' saying all the same.* There has been no attempt to place John's interpretation on the lips of Jesus. The resurrection metaphor is narrated after Jesus' quotation. E. P. Sanders writes, "John 2:19 shows how deeply embedded in the tradition was the threat of destroying and the promise of rebuilding the temple. It was so firmly fixed that it was not dropped, but rather interpreted."[7]

John takes this saying in one direction and Mark takes it in a different direction. This is what memory theorists might call "counter-memories." Mark is convinced that Jesus has been misunderstood and tells a story to set the record straight. John sees this saying in new light and tells a story to draw out the "true" meaning of the saying. Both are trying to *counteract* a previous interpretation of the temple saying. So we have here a common memory along two separate refraction trajectories. These two points can be charted to a common departure point. This is how we get the image of a triangle.

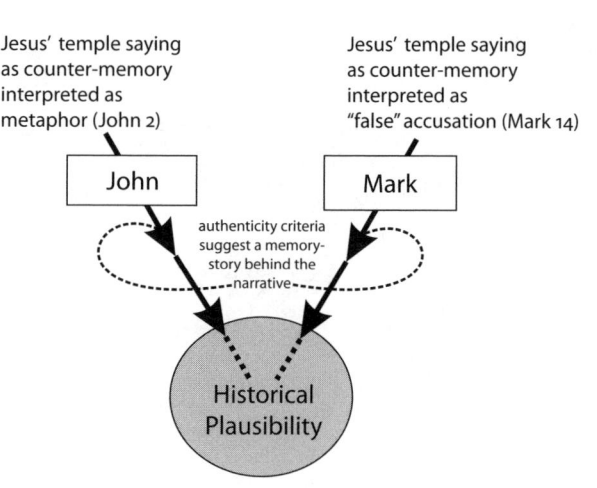

As the above sphere indicates, I am hesitant to use the image of a simple triangle, because talk of "points" suggests an exactness that the postmodern historian does not expect or require. I also should remind you that memory moves forward in spirals with several turns of interpretation along the way. What are here represented in linear fashion should be thought of as two spiraling memory trajectories. As discussed, memory trajectories are moved forward in certain interpretative patterns. Because of this, historical memories can be plausibly charted.

If Mark 14 and John 2 are best explained as counter-memories, we can say with confidence that there was a historical memory that motivated both counteractions. Perhaps this process could be thought of as following two branches back to the Y in the tree from which they diverged. Notice below that I've included several general ideological trajectories to fill out the historical context. Still, the two branches that most interest us are John and Mark as they point backward to a common sphere of historical plausibility.

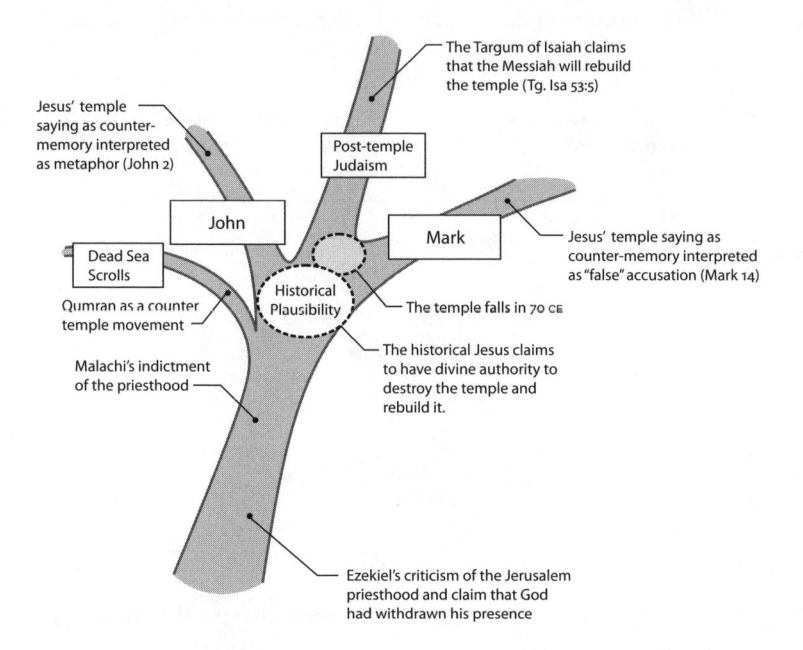

The Targum of Isaiah claims that the Messiah will rebuild the temple (Tg. Isa 53:5)

Jesus' temple saying as counter-memory interpreted as metaphor (John 2)

Post-temple Judaism

John

Mark

Jesus' temple saying as counter-memory interpreted as "false" accusation (Mark 14)

Dead Sea Scrolls

Historical Plausibility

Qumran as a counter temple movement

The temple falls in 70 CE

Malachi's indictment of the priesthood

The historical Jesus claims to have divine authority to destroy the temple and rebuild it.

Ezekiel's criticism of the Jerusalem priesthood and claim that God had withdrawn his presence

Each branch represents a pattern of memory refraction. Mark remembers Jesus differently than John. These differences in memory can be analyzed to determine certain editorial tendencies. In this case, we have a similar saying remembered along two diverging patterns. By determining the most likely single cause that best explains both branches, the historian can make a historical claim with confidence.

Please do not miss the beautiful irony here: It is when the editors of these stories disagree the most that we can most confidently postulate historical memory! *The fact that the memories of Jesus were refracted* (bent in different directions) *is the very fact that allows the historian to postulate the historical event.* Like a telescope lens which bends light so that an invisible object can be approximately seen, refracted memories of Jesus allow us to tell the story of the historical Jesus.

We now return to the story.

When Jesus told the demons to leave, they left. Other exorcists used special roots, rings, and bowls. Jesus used no props, tools, or trinkets; he was uniquely gifted. Jesus seemed to have an uncanny ability to simply speak spiritual healing into reality. Moreover, this "spiritual healing" seemed to have a direct relationship to the physical world. Reports of physical healing spread like wildfire. Jesus had come to the conclusion that God was at work in his very words and that these words had the authority to subvert power structures. He believed that God had given him "dominion, glory and a kingdom" (Dan. 7:14). He viewed the world with apocalyptic eyes and was determined to act out the role of Daniel 7's "Son of Man." So when Jesus took his lungs and tongue to the seat of Jewish power, he fully expected to see tangible results.

There is a story in Hebrew Scripture of a leader named Joshua (Jesus is the Greek form of the name Joshua) who marched around the walls of Jericho (Josh. 6). He guided the children of Israel around the city walls for six days. Then his little army shouted out in unison and the walls fell.

I read this story as legend — I just can't help myself. Try as I may to open my mind, this story doesn't reflect the reality I perceive in my world. But Jesus didn't have such limitations of perception. He really believed that such things were possible. He wasn't alone. The Jewish historian Josephus tells us of a contemporary of Jesus who claimed to be able to shout down the walls of the city.[8] In Jesus' culture, people perceived a different reality than we do. Jerusalem's power elite knew this all too well.

This is why Jesus, armed with nothing but wit, wisdom, and an absurd claim concerning the temple was perceived as a threat to the power structure in Jerusalem. It might have seemed like an absurd claim to some, but when Jesus claimed to destroy the temple and build another, Jerusalem's high priest took notice. That kind of claim had the power to rouse grand expectations in the masses. The power of his words earned him a trial, and Jesus finally got his chance to speak truth to power.

The high priest had a responsibility to keep the peace. In order to keep the peace with Rome, the Jerusalem priesthood couldn't afford to have a madman stirring up trouble, especially during Passover when the stories of liberation were present to mind. The people of Israel had a long history of reenacting their national narratives. Jesus would have to be handed over to the local Roman authorities. Jesus would be executed because in politics, perception is reality.

New Beginnings

Nothing endures but change.

Heraclitus

Jesus was a prophetic voice for religious reform and political restoration in a time when the common sentiment was for violent uprising. Like Moses, Jesus aimed to liberate his people from oppression. But unlike Moses, Jesus' fight wasn't with the "Evil Emperor" but with the hand that moved the political puppets. Though some thought he was insane, Jesus was convinced that he was establishing God's heavenly kingdom on earth by defeating the spiritual armies of Satan. In this way, his voice was his best weapon against oppression.

The power of Jesus' words got him noticed, attracted crowds, created controversy, and got him killed. Even his most embarrassing words were remembered. Jesus made his chief historical impact by the power of his words. With this in mind, we *must* conclude that the initial force of his words set memory trajectories in motion. We *must* conclude that the initial perceptions of Jesus by his contemporaries were shaped by what was most memorable about him. Furthermore, there *must* have been some continuity between his historical impact and how this impact was remembered.

Given what we now know of perception, we should expect that Jesus' impact was bent by narrative refraction from the very beginning. Jesus was raised in a culture that acted out their cultural stories. Jesus himself told these stories, interpreted these stories, and mimicked these stories. It stands to reason that Jesus was perceived through the lenses of narrative memory and that memories of him were bent further in this direction.

Subtle refractions of the stories about Jesus occurred with every retelling. Each retelling was a magnifying lens that further bent the story. Each retelling represented a new interpretation of these memories conforming to each new external context. This is how historical memory functions. We can analyze these memories with confidence because memory is refracted through lenses that follow certain patterns. Sometimes these memories are bent in dramatically different directions. This dual effect suggests a common sphere of historical memory that can be plausibly charted.

This is the task of the historian within a postmodern paradigm. The historian's job is to tell the stories of memory in a way that most plausibly accounts for the available mnemonic evidence. With this in mind, the historical Jesus is not veiled by the interpretations of him. He is most available for analysis when these interpretations are most pronounced. Therefore, the historical Jesus is clearly seen through the lenses of editorial agenda, theological reflection, and intentional counter-memory.

I perceive a new beginning of historical Jesus research, one that does not lament that the ancient past is unknowable. I suggest a new beginning that is rooted in the notion that the interpretation of memory refraction is the historian's best way forward. The seeds of this new beginning have already been planted by better works than this. I only hope that this book focuses good light on fertile soil.

World of Dreams[1]
Mr. Isaac Newton tested everything
Poked and prodded, then said
"Solid things are as real as they seem"
Mr. Albert Einstein pondered light and speed
And with his mind's eye, declared "oh my,
This is a world of dreams"

When we investigate the highest heavens
They seem to race away faster than we can follow
And when we penetrate the heart of atoms
We find there something strangely resembling
Nothing at all

In the smallest measure of anything at hand
Entities of energy are alive in a whirling dance
Even our own bodies are not as we perceive
But made of the same stuff our thoughts are made
In this world of dreams

So do we live and move amidst illusions?
Has what we're seeing fooled us
And only exists in our minds?
And what are we to do with such conclusions?
For what cannot come true in a world of a
Mystical kind?

Mr. Albert Einstein woke one day from sleep
To arise, to his surprise, in a world of dreams
So as we move closer, the farther we must reach
We may fight for what we like, but this is a world of dreams
We may feel that this is real, but this is a world of dreams
Or proclaim no, it can't be so
But this is a world of dreams

Notes

Notes to "Beginnings"

1. One of my primary interests is historiography, by which I mean the study of the nature of history. It is important to define this in contrast to the other prominent use of this word: *the product of the writing of history.* This second definition understands the term to describe a particular approach to the writing of history. The former deals with the writing *about* the discipline of history, while the latter attempts a writing *of* history. The reader should be aware from the start that it is the first definition and not the second that will serve to navigate the present book. While some may insist that historiography is a subset of the philosophy of history, the semantic range of the term has evolved in recent years so that historiography and the philosophy of history are practically synonymous. I will assume as much.

2. Many people mistakenly use the term as a synonym for relativism, existentialism, or just contemporary life in general.

3. It is for this reason that many speak of postmodernism as "social discourse" rather than a unified philosophy. Cf. D. Harvey, *The Condition of Postmodernity* (Oxford: Blackwell, 1990), p. 9.

4. The mantra that "form follows function" is entirely relative to what the perceived function of something is.

5. I've heard this kind of criticism leveled toward existentialist scholar Rudolf Bultmann: "Jesus and Paul weren't existentialists! So why apply existentialist philosophy to the New Testament?"

6. Socrates (c. 469-399 BCE) was a classical Greek philosopher and is commonly considered the father of philosophy. He is known primarily through the writings of his students (for example, Plato). He was executed for "corrupting youth."

7. But before we get anachronistically arrogant, we ought to admit that most people in contemporary society can't describe the anatomy of the human eye ei-

ther. This just goes to show that most people don't care to know how or why they look at the world the way they do. This kind of reflection is generally considered a luxury. It isn't until we have a problem with our vision that we seek out those who have researched such matters. In the same way, philosophers generally go unheeded by the general public.

8. See quote on page 3; G. Vico, *The New Science of Giambattista Vico*, trans. Thomas Goddard Bergin and Max Harold Fisch (Ithaca, NY: Cornell University Press, 1968), p. 331.

9. I most often hear the first challenge from scholars who unabashedly approach the Bible from a faith perspective. This group believes that biblical scholarship is only valuable if it is ultimately edifying to the church. Let me first commend the underlying concern here. There is a great need to bridge the gap between biblical scholarship and the church pew. If more scholars took this relationship seriously, we might see less abuse of the Bible in the way of social inequality, partisan politics, and religious violence! So I must encourage these scholars in their goal to "edify" the church.

10. Historical criticism is interested in the world "behind the text" with questions of date, authorship, earlier forms, later redactions, etc.

11. Literary critics are interested in the world "of the text" with questions of theme, motif, narrative structure, characterization, etc.

12. See my discussion of how this plays out in Mark 12:35-37 in my *The Historiographical Jesus* (Waco, TX: Baylor University Press, 2009), pp. 221-58.

13. Those familiar with Rudolf Bultmann's legacy will recognize a certain affinity between his theology and the first challenge. I have the highest respect for the late great theologian. I do not wish to contribute to the caricature of his theology that is normally put forth in books like this. I deal more directly with Bultmann in my *Historiographical Jesus*, pp. 32-39.

Notes to "Perception I: Thinking from the Outside In"

1. Here I risk offending analytic philosophers by lack of clarity and everyone else by using jargon. On the one hand, we must ask whether it is proper to speak of thought as a filter, or of mental content as something to which we must relate. On the other hand, attempting to parse this out would make this chapter virtually unreadable. In my following description of mental content, I presume that most readers will associate "mental content" and "thought-categories" as stuff that happens inside our heads to help us make sense of the world around us. Moreover, I acknowledge that such terminology might be examples of "paleonymic" language. Language often imports old worldviews into contemporary speech. For example, very few modern people think that the sun is moving upward when they use the

word "sunrise." We know that the sun does not "rise" over the Earth. But the language remains (it is paleonymic) and continues to be useful.

2. A good place to start is the *Stanford Encyclopedia of Philosophy*'s introduction to the life and works of Descartes: http://plato.stanford.edu/entries/descartes-works/.

3. Plato's *Philebus*, Loeb edition, trans. Harold North Fowler (Cambridge, MA: Harvard University Press, 1952), here 34A, 35A-D, 39A.

4. Plato's *Theaetetus*, Loeb edition, trans. Harold North Fowler (Cambridge, MA: Harvard University Press, 1952), here 191D, 193C. My gratitude to Tom Thatcher for this quote.

5. In fact, Descartes thought that a person's access to his thoughts was more trustworthy than vision. This presupposition was later challenged by Empiricist philosophy, which emphasized knowledge gained by sensation over that of knowledge gained by abstract thought.

6. G. E. Rawlinson, "The Significance of Letter Position in Word Recognition," Ph.D. thesis, University of Nottingham, Psychology Department, 1976. In summary, Rawlinson writes "that randomising letters in the middle of words had little or no effect on the ability of skilled readers to understand the text. Indeed one rapid reader noticed only four or five errors in an A4 page of muddled text." For this summary see http://www.newscientist.com/article.ns?id=mg16221887.600 for a published letter from Rawlinson to *New Scientist* (29 May 1999); see also http://www.mrc-cbu.cam.ac.uk/~mattd/Cmabrigde/rawlinson.html for a more thorough summary of his and related works.

7. I intend no offense to the fine people of Nottingham. Being a graduate of Durham University, I am well aware that the quality of a university should not be measured by its popular repute.

8. Feel free to skip ahead to Perception — Part Two if you'd like to see this discussed in more depth.

Notes to "Memory I: Family Matters"

1. For more on this see Bruce Chilton, *Rabbi Jesus: An Intimate Biography* (New York: Image/Doubleday, 2000), ch. 1.

2. Here I have adapted a well-known thought experiment of Anti-Individualism where a man is transported from Earth to a parallel reality called "Twin-Earth." Twin-Earth is exactly the same as Earth in every way except, instead of water, they have a substance that looks, tastes, and feels just like H_2O. But instead of water, Twin-Earth has twin-water or "twater." Since the man has no clue that his new life on Twin-Earth is devoid of water, he has no reason to believe that twater is not the same substance he has known for his entire life. Indeed, he remembers his former life on Earth when he would drink, wash, and swim in H_2O through the lens of

twater and not know that his memories have been reshaped by his new experience with twater.

For those well versed in philosophy of mind, this kind of thought experiment is nothing new. There is often a parallel world or an evil magician involved in these illustrations. For those *not* well versed in philosophy, such science-fiction examples can seem fanciful and outlandish. It is for this reason that I've chosen a more mundane illustration.

3. Halbwachs, *Les Cadres sociaux de la mémoire* (Paris: F. Alcan, 1925); *On Collective Memory,* trans. and ed. Lewis A. Cosner (Chicago: University of Chicago Press, 1992).

4. Castle Rock Entertainment/Columbia Pictures, 1989.

Notes to "History I: A Type of Now"

1. Added to this gloss is the act of projection; historians project possible reconstructions onto the data available to them (more on this later). One might also mention that much of natural and anthropological history has not been relayed through human memory. What does not survive by way of memory may be thought of as artifact (pottery, architecture, etc.) or natural evidence (geography, celestial data, etc.). Still, memory plays a crucial role in the analysis of this data as well.

2. This idea was never better explored than by B. Schwartz, *Abraham Lincoln and the Forge of National Memory* (Chicago: University of Chicago Press, 2000).

3. http://www.suntimes.com/news/sweet/213786,CST-NWS-obama17.article.

Notes to "Jesus I: Dysfunctional Family"

1. Harishchandra was a king who became legendary for truth-telling and promise-keeping, even at the expense of losing his entire kingdom.

2. The doctrine of the Incarnation teaches that Jesus was both fully human and fully divine. While Jesus' sexuality is not presupposed in this doctrine, I take the liberty of supposing that human sexuality is included in being "fully human."

3. The canonical gospels are those that were deemed divinely inspired and included in the Bible, i.e., Matthew, Mark, Luke, and John. This study will assume that other gospels are also of historical value, such as "Thomas" and "Q." Q is thought by many scholars to have been a collection of sayings used as a source for (primarily) Matthew and Luke. Many believe that the overlaps between Matthew and Luke (that have not been derived from Mark) suggest that both were privy to an oral source.

4. Matt. 19:12 reads: "For there are eunuchs who have been so from birth, and

there are eunuchs who have been made eunuchs by men, and there are eunuchs for the sake of the kingdom of heaven. He who is able to receive this, let him receive it."

5. There are several different kinds of criteria. In this chapter, I'll introduce only three. The so-called authenticity criteria are a carryover from previous generations of historical Jesus scholars. I am of the mind that these criteria do not "authenticate" historical facts, as many previous scholars supposed. Rather I find these criteria useful to measure early and/or widespread historical memories. Finally, while all historians use some set of criteria when they construct images and stories of historical memory, it is the *telling* of this history that defines the historian's task. For a more detailed description of criteria in Jesus research, see my *Historiographical Jesus,* pp. 87-92.

6. To be accurate, it would be better to say that this is a Semitic idiom. "Semitic" would include either Hebrew or Aramaic.

7. The Pseudepigrapha is a group of texts written between 350 BCE and 150 BCE and ascribed to various prophets and kings of ancient Jewish tradition.

8. The categories of memory and invention cannot be separated so neatly. A large part of invention involves memory and vice versa. I will pick up this thread further below. For now, it is necessary to say only that there is a difference between a story/saying that reflects life experience and one that reflects only the storyteller's imagination. Unless the storyteller intends to deceive, both teller and audience presuppose a distinction here. As historians we must consider how these overlap, but there is a greater danger in collapsing genres altogether.

9. See also Jesus' most direct challenges to "traditional" family in Luke 12:51-53 and 14:26. I interpret these sayings as hyperbole intended to subvert the common notions of extreme blood loyalty, which leads to xenophobia.

10. Thomas is a non-canonical gospel that seems to have warranted interest by Gnostic Christianity. I agree with the academic majority that Thomas solidified as a written document close to a hundred years after the writing of Mark and Luke. I also agree that Thomas does indeed contain valuable historical data.

11. He wrote: "To speak of studying the mind of Jesus from within may seem presumptuous; but no other method is of the slightest value" (R. G. Collingwood, *Philosophy and Religion* [London: Macmillan, 1916], pp. 42-43).

Notes to "Perception II: Understanding Is Construing"

1. "Hermeneutics" is the study of how people approach interpretation. For example, a judge must interpret the law using a certain set of guidelines, say, the U.S. Constitution. A commitment to such guidelines can be thought of as a hermeneutic. And on a deeper level, every judge will bring presuppositions to the law by way of upbringing, social class, gender, race, religion, philosophy, etc. Each of these would also be considered examples of hermeneutics. The rest of this chapter will

discuss the "circular" nature of hermeneutics. Hermeneutics is the study of the ways and methods people use to interpret.

2. For a more thorough description of Schleiermacher's circle, see Hans-Georg Gadamer, *Truth and Method* (New York: Continuum, 2004), pp. 190-92.

3. Friedrich D. E. Schleiermacher, *Hermeneutics: The Handwritten Manuscripts* (Missoula, MT: Scholars Press, 1977), p. 41.

4. *Notes,* 1809; as quoted in K. Mueller-Vollmer, *The Hermeneutics Reader* (New York: Continuum, 1985), p. 8; set together, the two-part definition reads: "Everything is understood when nothing nonsensical remains. Nothing is understood that is not construed." Hans-Georg Gadamer, in *Philosophical Hermeneutics* (Berkeley: University of California Press, 1976), p. 7, rightly places the first part of this definition within the context of historical romanticism and questions its usefulness for contemporary interpreters.

5. Dilthey argues that our worldviews are products of our lived experience and since experiences vary from person to person, culture to culture, so do worldviews (H. A. Hodges, *The Philosophy of Wilhelm Dilthey* [London: Routledge & Kegan Paul, 1969], p. 31). Cf. discussion in S. J. Grenz, *A Primer on Postmodernism* (Grand Rapids: Eerdmans, 1996), pp. 99-103. Cf. also http://plato.stanford.edu/entries/dilthey/.

6. W. Dilthey, "The Development of Hermeneutics," in *Dilthey: Selected Writings,* ed. H. P. Rickman (Cambridge: Cambridge University Press, 1976), pp. 258-59.

7. It is important not to confuse existentialism with postmodern philosophy. I see the former as a forerunner to the latter, but a firm distinction must be maintained.

8. In his *Being in Time* Heidegger often raises objections to his own arguments to further the discussion. One question that he raises concerns the problem of understanding. His goal was to put forth a means of understanding *Dasein* (i.e., the person who lives responsibly and authentically in the midst of his "thrown-ness" into existence). He grants that in order to do so, one must already have at least a vague understanding of what "being" is. Recognizing the circularity of this, he argues that all understanding is circular in that we always project possibilities onto the world around us. This is the larger context of his application of the hermeneutical circle. See discussion in R. Polt, *Heidegger: An Introduction* (London: Routledge, 1998), pp. 30-31, 70-71.

9. In the original German: "Vorhabe, Vorsicht und Vorgriff"; M. Heidegger, *Sein und Zeit* (Tübingen: Max Niemeyer, 1961), pp. 150-51. Later, Paul Ricoeur would attempt to lessen the paradoxical nature of "fore-conception" by describing the circle in terms of "guess" and "validation" (*Interpretation Theory: Discourse and the Surplus of Meaning* [Fort Worth: Texas Christian University Press, 1976], p. 79).

10. M. Heidegger, *Being and Time,* trans. John Macquarrie and Edward Robinson (London: SCM, 1962), p. 194.

11. Heidegger, *Being and Time,* p. 194 (translator's emphasis).

12. Heidegger, *Being and Time*, p. 195.

13. This, of course, is not the end of Heidegger's interpretive process. Gadamer (*Truth and Method*, p. 267) sums up Heidegger's model by stating that "interpretation begins with fore-conceptions that are [eventually] replaced by more suitable ones." Such "more suitable" conceptions are then projected as fore-conceptions of meaning onto subsequent perceptions.

Notes to "Memory II: Variation and Stability"

1. "No Direction Home." Directed by Martin Scorsese. *American Masters;* Public Broadcasting Service, 2005.

2. *Historiographical Jesus: Memory, Typology, and the Son of David* (Waco, TX: Baylor University Press), pp. 41-64.

3. That I could actually discern a difference between the recorded versions of this song from the live version suggests that my culture's default position is that of literacy mediated through technological device. Those reared in an oral culture with no means to record sound might perceive less variance.

4. I have a confession to make: Whenever I play this game, I intentionally invent a new phrase bearing no resemblance to the one whispered to me. The more absurd, the better.

5. While Maya culture was known for its fully developed written language, like early Britain, most of its common people were illiterate and thus an oral culture by default.

Notes to "History II: Between Certainty and History"

1. Lessing was quoted at the beginning of this section.

2. Leonard P. Wessel, *G. E. Lessing's Theology: A Reinterpretation* (The Hague: Moulton, 1977), pp. 54-55.

3. Gotthold Lessing, "On the Proof of the Spirit and of Power," in *Lessing's Theological Writings,* ed. H. Chadwick (London: William Clowes & Sons, 1956), p. 52. Italics mine.

4. Lessing, "Proof," p. 53 (translator's emphasis).

5. This, of course, does not solve the problem of miraculous reports. To many (including myself), reports of the supernatural seem highly implausible. However, the postmodern historian ought not begrudge those with worldviews that incorporate supernatural possibility. Indeed, those who believe in miracles are more likely to perceive them. This point will be made with fuller voice in Part Three.

6. This is a very conservative estimate. Most scholars believe that Mark (our earliest written gospel) was composed around 70 CE.

7. See the suggestions for further reading at the end of this chapter and the previous chapter.

8. Another plausible solution is that the motivation to write down a composition allowed an individual composer to represent the story in a different artistic medium that presented unique aesthetic and theological possibilities. So T. Thatcher, "Why John Wrote a Gospel: Memory and History in an Early Christian Community," in *Memory, Tradition, and Text: Uses of the Past in Early Christianity,* ed. Alan Kirk and Tom Thatcher, Semeia Studies 52 (Leiden: Brill, 2005), pp. 82-83.

9. Here I use the example of textual criticism to demonstrate only one problem with modern historiography. This does not negate the study of textual variants. What I hope to have shown is that the attempt to achieve "an original" does not move us any closer to history "as it actually happened."

10. Rudolf Bultmann, *Jesus* (Berlin: Deutsche Bibliothek, 1926), more popularly known as *Jesus and the Word* (New York: Scribner's, 1934), p. 13; cf. "Aber wie weit die Gemeinde das Bild von ihm und seiner Verkündigung objectiv treu bewahrt hat, ist eine andere Frage" (Bultmann, *Jesus,* pp. 16-17).

11. One might think here of how technology (such as video) has changed our ability to measure the veracity of memory. If the assassination of President Kennedy teaches us anything, it is that the more a video is replayed the more interpretations of that memory will vary.

12. See chapter 4 of my *Historiographical Jesus.*

13. Read, for example, the book of Malachi with special attention to Malachi 3:1 and 4:5. The Baptizer is remembered for having appealed to Malachi when he preached.

Notes to "Jesus II: Talking Politics"

1. I have italicized the text quoted from Malachi 3:1.

2. Matthew, writing for a Jewish Christian audience, prefers the slogan "kingdom of Heaven" because he tries to avoid using the word "God." Readers of Matthew should be aware of this. He is not talking about Heaven as a place; "Heaven" is way to refer to the person of God in reverence. Thus the slogan "kingdom of Heaven" means exactly the same thing as "kingdom of God."

3. One wonders if this isn't exactly what happened to the boy who ran away naked during Jesus' arrest (Mark 14:51-52).

4. In Mark's appendix, Jesus sits down at the right hand of God in Heaven (16:19). The metaphor here is thick (compare Daniel 7–9). Does God have literal "hands"? Does God have a literal throne room just beyond the clouds? No, this is the language of apocalyptic visions. The most natural reading of this language for both ancient and modern readers is that this is metaphor.

5. The author also employs Elijah typology in Luke 7:1-16 where two stories

about Jesus closely mirror stories of Elijah. This leads nicely into Jesus' interaction with the Baptist's disciples where Jesus overtly appeals to Elijah typology.

6. In addition, Luke most likely didn't see a dual typology as a problem in this case because of the Elijah-Elisha link.

Notes to "Perception III: Believing Is Seeing"

1. Hans-Georg Gadamer, *Truth and Method* (New York: Continuum, 2004), p. 295.

2. Photos of the girls can be seen at http://www.usatoday.com/news/nation/ 2006-05-31-indiana-mistaken-identity_x.htm. I have not included the girls' photos here out of respect for their families.

3. http://www.msnbc.msn.com/id/23849928/.

4. http://www.msnbc.msn.com/id/23849928/page/10/ (bracketed comments mine for clarification).

Notes to "Memory III: Through a Glass Darkly"

1. Michael Schudson, "Dynamics of Distortion in Collective Memory," in D. L. Schacter, ed., *Memory Distortion: How Minds, Brains, and Societies Reconstruct the Past* (Cambridge, MA: Harvard University Press, 1995), p. 346.

2. Jan Assmann, "Ancient Egyptian Anti-Judaism: A Case of Distorted Memory," in Schacter, ed., *Memory Distortion*, pp. 365-78.

3. Schudson, "Dynamics," p. 348. However, Schudson (p. 361) rejects the notion that such a position demands an agnosticized approach to memory (or history). Rather he asserts, "If interpretation were free-floating, entirely manipulable to serve present interests, altogether unanchored by a bedrock body of unshakable evidence, controversies over the past would ultimately be uninteresting. But in fact they are interesting. They are compelling. And they are gripping because people trust that a past we can to some extent know and can to some extent come to agreement about really happened."

4. This only confirms how entrenched our patterns of perception are within language categories.

5. Schudson, "Dynamics," p. 348.

6. This is similar though not identical to Paul Ricoeur's treatment of literary/ hermeneutical distanciation ("The Hermeneutical Function of Distanciation," *Philosophy Today* 17, no. 2 [1973]). The concept is perhaps best summed up by Nietzsche, who stated that the human animal's default position is that of forgetfulness but, by breeding memory into humanity "forgetfulness can be suspended in certain

cases" (*The Genealogy of Morals* [Garden City, NY: Doubleday Anchor Books, 1956 (1887)], p. 39).

7. Elsewhere, I have added a fifth: (5) articulation: the tendency for memories to conform to language conventions.

Notes to "History III: If Memory Serves"

1. "Hurricane's Eye," *You're the One* (Warner Bros. Recordings, 2000).

2. Hayden White, *Metahistory: The Historical Imagination in Nineteenth-Century Britain* (Baltimore and London: Johns Hopkins University Press, 1973), p. 7.

3. A. Le Donne, "Theological Memory Distortion in the Jesus Tradition: A Study in Social Memory Theory," in Stephen C. Barton, Loren T. Stuckenbruck, Benjamin G. Wold, eds., *Memory and Remembrance in the Bible and Antiquity* (Tübingen: Mohr Siebeck, 2007), pp. 163-77.

4. http://www.afterthechase.com/songs/simple.html.

5. A mnemotechnique is a "memory vehicle." It is a method by which we package our memories to make them readily accessible and relevant. Song is a good example of a mnemotechnique. The alphabet is often committed to memory by cementing it into verse and rhyme.

6. James Fentress and Chris Wickham, *Social Memory: New Perspectives on the Past* (Oxford: Blackwell, 1992), pp. 72, 73-74.

Notes to "Jesus III: The Big Stage"

1. The Targums are Aramaic paraphrases of the Hebrew Bible that often include editorial commentary.

2. Indeed, this is the historical context for the community at Qumran who collected the Dead Sea Scrolls. The Jewish sect by the Dead Sea thought of themselves as the true priesthood and awaited the restoration of a purified kingdom and temple.

3. The early church tended to be fond of the titles "Christ," "Lord," and "Son of God." "Son of Man" is not altogether forgotten, but it pales in popularity beside these other titles. It is therefore likely that Jesus' self-designation as the Son of Man was his own invention. He used it enough to make it stick in the memories of his disciples, but it was ultimately overshadowed by other titles.

4. Keep in mind that there is no non-story form of events behind the story. Mark formed his larger narrative from memories that had been previously narrativized in the mnemonic process.

5. While these passages share a conceptual kinship, there are enough differences to think that this saying was remembered in different groups independently

(C. H. Dodd, *Historical Tradition in the Fourth Gospel* [Cambridge: Cambridge University Press, 1963], pp. 90-91; R. Bultmann, *The Gospel of John* [Oxford: Blackwell, 1971], p. 126; Raymond Brown, *The Gospel According to John* (Garden City, NY: Doubleday, 1966), vol. 2, pp. 120-21; G. R. Beasley-Murray, *John,* WBC 36 [Nashville: Thomas Nelson, 1999], p. 38). So the Criterion of Multiple Attestation can be applied. See my definition of Multiple Attestation on page 50. There are, of course, other sayings in the Jesus tradition with similar content that solidify this appeal (Mark 15:29-30; Thom. 71). And if Mark 11:23; 13:1-2 were to be included as related sayings, one could also appeal to the Criterion of Multiple Forms.

6. "All of the evangelists have to face the difficulty that Jesus did not literally fulfill the promise involved in this saying" (Brown, *The Gospel According to John,* vol. 2, p. 120). Both evangelists seem to have included this saying in reaction to a previous (perhaps embarrassing) perception of Jesus. Both seem intent to counteract a similar perception — that Jesus claimed to be able to destroy the temple. This is evidence that these passages are reacting to an early and widespread memory of Jesus. So the Criterion of Embarrassment is warranted. On the basis of the above criteria, it is highly unlikely that this saying was invented by the early church. Rather it was remembered to have been uttered by Jesus himself.

7. E. P. Sanders, *Jesus and Judaism* (London: SCM, 1985), pp. 72-73.

8. *The Antiquities of the Jews* 20.8 § 169-72.

Notes to "New Beginnings"

1. http://www.petermayer.net/music/?id=5.

HORMEGEDDON

HOW TOO MUCH OF A GOOD THING
LEADS TO DISASTER

BILL BONNER

For information about this title or to order other books and/or electronic media, contact the publisher:

LIONCREST
PUBLISHING

Library of Congress Control Number: 2014942933

ISBN:
978-0-9903595-3-1 (print)
978-0-9903595-1-7 (mobi)
978-0-9903595-2-4 (epub)

Printed in the United States of America

Cover design by: Erin Tyler
Interior design by: 1106 Design

Acknowledgments

SPECIAL THANKS to Nassim Taleb for taking the time to read the manuscript carefully and making several valuable suggestions.

I would also like to thank my sons for helping me with this book: Will, for managing the publishing process. Jules, for editing the English language version. And Henry, for editing the French version. As far as I know, I am the only author who has been aided by three sons on a single book project; I take more pride in this than in the book itself.

TABLE *of* CONTENTS

Chapter 1
TOO MUCH INFORMATION

"Perhaps there is a realm from which
the logician is exiled."

—FRIEDRICH NIETZSCHE

December 21st, 2012

I was in Paris when the end of the world came.

My company, Les Belles Lettres, has been publishing the Greek and Latin classics there since 1919. We've translated approximately 900 of the 1,200 texts that still exist. It seemed a shame that the world would end before we completed our work.

So I went into the office, where, amidst a thick blue fog, I found Caroline—the CEO—energetically working her way through a carton of Marlboros. She was determined to go out doing the two things she loved most: promoting Aristotle and chain-smoking at her desk—screw the workplace tobacco ban; they can fine me in hell!

Impressed with her attitude, I considered writing a very nasty letter to the IRS, maybe I'd park in a handicapped spot while I was at it…but first I needed to get coffee.

At the nearby "café bar bistro," however, there was no mention of the impending apocalypse. Apparently, management had decided to continue serving coffee right through the end of the world. *Servi kaffe, pereat mundis.*

I looked at my watch. It was 11 AM, the supposed ETA of our apocalypse. We were all still there.

I was perplexed. Could it be that the Mayans were just as thick as the rest of us? Was it all just meaningless guesswork? What if their chief astrologer was one of Paul Krugman's ancestors?

Then it hit me: the Mayans were based in South America. They probably used Eastern Standard Time!

But 11 AM EST rolled around, and the world was no more destroyed. Caroline tossed her empty carton in the trash and sighed.

The cosmos had spared us.

That's the trouble with natural disasters. They never quite show up when they're supposed to. And for card-carrying doom and gloomers like me, they are a source of much disappointment.

Manmade disasters, on the other hand, are not only far more frequent, but far more predictable. They're also extremely entertaining…assuming of course, you're into that sort of thing.

Take, for instance, one of the worst military campaigns in history: Napoleon's invasion of Russia.

Up until then, Napoleon's career had been a spectacular success. He could seemingly get away with anything. By the time the French senate proclaimed him Emperor in 1804, he was already regarded as the greatest military genius who ever lived. So when he decided to invade Russia, no one blinked. No one besides Armand Augustin Louis de Caulaincourt, Napoleon's long-time aide-de-camp. He knew better. He had actually been to Russia. Napoleon was the one who sent him there as France's ambassador to St. Petersburg. He knew invading Russia was a bad idea. He warned the emperor of the terrible weather, the bad roads, and the savage people. He begged him not to go. It would be the ruin of France, he said.

The Emperor ignored him and a few months later there they both were, freezing their rear ends off as they fled the smoldering ruins of Moscow.

We have a chart in our library at home that shows what happened next. It records the temperature dropping to minus 30 degrees centigrade…as the size of the French army dropped along with it. Soldiers burned down barns to try to get warm, but many of them froze. Many of those who survived the cold got shot by the Russian army while still others were attacked by partisans on the roads, packs of wolves in the forests, and prisoners the state had released into the city streets. If that didn't get them, they starved to death. Napoleon entered Russia with 300,000 troops. Only 10,000 got out.

I told this story to my kids over and over again as they were growing up. And I can tell you with some confidence that it has had beneficial effects. None of my children will ever invade Russia. They won't make that mistake!

Knowledge of Napoleon's 19th century disaster, however, didn't dissuade Hitler from repeating it in the 20th century, on a larger scale. And he was certainly aware of the dangers. The famous German war historian, Clausewitz, wrote extensively on Napoleon's ill-fated invasion.

August von Kageneck's history of the German army's 18th regiment on the Eastern Front in WWII contains a delightful anecdote to this end. The regiment had been annihilated, rebuilt, and annihilated again. Finally, near the end of the war, the remnants of it were captured by the Russians. A Soviet interrogator with a sense of humor posed a question to the survivors: "Haven't any of you ever read Clausewitz?" None of the prisoners raised his hand.

Why do these disasters happen? That's what I set out to explore in this book. To use the words of the Scottish poet Bobby Burns, the best laid plans of mice and men 'gang aft aglee.' Is that Scottish? I don't know. But the sense of it is probably best captured in the old Navy expression: go FUBAR. The last three letters of that mean "beyond all recognition." The first two, I leave you to figure out for yourself.

History is a long tale of things that went FUBAR—debacles, disasters, and catastrophes. That is what makes it fun to study. And maybe even useful. Each disaster carries with it a warning. For example, if the Sioux have assembled a vast war party out on the plains, don't put on your best uniform and ride out to the Little Big Horn to have a look. If the architect of a great ship tells you that 'not even God himself could sink this ship,' take the next boat! When you are up against a superior force, like Fabius Maximus against Hannibal, don't engage him in battle; instead, delay…procrastinate… dodge him, wear him down, until you are in a better position. And if the stock market is selling at 20 times earnings…and all your friends, analysts and experts urge you to 'get in' because you 'can't lose'—it's time to get out!

You can learn about these disasters by reading history. But be careful. Histories are narratives. They are stories. One theme is examined in detail, while all the others are ignored. More is ignored than examined, simply because there is always much more that happened than any one story can include. A single storyline makes its teller more in demand at dinner parties, but it also turns him into a fool, because most of what really happened has been shaken out of his history book and left lying on the ground.

"We never know what we are talking about," cautioned English philosopher Karl Popper. He had a point.

But the Austrian logician, esteemed philosopher and suspected lunatic Wittgenstein had an answer for him: then, shut up.

Silence isn't much fun though. Instead, we reach…we stretch…we strain to understand things we can never really hope to understand at all. The Truth is too big, involving a connection between all things animate and inanimate, from the beginning of time to the universe's very last breath. We can't see so much. The best we can do is try to catch tiny glimpses of things that are *true enough.*

This book has a modest ambition: to catch a faint glimmer of truth, perhaps out of the corner of our eye. What truth? It is a phenomenon I call Hormegeddon.

German pharmacologist Hugo Schulz first described its scientific antecedent in 1888. He put small doses of lethal poison onto yeast and found that it actually stimulated growth. Various researchers and biochemical tinkerers also experimented with it in subsequent years and came to similar findings. Finally, in 1943, two scientists published a journal article about this phenomenon and gave it a name: "hormesis." It is what happens when a small dose of something produces a favorable result, but if you increase the dosage, the results are a disaster. Giving credit where it is due, Nassim Taleb suggested applying the term beyond pharmacology in his 2012 book, *Antifragile.*

Disasters come in many forms. Epidemic disease is a disaster. A fire can be a disaster. A hurricane, an earthquake, a tornado. All these natural phenomena are the disastrous version of normal, healthy environmental processes. But this book is about another kind of natural disaster. Public policy disasters.

Generally speaking, public policy disasters are what you get when you apply rational, small-scale problem-solving logic to an inappropriately broad situation. First, you get a declining rate of return on your investment (of time or resources). Then, if you keep going—and you *always* keep going—you get a disaster. The problem is, these disasters cannot be stopped by well-informed smart people with good intentions, because those exact people are the ones who cause these disasters in the first place.

You will find, as you read this book, that the disasters we cover all have the following elements.

1. **They are the products of rational thinking.**

2. **They are the results of large scale planning, usually backed by the police power of government.**

3. **The feedback loop is twisted.** Typically when a mistake has been made you feel the pain of adverse consequences. The pain initiates a change in behavior. This is how a feedback loop is supposed to work. Public policy disasters twist that loop and put the pain onto someone else, leaving those who made the original bad choices free of consequences and free to continue their bad behavior (more on this in the chapter on Corrections).

4. **They create their own support.** Rather than self-limiting, public policy disasters are self-perpetuating. They create 'zombies.' That is, people who gain from wealth-destroying activities.

"Hormegeddon" is my shorthand way of describing what happens when you have too much of a good thing in a public policy context.

Economists describe the 'too much of a good thing' phenomenon as 'declining marginal utility.' The idea is well known and understood:

You invest money. The first money you invest produces a good return. Then, the rate of return goes down...eventually to zero. When you get *below* the rate of return, on a 'risk-free' Treasury bond for instance, you're no longer earning anything for the risk you take; you're losing money. If you keep investing at this point, your losses will increase. What was just a bad investment becomes a disastrous investment. Economics has no special term for this stage—where marginal returns sink below zero, and you begin to get negative returns that, eventually, lead to hormegeddon. Nor is this phenomenon specific to just finance.

Take exercise. Your muscles need to push against something or they will atrophy. A little bit of exercise is surely a good thing. Even a moderate amount of exercise is beneficial. But soon you reach the point of diminishing returns. Participants in Crossfit—a high intensity interval fitness regimen that ranks somewhere between D-Day and a cage fight in Bangkok—are routinely warned to watch out for symptoms of "rhabdomyolysis," a potentially fatal condition wherein over-strained muscles explode and cause kidney failure. The damage is often irreparable. The founder of Crossfit, Greg Glassman, was recently quoted saying, "It can kill you. I've always been completely honest about that."

Or take food. A good thing. A necessary thing. A little bit of food can be the difference between survival and death. A very high return on investment, in other words. But it's obvious that the return goes down the more you eat. That's declining marginal utility. Each additional bite produces less of a benefit. Keep chowing down and soon you enter into a new phase. This is the territory of the downside, where the returns go below zero. The more you eat the worse your health becomes. You feel bad. You look worse. Eat enough and your life expectancy will fall. That's why few reasonable people regret skipping a second helping of chocolate custard or declining a third glass of bourbon.

Is everything subject to the law of declining marginal utility? Maybe not love, beauty and grace, but almost everything you can measure seems to obey the law. Mae West famously remarked, "too much of a good thing is wonderful." As to what she had in mind, I have my doubts. Typically, the marginal rate of return declines as you add to your investment. But does too much of a good thing always end in disaster? The phenomenon I describe in this book applies only to large-scale public policy disasters. But there are parallels in the rest of life.

An oddball story circulated in the news media during the summer of 2012 about a man in Africa with five wives. He had recently taken a new, younger sixth wife. The older wives got jealous. Apparently, as the story goes, they burst in on him when he was making love to the new wife and demanded the same treatment. The man was in the midst of complying with their request when the strain of it got to him. He had a heart attack and died.

Still, despite its prevalence in this world, hormegeddon trudges on in anonymity, ignored by just about everyone on the planet.

The reason is simple: our intellectual traditions give us no purchase on it. Western thought is largely dominated by rational problem solvers. They presume that individual human beings can consciously determine where they want to go and how to get there. I will pass over the fact that not a single human being on the planet actually got where he is by rational thought alone. Instead, we are all products of forces we can barely begin to fathom, let alone control. But the idea that there are forms of collective human activity that cannot be controlled or improved by planning is still a shocking and unsettling notion to most people. We have no words to explain it. As for the disasters themselves—specific instances of hormegeddon—most people are content to pass them off as 'mistakes' or the works of 'bad people.' In a sense, they are both. But it is worth taking a closer look at how these 'mistakes' are made and how even good people—assuming we can tell the difference—make them.

As a society, we believe we make progress by considering a range of possibilities and choosing the way forward that seems most promising. We propose a hypothesis; we test it by moving forward; then, we improve our plans based on the results. But human behavior is not as simple as that. In a previous book with Addison Wiggin, *Empire of Debt,* we noted that societies seem to follow patterns of boom and bust that have little to do with conscious decision making. 'When do nations begin to throw their weight around...and assume the role of an empire,' we asked. 'When they can,' we answered.

Markets, too, follow patterns that are neither controlled nor intended by human designers. Unpredictable in detail, these patterns are still faintly recognizable—though not fully understood. We can recognize patterns in music, for example, and cringe when the music goes off key, yet forever be unable to explain why. We can even create decent music without fully understanding, consciously or intellectually, what we are doing. So can we recognize market movements, and even simulate them, without ever being able to control them. Form never precedes function; that is the folly and the vanity of theory. Instead, markets are what *results* when individuals make their own choices, each competing with one another, each trying to make the most of what he has while avoiding the mistakes he sees others making. Every individual may be as rational and calculating as he can be. But that doesn't mean markets act as 'rationally' as we would like. The world's smartest mathematicians and logicians try to model them; none has had more than a trifling success.

In a later book with Lila Rajiva, *Mobs, Messiahs, and Markets,* we showed that collective action in markets, mobs, and democracies also follows broad, recognizable patterns. We explained, as part of that work, why large groups of people seemed to do such extraordinarily pig-headed things from time to time.

Republicans can drive a car more or less as well as Democrats or Communists. Of the millions of autos on the road, driven by Rosicrucians, Rotarians, River Keepers and all manner of people with all manner of ideas, there are relatively few accidents. Making their own decisions about their own lives, people of all sorts get along passably well—even when they are driving automobiles at high rates of speed with a Democrat headed right for them. They obey simple, general rules—keep to the right (or left)!—and decide the minor details for themselves. Usually they get where they are going. But trust these people with public affairs and there's a good chance you'll wind up driving tanks through Poland.

The human brain is well adapted to driving a car and to looking out for itself. Without conscious thought, it makes life and death calculations on a second-by-second basis, for the most part successfully. But it evolved while living in small groups without the abstractions of large-scale, modern public life. The ability to do abstract thinking, or to understand the dynamics of large groups, was unnecessary. That is probably why the ability to do this kind of thinking is so rare. The typical brain is not equipped for it. Ask the human brain to coordinate the ordering of a pizza for a family of five and the results are outstanding. Put it to work on Obamacare, NSA snooping, firearms control or public finance and the results can be astonishingly silly.

Ambitious people pretend this isn't the case. They feel it is their responsibility to read the papers and try to understand the headlines. They identify the hero, the villain, the love interest and the conflict. They root for the good guy, curse the guy in the well-tailored business suit, and pray their side will win. They cannot imagine a team without a captain or an army without a general or a war without a victor. They need to think someone is in charge; someone who can win this struggle against an uncertain Fate.

Few people can stomach the idea that public life is out of the conscious control of the authorities in whom they have placed so much faith. They lack what Nietzsche referred to as an 'amor fati'…a faith in, and an affection for, Fate. People don't like Fate. Fate is the bad stuff that happens when no one is in charge, when chaos reigns. Instead, they believe in the ability of right thinking experts to 'do something' to bring about a better outcome than Fate had in store for them. They want a leader who will slay their enemies and bring the home team to victory. They want officials to deliver up full employment, someone else's money, the America's Cup, and free beer on tap 24/7. They want someone in the driver's seat who will take them where they want to go. But where do they want to go? They don't know. And history is largely a record of fender benders, sideswipes and pile-ups on the way there—a place, it turns out, they really shouldn't have been going in the first place.

History ignores the trillions of very good decisions made by private citizens in their private lives. We don't see the calculation of the boatmen, bringing their barks to shore just before the tide turns. We hardly notice the bowman, who sends his arrow to a spot just a few feet in front of a racing rabbit. Nor does history spend much time on the brakeman, who carefully brings the 11:07 AM from New York to a halt directly in front of travelers standing on the platform at Pennsylvania Station in Baltimore.

But the competence of the brakeman, boatman and bowman make us overconfident. If we can bring a train to rest at exactly the right spot, why not an economy? If we can impose our will, by force, on a rabbit…why not on Alabama? If we can drive a car, why not a whole society?

It seems reasonable enough. And it agrees with our core intellectual bias—well established since the time of Aristotle and re-established during the Renaissance—that we are able to see, understand, and direct our future.

But if that were true, history would be a lot less colorful than it is. What actually happens is that people take on big projects. And fail miserably. For instance, the people of nation X demand cheap bread. The government assigns its finest minds to the project. Soon, people are starving.

Military history offers plenty of examples of strategic miscalculations, misunderstandings and gross recklessness. These various buffooneries appear antiseptically in the historical record as simple 'errors.' But they are errors of a special sort. They are the kind made when you undertake large-scale projects in the modern world using brains evolved and adapted for much smaller problems.

Before we get into some of the more staggering examples of major disaster, it is important to note here that none of the ideas or themes in this book is entirely original. Many writers and economists have tried to explain these phenomena in different terms.

In the 1960s, American economist Mancur Olson explained that large groups don't necessarily work together to improve their collective well-being. Instead, individual members or smaller groups become predatory on the larger group. He raised the issue of the "free rider" who takes advantage of collective goods without paying his fair share of the costs. These predatory sub-groups, which I call 'zombies,' are part of the reason a public policy 'mistake' cannot be corrected. They are also the reason that cooperation in human societies is cyclical. When a group gains the advantages of cooperation, the less incentive the individual participant has to cooperate.

Olson also noted in *The Logic of Collective Action: Public Goods and the Theory of Groups* that as the size of a group increases so does the cost of organizing. The cost of organization is an overhead expense that reduces net output. This is another way of saying that the return on investment goes down as the scale goes up. It's another part of the reason public policy solutions to collective problems are subject to the law of diminishing returns; they become more and more costly.

Olson favored rigorous preventative measures. But Austrian economist Josef Schumpeter had a different solution: 'creative destruction.'

Simply put, to avoid being overrun by zombies, you just let nature take its course. The inefficient, the incompetent, the imprudent, the passé—all are supposed to be swept aside naturally in the trial and error of a free market system. The market cleanses itself. Businesses that are no longer productive are pushed aside by new competitors. Rich people who make mistakes are soon no longer rich. Industries that are uncompetitive disappear.

But this doesn't always happen the way it is supposed to. Gradually, the zombies erect barriers to protect themselves, prevent change and stabilize the system. They use the power of government to hold onto what they've got and get more. Entitlements are offered. Bailouts are given. Contracts are awarded. Bureaucracies grow. Whole industries are shielded from competition. Whole classes of society are given special privileges. Before he died, Schumpeter himself predicted that bourgeois western societies would tend to elect politicians committed to softening, temporizing, and blunting the blows of creative destruction. That is just what has happened.

One of Schumpeter's students, Hyman Minsky, described what happens next with his famous dictum, 'stability leads to instability.' Success, as it turns out, leads to failure.

Success, stability, even civilization itself, is largely cyclical. Stability—or the illusion of it—lures people to reach further and take bigger gambles. Why? Stability leads them to believe they have nothing to fear. A man who doesn't get caught with one mistress might take up with another one. A woman who drinks and drives without incident may be tempted to step on the gas. A marginal enterprise that might have gone broke in a dynamic economy may be subsidized and protected in a stable one. In some cases, incompetence itself becomes a virtue. Think about General Motors. Being totally incompetent at making cars was perhaps the best thing that ever happened to it. After Washington gave the company $49.5 billion, GM's CFO, Ray Young, was ecstatic, calling the bailout a "once-in-a-lifetime opportunity."

Meanwhile, with no fear of negative consequences, people take more and more risks, reaching for higher and higher returns. The stability of the system reassures and misleads them. They think the lack of corrections in the near-past means there will be none in the proximate future. They begin to think they can't lose. Their actions become more and more reckless, and then the whole system becomes, to use Nassim Taleb's word, 'fragilized.' It becomes unstable...and eventually blows up.

"Stability" is what you get when you successfully avoid creative destruction. It is what governments crave. As you will see in subsequent chapters, governments represent existing configurations of power, wealth and status. Their chief goal is to preserve them. But, the more successful you are at avoiding creative destruction, the more pent-up destruction you have in store.

The anthropologist Joseph Tainter explained that civilizations collapse when they become too complex. His idea is that over time civilizations are confronted with challenges that they meet by introducing new, more complex solutions. It could be a flood-control system, or a bureaucracy to prevent people from smoking, or high walls to protect against invasion. Whatever they are, the solutions cost time and energy. Eventually, and especially as the economy becomes larger, the costs become too high. The whole system is whacked, first by declining marginal utility, then by negative utility and finally, if it continues, hormegeddon.

Olson, Schumpeter, Minsky, Tainter, Taleb—these observers all point us in the same direction: There's no standing still. And no progress in public affairs without backsliding.

WHY CENTRAL PLANNING FAILS

There is a difference between science and engineering on the one hand and philosophy and poetry on the other. Science and engineering, applied to the right subjects, have no known upward limits. We can make incremental improvements. We can know things with reasonable certainty. One innovation leads to another. Gradually, over time, we get better at building bridges and flying airplanes.

But some things don't get better. Is a kiss, properly rendered, any better today than it was 2,000 years ago, when Cleopatra—famous for the art of love—planted one on Marc Antony's lips? Some things—especially those things considered "art"—are not susceptible to the scientific method or improvement. No progress is made, or possible.

What about economics? What kind of thing is it? A science? Or is it an art? Is a good central banker like a good mechanical engineer, who can improve our standard of living, or is he like a good poet... or a good judge? As far as we know, judges today are not a bit better than those from the time of Solomon, or Lord Denning, or Judge Learned Hand. They listen to the pleas. They sort out the evidence. They try to make the right decision in accordance with the rules in place at that time.

But there are those who believe they can make the right decision more right, or the poet more poetic. And while many of these snake oil salesmen content themselves with a quick buck and the next train out of town, some of them go for the long con. These are the central planners.

The illusions, mistakes and misconceptions of central planners take their toll in a great variety of ways—mostly as costly nuisances. Occasionally, when they are particularly ambitious, they make the history books. Napoleon's march on Moscow. Mao's great famine. The Soviet Union's 70-year economic experiment. These fiascos are caused by well-meaning, smart public officials. They are the Hell to which the road paved with good intentions leads. Sometimes, a mistaken public policy can be reversed or abandoned before it has done serious harm. Mostly, however, a combination of special circumstances makes correction impossible. The disastrous policies are reinforced until they finally reckon themselves out in a catastrophic way.

Large-scale planners fail because they believe three things that aren't true. First, that they know the exact and entire present state of the community they are planning for (wants, desires, hopes, capabilities, resources); second, that they know where the community ought to go (what future would be best); third, that they are capable of creating the future they want.

None of those things is more than an illusion. Together, they constitute what F. A. Hayek called "the fatal conceit, that man is able to shape the world around him according to his wishes."

Full knowledge of current conditions would require an infinite amount of real information. As 19th century philosopher, Samuel Bailey, wrote in 1840, it would require "minute knowledge of a thousand particulars which will be learnt by nobody but him who has an interest in knowing them." The planners have nothing like that. Instead, they rely on a body of popular theories, claptrap and statistical guesswork.

As to the second point—that they are blessed with some gift that tells them what the future should be—we pass over it without argument. No one really believes that people in the United State Congress or the French National Assembly, or in the bureaucracies and think tanks of these nations, have anything more to guide them than anyone else. Which is to say; all they have is their own likes and dislikes, prejudices and fears, and self-serving ambitions.

Each man always does his level best to shape his world in a way that pleases him. One wants a fat wife. One wants a fortune. One wants to spend his time playing golf. Each will try to get what he wants depending upon the circumstances. And the future will happen.

The pretention of the central planner is that he knows a better future—one that he can design and bring about. The god-like vanity of this assertion is staggering. No one really knows what future is best for humankind. People only know what they want. For the limited purpose of this book, I presume that the best future is the one in which people get what they want...or at the very least what they deserve. A man burning in hell may want ice cream; it doesn't mean he will get it. But the central planner presumes to know not only what he wants, but what he should have. It is scarcely worth mentioning, additionally, that the central planner's hands are as empty as his head. He has no ice cream to give anyone.

Where individual plans and evolution will take us collectively, no one knows. Fate will have the final say. But the central planner will have his say first, disrupting the plans of millions of people in the process. He certainly has no 'amor fati.' It would put him out of business. Instead, he steps in to impose his own version of the future. And as soon as the smallest bit of time and resources are shanghaied for his ends rather than those of individual planners, the rate of natural, evolutionary progress slows. That is, the millions of private trials that would have otherwise taken place are postponed or canceled. The errors that might have been revealed and corrected are not discovered. The future has to wait.

Even when they are applied with ruthless thoroughness, central plans inevitably and eventually go FUBAR. No 'workers' paradise' ever happens. The War on Drugs (or Poverty...or Crime...or Terror... or Cancer) ends in a defeat, not a victory. Unemployment does not go down. The 'war to end war' doesn't end war. The Domino Theory falls; the dominoes don't. Or, if any of these grand programs 'succeeds,' it does so by undoing previous plans often at a cost that is far out of balance with the reward. World War II is an example of central planning that seemed to work. But the Allies were merely nullifying the efforts of more ambitious central planners in Germany and Japan.

Generally, life on planet Earth is not so 'rational' that it lends itself to simpleminded, heavy-handed intervention by the naïve social engineer. Sure, we can design bridges. Houses too. And particle accelerators. But we cannot design economies. No more than we can invent real languages.[1] Societies. Customs. Markets. Love. Marriages. Children. Or any of the other important things in life.

Not to overstate the case, however, it is also true that humans can design and achieve a certain kind of future. If the planners at the Pentagon, for example, decided that a nuclear war would be a good thing, they could bring it about. The effects would be huge. And hugely effective.

This extreme example reveals the only kind of alternative future that the planners are capable of delivering. Large-scale central planning can be effective, but only by pulverizing the delicate fabric of evolved civilized life. It is a future that practically no one wants, because it means destroying the many different futures already in the works—marriages, businesses, babies, baptisms, hunting trips, shopping, investment and all the other activities of normal life.

Not all central planning produces calamities on that scale, of course. But all, to the extent they are effective, are repulsive. The more they achieve the planners' goals, the more they interfere with private goals, and the more they retard or destroy the progress of the human race.

Still, this view I am putting forth is hardly accepted wisdom. Most people would dispute that it is wisdom at all. It is a minority view, held by such a small group that all of its members together could be soused with a single bottle of good whiskey.

TRUST AND COOPERATION

Highly organized Roman and Greek armies almost always won against less disciplined fighters, no matter how brave and bold they may have been individually.

A soldier must trust his comrades to 'do their duty.' If they break ranks and run, he will be placed in a vulnerable position. His flank

---

[1] My apologies to L. L. Zamenhoff.

exposed, he may break and run too, leaving the whole army open to disaster.

But as the benefits of cooperation increase for the group, the individual finds that he has more and more reason not to cooperate. If his army is going to win anyway, why should a soldier give up his life in a battle? As cooperation reduces the danger, the individual has less and less reason to sacrifice himself.

We can see a version of this in mass vaccinations. Vaccination against diseases such as measles, diphtheria, and pertussis provides not just the individual, but the group, with benefits. These diseases find fewer hosts and become less common. When so many others are vaccinated, even a person who is not immunized is much less likely to get these diseases.

In rare cases, an individual may be harmed by the vaccination. At this point he has a choice: to vaccinate or not to vaccinate? One hundred years ago, this choice required a true cost-benefit analysis. Not anymore. Today, as a greater percentage of the population is immunized, the individual has more and more reason to break ranks. He will get the benefits of immunization without the risks of taking the vaccine himself. It's okay Doc, you can put the needle away.

A version of this plays out in the financial world too. The lender needs to trust that he will get repaid. As trust builds, risk of non-payment goes down. Interest rates decline. But the easier lending standards bring forth more marginal borrowers. And as the benefits of cooperation grow, these marginal borrowers (and marginal lenders) have more and more incentive to break ranks. At the extreme, people without incomes or assets borrow at very low rates to buy houses they cannot afford. They get the benefit of a high-trust society, without actually being trustworthy themselves. Over time, the quantity of lending increases. But the quality of debt must go down.

If this sounds a lot like the European debt situation, you'd be right. When the states of Europe came together to form a European Union with a single currency, the euro, the cooperation led to growth and prosperity. This cooperation gave countries like Greece, Italy and Ireland an advantage. They were able to borrow at low, German interest rates. But they did not necessarily share those Germanic qualities of hard work, honesty, thrift and discipline that made them so creditworthy.

The trust and cooperation that bring low rates and economic progress also increase economic returns to the non-cooperating rule breaker. He may borrow money, at low rates, with no plausible way to repay the loan. Or, sensing trouble, he may sell his own debt short… speculating against the system by taking positions that not only reap huge rewards when Humpty Dumpty falls, but actually help push him off the wall.

Instead of an orderly retreat from excessive debt, what usually results is a panic, a credit market rout. Trust breaks down quickly and short-term interest rates skyrocket. Then, after the excessive debt is purged from the system—by bankruptcies, defaults, and write-offs—a new phase of trust-building and cooperation can begin. This should not be news to anyone. For it is the same cycle that nearly every natural phenomenon follows—be it life, death, the price of bonds, or the quality of the food at a popular restaurant.

Obviously, these inevitable cyclical shocks are a lot easier to bear for a small group than for a much larger one. In a small group, you can know what is going on in a direct, personal way. In a large group you don't know your leaders or have any real understanding of the public activities that affect your life. It is this distance between you and modern public life that makes large-scale disasters possible. The greater the distance, the greater the chance that things will go FUBAR. That's why government too obeys the rule of declining marginal utility. Small, modest governments seem to work better than big, ambitious ones. Switzerland, with its emphasis on local, canton-level politics, seems to provide better service than, say, the big, centralized government of the United States of America.

Aristotle's ideal world consisted of a small, localized society where everyone could be equally informed by the 'sound of the herald's cry.' Since everyone had access to the same set of facts and shared the same interests—the health, prosperity and safety of the community of which they were all part—they could all sit down together and make plans guided, perhaps, by a 'philosopher king.' In such a context even central planning—on a small scale—might be beneficial. At least, that seems logical.

However, it was not logic, but evolution, that brought mankind to his present condition. This is what you get after countless trials and innumerable errors, by millions of poor, battered souls and small hapless groups, each trying to better its position, each trying to gain an advantage, each trying to survive and improve its status, its wealth, and its power in the easiest possible way.

Aristotelian logic was a forerunner of 'positivism,' in which all truth can be determined by objective conditions and scientific reasoning. "Give me a problem and give me the facts," says the positivist, confidently. "Let me apply my rational brain to them. I will come up with a solution!"

This is fine, if you are building the Eiffel Tower or organizing the next church supper. But positivism falls apart when it is applied to schemes that go beyond science, engineering and the reach of the 'herald's cry.' That's what Aristotle, himself, said. Only in a small community would all the people share more or less the same information and interests. In a large community, you can't know things in the same direct, personal way. It's even harder for large groups to work together on common projects, without the addition of force and coercion.

THE WORST KIND OF INFORMATION

We are products of the Paleolithic age, a period of many thousands of years in which the *Homo* species developed the unique adaptations that make them human. In the Paleolithic period we lived in small tribes. The information we had was limited. But it was reliable. When a fellow tribesman came running into camp with word that another tribe was about to attack, we had a pretty good idea of how real and how important that information was. We grabbed our spears.

Now, we have a lot more of a different kind of information for which our Paleolithic brains are not well adapted. It is high in quantity, low in quality. Nietzsche referred to it as 'wissen.' As opposed to 'erfahrung,'—direct, personal, particular knowledge. Wissen refers to 'what everyone knows'; like we might know that America has a problem with violence or we might know that Berlusconi is a rascal or that Abraham Lincoln loved the slaves. It's the stuff you read in the newspapers and hear on TV.

Until the invention of TV, radio and the Internet, the volume of this 'public information,' as I like to call it, was only a fraction of what we get today. Just recently, a *New York Times* article estimated that the typical American receives as many as 5,000 advertising messages every day.[2]

Advertising, news, opinions, data of all sorts—it is remarkable how much more we "know" today than we used to. In 2013, we knew, for example, that the unemployment rate was above 7%. We knew Iran posed a threat to our safety. We knew education was the way to get ahead. We knew the Republicans were trying to block tax increases and that global warming could tip the world into a climatic disaster. Joe Jones, running for the office of Sheriff, was a 'friend of the people.' LavaX—a cleaning product—would leave your tub "as clean as an operating table." But what did all these things mean? Were these things even true? Did anyone know? Was there *any* way of knowing for sure?

Like infectious social diseases, public information is made possible by modern, large-scale life. Millions of people can now have a

---

[2]   Being as it is 'public information' that number is probably wrong and not to be taken entirely seriously. Yet, given the existence of cable television, it is probably not too far off.

conversation about something none of them really knows anything about. It can be fun. But it can lead to serious itching, or as I call it, 'public thinking.'

At an investment conference in 2002, a guy came up to me making conversation. 9/11 was fresh in our minds. And the Bush Administration was pushing for an invasion of Iraq.

"I guess we'll have to go in and clean that place up," he said.

Had he ever been to Iraq? Had he ever met an Iraqi? Did he speak the language? Where was the detailed, specific, precise real knowledge that you would need to make sense of it all? What, exactly, was unclean about Iraq? And how would this lack of hygiene be scrubbed up by a foreign invasion?

A million nuances, an infinite number of real 'facts' based on experience and direct observation, a whole universe of assumptions, misapprehensions, muddled thinking, all reduced to a single phrase. And that, there, is 'public thinking.'

Constructing a public policy out of public thinking is like building a skyscraper out of marshmallows. The higher you go, the squishier it gets. Because the information blocks themselves are not solid. Instead, they are combinations of theory, interpretation, guesswork, spin, hunch and prejudice. They are memes, not real information.

It takes a certain kind of brain to appreciate the emptiness of public information. Most of us are too earnest, which is to say most people are better adapted to the time in which they evolved. Most of us have stone-age brains. We regard all information as though it is rock hard. When Colin Powell told the world that the Iraqis had 'weapons of mass destruction,' most people—trapped in the noise of modern life—believed him. They took it as information of the same quality as the alarm sounded by the fellow who ran into camp warning of an imminent attack.

'Public information' contributes in an important way to hormegeddon. Like sugar, human consumption of news and information has soared since the 18th century. Both sugar and public information are tasty in small quantities. But eating large quantities of sugar rots your teeth and may give you diabetes. It is also self-perpetuating, as eating sugary food takes away your appetite for real food. So too with public information, your ability to make good decisions rots as your appetite for useful information decreases.

Public information is the stuff on which our governments, our social programs, our wars, and our money (including fiscal and monetary policies) now depend. It is the body of facts with which our consent is informed. It is the faux-granite upon which our public policies—involving trillions of dollars and interfering with countless private plans—are erected. And like everything else, public information obeys the rule of declining marginal utility. A little may be a good thing. But 'too much' leads to trouble. It gives you the impression that you know something that is really unknowable. Phony knowledge then leads to foolish action. Soon, you are on the road to hormegeddon.

MONEY, LAWS AND PRE-CIVILIZED DISASTERS

Civilization came into being only about 10,000 years ago with the advent of animal husbandry and sedentary agriculture. Then came larger groups. Then came money. Then came international trade.

We soon reached the point where we ate food prepared by people we didn't know with ingredients we didn't grow. We did so because we trusted that the people preparing the food were following the rules of civilized life. Those rules were developed over time, and expressed clearly by Jesus Christ in his Sermon on the Mount when he said, "do unto others as you would have them do unto you." Or, in the negative, as explained by Hillel, "that which you don't want someone to do to you, don't do to someone else." Both are statements of another universal law, the Law of Reciprocity, from which the basic rules of civilized life can be derived. The consumer did not have to know the baker personally. He only had to have confidence that the baker wasn't poisoning him. For his part, the baker didn't have to trust that the consumer might give him a haunch of meat when he came back from his next hunting expedition; he was happy to take a coin in payment.

Trustworthy money and trust, generally, allowed for diversity, further elaboration of the division of labor, and greater material progress. People could worship different gods, speak different languages, follow different customs and nevertheless cooperate—even without intending to do so—to their mutual advantage.

But that didn't mean the instincts and thinking patterns developed over hundreds of thousands of years had disappeared. Another feature of the human Paleolithic brain was that it had a strong sense of solidarity. In other words, it was probably more important in Stone Age tribes to all think the same thing than to think independently. Human survival was a close call. Hunting big game required coordination. Surviving in times of scarcity required group cohesion and discipline. There was probably not enough surplus to support a lot of 'out of the box' thinking.

When we read today about how Socrates died—he was a gadfly thinker who was put to death by the Athenian authorities for "corrupting the youth"—the story is hard to understand. Surely, Athens could have accommodated a harmless iconoclast. But putting up with alternative opinions may be a modern luxury, a feature of civilization, not of our barbarous past.

Today, truly independent thinking isn't illegal, but it is rare. Psychologists have done a number of studies proving that most people will ignore obvious facts and conclusions in order to remain steadfast with the group. That is, they prefer solidarity to truth. They prefer public information to private information, even though the former lacks meaning, cannot be verified and often is contradicted by personal observation and experiences. That is why people stand in line in airports watching an old lady get patted down by TSA agents, even though everyone knows perfectly well the old gal poses no threat.

It is also why most people can see little difference between a sporting event and a war. In both instances an instinct—developed over thousands of years—causes them to support the home team without quibble or equivocation. Their brains are not adapted to the kind of abstract thinking required to separate one competition from the other. For 99% of our time on earth there was no need.

These instincts make people easy to deceive, especially when they are out of range of the herald's voice. They are encouraged to believe that the collective projects are beneficial, whatever they are. Often, in a spirit of solidarity, they go along with the gag—for decades—even as the evidence from their daily lives contradicts its premises and undermines its promises. How else do you explain WWI, in which all major combatants continued making extravagant investments in a war, year after year, with no positive return? By the time the war ended there were 37 million casualties and the leading participants were bankrupt. What was the point? What was at stake that would justify such an investment of resources? Apparently, nothing. Nor did the Russians or Chinese readily give up their experiments with communism even when their schemes disrupted the private plans of nearly a billion people over three generations. And already, America's War on Terror has loomed over us for more than 10 years, even though there have been far more sightings of Elvis and Jimmy Hoffa than actual terrorists.

Not everyone goes along, however. First, a few "out of the box" thinkers question the program. Then, the masses begin to grumble and complain. Unfortunately, that's when the planners make even more plans. Typically, they urge people to make sacrifices. They promise that it will all turn out right in the end. "You can't make an omelet without breaking some eggs," said Lenin. People go along with breaking a few eggs for a while, particularly if the eggs belong to someone else. But ultimately, the problem is not the eggs, it's the omelet. It has the right shape, it appears sensible and rational. It should taste good. But it's disgusting. When you cut into it, it's burnt and runny. There are things inside you didn't order. There's probably a hair. And that's when you realize that you never wanted an omelet. You just wanted some eggs.

Chapter 2
TOO MUCH ECONOMICS

"Can you by legislation add one farthing to the
wealth of the country? You may, by legislation, in
one evening, destroy the fruits and accumulations
of a century of labour; but I defy you to show me
how, by the legislation of this House, you can
add one farthing to the wealth of the country."

—RICHARD COBDEN

FRIEDRICH HAYEK MADE THE POINT on numerous occasions that the more a person has been educated, the greater the likelihood he is an idiot. That insight may or may not be true of those who spent their school years in engineering and science; it is certainly true for those who have studied economics. The more they have learned, the dumber they get. Like a cloud rising against a mountain, when a young person enters the economics department, the higher up the academic slope he goes, the more the common sense rains out of him.

The trouble with *The Economist*, *The Financial Times*, the US Congress and most mainstream economists is not that they don't know what is going on, but that they don't want to know. It would be counterproductive. Nobody gets elected by promising to do nothing. Nobody gets a Nobel Prize for letting the chips fall where they may. Nobody attracts readers or speaking fees by telling the world there is nothing that can be done. Instead, they meddle. They plan. They tinker. Usually, the economy is robust enough to thrive despite their efforts. But not always.

From 2007–2012, Nobel Prize winning economists Paul Krugman and Joseph Stiglitz, along with celebrity economist, Jeffrey Sachs, and practically all their colleagues, failed to notice the most important happening in their field. This in itself was not news. Not noticing things came easily to them, like second nature. In fact, you might say they built their careers on not noticing things.

Blindness was part of their professional training. It was what allowed them to win coveted prizes and key posts in a very competitive occupation. Had they been more reflective, or more observant, they would probably be teaching at a community college.

Their obstinate dedication to obliviousness marks the culmination of a long trend in economics. By the mid 20th century, leading economists *preferred* not to look. They closed their eyes to what an economy actually is (to how it works) and focused on their own world—a make-believe playground of numbers, theories and public information, with little connection to the world that most people lived in. Not surprisingly, they missed things...

Irving Fisher, one of the greatest economists of the 20th century, on September 5, 1929: "There may be a recession in stock prices, but not anything in the nature of a crash."

Julius Barnes, head of Hoover's National Business Survey Conference, announced in 1930: "The spring of 1930 marks the end of a period of grave concern. American business is steadily coming back to a normal level of prosperity."

And now, in the 21st Century, more than 75 years later, economists are up to more mischief. And part of the mischief involves not noticing things that are under their noses, including the fact that their discipline is 90% claptrap.

Minutes of the Federal Reserve's Open Market Committee meetings, released in 2013, showed that neither Ben Bernanke, the Fed chairman, nor other key decisions makers had any idea what was coming their way in 2007.

"My forecast for the most likely outcome over the next few years," opined Fed governor, Donald Kohn, "is...growth a little below potential for a few quarters, held down by the housing correction, and the unemployment rate rising a little further."

Ben Bernanke set the pace for his fellow Fed officials back in 2005, with a stunning display of arrogance and ignorance about the threat derivatives posed to the global financial system:

> They are traded among very sophisticated financial institutions and individuals who have considerable incentive to understand them and to use them properly. The Federal Reserve's responsibility is to make sure that the institutions it regulates have good systems and good procedures

for ensuring that their derivatives portfolios are well
managed and do not create excessive risk...

Then, two years later, he was at it again:

At this juncture...the impact on the broader economy and
the financial markets of the problems in the subprime
markets seems likely to be contained...

And again, in 2008:

Fannie Mae and Freddie Mac were "adequately capital-
ized," he said. They were "in no danger of failing."

In the financial pile-up of '08–'09, derivatives did, in fact, create
so much risk that the system couldn't handle it. Subprime crashed.
Almost every financial school bus was dented. Practically all of Wall
Street—Fannie and Freddie too—had to be towed away.

And then, in 2013, Ben Bernanke, as blind to the approaching
financial disaster as a pick-up truck to a brick wall, was driving the
whole world economy.

That economists are incompetent hardly needs additional evidence
or argument. But they are far from being idiots. On the contrary, they
are too clever by half. They are such able swindlers and accomplished
charlatans that they convince themselves of things that couldn't possibly
be true. They do so for reasons of professional vanity...and for money.

AIN'T NO AVERAGE MAN

Ben Bernanke's ridiculousness was not the exception to the rule. It
was the rule. He was following a hallowed tradition. These economists made themselves into useful stooges by creating a simpleton's
model of the economy. For simplicity's sake, I will refer to this model

as the Simpleton's Economic Model, or 'SEM' for short. So stripped down, shorn of all nuance and ambiguity, it bears no relationship or resemblance to a real economy. It is like a stick figure that is meant to represent a real human being.

Still, SEM is something economists can work with. It brings them PhDs and Nobel prizes. It makes people think they know what they are talking about. It both justifies and permits dangerous intervention—like a surgeon whose only training comes from studying stick-figure diagrams.

At its most basic level, SEM requires that complex economic transactions be reduced to numbers and statistics. This alone is fraudulent, as we will see. Then, based on these numbers economists are able to do math—the more complex the better—to arrive at results that are internally coherent but describe life in a parallel, artificial and unreal economic universe. The SEM begins with a statistical construct—the average man—who doesn't exist (nor has ever existed) in reality. There is a simple example that illustrates how hollow this construct truly is:

Imagine that Warren Buffett moves to a city with 50,000 starving, penniless beggars. This is what economists would say about that city: "Stop whining…the average person in the city is a millionaire."

Statistically speaking, the economist would be correct, but only by peddling a form of information with negative content. After you heard it you would actually know less than you knew before. This, by itself, is destructive enough, but it's what happens next that is the real problem.

On the foundation of fraudulent numbers and empty statistics like these, economists build a whole, elaborate tower of hollow, meaningless facts and indicators: the unemployment rate, consumer price inflation, the GDP. None are 'hard' numbers, yet the economist uses them as a rogue policeman uses his billy club…to beat up on honest citizens. These numbers, these soft numbers made hard by the velocity with which they are thrown around, are an essential ingredient for hormegeddon.

Unlike a real, hard science, you can never prove economic hypotheses wrong. There are too many variables, including the most varied variable of all—man. He will do one thing sometimes, another thing the next time, then something else the time after that. Sometimes he seems to respond to economic incentives. Sometimes he's out to lunch. Why? Because every man is different. Unique. Infinitely complex. And thus, ultimately unknowable.

The problem with this is that you can't do much central planning in an economy where all the key component parts are unique and unknowable. You'd have to strip them of their particularities, reducing them to a simpler figure that you can work with—the average man. This 'average man' bears no resemblance to a real man. But he is useful to the economics profession. He is predictable, whereas real men are not. He will do their bidding; real men will not. He is like an interchangeable part in a vast machine, a cog; again, real men are not that way.

You turn a man into a stick figure with numbers. You say that he has 2.2 children. Or that he earns $42,500. Or, that he is 7.8% unemployed. None of it is true. It is all a convenient fabrication.

If you could get man to do what you wanted, you could, in theory, operate a centrally planned economy successfully. It has never happened. Because man is an ornery fellow, prone to putting a stick in the economists' wheels. Not that he is malicious or obstructionist. It's just that he and only he really knows what he wants; and he changes his mind often.

THE ECONOMY OF STUFF

Ultimately, economics is about material wealth. It's about stuff. Economists' conceit is that they can help people get more of it, that they can bring the average man more wealth, by improving the unemployment rate or boosting the GDP growth rate or increasing some other fraudulent number they created with one of their prize-winning theories. With more stuff, they contend, the average man will be better off.

But stuff doesn't automatically have a fixed value. What is yesterday's newspaper worth? How about a painting? Or an ounce of gold? Or a pound of frogs' legs?

The value of Stuff is established by people. They declare their interest in stuff by bidding for it in the market. Thus do they set the price for a loaf of bread, a share of Google, or an hour of someone's time. Markets are not perfect. They never "know" what the price should be. And they are subject to fits of panic, disgust, greed, and infatuation, just like the individuals who participate in them.

The market gods play tricks...they set traps...they toy with us...they seek to ruin us...and they discover exactly the right price—set by willing buyers and sellers—every day.

In financial terms, the market 'clears' when buyers and sellers figure out the price that will get the deal done. Then, they can regret it later.

The price is essential. It is what tells farmers they overplanted or homebuyers that they have waited too long. It's what causes speculators to look for open windows and investors to postpone retirement. It is what tells the producer what he should have produced and the consumer what he wished he could consume. It's what tells you what people *really* want.

Since real wealth can only be measured in terms of what people really want, any distortion of prices is misleading, vain, and potentially impoverishing. Bend prices and you send producers off in the wrong direction, making stuff that people don't really want. Everyone is poorer as a result. Even the smallest amount of central planning, where it disturbs private, individual planning to the slightest effect, reduces the sum of human happiness.

Taxes, tariffs, import restrictions, quotas, subsidies, bailouts, product specifications—every meddle is a fat thumb on the market scales. The price data is corrupted. The producer doesn't know what the consumer wants. The consumers' choices are sub-optimal. The whole economy is hobbled. Everyone gets less of the stuff he really wants and more of the stuff he doesn't.

If you agree with that, guess what…you're going against an entire century of economic theory and practice. The modern economist believes he can improve the way people invest, save, spend and do business. In the United States he has been hard at it—manipulating, interfering, controlling—for a century, since the Federal Reserve system was founded in 1913. Is there any evidence that all this sweat and heavy breathing has actually worked? That it has actually improved the way economies function? None that we have seen. But now after 100 years of meddling, economics itself is sinking below the zero barrier, down into the dark under world of hormegeddon, where the return on further effort will be starkly, catastrophically negative.

The Original Economists

There was a time when economists were not so conceited, not so bold and arrogant, not so ambitious…and not such dumbbells. The original practitioners of the trade saw themselves as natural or moral philosophers.

It was 'moral' in the sense that when you make a mistake you have to pay for it. You don't watch where you're going and you step on a rake, the handle comes up and hits you in the face. You go away on a trip and forget to pay the electric bill, you come home and the lights don't work. There is no complex mathematics that will bring the lights back on. There are no abstract theories—such as countercyclical fiscal policies—that will do it either. The solution is simple: you have to pay the bill. You have to suffer the consequences of your own mistake to set it straight. That's moral philosophy.

When your washing machine breaks down, you turn it off and try to fix it. A few whacks with a hammer and some choice swear words can often work wonders. This is a mechanical—not moral—system, and not a particularly complex one at that. The trouble is, economies are not washing machines. They are complex systems that cannot be adjusted by a mechanic and only dimly understood by a moral philosopher. Economies require a deft, nuanced touch. But economists have clubs for fists. They come up with theories and 'fixes' that are as clumsy as a wrench and as blunt as a hammer. They almost always lead to trouble.

The Ur-economists of old knew better. They observed animals and nature and tried to draw out the laws and principles that helped understand them. Same thing for man and his natural economy. They watched. They reflected. They attempted to make sense of it in the same way a naturalist makes sense of a beehive or an ant colony. 'How does it work?' they asked themselves.

In the 19th century, they were able to formulate "laws" which they believed described the way a human economy functioned.

The Wealth of Nations was Adam Smith's observation about how wealth was created. How did people know what to produce? How did they know what price to sell it at? How did they know when to shift to other things, or when to increase production? He saw individuals guided by an 'invisible hand' that led them to follow their own interests and thereby respond to the needs and desires of others.

Later, other economists focused on prices. Prices had an information content that was essential for everyone, that allowed producers and consumers to get on the same page. These economists understood that when you manipulate the numbers you confuse them both.

Among the other phenomena that these proto-economists discovered were Say's Law and Gresham's Law.

French businessman and economist, Jean-Baptiste Say, discovered that "products are paid for with products," not merely with money. He meant that you needed to produce things to buy things; you could not just produce money…has anyone ever mentioned this to the Federal Reserve?

Long before Say, a 16th century English financier named Sir Thomas Gresham noticed that if people had good money and bad money of equal purchasing power, they'd spend the bad money and hoard the good money.

Economists were like astronomers. When they discovered something new they named it after themselves. They were just observers back then and they needed some reward. No one hired them to 'run' an economy or to 'improve' one. They would have thought the idea absurd. How could they know what people wanted? How could a single person, or a single generation, improve an infinitely complex system that had evolved over thousands of years?

Central planners can rig the economy to produce anything— tanks, education, bridges, bureaucrats, assassinations, you name it. But none of these things are priced in the open market the way the original economists observed them at the birth of their discipline. These machinations are exceedingly annoying to the invisible hand. The reason is that it needs to see what things are really worth to us or it cannot properly allocate capital and guide consumers. Things that are not priced by willing buyers and sellers are like dark matter in the economic universe. They provide no light, no clarity, nothing that can help consumers, taxpayers, or investors decide what to do with their money. Many of the products and services commanded or provided by non-market entities are probably worthless; or worse, actually of negative value. That's when the invisible hand starts drinking early.

BY THE NUMBERS

What is the meaning of life? In the *Hitchhiker's Guide to the Galaxy*, Arthur Dent searches the interplanetary system for the answer. Finally, he finds a computer, Deep Thought, that tells him: "Forty-two."

Wouldn't it be nice if meaning could be digitized? Unfortunately for the deep thinkers in the economics profession, the important things in life involve qualitative judgments. Understanding them requires analog thinking, not digital calculations.

Numbers are a good thing. Economics is full of numbers. It is perfectly natural to use numbers to count, to weigh, to study and compare. They make it easier and more precise to describe quantities. Instead of saying I drank a bucket of beer you say, I drank two 40s. Then instead of saying 'I threw up all over the place,' you say, 'I threw up on an area four feet square.'

But in economics we reach the point of diminishing returns with numbers very quickly. They gradually become useless. Later, when they are used to disguise, pervert and manipulate, they become disastrous. Hormegeddon by the numbers. Ask Deep Thought the meaning of life then and the answer is likely to be "Negative Forty-Two."

At exactly what point does the payoff from numbers in the economics trade become a nuisance? Probably as soon as you see a decimal point or a greek symbol. I'm not above eponymous vanity either. So I give you Bonner's Law:

In the hands of economists, the more precise the number, the bigger the lie.

For an economist, numbers are a gift from the heavens. They turn them, they twist them, they use them to lever up and screw down. They also use them to scam the public. Numbers help put nonsense on stilts.

Numbers appear precise, scientific, and accurate. By comparison, words are sloppy, vague, subject to misinterpretation. But words are much better suited to the economist's trade. The original economists understood this. Just look at *Wealth of Nations*—there are a lot of words. We understand the world by analogy, not by digits. Besides, the digits used by modern economists are most always fraudulent.

"Math makes a research paper look solid, but the real science lies not in math but in trying one's utmost to understand the real workings of the world," says Professor Kimmo Eriksson of Sweden's Malardalen University.

He decided to find out what effect complicated math had on research papers. So, he handed out two abstracts of research papers to 200 people with graduate degrees in various fields. One of the abstracts contained a mathematical formula taken from an unrelated paper, with no relevance whatever to the matter being discussed. Nevertheless, the abstract with the absurd mathematics was judged most impressive by participants. Not surprisingly, the further from math or science the person's own training, the more likely he was to find the math impressive.

This is a formula from a research paper paid for by the Federal Reserve. It purports to tell us that when a house next door to you sells at an extremely low firesale price, your house gets marked down too:

$$Yi,j,t = \sum_{m=>0,>1} (\delta_{1,m} NearbyREO^m_{i,j,t-4} + ... + \delta_{9,m} NearbyREO^m_{i,j,t+4} +$$

$$\delta_{10,m} NearbyREO^m_{i,j,t} * Dist_i) + \alpha_j + \gamma_t + \beta X_{i,t} + \varepsilon_{i,j,t}$$

I attempted to put in another illustration, a model in which economists believe they calculate the effect of large-scale asset purchases by the Fed (aka: Quantitative Easing), but my trusty laptop computer rebelled. It wouldn't copy the formula. The 'clipboard' wasn't big enough, or so it claimed at least. I suspect moral and political indignation was the real reason; a laptop knows a digital fraud when it sees one.

Without coming to any conclusion about how good these formulae actually are, let us look at some of their components. Whereas the classical economist—before Keynes and econometrics—was a patient onlooker; the modern, post-Keynes economist has had ants in his pants. He has not the patience to watch his flock, like a preacher keeping an eye on a group of sinners, or a botanist watching plants. Instead, he comes to the jobsite like a construction foreman, hardhat in hand ready to open his tool chest immediately; to take out his numbers.

MEASURING QUANTITY VS. QUALITY

If you are going to improve something you must be able to measure it. Otherwise how do you know that you have made an improvement? But that is the problem right there. How do you measure improvement? How do you know that something is 'better?' You can't know. 'Better' is a feature of quality. It can be felt. It can be sensed. It can be appreciated or ignored. But it can't actually be measured.

What *can* be measured is quantity. And for that, you need numbers. But when we look carefully at the basic numbers used by economists, we first find that they are fishy. Later, we realize that they are downright fraudulent. These numbers claim to have meaning. They claim to be specific and precise. They are the basis of weighty decisions and far-reaching policies that pretend to make things better. They are the evidence and the proof that led to thousands of Ph.D awards, thousands of grants, scholarships and academic tenure decisions. More than a few Nobel Prize winners also trace their success to the numbers arrived at on the right side of the equal sign.

1...2...3...4...5...6...7...8...9...

There are only nine cardinal numbers. The rest are derivative or aggregates. These numbers are useful. In the hands of ordinary people they mean something. 'Three tomatoes' is different from 'five tomatoes.'

In the hands of scientists and engineers, numbers are indispensable. Precise calculations allow them to send a spacecraft to Mars and then drive around on the Red Planet.

But a useful tool for one profession may be a danger in the hands of another. Put a hairdresser at the controls of a 747, or let a pilot cook your canard à l'orange, and you're asking for trouble. So too, when an economist gets fancy with numbers, the results can be catastrophic.

On October 19, 1987, for example, the bottom dropped out of the stock market. The Dow went down 23%. "Black Monday," it came to be called, was the largest single-day drop in stock market history.

The cause of the collapse was quickly traced to an innovation in the investment world called "portfolio insurance." The idea was that if quantitative analysts—called 'quants'—could accurately calculate the odds of a stock market pullback, you could sell insurance—very profitably—to protect against it. This involved selling index futures short while buying the underlying equities. If the market fell, the index futures would make money, offsetting the losses on stock prices.

The dominant mathematical pricing guide at the time was the Black-Scholes model, named after Fischer Black and Myron Scholes, who described it in a 1973 paper, "The Pricing of Options and Corporate Liabilities." Later, Robert C. Merton added some detail and he and Scholes won the 1997 Nobel Prize in Economics for their work. (Black died in 1995.)

Was the model useful? It was certainly useful at getting investors to put money into the stock market and mathematically-driven hedge funds. Did it work? Not exactly. Not only did it fail to protect investors in the crash of '87, it held that such an equity collapse was impossible. According to the model, it wouldn't happen in the life of the universe. That it happened only a few years after the model became widely used on Wall Street was more than a coincidence. Analysts believe the hedging strategy of the funds that followed the model most closely—selling short index futures—actually caused the sharp sell-off.

"Beware of geeks bearing formulas," said Warren Buffet in 2009.

MAKING NUMBERS LIE

Cristina Fernandez de Kirchner, president of Argentina, will never be remembered as a great economist. Nor will she win any awards for 'accuracy in government reporting.' Au contraire, under her leadership the numbers used by government economists in Argentina have parted company with reality completely. They are not even on speaking terms. Still, Ms. Fernandez deserves credit. At least she is honest about it.

The Argentine president visited the US in the autumn of 2012. She was invited to speak at Harvard and Georgetown universities. Students took advantage of the opportunity to ask her some questions, notably about the funny numbers Argentina uses to report its inflation. Her bureaucrats put the consumer price index—the rate at which prices increase—at less than 10%. Independent analysts and housewives know it is a lie. Prices are rising at about 25% per year.

At a press conference, Cristina turned the tables on her accusers:

> Really, do you think consumer prices are only going up
> at a 2% rate in the US?

Two percent was the number given for consumer price inflation by the US Bureau of Labor Statistics (BLS) in 2012. But in North America as in South America, the quants work over the numbers as if they were prisoners at Guantanamo. Cristina is right. The numbers all wear orange jump suits. The Feds are the guards. Waterboard them a few times and the numbers will tell you anything you want to hear.

The 'inflation' number is probably the most important number the number crunchers crunch, because it crunches up against most of the other numbers too. If you say your house went up in price, we need to know how much everything else went up in price too. If your house doubled in price while everything else roughly doubled too, you realized no gain whatsoever. Likewise, your salary may be rising; but it won't do you any good unless it is going up more than the things you buy. Otherwise, you're only staying even, or maybe slipping behind.

GDP growth itself is adjusted by the inflation number. If output increases by 10% yet the CPI is also going up at a 10% rate, real output, after inflation, is flattened out. In pensions, taxes, insurance, and contracts, the CPI number is used to correct distortions caused by inflation. But if the CPI number is itself distorted, then the whole shebang gets twisted.

You may think it is a simple matter to measure the rate of price increases. Just take a basket of goods and services. Follow the prices. Trouble is, the stuff in the basket tends to change. You may buy strawberries in June, because they are available and reasonably cheap. Buy them the following March, on the other hand, and they'll be more expensive. You will be tempted to say that prices are rising.

The number crunchers get around this problem in two ways. First, they make 'seasonal adjustments' in order to keep prices more constant. Second, they make substitutions; when one thing becomes expensive, shoppers switch to other things. The quants insist that they substitute other items of the same quality, just to keep the measurement straight. But that introduces a new wrinkle.

Let us say you need to buy a new computer. You go to the store. You find that the computer on offer is about the same price as the one you bought last year. No CPI increase there! But you look more closely and you find that this computer is twice as powerful. Hmmm. Now you are getting twice as much computer for the same price. You don't really need twice as much computer power. But you can't buy half a computer. So, you reach in your pocket and pay as much as last year.

What do the number guards do with that information? They maintain that the price of computing power has been cut in half! They can prove that this is so by looking at prices for used computers. Your computer, put on the market, would fetch only half as much as the new model. Ergo, the new model is twice as good.

This reasoning does not seem altogether unreasonable. But a $1,000 computer is a substantial part of most household budgets. And this "hedonic" adjustment of prices exerts a large pull downward on the measurement of consumer prices, even though the typical household lays out almost exactly as much one year as it did the last. The typical family's cost of living remains unchanged, but the BLS maintains that it is spending less.

You can see how this approach might work for other things. An automobile, for example. If the auto companies began making their cars twice as fast, and doubling the prices accordingly, the statisticians would have to ignore the sticker prices and conclude that prices had not changed.

Or suppose a woman buys a new pair of shoes for $100. She never wears them, so a year later she tries to sell them back to the store. The store refuses, saying they are out of style. So, she goes to a used clothing store and sells them for only $5—a 95% drop. Does that mean a new pair of shoes is 20 times better? If that is so, assuming she buys another pair for $100, has she really got a $2,000 pair of shoes? Hedonics, seasonal adjustments, substitutions—the quants can trick up any number they want.

BLS will give you a precise number for the CPI, as though it had a specific, exact meaning. But all the numbers are squishy. Nothing is stiff and dry. Not a single statistic can be trusted. Yet economists build with them as though they were bricks. A flapping cod is piled on a slippery trout on which is placed a slithering eel. And upon this squirming, shimmying mound they erect their central planning policies.

The problem with the "inflation" number runs deeper than just statistical legerdemain. It concerns the definition of inflation itself. Does the word refer only to the rise in consumer prices? Or to the increase in the supply of money? The distinction has huge consequences. Because, in the years following the '08–'09 crisis, it was the absence of the former that permitted central banks to add so much to the latter. In other words, their measurement of 'inflation' not only had far ranging consequences for bondholders, investors, retirees and so forth, it also created a huge distortion in the entire planet's monetary system. As long as consumer price inflation didn't manifest itself in a disagreeable way, central bankers felt they could create as much agreeable monetary inflation as they wanted.

Here again, their engineering was a marvel of contradictions and false pretenses. The real rate of consumer price increases in the US is unknowable. But it is not unimportant. People place their bets. Depending on the CPI number, some people win, some lose. And the outfit that has the biggest bet of all is the very same as the outfit that keeps score. The government wants the lowest CPI possible. It helps keep revenues up and costs down. Social Security payments, for example, are adjusted to CPI increases. So are the Fed's inflation-protected bonds. And taxes too.

Every investor has an idea of how much he has made. But none knows for sure. Because, if you calculated inflation the way they did in 1980 (the system has been modified twice since), you'd have an inflation rate today of about 9%, not 2%. And if that were true, the stock market gains from 1980 to 2012 disappear.

Meanwhile, the authorities keep inventing new ways to torture the numbers.

An article appeared in the press on Oct. 4, 2012. "Health care as 'income' for the poor." The *New York Times* reported that the Congressional Budget Office (CBO) had decided to include government's health care spending, dollar for dollar, as income to American families. In the blink of an eye, the numbers boys at the CBO increased the household income of the bottom 5th of the population by $4,600 per household, thus lifting hundreds of thousands above the poverty line.

The government does indeed spend nearly $8,000 on the average Medicaid beneficiary per year. As for the average Medicare recipient, the total rises to $12,000. So, the statisticians seem to be on solid ground in terms of adding this money to the 'income' of the people who receive it.

The NYT is much too earnest a journal to mention it, but this opens up vast new possibilities for the number crunchers. Do the poor not also receive their share of other spending? Their children are educated, almost entirely at the expense of the government. Take the median number of children. Take the cost of a private school education. Add that to the typical low-income household. Presto! They're now a middle-income household. No kidding. Do the math. Or make it easier. Take education spending, $809 billion. Add it to household income. You just increased the average household income of the lowest fifth of the population by $7,000.

And what about security? Don't American households benefit from US 'security' spending? If they don't, why do we spend the money? The feds spend about $800 billion on 'security.' And if you added in all the crackpot spending justified in the name of security—such as building a US embassy in Baghdad that can withstand a nuclear attack—the total is closer to $1.2 trillion. Divide that by 114 million households. Whamo, add another $11,000. Now we're talking!

In fact, what is the entire US federal budget—not to mention state and local budgets—if not a benefit to the citizens, residents, and illegal immigrants of the United States of America? So, take the whole damned budget and divide it up. And now we have the poorest people in America with household income of about $55,000. Voila, we have won the war on poverty without firing a shot.

This is an extreme example, of course. Or is it? All we have done is taken the logic behind adding healthcare to household income to its logical end. Extreme or not, this is the nature of modern economics. Most economists today think they work in a branch of hard science, not a branch of philosophy. They think they face bounded problems that can be reduced to numbers and then manipulated and solved. But there is no science in it. There are no reproducible results. The initial conditions are never controllable. And you can never disprove a hypothesis. As a result, the "theories" are all claptrap and the numbers are all meaningless. Just ask the bottom 20% of American households who were told they were no longer poor—or *less poor*—with a few clicks of an adding machine.

THE UNEMPLOYMENT RATE

The Bureau of Labor Statistics said, in the spring of 2013, that 7.8% of the workforce was unemployed. Simple enough. But what does that mean? What is the 'workforce'? And what does it mean to be 'unemployed'? Think of all those people who work for cash—the immigrant laborers waiting at gas stations and Home Depot for day work, the college students who babysit and tutor your children, everyone selling stuff on Craigslist or eBay. Are they unemployed? How about the guy who couldn't find a job, so he went back to school? Is he unemployed? What about the housewife who would like to find a job...sort of...but isn't actively looking for one? Are these people part of the workforce?

It's obvious that you can change the assumptions a bit and change the reported unemployment rate a lot. When statistician John Williams looks at the US data, for example, and applies the same formula for determining unemployment rates as was used up until the early 1990s, he comes up with a real unemployment rate of 23%—almost as high as the jobless rate in Spain.

And yet, the BLS tells us in early 2013 that American unemployment is 7.8%. Not 'around 7%.' Not 'less than one in ten.' But 7.8% exactly. The precise number pretends to tell you something, but once you have taken it in you know less than you did before, because what you think you know is largely a fraud. You have more information and less knowledge. That is the declining marginal utility of numbers, of economics.

The exact number of people who want a job and can't get one is immeasurable and unknowable. It is unknowable because people aren't stick figures. There is no average man who is either working or not working. Each person's situation is different and often the person himself doesn't know whether or not he is jobless.

I saw a bum on the street in Baltimore the other day. He stopped me and asked if I could spare a dollar. I said I couldn't give him a dollar. "Free money could adversely affect your moral character development," I explained.

Instead, I offered him a job. I had some work to do around the office; I thought I was doing him a favor. What do you think he said?

It begins with an "F".

Should that man be counted as unemployed? He certainly didn't have a job. But if you offer a job to most people, what will they say? *Maybe.* Because their answer depends on a lot of questions that even they don't have the answer to. How much will they be paid? How many holidays will they have? How far will they have to commute? Will they get health benefits? How much do they really want to work? How much responsibility are they really willing to take?

And those are just the obvious questions. If you're considering taking a job you also have to think: 'what are my other options?' 'Could I make more without working?' 'Maybe I should start my own business instead.' 'Let me see if I can get on disability first…'

That's why the old economists thought it was absurd to try to calculate an unemployment rate. It was just an empty number. And it was even more absurd to try to 'increase' employment; you might as well try to increase the sale of pumpkins. As long as buyers and sellers of labor were both free to make a deal, there would never be any 'unemployment' problem, or any pumpkin problem. There would merely be people who, given the current bid, decided to withhold their labor from the market.

The old economists knew their limits. They could describe the conditions under which people held jobs and come up with some general rules and principles that explained why some people had jobs and others didn't; but not much more. They could not say with any precision how many people were unemployed. And they certainly had no desire to interfere with employers' and employees' private arrangements. If people chose to work for one another, or to hire one another, it was their own business.

Modern economists, however, have a seemingly boundless, and very convenient, faith in their own abilities. Give them a number; they will make it tell the story they—or their employers—want to hear. You could take any of their numbers into protective custody and examine it. You'll find that each digit has been beaten up and dressed up to mask a bruise, a welt, a broken bone.

Today, economists tell us not only how many people are looking for work, but what to do to help them find it. How can they do that? The easy sleight-of-hand for increasing the employment rate would be to reduce the number of people in 'the workforce.' Fewer workers. Same number of jobs. The unemployment rate goes down.

If you're going to change the definition of workforce, however, you have to do that when no one is looking; which is exactly what they've done. Two major changes in the way the workforce was defined in the US—one in the '80s and the other in '90s—cut today's unemployment rate in half.

Or, how about this? Raise the taxes on overtime pay! This is exactly what Francois Hollande has done in France. He says it will increase employment. And maybe he's right. Because now it may be more expensive to pay someone to work overtime than it is to hire someone new. So, with a little luck, the unemployment numbers may look better in France.

Is that good? Are people better off? Who knows? The numbers certainly don't tell you. In America, the jobless numbers have been held down by lending people money to go to school. So instead of people officially counted as unemployed, they are counted as in school. They load them up with debt—now more than $20,000 per graduating collegian—effectively transferring more than $1 trillion from lenders and taxpayers to the education industry. School attendance goes up. Unemployment goes down. But is anyone better off? Economists don't know.

In an upcoming chapter, you'll see how Germany got unemployment down to zero…and then kept going.

The result: disaster.

GDP: THE BIG IMPOSTER

The Obama team celebrated the GDP news towards the end of 2012. According to reports, the US economy expanded more than forecast in the 3rd quarter. Bloomberg was on the case:

> OCT. 26 (BLOOMBERG)—The U.S. economy expanded more than forecast in the third quarter, paced by a pickup in consumer spending, a rebound in government outlays and gains in residential construction. Gross domestic product rose at a 2 percent annual rate after climbing 1.3 percent in the prior quarter, Commerce Department figures showed today. Michael McKee and Betty Liu report on Bloomberg Television's "In the Loop." (Source: Bloomberg)

> Gross domestic product, the value of all goods and services produced in the U.S., rose at a 2 percent annual rate after climbing 1.3 percent in the prior quarter, Commerce Department figures showed today in Washington. The median forecast of 86 economists surveyed by Bloomberg called for a 1.8 percent gain.

With the figure for the third quarter, it put the growth rate for the year at 1.7%.

Wait a minute. As the *Wall Street Journal* put it, 'we borrowed $5 trillion and all we got was this lousy 1.7% growth.' The economy added only about $270 billion of activity. But what sort of activity? Of the 3rd quarter's growth, at least a third of it was attributable to growth in government spending. The feds increased their own outlays at a 9.6% rate. Take that out of the picture, and the private sector was growing at a 1.3% rate.

This was described in the press as a 'fragile recovery.' Was it? The US population was growing at a 0.9% rate. That left actual growth per person at 0.4%. But that little soupcon of 'growth' was just a number, one that had been twisted by seasonal, qualitative, and other such 'adjustments.' In other words, there was so much fudge in the GDP figures that you could get tooth decay just looking at them.

And even if the number were "accurate," it still wouldn't tell you anything. In fact, you'd know less after learning the number than before. Which is to say, the GDP number subtracts from the sum of human knowledge. The declining marginal utility of economics is picking up speed.

Here's another headline from the New York Times that tells the tale:

Rise in household debt might be sign of a strengthening recovery.

Come again?

Yes, after falling for 14 quarters, households finally stepped up to the checkout counter, credit cards in hand, to do their patriotic duty. They were buying stuff. They were going deeper into debt. Auto loans, for example, were up almost 14% in 2012.

Since 2008, total household borrowing has gone down. Until 2012. Then it went up. Economists said it signaled a 'strengthening recovery.'

That is the trouble with this sad métier. Economics. Anything that will get consumers pumped up is, apparently, a good thing. Anything that brings them to their senses, discouraging them from spending money they don't have on stuff they don't need, is bad.

How could it be? When did going deeper into debt get to be a good thing? How could genuine wealth and prosperity be built on a foundation of greater debt? How could people be better off when they are actually consuming their wealth? Isn't that the definition of getting poorer? What kind of a recovery leads households to repeat the same mistakes they made in the bubble years?

Here's a story from the New York *Post*:

> They take a limousine to McDonald's, own his-and-her Segway scooters and have designed their new house with 23 bathrooms, each equipped with Jacuzzi tubs.
>
> Time-share magnate David, 77, and his beauty-queen trophy wife, Jackie, 46, were already Orlando's gaudiest couple when they decided to open their doors to film-maker Lauren Greenfield as they broke ground on a 90,000-square-foot monster home with a 120-foot Grand Hall modeled after France's Palace of Versailles.
>
> It's bigger than a 747-jet hanger. Designs include three swimming pools, 10 kitchens, a bowling alley, a skating rink and a garage that fits 20 cars. The home's mahogany doors and windows alone cost $4 million.
>
> "We never sought to build the biggest house in America," Jackie says in the film, titled *The Queen of Versailles*. "It just happens."

It has been described as tacky, trashy and tasteless, with the top three floors inspired by Las Vegas' Paris Hotel.

Trashy? Tasteless? And now it sits, unfinished.

But hey, it added to the GDP!

Are we getting richer or poorer? Are we better or worse off? "Hey gimme a break," says the GDP, "I just work here." Economists can't really measure quality. So their GDP number doesn't tell us if a new house adds to the world's wealth or subtracts from it. They can only measure quantity. And speed.

An article in the *Wall Street Journal* explained how strong family attachments were impeding Italy's economic growth. Half the young children in Italy are raised by their grandparents—their 'nonni'—while their parents work. No need for daycare.

How does this affect an economy? Well, because granddad is willing to watch after little Silvio or Maria for free, the transaction doesn't register in the GDP. No exchange of money, no 'growth.' The article also went on to say that people were reluctant to leave their hometowns to seek work elsewhere because they relied on the family for childcare. Theoretically, a mobile population increases GDP too. People need to move, buy new houses and furniture, sign up for health clubs, daycare and so forth. All these things add to GDP growth. But they may do nothing to really increase quality of life. In other words, we know they add 'more,' but we have no idea about 'better.'

That is the thinking that has driven the profession of economics—and much of the world economy—to absurdity. Throughout the last 50 years, more looked so much like better, no one worried too much about the difference. More cars. More houses. More food. More gadgets. What was not to like?

As it turns out, the concept of GDP—and GDP growth—itself wasn't just vanity, it was a deceit; a total fraud. Because the cost was more debt. And by the 21st century the burden of debt had become so great that the system could no longer move forward. Here is how it worked, up until the early spring of 2007:

The Chinese, and others, made more stuff. The Arabs, and others, pumped more oil. Americans, and others, created more credit and used it to buy more stuff.

Rather than demand payment—in gold—for their excess dollars, as they would have before 1971, the exporters took the money and lent it back to the Americans. In this way, the US never really had to settle up. Approximately $8 trillion of purchasing power—the accumulated trade deficits between 1970 and 2007—was created in this way. Not needing to redeem the old credits, new ones were made available to Americans. Cheap credit drove up housing prices and gave Americans the collateral to borrow more money and buy more stuff. There is supposed to be 'no such thing as a free lunch' in economics. But for years Americans ate breakfast, lunch, and many of their dinners at someone else's expense.

But when the sub-prime mortgage market collapsed in '07-'08, suddenly US real estate prices stopped rising. This left millions of households in a bind. They could no longer borrow against rising home prices because housing was going down. They had to cut back on spending, which meant less stuff could be sold to them, which left producers with bulging warehouses full of unsold goods.

Economists looked at this situation and came to the same conclusion they had on the occasion of every other slowdown over the previous 60 years. The economy needed more "stimulus" to encourage consumers to buy more stuff. They did not care that consumers might already have too much stuff, or that they were now paying the price for buying more stuff than they could afford. Nor did they wonder whether consumers' lives might be better if they focused more on quality and less on quantity. 'More' is all they know; it is all they can do, because 'more' they can quantify. So they called for 'more stimulus,' more debt, more credit, more spending, and more stuff.

I cut your lawn. You trim my hedges. We pay each other. The GDP goes up. The more transactions per person per year—the greater the GDP of a country.

Is anybody better off? What really have the numbers told us? Has one single extra lawn been mowed? One single extra hedge cut down?

No. If a number—in this case, the GDP growth number—tells you that you're growing, but you're not really growing, what good is the number? It's a flimflam. An empty number. There's no good information in it. Worse, it misleads you. It has negative information content. And large public policy decisions based on it get us dangerously closer to disaster, and finally: hormegeddon.

STAMATIS THE GREEK

In the fall of 2012, one of four Greeks was unemployed. Half of young people were jobless. And the country was broke. Only the kindness of strangers in France and Germany kept the lights on.

An economist would use a technical term to describe the Greek economy—'basket case.'

But let's look more closely at one specific Greek: Mr. Stamatis Moraitis. The subject of a recent *New York Times* profile, Moraitis is remarkable man who was diagnosed with terminal lung cancer in 1976. Given 9 months to live, he decided to economize on his own funeral. In the US he figured it would cost $2,000. In his native Greece, on the other hand, he could be planted for less than $200.

It was such a good deal, Mr. Moraitis could barely wait to take advantage of it. He moved to the island of Ikaria; thirty-six years later, he's still alive.

Yes, the Greek beat cancer. The poor gravediggers got no tip. The undertaker delivered no bill. The children got no inheritance. They did not sell his house. They did not pay a realtor's fee. No remodeling was done, no moving company was engaged, no new kitchen was ordered, no heavy machinery was set to work in an Italian mountainside quarry to extract the rock for a fashionable countertop. Or headstone.

By *surviving*, Mr. Moraitis cheated the US economy out of a boost. Despite having terminal cancer, he sought no medical treatment. No chemotherapy. No radiation. No drugs. By living on Ikaria, a very poor island, he cheated the global economy too. He didn't build a new house; he moved into a small, cheap, old house with his parents. No new furniture. No new appliances. No new garage with two automobiles in it. And not only did he totally screw the housing industry, he slighted healthcare as well. Despite having terminal cancer, he sought no medical treatment. The man is practically an anti-consumer. No wonder the Greek economy is so weak!

Pity those poor islanders. With few jobs and unemployment at about 40%, Ikaria's 10,000 Greeks have no malls to go to, no fancy restaurants, no fast cars or paved roads to drive them on. What are they to do?

Well, they tend their gardens. They drink a lot of homemade wine. They visit with each other, often until late at night.

The *New York Times:*

> …their daily routine unfolded…wake naturally, work in the garden, have a late lunch, take a nap. At sunset, they either visited neighbors or neighbors visited them. Their diet was also typical: a breakfast of goat's milk, wine, sage tea or coffee, honey and bread. Lunch was almost always beans (lentils, garbanzos), potatoes, greens (fennel, dandelion or a spinach-like green called horta) and whatever seasonal vegetables their garden produced; dinner was bread and goat's milk. At Christmas and Easter, they would slaughter the family pig and enjoy small portions of larded pork for the next several months.

> Local women gathered in the dining room at midmorning to gossip over tea. Late at night, after the dinner rush, tables were pushed aside and the dining room became a dance floor, with people locking arms and kick-dancing to Greek music.

They spend their days in the sun and their nights in merriment. They beat cancer. And they seem to live a long time; Ikaria has one of the highest concentrations of 100-year-olds in the world.

But their economy is not growing.
Poor bastards.

THE STORY OF JACOB: THE WORLD'S FIRST ECONOMIST

Economists have no way of accurately judging the health of an economy, the quality of people's lives, or whether or not they are working. Yet, it may still be possible that they can do some good. We're not cynics. Perhaps they might keep the number of jobs up or boost raw output. Where's the downside in that?

The post-'07 'recovery' gives us the answer. By mid-2012, world trade was sliding and Europe, Japan and the United States were all facing the threat of relapse into recession. Despite trillions in cash injections, the world was seemingly poorer. There was your downside.

We won't play the blame game. This is no time for petty recriminations. Besides, we all know this is Keynes's fault.

John Maynard Keynes revolutionized the economics profession in the early 20th century. It was he more than anyone who created the Simpleton's Economic Model of today and changed economics from a refuge for keen-eyed observers and willowy philosophers into a hard-charging phalanx of delusional men of action. Keynes' big insight came right out of the Book of Genesis.

Pharaoh had a dream. In it, he was standing by the river. Out came seven fat cattle. Then, seven lean cattle came up out of the river and ate the fat cattle. A similar dream involved ears of corn, with the fat ones devoured by the thin ones.

Pharaoh was troubled. His dream interpreters were stumped. So, they sent for the Hebrew man who was said to be good at this sort of thing—Joseph. Pharaoh described what had happed in his dreams. Without missing a beat, Joseph told him what they meant. The seven fat cattle and seven fat ears of corn represented years of plenty with bountiful harvests. The seven lean cattle and thin ears of corn represented years of famine. Joseph wasn't asked his opinion, but he gave his advice anyway: Pharaoh should put into place an activist, counter-cyclical economic policy. He should tax 20% of the output during the fat years and then he would be ready with some grain to sell when the famine came. Genesis reports what happened next:

> ...the seven years of plenty ended and famine struck, and when Egypt was famished, Joseph opened the storehouses, and sold food to the Egyptians. People from all countries came to Egypt to buy grain, because the famine struck all the earth.

Why was this necessary? You'd think private investors would do the work more efficiently, for profit, buying grain at low prices when crops were busting out of their storerooms and selling them at high prices when crops failed. But there is no need to argue with the Biblical account. History shows us it sounds all too likely.

Keynes put forward the simple idea that modern governments should act like Pharaoh. They should run counter-cyclical fiscal and monetary policies. In the fat years, they should store up surpluses. In the lean years, they should open the doors of the granaries so that people might eat. This seems sensible enough, until you realize that modern governments do not run surpluses. Only deficits. The US hasn't run a real surplus (not including Social Security payments) since 1969. That's 44 years without closing the granary doors. Not surprisingly, when you look in there you won't find anything. Except I.O.Us. Instead of storing up grain in the fat years, the feds ate it. Now, come the years of famine, they have no grain to give out.

That might be the end of the story. But it's not. Economists insist that the feds can follow a pharaonic policy even with their bins empty. How? By borrowing money or, in the extreme, printing it. Would this have worked in Ancient Egypt?

Well, there's only so much grain available. Borrowing from those who still have some doesn't help. Like borrowing money, it just moves stocks from one granary to another. It doesn't increase the amount available. Nor could Pharaoh solve the hunger issue by handing out sawdust and pretending that it was whole wheat bread. It had to be digestible.

But modern economists have developed elaborate theories and mathematical proofs that allow them to flout the limitations of the real world that Pharaoh—and millennia of leaders after him—faced. The government may be deeply in debt, but it can go further into debt during the lean years, say the 'neo-Keynesian' economists, in order to offset the contraction in the private sector. Then, in a pinch, it can even print up some extra money. It doesn't matter to them that this paper money has no more nutritional content than sawdust. If the average dupe can be convinced that it's a superfood, everything is fine…for a time. But inevitably the counter-cyclical debt tonic becomes a poison. Someone drops dead, the seven trumpets sound, hormegeddon is unleashed, and the economists in unison cry out: "more poison!"

Chapter 3
TOO MUCH
SECURITY

"*The system itself could not have intended
this in the beginning, but in order to sustain
itself it was compelled to go all the way.*"

—MILTON MAYER

*THEY THOUGHT THEY WERE FREE:
THE GERMANS, 1933–1945*

MOST OF OUR NECESSITIES—water, oxygen, whiskey—follow a similar pattern of diminishing returns. For instance, a little water keeps us alive and healthy. Give us more water and we are no healthier, only more in need of a urinal. Keep giving us water and we develop a condition called hyponatremia wherein the brain swells and we die. In the same way, a nightly glass of hooch is a healthy habit. But show up at work Monday morning with a bottle of Rebel Yell and your co-workers will describe what you are doing as 'a tad excessive.' That's when the trouble starts.

Some things are excessive from the get-go. Even a little bit is too much. These are the things Adolph Hitler wanted to do. Anybody who's ever watched the History Channel knows Adolph Hitler was a xenophobic, genocidal maniac. But another way to look at him, for our purposes, is as a macro-economist with a plan for world improvement that quickly went too far, and became too much.

Germany felt under considerable threat in the 1920s and '30s. She had agreed to an armistice in 1919. Then, still subject to a starving blockade by the English navy and with no defenses left, the Allies slapped reparations on her to the tune of 132 billion gold marks.[3]

What would she pay with? Germany was broke. She could barely feed herself, let alone pay billions—in gold—in compensation to her former enemies. And when she failed to make the payments, the French invaded, seizing the richest and most productive industrial area of Germany, the Ruhr Valley.

The war debt could not be resolved by ordinary means. And since there was no honorable way out of the crisis, Germany took a dishonorable route. She made promises she could not keep.

In the years between the two world wars, when you begin looking for 'too much'—for the main ingredient of hormegeddon—you find it almost everywhere. Had not the war reparations been set *too*

---

[3] Approx. $581 billion in today's dollars

high, Germany, France and Britain might have been able to come to an agreement on more relaxed terms. Then, Germany might have been allowed into the company of civilized nations and WWII might have been averted.

Unfortunately in retrospect, the allies were *too eager* to assign the guilt to Germany, *too greedy* for reparations, and then *too block-headed* to pull back. Instead, they pushed Germany into a defensive, xenophobic, and ultimately delusional position.

Atop the mountain of 'too much' sat Adolph Hitler. He was the kind of man who should have worked as a housepainter, giving himself plenty of time on the ladder to let his over-heated brain nurse grudges and design grand strategies. He could have simmered in a local bar after work, hatching conspiracy theories and developing a bad case of lead poisoning, before eventually ending his days in a state mental hospital.

Instead, in the 'too much' era of the 1920s and '30s, history called him to do her dirty work, and he was on the job in a flash, ready to add hyperbole to overwrought situations. As if Germany didn't already have enough problems.

Hitler was a central planner's central planner. Not only did he have a plan for everything—each of which was a disaster of course—but he was also a modern economist. He saw a problem. He had a solution.

The biggest problem Germany faced as Hitler rose to power was the productivity of its farms. A lot of labor (mostly from women) went into producing relatively little food. Any decent economist could have explained why: there had not been enough investment in the farm sector. Germany had wasted its capital in the disastrous war that ended in 1919. Then, it was forced to redirect much of the national income to reparations payments. Had post-war Germany's market driven economy been left alone, farm prices would have gone up, drawing more capital to the farms. Agricultural investments would have almost certainly raised productivity and output. But the farmers were not left alone. Instead, when the National Socialists came to power in the mid '30s, they fell almost immediately to telling the farmers what to do, while systematically starving agriculture of the investment capital it needed.

In the 1930s, about 9 million people worked on German farms, compared to more than 10 million in the United States. But America had seven times as much arable land. This left German farmers with low incomes and little hope for improvement. Between 1870 and 1920, birth rates fell by half. This alarmed Nazi leaders, who feared a 'race death' for the German people. But rather than stand aside and allow modernization to lower farm population and raise farm incomes, Der Fuhrer proposed a solution. In 1933, he and the German leadership created a new legal entity—*the Erbhof.* These were farms meant to be the rampart of the German peasantry. They could be no bigger than 125 hectares, could not be sold or mortgaged, and they had to pass from father to son.

The advantage, from the farmers' point of view, was that the government would take away much of the burden of debt. But the disadvantage, which became apparent later, was that the farmers no longer had a way to finance expansion, equipment or periods of bad harvests. The Nazis wanted these farms for ideological reasons (Jews could not own an Erbhof), not practical economic ones, and the effect was to further retard capital investment on family farms while stymieing productivity, which remained low.

The Fuhrer had a solution for this problem too: invest more in the Wehrmacht (the German army). Then, he would use the army to take more farmland away from his neighbors. This may seem like a shocking and barbaric idea sitting here atop our 21st century high horse, but this was precisely what the English, French, Spanish and Russians had done in the name of rationality since the Enlightenment; a historical reality that Hitler was quick to point out. They had each seized huge territories, exterminated the people who were on it, and converted it to granaries that would feed their own people. The English got North America and Australia. The Spanish got South America. The French got huge areas in Africa. The Russians had taken over almost the entire Eurasian landmass, from the border of Poland in the West to the Bering Straits in the East, from the Arctic in the north to Mongolia to the south.

Germany had been largely left out of this grab for farmland. But why was it too late, Hitler wondered? There were huge areas of Poland, the Ukraine and Russia that were sparsely populated. Why not just take them from the natives the way the Americans took Kansas?

Hitler quickly shifted Germany's money from food production to war production. By 1939 an incredible 28% of output was directed towards the military, compared to less than 2% in the US. Nearly one out of every three German employees worked full time just to prepare for destruction and/or defense. You might think 28% is 'too much,' that this must be a case of 'declining marginal utility.' Almost surely, for each extra Reichsmark did not provide more 'security' than the mark that went before it. The rate of return not only declined, it soon dropped to zero. Then, it was negative. It no longer produced more safety and security for the German people. Quite the opposite: it increased the risk of violent confrontation between Germany and her neighbors.

No one could ignore the juggernaut growing in Germany. Not the French, the English, the Italians, the Poles or the Soviets. Each had to make an accommodation to it or prepare for war. As early as the late '20s almost everyone was geared up for fighting, spending an elevated percentage of their output just for military defense (or offense, as the case may be). By 1930 they were all spending 'too much'—far beyond normal defense needs. Soon the whole continent (the UK and America too) was in over its heads, far beyond the declining marginal utility of military expenses. Neither tanks nor barbed wire put bread on the table or fixed leaks in the roof. The Germans—and everyone else—were getting demonstrably poorer with each passing year. Those who spent the most lost the most.

While the French (before 1940) and the English had the advantage of an umbilical cord across the North Atlantic, the Germans had to make do with their own resources, which of course were not enough. Even before the war began they were running out of food. To solve this problem, the Nazis followed the time-trodden path of all central planners. They imposed one set of rules. When these caused other troubles (unintended consequences, in the language of classical economists), they imposed more rules to fix the problems caused by the first ones. Price controls were set up to avoid soaring prices for diminished supplies of food. Then, when hoarding and shortages began, they resorted to rationing. Food was rationed in Germany from the mid-'30s until after the end of the war. The combination of price controls and rationing was so lethal that Party bosses began to warn about a dangerous level of mal-nourishment, both on the farm and in the factories. By the late '30s, workers were beginning to drop dead from overwork and under-feeding.

Most remarkable about this period is that, at least before the invasion of Poland, much of the world applauded Nazi Germany's economic success. It was said that the Nazis may have been nasty, but at least they "made the trains run on time" and, by implication, made the entire economy work. This was untrue. In fact, the Nazi economy was a catastrophe from the very beginning. The trains didn't run on time. Even with the most disciplined and thoroughgoing efforts of the rail workers and their bosses, trains were often snarled up in hopeless tangles caused by sweeping strategic planning initiatives, almost all of which involved transport.

Coal, people, oil, ore, factories—all were moved around according to Hitler's strategic vision. This was the most centralized of central planning, concentrated in the warped brain of a single person, disrupting the plans of nearly every other person in Europe.

In the 1930s, France still had the largest and most powerful army in Europe. Hitler did not want to leave his key industries vulnerable to French attack, so he moved essential factories away from Germany's western border. Now increasingly cut off from the world market, rather than trade peacefully for raw materials, Germany was forced to make deals and shuttle supplies across improvised routes. After the Molotov Ribbentrop Pact, for example, the Soviet Union was the major source for many of Germany's raw materials, with Germany shipping finished weapons back to Moscow in return. All of this had to pass over a rail system designed primarily for trade with the West. And while the trains did not run on time, it was a major feat of engineering and ingenuity that any of the key elements of the economy ran at all.

Hitler's response to this difficulty was typically wrong-headed. He determined that Germany should achieve self-sufficiency in energy (sound familiar?) and other key economic ingredients by 1940. Rubber, for example, was to be made synthetically. Each of these contortions was 'uneconomic' in the sense that it was not the easiest, fastest or cheapest way to get the desired end product. But Hitler & Co. were marching to a different drummer. Economics mattered. But only as a tool. Economics was no longer a lens through which to observe or a set of insights with which to understand. It was a wrench, a sledge hammer.

Was farm production falling off? Were there too few trains to haul the troops or the coal? Had the price of oil spiraled out of control? Do not try to understand why. Bring out the sledge and whack away. Almost all of Germany's economic problems after 1936 could be traced to a single cause—too much spending on the military and too much central planning. But cutting back on military spending was out of the question. Herman Goering explained:

> No end of the rearmament is in sight. The struggle which
> we are approaching demands a colossal measure of

productive ability...the only deciding point in this case
is victory or destruction. If we win, then business will
be sufficiently compensated... It is entirely immaterial
whether in every case new investment can be amortized.
We are playing for the highest stakes... All selfish interest must be put aside. Our whole nation is at stake. We
live in a time when the final battles are in sight. We are
already on the threshold of mobilization and are at war,
only the guns are not yet firing.

The economy was not considered a life-like, infinitely complex
natural system—like an ecosystem—that you could study and admire.
It was a slave, to be bullied and bludgeoned into doing what you want.

Slave labor is one of those things that even a little bit of is 'too
much.' But so was almost every other feature of the Nazi economy—
from price fixing to rationing to strategic objectives and anti-Jewish
commercial laws. Every little fix stole from someone. Every little
regulation penalized someone and subsidized someone else.

Unemployment had been cut to 4%—essentially negligible—by
the mid-thirties in large part because the ruling elite believed it had
the right to direct labor where it wanted it. The Nazis wanted labor in
the arms factories. Since they paid the highest wages, they naturally
attracted workers from the fields and forests. This, however, left the
farms low on manpower. Of course, German farms had needed extra
labor for many years. It was traditional to attract seasonal workers
from Poland, for example. But the Poles were treated so badly under
Nazi guidance and labor rules that few signed up. It soon became
necessary to take a more muscled approach both with the Poles and,
later, with the French.

Was this a better approach? As we have seen, economists cannot
know what is 'better.' They can only know what is 'more.' They have
numbers. They can count. They can add up 'more'. So, in their little

minds, more is better. But then, we all know there are times when less is not only more, it's also better. One of those times was in the mid-1930s, when Germany faced this critical choice: More or Less?

Adam Tooze, a British historian, has written a marvelous book on the Nazi economy, *The Wages of Destruction*. He shows that, far from illustrating the success of intelligent central planning, the German economy of the Third Reich was a disaster. The National Socialists had their plans for Germany. They were determined to put them into practice, regardless of what the German citizenry may have wanted for themselves. They fiddled with one sector after another. When one fix failed to produce the desired results, bringing unintended and undesired consequences, they tried to fix the fix with a new fix. Most of these fixes involved spending money—if not on actual output, then on bureaucracies that regulated output. And most of them were directed towards a goal that only a demagogue politician or a lame economist would find attractive—making Germany self-sufficient. Imports cost money, they reasoned. Besides, international trade forced a nation to behave. Neither was attractive to the Nazis.

Like America in the 2000s, by the mid-1930's Germany's military machine was its biggest single expense. And it was a popular one. Not only did Germany face real enemies, but Hitler's investments in armament created a sense of purpose for Germany and a source of 'demand' that got its people working again. A welcome change for what was still a relatively poor country, with a standard of living only about half the US equivalent.

An autoworker in Munich, for example, could not expect anywhere near the same lifestyle as one in Detroit. Henry Ford paid his workers so well they were able to afford large houses with electricity and hot and cold running water. They could buy automobiles too, which gave a huge boost to America's heavy industry. When war began, the US could fairly quickly convert its auto factories to production of jeeps, tanks and trucks. Germany could not. In Germany, automobiles were still a luxury item. Few people owned them; certainly not the people who made them. Military orders made up for the lack of demand from the civilian population.

In this regard, some economists looked at Germany and labeled the rearmament program—from an economic standpoint—as a central planning success story. It 'put people back to work.' It 'got the economy moving again.' More stuff was being produced. 'More' worked! In July, 1933, the front page of the *New York Times* featured an article that began: "There is at least one official voice in Europe that expresses understanding of the methods and motives of President Roosevelt—the voice of Germany, as represented by Chancellor Adolf Hitler."

But vast spending on the military brought problems for the Nazi leadership. It lacked the raw materials needed to build heavy military equipment and the fuel needed to power a modern economy and modern war machine. Those could only be bought with foreign currencies, which it could earn by trade, or by drawing down its own hard currency reserves of gold. But while other economies had been forced off the gold standard, Germany held stubbornly to its strong mark policies. This only compounded problems as the German economy tried to recover from the destruction of WWI in the midst of the Great Depression and crippling reparations payments.

By 1936, it was clear that the government would run out of money in just a few months. The Nazi leadership had already 'fixed' the farm sector—with various jury rigs and many unintended consequences. The market system had largely been replaced by a system of bureaucratic meddles and price controls which, naturally and predictably, led to shortages that had to be reconciled by rationing.

Now, this same sort of meddling was causing shortages in the manufacturing sector too. If something were not done the whole rearmament effort could come to a halt. Germany was not rich enough to afford guns *and* butter—at least not on the scale promised by the Nazi

Party. And with their spreading system of bureaucratic mismanagement, neither the guns nor the butter were likely to last long.

At the time, Hitler was lucky to have at least one economist with a clearer head than most of his other advisors and henchmen. Carl Friedrich Goerdeler came from a tough, conservative Prussian family. He was smart. He was a good organizer. He was persuasive. Goerdeler seemed like a decent sort, too. After all, in 1933, as mayor of Leipzig, he refused to enforce the national boycott against Jewish businesses and ordered the police to release several Jews who had been taken hostage by the Brownshirts.

Goerdeler understood readily that you can't continue to spend more than you earn; he saw that Germany would have to adjust her priorities. 'More', he desperately wanted Hitler to understand, would no longer work.

While he knew Hitler was dead-set on military expansion, Goerdeler urged the Fuhrer to forget the whole thing. Germany could not afford both guns and butter, he argued, and the German people would be better off with butter. Abandon the program of breakneck re-militarization. Come to terms with England, France and America. Drop the hard-line anti-Jewish claptrap. In short, become a civilized nation with a market economy, rather than a centrally-planned war economy.

He wanted to take this message to Hitler personally, to talk to him, to try to persuade him. But his friends talked him out of it. Hitler had put Hermann Goering into position as his chief economic advisor. And Goering was a central planner—and Nazi—through and through. So, when Goerdeler prepared his memo for Hitler, he passed it instead to Goering who marked critical passages as "nonsense!" before putting it in front of the Fuhrer.

Instead of embracing Goerdeler's plan, Hitler came up with his own 4-Year Plan, released in 1936. It rejected a free-market economy altogether. Instead, Germany would have a war economy, in which all economic and financial decisions were subordinate to the interests of the military.

Like today's American neo-cons, Hitler told his followers that Germany was in a fight for its very survival. Therefore, the laws that applied to normal societies—including the laws of economics—no longer applied to Germany:

> The nation does not live for the economy, for economic leaders, or for economic or financial theories; on the contrary, it is finance and the economy, economic leaders and theories, which all owe unqualified service in this struggle for the self-assertion of our nation.

In the age-old battle between force and persuasion, civilization and barbarism, the market and politics, central planning and individual planning, the winner was clear. Politics was triumphant. Germany had gone over to the dark side. Hitler had chosen more military spending and more central planning. War was inevitable. So was Carl Goedeler's fate. He began to conspire against Adolph Hitler, including the attempt to kill him in 1944. For his trouble Goedeler was hung in 1945.

Bossing around an economy is another one of those things of which even a little bit is 'too much.' And yet, to economists, it appeared as if the German model really was working. Unemployment, for example, had been eradicated. The jobless rate was nearly 30% when the National Socialists came to power. By the end of the '30s, it was negligible.

Germany's economic growth rates were likewise impressive. They were the strongest in Europe, averaging about 8% per year in the years leading up to the beginning of the war. Where did Germany, short of resources, burdened by overbearing regulations and strangled by heavy military spending, develop the means and the wherewithal for such progress? There are two parts to the answer.

First, the 'growth' was fraudulent. Preparations for war are a form of economic activity, but they do not make people, generally, any better off. Instead, directing resources to weapons and ammunition makes them poorer; they end up with fewer of the goods and services they really want (and need).

Second, the Nazis were living on borrowed time and borrowed money. In the six years leading up to the invasion of Poland, the government received only 62 billion marks in revenue (the personal tax rate in Germany was only 13.7% in 1941). It spent more than 100 billion. Politics, Nazism, central planning, deficit spending, strategic visions— all were way past the point of declining marginal utility. They had no utility left. The Third Reich was neither on the rise, nor on a plateau. It had reached the downside and was preparing an ambitious plan to tunnel right through the bottom. Germany was headed for hormegeddon.

The downside for Nazi Germany began almost as soon as it started. The regime shifted national resources towards armaments as soon as the Enabling Law of March 1933 gave Hitler the power to rule by decree. More spending on the military left fewer resources for the consumer economy. As more and more men, steel and coal went into military output, non-military output declined, bringing down standards of living. The real wealth of the German people began to fall almost immediately. At first, the decline was modest. Economists didn't notice it. They focused instead on rapid industrial growth, falling unemployment, and belching smokestacks. But the typical German had less to eat, less to spend and less to buy. In the final years of the Third Reich, his standard of living was in free-fall.

The accepted rationale for security spending is that it is a necessary evil. Often times that is the only rationale that works when a particular expenditure does not increase standards of living. Few people wake up in the morning and say to themselves: 'what I really want is a tank.' Nor do they turn to their wives and say: 'Honey, we're out of ammunition.' That's because security spending is a state concern, not a private matter. Very few individuals want to use their time or money on weapons or defenses. A politician may say 'we'll be better off if we increase military spending.' A general may advise that the nation will be 'safer' if it hoards A-bombs. But how do they know? And just how many A-bombs are necessary?

Normally, we only know what things are worth by observation. We watch what people buy and what they do. If a gallon of gas is priced at $4 on the free market then that is what it is worth. If a dozen eggs are priced at $2, we can say that a gallon of gas is worth two-dozen eggs. We have no other reliable measure.

If allowed, people will use their time and money as they see fit. If people are 100% free to produce and to spend as they wish, we can presume they get 100% of what they want. Whether it is good or bad, we don't know. All we know is that prices reflect the relative value that people give to things and that the economy—which is the sum total of these prices and transactions—fully expresses the people's wants and desires.

This is, of course, a fantasy. Nowhere on Earth, at no time in history, did such an ideal economy exist. Everywhere, in every epoch, there were restrictions, laws, regulations, theft, subsidies, slavery and other distortions. Still, it is worth keeping in mind this ideal economy. Like an honest man or a virtuous woman, it gives us a standard against which to measure our shortcomings.

The Third Reich fell shorter than most.

No serious person argues that a command economy is the most efficient way to identify and produce what people really want. Instead, the meddlers argue that there are some things that are more important than economics; some things more important than what willing buyers and sellers actually want. Hitler said so:

> The job of the Ministry of Economic Affairs is simply
> to set the national economic tasks; private industry has

to fulfill them… Either German industry will grasp the
new economic tasks, or else it will show itself incapable
of surviving any longer in this modern age…

In 1936, he also proposed a law levying the death sentence to
anyone guilty of 'economic sabotage'—that is, not going along with
his plans. What he said—and what he wanted—was so good that it
made sense, at least to him, to dismiss the parliament and override the
wishes of his own constituents. He was merely doing what all central
planners do: replacing what the people wanted with what he wanted,
and replacing the whispers of the free market with the stentorian
sound of his own voice.

As far as we know, God does not speak to public officials and tell
them what would be best for the People. Instead, as far as we know,
people who control government always use it in an obvious way—to
get more of what they want and more of what they want others to have.
And since they have the government's police and military power to
help them do it (unless they are saints and geniuses) the downside is
almost always huge.

When people are allowed to spend their time and money as they
wish, the system adapts readily to changes in preferences. A fellow
wants a heavy coat in winter. In summer, he wants a bathing suit.
Tastes change. Buying patterns evolve. Who really gives a damn?
When a woman feels she has enough pairs of shoes, or a man feels he
has drunk enough whisky, they stop. There is no need to worry too
much about the return on investment. It is their own money; they
can squander it any way they want. Sure, they might not necessarily
get what they want, but at least they get what they deserve.

One of the under-rated qualities of an unplanned market is that
it so readily separates fools from their money. In government, it is the
fools who do the separating—taking money from relatively wise and
productive citizens and giving it to their friends, their pet industries,

and their own cockamamie projects. In private life, people often waste resources. But it is their own wealth they are wasting. And wasters quickly run out of money. Not so the feds. Given an opportunity, they can waste the output of a whole economy, and many decades of accumulated wealth.

In 1930, Germany was still recovering from the disaster of WWI. In terms of per-capita GDP, it had only 50% of America's prosperity and about 65% of Britain's. Yet, its factories were competitive. It had some of the world's best scientists and engineers and the strongest major currency in Europe. It was already manufacturing world-class tractors, automobiles and airplanes. Left alone, it probably would have increased production, cut costs, raised salaries and gradually joined the US, Britain and France as one of the world's most prosperous nations. As we have come to understand in this chapter, and from history, Germany took a different route.

Central planning can do a good job of imitating real progress, at least in the short run. As the decade wore on, Germany's economy began to look a lot like a success. Factories—reacting largely to orders from the military—began to recruit more labor. At the same time, the ranks of the army grew, removing able, previously "jobless," men from the workforce. The result was a lower unemployment rate. Joblessness had been as high as six million at the beginning of 1933, with capacity utilization as low as 50%. That was when the 'Battle for Work' began. Only six months later, East Prussia was declared "free from unemployment." How was this miracle achieved?

"The jobless of East Prussia were ruthlessly conscripted," explains Adam Tooze. "Thousands of married men were herded together in 'camps of comradeship.' Where they were subjected to a heavy program of earth-moving and political education…"

That's one hell of a central plan.

Economists, as we have established, are not good at measuring quality, only quantity. They cannot distinguish a ton of steel used in a battleship from the same quantity rolled out and pressed into automobiles. They cannot tell the difference between a man who is paid for tilling land and growing wheat from one who earns his living moving earth and distributing propaganda leaflets.

From an employment point of view—which is to say, and economist's point of view—the Nazis had an economy rarely surpassed. Unemployment went down after 1933 and kept going down for the next 12 years. When the end came, Germany not only had zero unemployed workers. It had a negative unemployment rate, with millions more people holding jobs than there were people in the German workforce.

How did it achieve this amazing result? Not by increasing the number of real jobs. It did it by reducing the labor force; not only in Germany, but throughout Europe. In Germany alone, 4 million men were taken out of the labor pool for service in the Wehrmacht. When they overran France in May of 1940, the Germans captured 1.2 million Frenchmen. And in 1941, the Third Reich relieved 3.3 million Russians—most of them permanently—from the need to seek employment. That is roughly 8.5 million people removed from the economy in less than two years.

Economists could do some fun ciphering with these numbers. The unemployment rate dropped to zero early in the war and then it kept going down. Women, who were not really part of the workforce since they had never worked in the job market and had no desire to get a job, nevertheless were dragooned into the factories to replace their fallen husbands and brothers. When this source was exhausted, the unemployment went negative even further.

As the war continued, Germany's labor force continued to shrink. Forty thousand people alone were killed in the firestorm set off by the British air force in Hamburg. But losses at home were nothing compared to the losses abroad. The Wehrmacht was then fighting on three fronts. East. West. And South. Stalingrad cost them 91,000 soldiers in the east. Tunisia cost 230,000 German and Italian troops in the south. As those fronts collapsed, losses to its armies had to be replaced for the main fighting in the west. This forced the planners to reach further into the population. And by this point, there was only reliable place to look: the farm population. By the war's end, a third of all boys born between 1915 and 1924 were either dead or missing.

A slave is not usually considered part of the labor pool. He is not someone who is looking for work. He is not someone who responds to an ad in the 'help wanted' pages. He is not someone who is likely to pay into a pension or sue his employer. And yet, bringing millions of these workers into the German economy had a remarkable effect on the unemployment rate. There were soon far more laborers than the entire measure of the labor force. By the end of the war, nearly one of every four workers was a foreigner—many of them there against their will.

The first large group of laborers were Poles. There was already a precedent for using these foreigners on a seasonal basis in German agriculture. As more German men left their farms, more foreign farm labor became necessary. At first, the Poles were recruited with promises of reasonable pay and food. Thousands signed up. However, the Nazis' ubermensch delusions soon spoiled the business. The civilian Poles were treated as badly as captured soldiers. They were housed in prisons and so poorly fed that many died. After a few months, they were so weak from hunger and mistreatment that they had to be shipped back to Poland. Tooze quotes an eyewitness:

> There were dead passengers on the returning train. Women on that train gave birth to children that were tossed from the open window during the journey…people sick with tuberculosis and venereal disease rode the same coach. The dying lay in cars without straw, and one of the dead was thrown onto the embankment.

Word got around. Recruiters could no longer get the Poles to sign up as voluntary 'Ostarbeiter,' an official term for forced laborers. But the demand for labor did not slack. And voluntary recruitment soon turned into outright slavery. The first slave laborers in the Fatherland were 300,000 Polish soldiers captured in the 1939 attack. Then, by the spring of 1940, another 200,000 Polish civilians were brought in. Then, after the attack on France, the number of slave laborers swelled by 1.2 million prisoners of war—most of them French.

The biggest source of slaves, or near-slaves, however, was the Soviet Union. Approximately 2.7 million Soviets are believed to have been rounded up to work in Germany after 1941.

Surprisingly one group who fared particularly badly in the hands of German employers was their own erstwhile ally—the Italians. Italy dropped out of the war in the autumn of 1943. Rather than let them go over to the allies, Germany took prisoner every Italian soldier it could lay hands on and worked them mercilessly during the following winter, with 32,000 succumbing to starvation and related diseases.

At the beginning of Operation Barbarossa, the plan was to starve captured Russians and Poles, eventually allowing them to die; Jews were murdered. But as the labor shortage worsened, even the Jews were given an opportunity to work for the Third Reich. As many as 1.65 million concentration camp internees were put to work for Germany during the war years. Approximately 75% did not survive the war.

While Germany enjoyed some of the lowest unemployment rates the world has ever seen, its economy boomed. Literally. The English, and then the Americans, were bombing the hell out of it. This too had a beneficial effect, at least from the point of view of a numbers-addled economist. Capacity utilization—a key measure of economic health—rose to almost impossible levels. Every factory. Every railway car. Everybody who could walk and every corner of every workplace serviced the war economy.

Full capacity. Full employment. As a percentage of the workforce, unemployment had reached a phenomenal level: about MINUS 25%. Economists must have been delighted. Their numbers had never looked so good. What was not to like?!?

As the war intensified, of course, so did the shortages. Farms lacked labor and equipment. Factories were converted to supplying guns, uniforms and ammunition. And homes were left to deteriorate or be destroyed. The distant drone of Allied bombers became commonplace as the war went on. America had brought in thousands of Mustang fighter planes that were faster and more maneuverable than the Luftwaffe's planes. They cleared the skies for massive daylight bombing raids.

Germany's builders had never had it so good. Domestic housing construction had peaked out in 1937. Five years later, there was hardly a house in the country that didn't need building...or rebuilding. A quarter of a million houses were damaged in the bombing of Hamburg alone. Trouble was, there were no domestic builders to fix them; they had all been drawn into the war effort, along with everyone else.

From the very beginning in 1933, the domestic economy was stripped in order to provide resources to the military. Food, housing, clothing all were soon rationed in order to prevent price inflation. Ration coupons for clothing, for example, helped cut demand. But nothing could boost supply, not when so many people and so much capital had been diverted to war. This left Germans with worse food, worse housing, and less income than they had before the Nazis took over. As early as 1941—in the first years of the war—civilian consumption was already down 18% from 1938...and the collapse was just beginning.

With so few workers and so many jobs, you'd expect a substantial increase in real incomes. But that presumes there is a freely functioning labor market. In Germany, central planners controlled the labor rates. And their main idea was to wring out as much wealth from the private sector as possible, so that it could be directed to the military industry. By war's end, there was little left.

In 1945, it was the Germans' turn to starve. In many urban areas, the daily calorie ration was no more than 1,000. Diseases linked to malnutrition were rampant. The birth weight of newborn babies was dangerously low. In terms of GDP per capita, Germany had wiped out six decades of progress in little more than a decade of megalomaniacal central planning. Not since 1880 had Germans lived with so little material output and comfort. But that assumes the GDP measured real, useful output. It did not. It measured primarily military output. The real living standards of Germans were much lower than even these numbers reveal.

It was horribly expensive and painful, but Germany had provided a good lesson.

"You can never be too safe," is an expression you hear from time to time. The government takes it upon itself to protect its citizens. It suggests that you can't spend too much on military preparedness and that defense is too important to be left to popular preference. Leaders think they know better; they insist. But is military spending really not subject to declining marginal utility? And what happens after even the marginal returns are gone?

Germans were probably 'safe enough' in 1933. Perhaps the first few extra tanks and airplanes didn't hurt. They may have been useful, maybe not. Perhaps they merely brought German security spending to the point of declining marginal utility. But then further investment in its military, above and beyond the point where diminishing returns become negative returns, soon brought the Third Reich to a miserable conclusion.

Not the first time, nor the last.

Today, the US has no worthy enemies. Still, it spends more than $1 trillion a year—fully loaded—to defend itself against them. For that kind of money, you'd think you'd at least get a little morbid entertainment. But the 'terrorists' and 'insurgents' it protects us against have no divisions, no trained officers, no sophisticated weapons, no heavy armor, no ships, no aircraft, no tanks and no marching bands. That is why the news from the front is so boring; the newspapers barely report it. There are no pitched battles. No Napoleonic charges. No breathtaking victories. No Stalingrads. No Gettysburgs. No brilliant strategies. No crushing defeats.

Oh, for another Battle of Kursk! That was the greatest land battle in history: a tank battle pitting the Germans' Tigers and Panzers (about 3,000 of them) against the Soviets' T-34s. The German tanks had greater range, but the Soviets' tanks were faster…and there were more of them (about 5,000 in the area). Wehrmacht forces numbered almost half a million men. The Soviets boasted 1.5 million soldiers. In February 1943, the ground was firm. The sky was clear. Both sides fielded experienced, battle-hardened troops.

This was a monster slugfest. Too bad both monsters couldn't lose!

It was a battle on a scale the world has never seen before, or since. The Soviets had many advantages. First, they had the Germans' battle plans, so they knew where the Panzer divisions would strike. The Soviets built eight defensive lines—including tank traps and mine-fields—which slowed the attackers down and wore them out. Second, the Soviets had shorter supply lines. They could rush more troops and equipment to the front much more easily than their enemy. Third, they had huge superiority in men and machines. Most importantly, after the defeat at Stalingrad, the gods of war had gone over to the other side. The momentum of the war had quickly turned against the 1,000-year Reich. Christmas fruitcake would last a little longer.

Even if the Germans had won the battle of Kursk, they would have gained little. It would have been an empty victory; there was no way to follow up. They lacked the forces to launch another big offensive into the Soviet heartland. Accordingly, the Germans were on the defensive everywhere. They had already lost North Africa and now were losing Italy too. A huge Allied invasion of France, though still a year away, was inevitable. With the US fully engaged, and Germany's Italian allies now on the other side, there was no hope for Hitler's strategic war aims.

If they had been smarter, they would have renounced their agenda of conquest, taken all their troops back to Germany itself—as fast as possible—begging forgiveness and promising never to set foot beyond the Rhine or the Oder ever again. Once there maybe they could have put up enough of a fight to force an end to the war without being totally annihilated.

Instead, Hitler gave orders to hold ground everywhere. The Battle of Kursk was not an offensive, it was a gambit from a defensive posture intended to give the Germans time. Time to what? Time to lose on a bigger scale! Germany had nothing to gain from continuing to fight, and everything to lose.

Germany would lose most of its soldiers and suffer the bulk of its civilian casualties—more than two million of them—in the last two years of World War II, when it was already a lost cause. She would throw most of her wealth down the rat hole too. After Kursk, Germany no longer had the muscle to protect itself on land, sea or air. From every direction, the nation was pummeled and punished until the entire country was in ruins and occupied by invading armies.

That is the nature of hormegeddon. Once you are in it, you tend to stay in it, until you reach the bitter end.

Chapter 4
TOO MUCH GOVERNMENT

"As restrictions and prohibitions are multiplied the people grow poorer and poorer. When they are subjected to overmuch government, the land is thrown into confusion."

—LAO-TZU

Poor Chuck Hagel. In early 2013, hardly a day went by without a good walloping from *The Wall Street Journal*. Brett Stephens called him a coward, a flip-flopper, a political opportunist, a bigot, and worst of all, a bad friend to Israel. Dorothy Rabinowitz whirled herself into such a frenzy over what a buffoon he was, it became hard to understand the words coming out of her frothing laptop. At the same time, over on Capitol Hill, Senators John McCain and Lindsay Graham went to work on him in a particularly clumsy and disgraceful manner, like a pair of goons trying to break kneecaps in the dark.

It was a bit of kabuki theater that was at once both distasteful and absolutely necessary. Those who would presume to meddle should have their own mettle tested first. In addition to getting roughly handled by the press and the politicians, candidates for any post—elected or appointed—should be subjected to certain ordeals. The object will not be to reveal weaknesses or shortcomings, but merely to allow the candidates an opportunity to demean themselves in petty and irrelevant ways. For example, a candidate for the Secretary of Treasury might have to fish a wedding ring from the bottom of a Manhattan sewer. A mayoral candidate might be locked out of his house, stark naked, just to see how he handled the situation.

Situations like that build character. They are also a tremendous source of humiliation and discouragement. And if we're lucky these ordeals will help to eliminate candidates altogether. Anyone with so little dignity as to submit to them isn't worthy of the office. And if he refuses, he should be denied the office too; because he hasn't been willing to comply with the requirements.

The world needs a lot fewer leaders than it has. Most of the time, people go about their business with no need for the expense and distraction of leadership. That is true in business as well as government. A leader just gets in the way, wasting everyone's time and energy.

Think about what you really want. Fixing the crack in the swimming pool before warm weather. Getting your father-in-law into a rest home or a casket. You want to figure out how to play "All of Me" on the guitar and how to make beef bourguignon on the stove. None of this requires leadership.

Most businesses probably work best without leadership. People work out how to get things done. They don't need interference from the top. Besides, the 'leaders' often have no idea how the business really works. This is especially true of celebrity CEOs whose real job it is to goose up the stock price. Often, a business will go along plausibly well, with the lower- and middle-level employees innovating as necessary. Then, a strong leader will take over, pulling the whole business down some dead-end road, typically by grandstanding with a large merger or acquisition. The CEO gets headline fame; later, the business goes broke.

The Secretary of State is meant to lead America's foreign policy. The Secretary of Defense is meant to lead America's military. But what need is there? Who needs them? Each American can perfectly well decide for himself where he will travel and with whom he will trade. He needs no leadership.

Many of the bruises on Chuck Hagel's face came from his claim that Iran's government is 'legitimate.' But who cares? Everyone knows perfectly well that Iran's government is as legitimate as any other, including the government of the United States of America. All democratic governments owe their legitimacy to the same thing—the decisions of misled voters, based on fraudulent representations by dishonest leaders.

Another faux pas that brought the blows down on Hagel was a years-old comment about a powerful "Jewish lobby." There isn't supposed to be a "Jewish lobby." And the one there isn't supposed to be isn't supposed to be powerful. Of course, everyone knows there is a very powerful lobby, composed largely of Jews, whose main focus is to protect the interests, as they see them, of a foreign nation—Israel. Leaders are just not supposed to say so. That was Hagel's big mistake. He slipped up.

That's what leadership is all about—solemn and pompous lying. Pretending you know something you really don't and asserting that your desires for other people are more important than their own desires for themselves. The greatest leaders are those who do it most grandly. Abraham Lincoln, for example. Without his leadership, the US would have probably split apart, which is to say the southern states would have been permitted to exercise their right to self-determination—laid out in the Declaration of Independence and later on in the United Nations Charter. They merely demanded to do what the thirteen colonies had done before them—to badly misgovern themselves rather than to be misgoverned by some foreign entity (Lincoln received not a single Southern electoral vote).

Lincoln—at Gettysburg—said the North was fighting to preserve the promise of the revolution, and that the war was a test of whether "any nation, so conceived...can long endure." In the end, General Grant and General Sherman, decided the matter. The answer was no.

The next greatest leadership debacle came in 1917. That was when Woodrow Wilson launched the US into someone else's war on the basis of a breathtaking deceit. It was a "war to make the world safe for democracy," he said. But if that were so, the US went in on the wrong side. Specifically, Britain and France ruled hundreds of millions of people—in Africa, Ireland, India, Southeast Asia—with no votes allowed! Germany, in comparison, was a model of democratic humbug.

There is no faster path to disaster than enthusiastic leadership. Exhibit A: WWI. Exhibit B came next—it was a disaster known as the Great Depression. In the previous depression, 1920–1921, US President Warren Harding and Treasury Secretary Andrew Mellon simply ignored it. No leadership required. Two years later the depression was over.

However, in 1929, when the next one came, Herbert Hoover and then Franklin Roosevelt met it with aggressive leadership. Advancing the preposterous notion that they knew better than business people and investors, they promised to mitigate the depression with 'counter-cyclical policies.' They blocked the markets from making necessary (but painful) adjustments, thereby stretching out the depression for almost an entire decade.

Recently, the US has been the victim of two leadership whoppers. After terrorists brought down the World Trade Towers in 2001, George W. Bush led the country in an attack on Iraq, based on the fraud of 'weapons of mass destruction' that a team of inspectors said, subsequently, the Iraqis didn't have.

Then, after the financial crisis of '08–'09, the Obama team provided leadership, with the now-familiar lie that bankrupt institutions need to be kept alive at all costs and that a slowdown caused by too much debt could be remedied by adding even more debt.

If George W. Bush had shown a little less leadership in military matters, the world would have saved 157,000 lives and as much as $6 trillion dollars. If Barack Obama had shown a little less leadership in economic matters, the liquidity crisis would have swept away incompetent managers and overpaid CEOs, bad debts would have been flushed out quickly, and the economic crisis would have ended in 2010.

Now just to be clear, I do not advocate for zero lying or zero leadership. I do not advocate for anything. And in fact I'm willing to agree that there are probably times when a lie is just what a group needs to stiffen its backbone or calm its nerves. Occasionally, a gifted leader can help guide a business or even a government. But those occasions are rare. As a rule of thumb, the man with the plan is usually an idiot.

So why do we let other people tell us what to do; are we not all equal? In many cases, are we not *better*? What is the purpose of government, then?

WHY GOVERNMENT?

Government claims the right to tell you what to do. Using the blunt instrument of 'government' a minority is able to categorize, regulate, tax, inspect, dragoon, conscript, enslave, bully, incarcerate, murder and push around other people. Why do the other people stand for it?

There must be at least 10,000 commandments Americans are expected to obey. The IRS code probably has that many by itself. We cannot build a house or cash a check without fulfilling hundreds of (often invisible) requirements. We pass through an airport and we submit to scandalous indignities, usually without question. We know the TSA agent is a moron. But "dress'd in a little brief authority," as Shakespeare put it, "most ignorant of what he's most assur'd, glassy essence, like an angry ape, plays such fantastic tricks before high heaven, as make the angels weep." Such is government bureaucracy.

Bill Buckler, The Privateer, reckons:

> Today, the US government 'GOVERNS' 310 million people with an annual budget of nearly $4,000 billion and TOTAL (funded and unfunded) debt approaching US$100,000 billion. It takes about 5,400 times as many dollars and about 37,000 times more debt to 'govern' about 3.35 times as many people as it did a century ago. Why? The answer is equally simple. Today, the US government 'governs' everything. It is all pervasive. It has taken over the economy from its people.

But what about the return on taxpayers' money? Do they get as good a deal from $4 trillion worth of government as they did from a $1 trillion government?

The famous economist Arthur Laffer explained to Ronald Reagan 30 years ago that there was no straight-line, direct relationship between tax rates and tax receipts. It was called the Laffer Curve. It showed that you can sometimes reduce tax rates and actually increase tax revenues; and by contrast, you can sometimes also increase tax rates and reduce your tax take.

So, modern, enlightened leaders try to find the optimum tax rate. Trouble is, the *vox populi* screams for more and more 'services,' regardless of the tax rate. It wants more regulations, more protections, more cushions to sit on, more bread…and more circuses. It also wants things that go far beyond money. It wants status, comfort, privileges, recognition and revenge. It wants to see its enemies punished, its arguments proven, and its fashions, prejudices, and gods imposed on everyone.

The number of government employees rose over the last 150 years. But so did the number of private sector employees who do work either required by the governing class or made profitable because of it. Tax lawyers, for example, would have no income were it not for the complications of the tax system. Naturally, tax lawyers support further complications.

Whole industries are perverted and corrupted. The Pentagon revealed a program in which bundles of $100 bills were shipped to Iraq—presumably to pay bribes and bills. A total of $12 billion was packed onto 21 huge C-130 Hercules aircraft. Where did the money go? No one knows. But a Special Inspector General for Iraq Reconstruction said $6.6 billion was probably stolen—the largest theft of funds in national history.

In the health care industry, which is supposed to be in the private sector, Healthcare Analytics estimates that as much as $840 billion was wasted in 2009, thanks to various frauds, canoodles and federally-imposed mandates. Chief among these were the unnecessary interventions performed on patients simply because they don't pay their own costs or because health care professionals fear being sued by government-protected tort lawyers. Better safe than sorry. Hold still, it's just a needle.

In the education industry, also largely underwritten by state and federal subsidies, the number of 'administrators' has been growing at about twice the rate as the number of teachers—for at least the last thirteen years. Students and their families pay more and more for a degree but get less and less out of it. And the poor student leaves school with a burden of debt that he will carry for many, many years.

More about these things in subsequent chapters. In this chapter we look at government itself. As we will see, not only do higher tax rates not necessarily produce more tax revenue, neither does more tax revenue—or more government spending—produce more real benefits and services. More is not always better. Sometimes it is worse. And it doesn't take long before the marginal rate of return sinks below zero. Next stop, hormegeddon.

Origins of Government

We know very little about the actual origins of government. All we know, and this from the archeological records, is that one group often conquered another. There are skeletons more than 100,000 years old, showing the kind of head wounds that you get from fighting. We presume this meant that 'government' changed. Whoever had been in charge was chased out or murdered. Then, someone else was in charge.

Tribal groups had "chiefs." They could have been little more than bullies, or perhaps respected elders. Over the millennia there were probably as many different examples of primitive 'government' as there were tribes. Some elected their leaders. Some may have chosen them randomly. Some preferred consensus. Others probably had no identifiable leaders at all. But it seems to be a characteristic of the human race that some people want to lead and others want to follow.

In times of adversity, there may have been an advantage to having a leader. There were group decisions to be made—how food was stored up or rationed out, for example—that could affect the survival of the whole group. Under attack from another group, a strong, able leader might be the difference between life and death.

We don't have to look back 100,000 years to see what happens in small political units. We can see them today. They are all around us. Every corporation, group, club, association, every place where humans get together seems to develop a political/social order. Rules evolve. Leadership arises. Informal groups typically yield to the strong personality. Juries try to control it. Families resist it. Dinner parties try to avoid it.

But that's just the way it is. Some people seek to dominate. Others like being dominated. Trouble is, there is usually more than one person or one group that wants to do the dominating. This leads to conflict. To treachery. To mass murder. To war. And to elections. But let's not get ahead of ourselves. First let's try to guess how it all originated.

On a small scale, we imagine that primitive governments were both extremely variable in form and extremely limited in scope. After all, how much governing can you get away with in a small group? Not much. You can boss people around, but they won't take too much bossing. And there is always a rival would-be boss who is ready to topple the big boss if he should lose his support. In a tribal setting, the strongest, fiercest warrior might have been able to set himself up as the governing authority. But he could easily be stabbed in the back as he slept, or even fragged in a hunting 'accident.' Under the best of circumstances, his reign wouldn't last much longer than his own strength.

In a small town, government proceeds tolerably well. There is not much distance between governors and the governed. The latter know where the former live, how they live, and how little difference there is between them. If the governors over-reach, they are likely to find themselves beaten in the next election…or in the middle of the street.

But as the scale increases, the distance between the governed and the governors increases. Government becomes a bigger deal. More formal. More powerful. It can do more governing. The feedback loop between decisions and consequences is stretched out, and then bent. The governors are protected from the people they govern by distance, rank, and armed guards.

THE FIRST BIG GOVERNMENT

The first large scale, long-term government we know about was in Egypt. After the unification of the upper and lower kingdoms in about 3,150 BC, the dynastic period began. It continued for three millennia, not ending until the Romans conquered Egypt in 30 BC. We don't know exactly how government worked during those many centuries, but we know that a theory of government arose out of them. At the time, it was not considered a theory at all, but a fact. The ruler was divine. A god.

As a theory it is a good one. It answers the question: why should you take orders from another human being? In Ancient Egypt the question didn't even come up. Because Pharaoh was not another human being. He was something else. Precisely what he was, or what people thought he was, is not clear. But the record shows that he was treated as though he was at least a step or two higher up the ladder than the rest of us. If not a full god, he was at least a demi-god—on a rung between man and the heavens.

You might think that would be the end of the story. It was not. There were Asiatic settlers—the Hyskos—in the delta area who had a different idea. So did the Thebans. And the Nubians. And the Assyrians. And the Hittites. There were hundreds of years of internal warfare against dozens of different groups; not to mention the struggles within the divine families themselves.

If God had wanted his man on the throne, you'd think he would have done more to help him. Or at least you'd think he would have been a little clearer about who His man was. Why let people guess and rumble, trying to decipher God's choice? But who can figure the mind of God? Maybe God liked to see His man get a workout. We can't know.

Pharaohs may have lived like lords. They may have governed like gods. But they died just like everyone else. And after the 30 dynasties, as counted by Menetho, the Egyptian historian from the 3rd century BC, the whole system went kaput. Cleopatra—descended from one of Alexander's generals (Ptolemy), who had taken over as leader of Egypt—got herself rolled up in a carpet so she could spin out at the feet of Julius Caesar. She had a child by him, then went over to Marc Antony's side. That proved a mistake. Caesar's nephew, Octavian, was better organized and a shrewder politician. Antony's army was beaten at Actium.

That was the end of Pharaonic power in Egypt. But the idea of a divine ruler survived. Antony had already begun to feel the blood of divinity pumping in his veins. And then, after he was out of the way, hardly had the half-god pharaohs gone to their graves in Egypt before the half-mad Caesars in Rome started to sprout wings.

THE SOURCE OF GOVERNING POWER

All this internal and external strife begs the question though: if the authority of government came from God, who are we—who were *they*—to question it?

Caesar took the role of emperor of the whole Roman world. He did not seem to be too concerned about the theory of it. People bowed to him and paid tribute. That was how an empire worked. He didn't have too much time to think about it anyway. He was cut down on the Ides of March at the age of 55 in 44 BC.

But the appeal of divinity did not die with the Ptolemies. Four score years after Cleopatra's death, the emperor Caligula declared himself a god. Perhaps he didn't do it right . Romans came to the conclusion that he was not divine at all, just insane. His own guards murdered him soon thereafter.

Rome struggled on for another four centuries. If there was a guiding theory to dignify one man's bending to another we aren't aware of it. It was considered normal and natural. Those who got control of the government of Rome were able to exercise the rights of governors. They were victors on the field of battle and in the halls and assemblies of Roman government.

What did they do with this power? "Ad victorem spolias." Simple enough. You defeat someone, you take his stuff: His land. His wife. His children. At least there was no humbug about it. And the rules were simple. Government operated in its naked form. As Mao described it two millennia later, political power came "from the barrel of a gun," not from the Rights of Man or the Social Contract.

In the exploits of Genghis Khan and Tamerlane, too, we find a very pure form of government at work and a very clear theory about it. Genghis announced his theory of government as follows:

> Man's greatest good fortune is to chase and defeat his enemy, seize his total possessions, leave his married women weeping and wailing, ride his gelding, use his women as a nightshirt and support, gazing upon and kissing their rosy breasts, sucking their lips which are as sweet as the berries of their breasts.

Tamerlane was no less direct. He saw government as a legitimate enterprise. He raised troops with the intention of conquering other peoples and replacing their governments with his own. His warriors were paid in booty—jewels, coins, horses, women, and furs. He was paid in loot, tribute and taxes.

This is not to say that there was anything wrong with running a government in such a way. I am not giving advice or making suggestions. I am just trying to understand the essence of what government is so we can understand how it might be subject to the type of declining marginal utility that leads inexorably to hormegeddon.

THE NATURE OF GOVERNMENT

The idea that government's mission is to make things better is false. Government is best understood as a naturally occurring struggle between the outsiders and the insiders. By definition, insiders always control the government and use it to 1) maintain existing power, status and wealth relationships and 2) exploit the outsiders.

Everybody—or everyone who isn't either feebleminded or a saint—wants wealth, power and status. And the easiest, fastest way to get it usually is to take it away from someone else. Taking wealth away from someone else gives you a clear advantage: he has less; you have more. If you make these transfers law, your opponent is at even more of a disadvantage. Thus, the popularity of government.

After Rome fell, barbarian tribes swept over Europe. Local strongmen set up their own governments. There was little theory or justification involved. They used brute force to take what they wanted. Then they settled down to govern. One local lord provided protection from other local lords. All demanded payment, tribute, wealth and power. In the largely un-moneyed economies of the Dark Ages, taxes came in the form of a share of output and/or days of labor. A serf typically worked one day in 10 for his lord and master.

The local warlord and his entourage were the insiders. They took from the outsiders as much as they could get away with. Some even asserted a *droit du seigneur,* known in colloquial French by the more carnal expression, "the right to the thigh." The local chief demanded the right to deflower the brides of his peasants. Even as recently as the beginning of the last century, Kurdish chieftains claimed the right to bed Armenian brides on their wedding night.

THE DIVINE RIGHT OF KINGS

As the Dark Ages progressed, government became less locally peculiar. Across Europe, serfs, lords, and vassals knit themselves together into the feudal system. One governed a small area and was in turn governed by another, who governed a bigger one. At the top was the king, who owed his allegiance to God himself.

Justifying and explaining the phenomenon of government also evolved. How to make sense of it? Why was one man powerful and rich and another weak and poor? Europe was Christianized by then. All men were supposed to be equal in God's eyes. How come they were so different in the eyes of each other? Reaching back into antiquity, the doctrine of the "Divine Right of Kings" was developed to explain it. Scholars did not maintain that kings were divine, because that would undermine the foundations of Judeo-Christian monotheism. Instead, they claimed that kings had a special role to play, that they were appointed—and anointed—by God (through his ministers in the church of St. Peter) to rule. Some people thought the kings were descended directly from the line of Jesus Christ. Others thought that God gave kings a "divine" right to govern in His name. Either way, in the words of Mel Brooks, it's good to be the king.

In the fixed order of the world, each person had a job to do. One was a hewer of wood. Another was a drawer of water. A third was a king. Each man did his duty.

Scholars in the Middle Ages spent a lot of time on the issue. As a theory of government it seemed coherent and logical. But there were traps and dead ends in it. If the right to rule were given by God, man could not contradict Him. But men did. One divinely appointed ruler met another divinely appointed ruler on the field of battle. Only one could win. What kind of game was God playing?

And if God granted a man the right to rule other men, did that mean that every order he gave must be obeyed, just as though it had come from the mouth of God himself? And what if the king seemed not to be doing God's work at all? Adultery was clearly a no-no. God disapproved of it. But kings often made it a habit and a sport. Did not the king defile his body and betray his Lord? In an effort to explain away the problem, scholars put forth the idea that the king actually had two bodies. One sacred. One profane. But which was which?

"The Divine Right of Kings" was a theory of government that held water. But you had to put the water in the right container. You had to believe in God. You had to believe that He gave out job assignments.

You also had to believe that He didn't mind when His employees and agents made a mess of things; or even when they contradicted His own orders. Looking at the history of the monarchs granted this divine authority, you would have to conclude that God was either a very tolerant taskmaster or a very negligent one. Adultery, murder, thieving, lying—there was hardly one of God's commandments they did not flout at one time or another.

Taken all together, it became very difficult to believe in the divine right of a king, without also believing that God was choosing His most important managers at random. Kings were not especially smart. Not especially bold or especially timid. Not especially wise or stupid. For all intents and purposes, they were just like everyone else. Sometimes smart. Sometimes dumb. Sometimes good. Sometimes evil.

Ultimately the system came apart for two reasons: 1) it made God look like a fool, and 2) the rising wealth and power of the productive classes required a new idea. Finally, the "thinkers" tossed out the divine theory and the kings at the same time. Towards the end of the 18th century, the church, the monarch and the feudal system all lost market share. The Enlightenment made people begin to wonder. Then, the beginning of the Industrial Revolution made them see things differently.

GOVERNMENT AND THE SOCIAL CONTRACT

People only understand the world by analogy. The deals and documents of a manufacturing, merchandizing economy suggested an explanation for government—that it was a kind of 'social contract.' But a 'social' contract is to a real contract what an inflatable sex doll is to a real woman; it may be good enough in certain ways, but not the essential ones.

Government is an expression of power relationships, in which some people seek to dominate others by force. These dominators gather 'insiders' together so that they can take money, power and status away from other people, the 'outsiders.' That is not how contracts work.

If it were a contract, what kind of contract would it be? A services contract? Many people think that government provides some service. That is true, but it is incidental. Governments often deliver the mail. But they don't have to. They would still be governments even if they didn't control the Post Office. And what if they didn't have a department of inland fisheries, or a program to promote self-esteem in obese tollbooth operators? They would still be in the government business. They would still have their helicopters, chauffeurs and expense accounts. But if they lost control of the police or the army, it would be an entirely different matter. Written "contracts" and constitutions are decorative details of government; force is the essence of it. Andrew Jackson understood this all the way back in 1832 when he essentially told Chief Justice John Marshall to pound sand after the latter issued the Court's opinion in Worcester v. Georgia. "John Marshall has made his decision," Jackson is reported to have said, "Now let him enforce it." Without armies and police, governments would no longer be governments.

At the end of the 19th century, people were asked what they thought the new century would bring. Almost universally they predicted that government would grow smaller. Why? Because people were becoming much richer and better educated. People who were rich and well-educated could solve their own problems and organize themselves to provide the services they wanted. The thinkers of the time thought there would be less need for government.

It didn't turn out that way. Because the thinkers misunderstood what government really is. Government is not an organization that contractually provides benefits and services, and therefore shrinks as the need subsides. As a society grows richer it can afford more illusions, more entertainments, more re-distribution of wealth, more regulation, higher taxes, and more unproductive people. The insiders take more, because there is more to take and because outsiders can afford more exploitation. Not surprisingly, governments grew tremendously in the 20th century.

The "social contract," is a fraud. You can't have a contract unless you have two willing and able parties. They must come together in a meeting of the minds—a real agreement about what they are going to do together.

There was never a meeting of the minds to establish a "social contract" with government. The deal was forced on the public. And now, imagine that you want out. Can you simply "break the contract?" Imagine refusing to pay your taxes or declining the services of the TSA and other government employees. How long before you wound up in jail? Ask Wesley Snipes; he can tell you.

What kind of contract is it that you don't agree to and can't get out of? Also, what kind of a contract allows for one party to unilaterally change the terms of the deal? Congress passes new laws almost every day. The bureaucracy issues new edicts. The tax system is changed. The pound of flesh they already got wasn't enough; now they want a pound and a half!

INSIDERS VS. OUTSIDERS

Insiders always use government to transfer power and money from the outsiders to themselves. When wealth was easy to identify and easy to control—that is, when it was mostly land—a few insiders could do a fairly good job of keeping it for themselves. The feudal hierarchy gave everybody a place in the system, with the insiders at the top of the heap. But come the Industrial Revolution and suddenly wealth was accumulating outside the feudal structure. Populations were growing too, and growing restless. The old regime tried to tax this new money, but the new 'bourgeoisie' resisted. It wanted to be an insider too.

"No taxation without representation!" The outsiders wanted in.

There never is one fixed group of people who are always insiders. Instead, the insider group has a porous membrane separating it from the rest of the population. Some people enter. Some are expelled. The group swells. And shrinks. Sometimes, a military defeat or a revolution brings a whole new group of insiders sweeping into power. Elections, if they happen, then change the make-up of that core group.

But the genius of modern representative government is that it cons the masses into believing that they are insiders too. They are encouraged to vote and to believe that their vote really matters. In some places the outsiders are *required*, by the insiders of course, to vote.

The common man likes to think he is running things. And he pays dearly for it. After the insiders brought him into the voting booth, his taxes soared. In America, with taxation without representation, before the war of independence, the average tax rate was as little as 3% or so. Now, with representation, government spends about a third of national income. And if you live in a high-tax jurisdiction, such as Baltimore, California or New York, you will find your state, local and federal tax bill run up to 50% or more of marginal income.

In short, the insiders pulled a fast one. They allowed the rubes to feel like they had a solemn responsibility to set the course of government. And while the fellow was dazzled by his own power…they picked his pocket!

It didn't stop there. Under the kings and emperors, a soldier was a paid fighter. If he was lucky, his side would win and he'd get to loot and rape in a captured town for three days. Relatively few people were soldiers, however, because societies were not rich enough to afford large, standing armies.

The industrial revolution changed that too. By the 20th century, developed countries could afford the cost of maintaining expensive military preparedness, even when there was not really very much to be prepared for. But the common man was skinned again. Not only was he expected to pay for it, still under the delusion that he was in charge, he also believed he had a patriotic duty to defend the insiders' power by *doing* the work he was paying for! No wonder the modern democratic system has spread all over the world. It is the best scam in town. Nothing can compete with it.

In 1776, Adam Smith published his *Wealth of Nations,* arguing that commerce and production were the source of wealth. Government began to seem like an obstruction and a largely unnecessary cost. Its beneficial role was limited, said Smith, to enforcing contracts and protecting property. The school of laissez-faire economics maintained that government was a "necessary evil," to be restrained as much as possible. The "government that governs best," as Jefferson put it, "is the one that governs least."

Government—according the Liberal philosophers of the 18th and 19th century—was supposed to get out of the way so that the 'invisible hand' would guide men to productive, fruitful lives. Smith thought the arm attached to the invisible hand was the arm of God. Others believed that not even God was necessary. Men, without central planning or God to guide them, would create a 'spontaneous order' which, guided by an infinite number of private insights, would be a lot nicer than the clunky one created by kings, dictators or popular assemblies.

The more government got in the way, the less useful it became. In other words, the more it became subject to the law of declining marginal utility. A little government is probably a good thing. The energy put into a system of public order, dispute resolution, and certain minimal public services may give a positive return on investment. But the point of diminishing returns is reached quickly.

MODERN GOVERNMENT: TOO MUCH OR NOT ENOUGH?

The modern social welfare state was invented by Otto von Bismarck in the mid-19th century as a means to gather working class support for the Prussian Empire, stem emigration to America, and—most importantly—stick it to his socialist opponents. Before then, Republican France had taught the world you could get a lot more out of 'citizens' than you could out of 'subjects.' Monarchs might retain the loyalty of their subjects. They could claim some of their money, too. But even the Sun King, Louis XIV, the man for whom the term 'absolute monarch' was coined, was lucky if he collected 5% of the kingdom's GDP in taxes. As for his soldiers, every one of them wanted payment. In real money.

In the course of the 19th century, monarchy was gradually replaced by some form of representative democracy or republicanism. In theory, a democratic system is more flexible and more adaptable than other forms of government. Periodic elections should correct mistakes. In practice, just the opposite may be true: democracy may allow the biggest and most stubborn errors of all.

Even kings had bits in their mouths and a hand on the reins. According to the 'divine right of kings' doctrine, a king was a servant of God. A king was subject as well as monarch. God himself had given them the post; they could not refuse it. Nor could they refuse to carry out the job on the terms that they believed God had prescribed (minus a few pesky commandments, of course). God could pull on the reins whenever He wanted.

In the famous example from the 11th century, Pope Gregory VII got into a dispute with Henry IV, the Holy Roman Emperor. Henry was excommunicated. How much harm Gregory's excommunication would do him, Henry might not have known. But he didn't want to find out. He dressed as a penitent and waited three days outside the Pope's refuge at Canossa. Then, he was admitted and forgiven.

The democratic majority, on the other hand, recognizes no authority—temporal, constitutional, or religious—that can stand in its way; no limit on how big it can get or what it can do. And thus it deludes itself into thinking that it is the master of itself, its own government and its own fate.

"The government is all of us," said Hillary Clinton.

Thus, with not even the power of the Almighty to hold them back, modern democratic governments launch themselves headfirst towards hormegeddon.

That is exactly what happened in the early 20th century. Government central planners, with no realistic limit on their ambitions, and no direct penalty for their mistakes, reduced the standards of living of half the world's people, retarded economic growth (thus clipping life expectancies), caused major famines that killed millions, then killed tens of millions more in wars, concentration camps, gulags, forced marches, and other hellish catastrophes.

Under those circumstances, it is not hard to see that people had too much government. But was it really 'too much,' or just not enough of the right kind?

Bismarck realized that the masses must be rewarded for their support. They must see their relationship with the modern welfare state as a good deal. His innovation was to collect money from all of them and then give much of it back to some of them. This would hardly have been much of a bargain, had it not been for the industrial revolution itself. The insiders do not run government as a charity. They need to get something out of it. And the costs of administering large transfer schemes—especially for health care—tend to be very high and subject to considerable padding. This leaves the amounts available for return to the taxpayers substantially lower than what the taxpayers paid in the first place. And it means that most taxpayers could get much more for their money—pensions, health care, education—from more efficient private providers.

The grand bargain of the welfare state only worked because economies were growing fast. Growth is what made it a good deal for citizens. And growth, in the mid-1900s, was as sure as sin. The population of Europe was exploding. GDP rates were high and rising, as machines, powered by fossil fuels, began to increase output.

Canals, then railways, then highways, made commerce easier, faster, and cheaper. Steam engines, then internal combustion and electric turbine engines turned wheels that made things and moved things. Mechanized looms, mills, trains, boats—GDP was rising fast. The next generation would be richer and bigger than the last. And as long as this was so, government could promise voters a bargain that they couldn't resist. No matter what they paid into government coffers, they would get more back, financed by the next generation.

The story of America's first social security system payee illustrates how it works. Ida May Fuller paid in $24.75. She got back $22,888.92 in retirement benefits. It was all well and good because there were 42 workers for every person receiving benefits. But now people live longer. And have fewer children. The ratio is reversing. There are only 2.8 people working for each retiree. The Social Security system now operates at a deficit, with $48 billion more paid out in 2012 than paid in; at the present rate it will be insolvent by 2033. And for the first time ever, a married couple retiring today cannot expect to get as much back from Social Security as they paid in during their working lives.

Likewise, in the UK, Lord Beveridge proposed in 1942 that the initial benefit level for a retired couple be just 32 shillings a week (about $100 today). These were to be paid out of a fund managed by the government, but financed according to actuarially-sound principles. The system was to be compulsory, but what people got out—in the aggregate—was supposed to reflect what they put in. Almost immediately after the system was set up after WWII, benefits grew faster than contributions. And today, the UK government strains to keep up. And on both sides of the Atlantic government is being forced to forego other activities in order to keep the "entitlement machine" working. In the US, in 1978, these transfer payments consumed less than 10% of GDP and only 45% of federal spending. By 2010, they were up to 14% of GDP and 60% of federal outlays.

As long as strong growth continued, the bargain was reasonable from a citizen's point of view. He got paid more than he put in. He was getting a good return on his investment, he didn't care that the government was redistributing money from the next generation in order for him to get it. But in the second half of the 20th century, it became harder and harder for the government to keep this promise: growth rates were slowing down.

After 1945, the focus of modern government shifted—especially in Europe—from killing people to protecting them. They are to be protected from joblessness, hunger, poor diet, poor childrearing practices, disease and physical disability, unsafe food, unsafe products and houses, dangerous work conditions, working too many hours, pollution, racial epithets, news bias, cancer, you name it! But all of this costs money. Government imposes the expenses of 'complexity'— including the many indirect costs that come from complex regulation and pettifogging restrictions—on its citizens.

As those costs rise, the ability of the economy to support them declines—just as Tainter tells us. At the end of 2013, almost every government in the developed world was so encumbered by complexity it had only two choices: downsizing or disaster.

Government is essentially, and incontestably reactionary. Even when it claims to be revolutionary. Its aim is to protect existing power arrangements and existing capital. It may from time to time shift capital from one group of insiders to another group of insiders, but always and everywhere, it looks backwards. It always tries to prevent the free-wheeling, unpredictable workings of a healthy, civilized, dynamic economy from redistributing the insiders' power, status and money. One brief, telling example: during the time of the bubonic plague, so many people died that labor came to be in short supply. Naturally, wages rose. What did government do? It put on wage controls, trying to hold down the cost of labor. In short, government's mission is to look into the future…and prevent it from happening.

Why is that? Simple. The unborn pose no threat, so they don't have to be bribed or bought off. They don't make campaign contributions. And they don't vote.

As the 20th century progressed, modern welfare states found that they had reached a point where squeezing more blood out of their taxpayers depressed growth rates and reduced tax revenues. The harder they squeezed, the less blood the feds got. Tax rates were above optimal levels. So, they switched from squeezing existing taxpayers to draining those who hadn't even been born yet. The obvious advantage: the future didn't complain. After 1980, when Dick Cheney proclaimed that 'deficits don't matter,' debt to GDP ratios rose steadily in almost all the developed nations. Then, in the first ten years of the 21st century, they exploded.

In its zeal to protect itself, its insiders and its supporters—that is, to prevent the future from happening—government has invested more and more resources in activities with less and less real return on investment. Defense, education, health care, domestic regulation of all sorts—all now yield little or no positive return. Meanwhile, peacetime debt levels rise to levels never before seen in world history, with no plausible plan for reducing them.

How will it end? In hormegeddon, of course.

Chapter 5
CORRECTIONS

*"Good judgment comes from experience.
And where does experience come from?
Experience comes from bad judgment."*

—MARK TWAIN

EVERYONE KNOWS THAT EVEN THE best-laid plans go FUBAR. As Mike Tyson famously remarked, "everyone has a plan, until he gets punched in the face."[4] Life punches us often. We step on rakes. We forget to pay the electric bill. We learn. We adapt. Or, we go broke. And we all die anyway. There are some errors you can't correct and some unpleasant results you can't escape, no matter how smart you are.

We should pause here and say a prayer of thanks for the dunderheads, idiots, and jackasses who have gone before us. We owe them all a debt of gratitude. Those people who went bankrupt, those who touched the third rail, those whose selflessness is honored in the Darwin Awards. Not only do they cleanse the gene pool, they also help us avoid doing the same thing—assuming we bother to pay attention.

THE SECOND GULF WAR

The 20th of March, 2013, marked the tenth anniversary of a great undertaking: the invasion of Iraq.

For a mere $1.7 trillion (not counting the estimated $6 trillion that war veterans will begin to receive in the coming years), we got around 189,000 people killed, at least 134,000 of which were Iraqi citizens. In a sense, the Bush administration accidentally surpassed its goal. The Iraqis were not only liberated from Saddam, but from the mortal coil itself.

Jonathan Schell decried the war's "unbroken record of waste, futility and shame." By his account it was not only a meaningless war, it was a badly run one.

---

[4] In popular culture, the quote varies from "punched in the face" to "punched in the mouth" although Tyson himself says it was simply "gets hit," which is markedly less poetic.

And to top it all off, it was a war we lost, as Iraqi blogger, Riverbend, explained in 2007:

> It's over. You lost. [...] You lost every sane, red-blooded Iraqi when the Abu Ghraib pictures came out [...] You lost when you brought murderers, looters, gangsters and militia heads to power and hailed them as Iraq's first democratic government.

To say that it was a 'mistake' hardly does justice to a war that killed more than a hundred thousand people and cost more than WWII. Calling it a 'calamity' or a 'catastrophe' makes it sound like an accident, or a natural disaster. This was no accident. Not even a case of negligence, like manslaughter. It was pre-meditated murder.

There arose, in those days, a sort of contest between journalists, moralists, and geo-political illusionists to see who could find bigger, better words to properly describe the magnitude of the disaster.

Peter Van Buren, witnessing the "end times for the American Empire" first hand, described the rebuilding of Iraq as a chicken processing plant that never processed a single chicken.

Still, it was a great success. Every time the press came to call, the actors put on their sanitary outfits, turned on the processing lines, and put on a good show.

The contractors profited. The Pentagon profited. The consultants, experts and hangers-on all got paid. So what if it didn't do the Iraqis any good? So what if the taxpayers spent millions on nothing?

As Taleb points out, among the relics of ancient Mesopotamia, discovered in the very ground on which the US military complex carelessly plodded, was a stone dating from about 1772 BC. Now in the American Museum of Natural History in New York, it gives us Hammurabi's laws, number 229 of which is as follows:

If a builder builds a house and the house collapses and
causes the death of the owner of the house—the builder
shall be put to death.

When the Romans built a bridge, the architect would have to
stand under it when the scaffolding was removed. If he did his work
badly, the bridge fell down and he was killed.

But where were the feet poking out of the rubble of the Iraq War.
Rumsfeld? Bush? Cheney? All the jackasses in Congress who went
along with it?

And where were the intellectuals who pushed the war: Irving
Kristol, Norman Podhoretz, Paul Wolfowitz, Richard Perle, Douglas
Feith, Scooter Libby, John Bolton, Eliot Abrams, Robert Kagan, Michael
Ledeen, William Kristol, Frank Gaffney Jr.? Were there no gallows?
How come they walked around and still made TV appearances?

They claimed that US troops would be greeted like liberators.
They claimed the war would pay for itself with Iraqi oil. Thomas L.
Friedman said an invasion of Iraq would be one of the great revolu-
tionizing events of history. The American GIs weren't really fighting
men, they were 'nurturing' a great new democracy. Surely there is
some corner of Hell, dark and hot, reserved for these miscreants.

And what about the soldiers themselves?

"Active duty military personnel in uniform, and people needing a
little extra time or assistance, are free to board at this time," came the
announcement at the US Airways gate for the flight from Washington
to Charlotte. Apparently, the airline accorded the same treatment to
soldiers as to people on the short bus—cripples and mental defectives.
Perhaps they really needed help.

The *Wall Street Journal* told the tale of one of them, Marine
Lance Cpl. Williams. The only survivor of a roadside bomb, now
back in civvies, he couldn't seem to enjoy himself. The WSJ said he

wondered why he alone was spared while all the other members of his squad—his "family"—were killed. Perhaps, too, he wondered why any of them had to die.

Back to 'normal' life, the veteran faced a familiar enemy: himself. Statistically, in uniform or at home, he was more likely to kill himself than be killed by someone else. This was a first in world history: in which a fighting force was literally its own worst enemy.

The war against Iraq was a very popular war in the beginning. Americans wanted to strike a blow against someone—anyone—and Iraq was available. But after a few years, the public lost interest and then turned against it. It wasn't worth it, they thought. Some felt betrayed, led into the war under false pretenses. A few soldiers, too, saw they were being badly used. And more than a few taxpayers counted up the cost and didn't like the numbers. From any angle you looked at it, the Iraq War was an error.

It was "the most disastrous foreign policy decision of my lifetime... worse than Suez," said British minister Kenneth Clarke on the BBC. Why disastrous? Because there are now more Al Qaeda fanatics than ever, who are more determined than ever to cause trouble. And any real enemy of the United States of America learned that it had better get real weapons of mass destruction—and fast. Not having them would not save you from invasion.

In terms of the financial cost, when it was launched I estimated that the war in Iraq would cost $1 trillion. Readers of my newsletter wrote to say I was crazy. It was a cakewalk, they said. It could be accomplished for pennies, they insisted. But even $1 trillion was far too low. Nobel Prize winner Joseph Stiglitz puts the cost at over $5 trillion—perhaps as high as $6 trillion—when the final bill for missing limbs and life-long psychological care is tallied. Was it worth the expense? You decide. But first, consider what kind of expense it was. Not a necessity; there was never any need. Was it an investment? At first, some war proponents cited the return on investment they'd get from oil concessions. But most of those have gone to foreign companies, and oil is sold at world prices anyway. That leaves entertainment.

At $80,000 per family-of-four, the Second Gulf War was far more expensive than cable TV. But less than a beach house. Several novels and big-budget movies came out of it. Americans watched its progress on prime time TV—like a Super Bowl with mortal stakes. And thinking Americans surely got their juices flowing, with laughter or outrage. At Tony Blair, for instance, who said there was "no doubt" they would "find the clearest possible evidence of Saddam's weapons of mass destruction." And at Dick Cheney, who said the invaders would be "greeted as liberators." And George W. Bush, who claimed "the establishment of a free Iraq at the heart of the Middle East," would be "a watershed event in the global democratic revolution."

But there is one other way in which the war against Iraq may have been worth it. True, it was a disastrous adventure from almost every perspective. But mistakes are always more valuable than successes. The whole progress of mankind depends on them. You make mistakes, you learn, and you correct them.

The trouble with the Iraq War is that the people who made the mistake seemed to have learned nothing. The lies and delusions behind the war never blew back into the faces of those responsible for them. Instead, soldiers, taxpayers, and innocent Iraqis civilians paid the price. Politicians, the military brass, and the war-mongering pundits who promoted the war still walk on two legs and sleep soundly at night.

Too bad they can't share, more directly, in the war's pedagogic benefits. Perhaps, in genuine solidarity for the victims, they could cut off a leg or at least, in a dark night of moral desperation, say a prayer for the 2,700 US soldiers who have blown their brains out.

LEARNING FROM OUR MISTAKES

"I told him not to take her back," said Calvin.

Calvin was my first boss. I went to work at 16. In 1964. He was a painter who loved to talk, joke, and sing. It was a pleasure to work for him. He knew everyone. And everyone's business. And he had his own code of conduct, which he was happy to share.

"I told him not to take her back. When a woman runs off one time, she'll do it again. Besides, if you have a woman you have to worry about, you don't have a woman worth worrying about."

It was a no-nonsense judgment. Probably a good one.

"So what happened?'

"She ran off again. With the same guy."

"Oh, so then what did he do…"

Tommy, her husband, took a philosophical approach.

"Oh, Tommy told me that he didn't take it personally. She was just that kind of woman. You couldn't trust her."

Tommy may have learned something valuable from the experience, or not. But that's what life does to you. You live. And learn. You can make a mess of things. You can learn a valuable lesson. You might lose money. You might lose a friend. Your business or career might take a hit. You go on…

But if you don't try, and you don't make errors. you get nowhere and learn nothing.

Suppose, though, we never suffered from our own mistakes. Suppose someone else did the suffering for us? Sitting in our cozy living room in Baltimore, I put my hand in the fire and feel no pain, but someone in West Virginia gets blisters. I invest recklessly and someone in New York loses money. I moon the mayor at her next press conference and someone in Seattle gets arrested.

What if I never personally paid a penalty for making a mistake? What could I possibly learn from that?

SUCCESS IS IN THE STRUGGLE

Sultan Osman III was the leader of the entire Ottoman Empire, briefly, in the 17th century. Here was a guy who had everything. Power. Money. Sex. Food. He had it all. While he was waiting to take over as Sultan, he was put in the harem to keep him from causing problems. The Ottomans confined their princes in the harem so they wouldn't challenge the authority of the Sultan himself.

So, Osman III spent his life among the women of the harem until he was 56 years old. He got all the food and sex he wanted. What happened? He got fat and hated women. He put on iron boots so that women could scurry out of the way and he wouldn't have to see them.

And then, when his father finally died, he took power. What kind of an emperor was this man? With no training. No experience. No mistakes. No successes. No lessons. No failures. Nothing except the intrigues of harem life. We don't really know. He died three years later.

The newspapers and tabloids are full of stories of people who have had too much luck. They won the lottery. They were born into rich families. They have a way with women, or men. They toil not. Neither do they spin. Often, they are walking disasters.

Humans were showed the door from Eden a long time ago. Now, we live in imperfection and need correction. We need an adversary. We need setbacks. We need to push against something. Our muscles need to strain in opposition to some force—or else they wither. So do our characters and our minds. "Too much" is not a blessing; it is a curse. We benefit from scarcity, not from having too much. When things are too plentiful and too easy—when we're able to get what we want without resistance—we're headed for weakness, for fragility, and for disaster. We flourish when things are hard, not when they are easy.

The story of human life is a story of conflict and of challenge. It is the story of evolution, constantly flushing out the weak, constantly making the strong stronger through adversity. We face problems and conflicts; we find ways to rise above them. Or we sink.

Humans are better off, generally, when things go wrong rather than when they go right. The hero doesn't become heroic unless he faces an antagonist. He can't triumph unless he has something to triumph over.

When there is no real challenge, we invent them. We suffer from imaginary ailments. We pick unnecessary fights. We find unworthy enemies and make war on them. That is the real backstory to the war on terror. After the fall of the Berlin Wall, the US had no enemy. It had to invent one.

Whether you are talking about human muscles, human bones, human careers, or families or enterprises—without real challenges, they become fragile. Like bones in space, they lose their density and their strength. It is the osteoporosis of Life.

As Nietszche tells us, "that which doesn't kill you makes you stronger." I'm not sure that is literally true, but it true enough. You don't get very strong if you have nothing to push against. You get weak.

What happens if you give all the kids in a math class an A? What happens if you make the playground so safe that the kids never get hurt? What happens if investors never lose money, businesses never go broke, and banks always get bailed out? What happens if the economy is not allowed to go through a depression?

Well, can you imagine what you would look like if bad barbers were never forced out of business? Or how well your business would do if you never fired anyone?

What kind of success will your children have if they are not allowed to fail?

'Having it good' is, in fact, a leading cause of hormegeddon. Starting out in life, the worst kind of luck you can have is good luck. Imagine that you get As in your classes without working. Imagine that all the pretty girls you meet like you. Imagine that your first investments are great successes. If you have that kind of success, you're doomed. You learn nothing from success. Like so many other things, good luck reaches the point of declining marginal utility quickly—just ask any child movie star. Starting with bad luck is much, much better. Because it's failure that teaches the important lessons.

SMALL PRIVATE ERRORS

Government is the biggest institution on the planet. Talk about large-scale catastrophes and you are necessarily talking about government in action. But, relative to their size, is there any reason to think that governments mess up more often or more catastrophically than private businesses or households? Yes! Smaller institutions—including businesses and individuals themselves—make plenty of errors, but their mistakes are usually corrected before they become major disasters.

Let's say you make investment errors. You buy subprime mortgage-backed debt in 2007. Then, bam! The market falls apart. You lose all your money. The bad decisions self-correct. Soon, you have no money. You can make no more bad investment decisions.

Or maybe you thought the world would end on the 12th of December 2012, as the Mayan Calendar seemed to suggest? You jumped off a high building just as the moment arrived, hoping to be taken up in rapture. That's not a mistake you can make twice. Problem solved!

Or maybe you entered into a bad marriage, but you are a good Catholic. You suck it up. You stick it out. Then, your wife runs off with the priest. You won't do that again!

In the private world, a bad driver pays higher insurance premiums. A bad chef loses his job, and his restaurant. In the public sector, a bad economist becomes head of the Fed.

Little on-going corrections prevent small mistakes from becoming major disasters. A ship's captain, leaving Belfast en route to New York, checks his bearings. If they are off, he corrects them. If he fails to do so, even a minor error early in the voyage could send the ship to Greenland or the South Pole.

Likewise, a driver corrects his automobile almost continually, with light movements on the steering wheel as needed. He cannot read the paper. He cannot take a nap. He must make corrections! He knows when to make course corrections by looking, by observing, and occasionally by the sound of crunching gravel that serves as notice that maybe he needs to be paying closer attention.

Not only does the driver get the feedback necessary to know when he is making a mistake, he also has a keen interest in paying attention. He is motivated by the fact that the consequences—the downside—will be immediate and painful. Errors committed in private life are suffered most by the person who commits them and those immediately around him. There is a feedback loop that takes your mistakes and delivers the consequences of them back to you, with interest. You feel the pain. You suffer the loss. You cringe with embarrassment and shame.

On a bigger scale, embarrassment and shame is no less a driving force for private companies. If an automobile doesn't work, the disturbing information soon finds its way back along the commercial chain from the dealer to the manufacturer. Everyone involved has more or less the same interest—all want to correct the problem as quickly and as inexpensively as possible, since it means losses to all of them.

BIG GOVERNMENT MISTAKES

This corrective mechanism does not operate so well in a government program. Failure is often not noticed. And if it is noticed, there may be little incentive to fix it. In fact, the incentives could face the opposite direction; a failure may bring more or continued financing whereas a success may make the project self-extinguishing.

Most often, however, the government employees need not worry. Programs are rife with vague and immeasurable goals. Many are constructed in such a way that they could never actually succeed. And most are purely BS anyway.

Thus small corrections don't come easily, as the public sector protects itself from having to make them. All this works wondrously to the benefit of central planners, while simultaneously highlighting why central planning doesn't work: The planners are protected from small setbacks.

To any problem, there are infinitely more solutions that won't work than those that will. The one that will work has to be found by a combination of theorizing and trial and error. The typical trial is likely to end in failure. In private lives and private businesses, of course, these failures are stepping stones to success. Each one eliminates another erroneous path until we are pointed in the direction of something that might work.

Central planners operate in a different way. The trials tend to be much bigger, affecting not just a few people, but many. Then, cut off from the consequences of their mistakes, the failures are hidden. Instead of correcting errors, the planners tend to double down on their bets. When a little investment of public resources doesn't pay off, more energy and money are put to work. The marginal rate of return declines and then, *voila!*, the rate of return goes negative. Still the planners keep at it, because that's their job, and the results are often catastrophic. If they persist, and the scale is large enough, the result is hormegeddon.

THE CORRECTIVE INFLUENCE OF MILITARY FAILURE

In WWI, England's top generals organized and executed their battle plans from the comfort of London. This distance protected them from bombs and snipers, but it meant that they were a bit out of touch.

Offensive campaigns against entrenched forces had been obsolete at least since America's War Between the States. Rifled, breech-loading weapons made the attacker's job almost suicidal. Confederate General Stonewall Jackson noticed that the attackers almost always lost. He was called 'stonewall' partly because he was said to stand "like a damned stone wall," in the heat of battle, and partly because he often remarked about the futility of attacking against troops who were ensconced behind a stone wall. "Remember the stone wall," he repeated.

A trench is like a stone wall. One that doesn't yield easily to artillery fire. Sending men across a 'no man's land' towards the enemy trenches was not war; it was military manslaughter. That is, it was a mistake with lethal consequences.

This was obvious to practically everyone on the front lines. But from the safety of Whitehall, the feedback loop was long and muffled. If one attack failed, the generals decided to try another. The death tolls mounted.

That was the story of the Battle of the Somme, for example. The planners thought they would knock the Germans out with artillery fire before sending their Tommies "over the top." British general Rawlinson told his men that, "the infantry would only have to walk over to take possession."

But the Germans were not only entrenched, they had double and triple rows of barbed wire in place, protecting two or even three lines of trenches, each punctuated by concrete sentry posts, deep dugouts and all connected with communication wires. The defenses were well-built, with the second trench line far enough behind the first to protect it from the initial bombardment and give defenders a second killing field in which to do their work.

The first day of the battle cost Britain 60,000 casualties—the worst day in its military history. But that didn't correct the generals. They were not among the casualties. They kept giving bad orders. When the campaign was over, the total of those killed on both sides had surpassed 300,000. And on the list of the dead was not a single central planner.

The ancient Greeks were the champions when it came to military feedback. No enterprise is more dangerous and expensive than war.

So, you want to make sure war is undertaken with serious forethought and that mistakes are corrected as quickly as possible. The Greeks achieved this by putting their war leaders at the very front of their armies. Greek battle phalanxes were often composed with the most experienced of their warriors in the lead. Younger soldiers filled in behind them. As the formation drew up and joined the enemy, the leaders were most exposed. Many died in the first contact with the enemy—impaled on enemy spears or cut down by his swords.

This was a healthy feedback loop. Those responsible for war paid the price for it. Those responsible for tactical or strategic errors were soon unable to give further orders. Leonidas, famously cut down at Thermopylae, could not repeat his mistake.

In life, failure is more instructive than success. In war, defeat is often better than victory. Imagine that the Russians had driven Napoleon back at Smolensk. He might have decided to forget the whole thing. Imagine that Hitler had been beaten back by the Poles at Bzura; he might have withdrawn and renounced his dreams of conquest. But corrections in military history rarely happen voluntarily.

The longer military success is allowed to continue the greater the eventual correction (no imperial power lasts forever). In WWI, the combatants kept right on going—with much assistance from American meddlers—until all of Europe was bankrupt and nearly an entire generation had been wiped out.

Part of the reason the Germans were such formidable soldiers in WWII—despite huge supply problems—was that the officers and men were all close to the action; few were spared their own mistakes. Germany's officer class had a quick feedback loop, bringing the officers themselves both faster and better information…and making them suffer, personally, the effects of war. Claus von Stauffenberg, for example, was still on active duty when he plotted to kill Hitler, even though he was missing one eye, one hand, and several fingers on the other hand. On the Eastern Front, survivors were scarce. Those without at least one or two serious wounds were almost nonexistent. By the end of the war, there was hardly a field commander of any rank fully intact.

In WWII, America's soldiers were largely amateurs by comparison. Commanders learned quickly they couldn't allow officers to escape the consequences of their own mistakes.

In June 1944, Brigadier General Jay MacKelvie failed to engage the enemy in Normandy. He was found crouching in a ditch by Brigadier General "Hanging Sam" Williams.

"Goddam it, General, you can't lead this division hiding in that goddamn hole," Williams shouted to him. "Get the hell out of that hole...or you'll have this whole division wading in the English Channel."

McKelvie was relieved of his command after one of his battalions, with 265 soldiers, surrendered to a German patrol of only 50 men. General Omar Bradley, America's top military commander in France, oversaw firing not only McKelvie, but his replacement too, along with 16 other field-grade officers.

"We're going to make that division go, if we've got to can every senior officer in it," said Bradley.

Hitler assumed personal responsibility for the war effort after '43. Talk about distance from the battlefield and a stretched out feedback loop! He was so far removed from the consequences of his decision-making, his management of the war became an amateur fantasy. He should have been relieved. But by whom? Weeding out incompetents stops when hormegeddon begins. Privates may still be punished for having unpolished shoes, but the deciders are rarely replaced or reprimanded.

Today, America's Pentagon brass are probably more protected from personal consequences than any in history. Even in war zones, officers live in relative comfort and safety—with extra pay, bonus career boosters, and no fear of correction. At home and abroad, they have chauffeurs, pilots, secretaries and assistants. And despite military engagements all over the world, none fears for his life. Nor is there much career risk. The US military has not won a serious war since 1945. Yet the officer class grows richer and more ubiquitous.

Note also that General Petreaus, hero of 'The Surge,' had no battle experience whatever when he was put in command of US forces in Iraq. He had never suffered any injury or casualty in the field. He was in no danger to life or limb while he was the supreme commander. And a failure—given the vague war aims involved—might not even be noticed. His career was undone, not by the valor of his enemy, but by the recklessness of his friends, namely his ego-stroking, bio-penning mistress.

Mistakes are not like head colds. They don't go away if you ignore them. Bad money doesn't turn into good money because you add more to it. If you turn the wrong way when you are driving, the longer you go on the further you will be from where you want to go. If you drink too much on Monday night, you won't feel any better if you drink too much on Tuesday and Wednesday too.

THE ANATOMY OF CORRECTIONS

Repetition doesn't make mistakes disappear; it just makes them worse. Unfortunately for central planners, economists, and governments, nothing gets worse forever. Which means at some point there must be a day of reckoning. Then, what must happen 'sooner or later' does happen. It isn't very pretty. The longer the correction has been dodged and denied, the uglier it is.

The tricky thing is, uncorrected mistakes don't simply become more hideous gradually and obviously. Instead, they often look rather fetching until, suddenly, a mirror cracks. Imagine that you have had too much to drink and you are driving too fast through a busy, crowded city. That is a mistake. Your wife warns you to slow down. Annoyed, you step on the accelerator and go even faster. Keep it up and the chances of a disastrous outcome multiply. Every additional minute that you speed may have exactly the same risk component as the minute that preceded it. But the odds of an accident accumulate. Keep making the same mistake long enough and a terrible result is almost guaranteed. The negative feedback can go from zero to 100% in the bat of an eye.

This phenomenon is like the consequences of falling out of a window 30 stories high. The first few moments are probably uneventful. As Percy Sledge put it, "but it's not the fall…that hurts him at all… it's the sudden stop."

The stop is called a correction. The further you fall without correction, the faster you're going when you hit the street. And there's no terminal velocity. Nor do negative consequences rise regularly. Between the top of the ground floor and the street, they rise suddenly. The average moment of your descent may be more or less agreeable. It's the final moment, however, that ruins the adventure.

As the scale of the mistake increases the eventual collision with reality becomes much more dramatic. It is one thing for a single business or single household to make a mistake. When millions of them make the same mistake, it is a very different sort of problem. Not just bigger…different.

Look at it this way: people die all the time. In a nation of 300 million people, you can assume that more than two million a year must go to their graves. And over a period of about 100 years, almost all of them will. They do so in an orderly fashion, with no disruption to the rest.

Suppose the death rate suddenly went up. Suppose 20 million died in a single year? Or 100 million? At two million deaths a year, the pain is local and private. Acceptable. Those who have no death in their immediate families are not especially affected.

At 100 million deaths, it's an entirely different thing. Trains stop running; restaurants shut down; the mail is no longer delivered. The whole society is whacked. It would be like the Great Plague in Europe, which carried away a third of the population in many areas. Fields went untended. Houses were abandoned. Normal life was disrupted. Even the survivors suffered.

THE FOLLY OF DEBT CORRECTION

In an economy, too, as the scale increases arithmetically, the damage multiplies. If one person borrows too much, he will later make his peace with the financial world. Either he cuts back in time and pays down his debts. Or, he will go broke. Like death, this is something that happens all the time. There are always a lot of people who make mistakes and find themselves in difficulty. One way or another, their mistakes are corrected. Life goes on.

But what happens when millions of people find themselves in financial trouble at the same time? That is when you get what economists call a "liquidity trap" or a "debt trap."

"One man's spending is another man's income," they say. The baker relies on the butcher and the carpenter for his cake sales. The carpenter counts on the baker to remodel. The butcher expects both to buy a nice cut of beef from time to time. One cuts back, then another's income goes down. This is generally no problem, because for everyone who is slowing down there is another who is speeding up. That is how a private sector economy works.

But sometimes, the trends are more massive. The central bank—eager to avoid correction—may press down on the accelerator. It may hold interest rates down. This may encourage people to borrow. In this manner, they become not individually over-indebted, but collectively over-indebted. Then, the correction is a much bigger problem.

In this example, we already see how the effect of central planning has turned a small excess of debt into a big excess of debt. Then, the correction that follows runs into the aforementioned "debt trap." It becomes a problem of a whole new dimension. Because when millions of people try to cut back simultaneously, it is as if the gates of economic Hell had opened up for them all. The baker's sales go down.

The carpenter finds he has no work. The butcher hesitates before buying another cow, fearing that there will be no one to buy the meat.

A man on his own may need to trim his spending by 20% in order to get himself out of the hole. But in this debt trap, his income goes down too. Now, he must cut back by 40%—reducing even further the income available to others. Instead of a small brush fire, now we have a huge forest fire, and the feds rushing to the scene with gasoline.

Of course, the authorities will be alarmed. They will not accept responsibility for the problem their monetary policies caused. Instead, they will take on new responsibilities—wanting to stop the correction in the worst way possible. What is the worst possible way to stop a debt correction? By adding more debt, of course!

That is exactly what has happened since 2008.

"We are dealing with waste and extravagance, incompetency and inefficiency," said former Fed chairman William McChesney Martin in 1958. We have "to take losses from time to time. This is a loss economy as well as a profit economy."

Half a century later, Mr. Martin's good advice was forgotten. The Fed of 2008 did not want to permit losses. It doubled down on its mistakes of 2001–2005, when it left interest rates too low for too long. Banks were not allowed to go broke. GM, AIG and Fannie Mae, too, were all spared. Debt was not corrected, it was encouraged.

TARP AND THE FINANCIAL SYSTEM

Rather than let the banks get the comeuppance they deserved, the government wrote them a check. It was the biggest bailout in history. So Neil Barofsky, Inspector General of the Troubled Asset Relief Program (TARP), thought he should at least make sure the American people were getting their money's worth.

The idea behind the $700 billion bank bailout was that it would help the economy recover. The banks were supposed to use the money to increase lending.

The money went out from the US Treasury. But Barofsky found that no one knew what the banks did with it. And no one wanted to ask. To be more precise, no one wanted him to ask either. He decided to ask the question anyway. It was obvious that the money hadn't increased lending at all. Instead, the banks had reduced credit, by paying off loans to each other.

Barofsky also discovered that the Treasury was offering loan guarantees to almost any large institution that asked. This was not included in the $700 billion. In fact, it wasn't included in any budget. And no one knew how much money was at risk. Again, he decided to find out. And again, he discovered that he was getting information that few people in Washington or on Wall Street wanted to know.

The figure was astounding—$23 trillion. But the press largely ignored it. Nobody wanted to hear about it. And nobody seemed to understand that most of it was going to the very people who had proved they were unreliable stewards of others' money. Normally, when you run a bank badly, a crisis comes and you pay a penalty. If you're able to get credit at all, you pay a higher rate of interest for it.

You learn from experience. This kind of bitter experience—a panic or a bear market—cleans out the worst of the players and leaves the survivors with a much more cautious approach. Punished for making mistakes, they won't do it again!

The United States had a financial panic in 1907. This was before the establishment of the Federal Reserve in 1913, so it shows us how panics worked before economists began interfering with them. We didn't have a Fed back then, but we had J.P. Morgan—the leading banker in Manhattan at the time. He didn't have a target for unemployment. He didn't have a GDP figure to watch or a CPI to distort. Most important, he didn't have a printing press. America's currency was backed by gold. What he did have was a small group of auditors and accountants with green eyeshades and sharp pencils. He also had a lot of money. Real money. So when the panic hit, debtors came to Mr. Morgan for help. Mostly bankers. They needed money. He had it.

At the peak of the panic, short-term financing was almost impossible to find. Call money interest rates rose as high as 80%. So, people who needed credit went to see Mr. Morgan. And he put his auditors to work. Day after day, night after night, they studied balance sheets. If the balance sheets were weak, Morgan refused to lend and the would-be borrower went broke. If the balance sheets were strong, on the other hand, he made the loan. But not without strings attached. Not only did he want a healthy rate of interest, he often insisted on firing the managers and owners of the banks that had gotten themselves into trouble. Neither weak balance sheets nor weak managers were tolerated.

In that manner, the Panic came and went in a few short months during the autumn of 1907. Cleaned up and strengthened, the banking system went for another 14 years without major incident.

Corrections work. They are how we learn. They are how the future happens, by culling errors and backing out of dead-end alleyways. Corrections can never be eliminated. Corrections are how we avoid 'too much of a good thing.' When the marginal utility of further inputs goes negative, nature cuts her losses. Without them, the process of evolution cannot work. And the longer they are prevented, delayed and dodged, the worse the corrections will be.

Chapter 6
TOO MUCH ENERGY

"What most consider virtue, after the age of 40 is simply a loss of energy."

—VOLTAIRE

THE DIFFERENCE BETWEEN a dead man and a live one is more than a pulse. Most important, the dead lack the ability to turn matter into energy or energy into matter.

Life cannot exist without energy.

Airline travel, massages, electronic books, church services: you name it, it all takes energy. Even quiet reflection, sitting in a dark room, takes energy. The brain transforms energy into thoughts. That's why dead men don't eat apples, burn firewood, or flip the pages of dirty magazines. They don't have the energy for it.

Could it ever be any other way? Could you ever have anything without energy? And if it is so, could you ever have too much energy?

CLIMATE CHANGE

Until recently, Holland Island in the Chesapeake Bay was home to several families. They farmed. They fished. They built large, handsome houses and enjoyed life—for generations—in "the land of pleasant living."

But then, the bay islands began to sink. Or, rather, the water rose. Sharps Island—900 acres, with several farms, houses and a hotel—disappeared in 1962. Holland Island was underwater by 2010. Its last resident waited until the water was at his door, then he waded to a boat and said goodbye.

Was this a result of 'too much' energy? Had too much energy use raised the high tide level in the Chesapeake Bay? I don't know. But whatever the case, there is little debate that water plays a vital role in civilized life.

In the case of the Classic Maya, the civilization seems to have ebbed and flowed along with the rainfall. Scientists studied stalagmites from a cave in Belize and were able to track rainfall on an annual basis as far back as 1500 years ago. Comparing the rainfall record to the traces left by the civilization, they found that building increased in the wetter periods and decreased when the climate turned dryer.

Between 1020 and 1110 a severe drought hit southern Belize, finishing off what remained of the Classic Maya in the region. Here too, on the surface, you would say that 'too little' water marked the decline. But you could turn that around; the wetter years were perhaps 'too wet,' since they provided energy for growth that couldn't be sustained in the inevitable dry years.

Jeffrey Sachs, director of the Earth Institute at Columbia, would argue that using too much energy brings about its own disaster. He's not alone. Many people think the world already uses too much fossil fuel, causing the heavens to fill up with noxious 'greenhouse gases' and the polar ice caps to melt. They think the downside of all this energy use will begin soon, or maybe it already has.

Perhaps a catastrophe is coming. Nature likes symmetry; the disaster could be equal to and opposite the remarkable progress of the last three centuries. According to Genesis, a great flood wiped out much of the human population thousands of years ago. Might it do so again?

The concentration of greenhouse gasses has never before increased so fast. Nor, apparently, has the melt-off of the North Pole ice and snow cover ever happened so quickly. Once the ice cap is gone, then, instead of reflecting the sun's heat, the Artic absorbs it. No one knows where this leads, but it could possibly trigger a sudden (in decades rather than millennia) rise in sea levels. At least one expert, John Englander, believes a 212-foot "High Tide" is coming, perhaps sooner than anyone expects.

Englander is not so much concerned with trying to change or protect the world's climate as he is with what is likely to happen and how it will affect our lives. He writes:

> The last truly abrupt changes in the Earth's climate occurred more than 50 million years ago. During that period, carbon dioxide increased about 100ppm over a

million years. The global temperature spiked by about 9 degrees F…over 10,000 years. While that may sound slow, in geologic time it is considered quick and drastic.

At our current rate of carbon emissions, we will increase carbon dioxide levels by that same 100ppm in just 30 to 40 years. In other words, we are increasing carbon dioxide levels roughly 20,000 times faster than at any time in the last 540 million years. Temperatures, which can lag behind the rise of carbon dioxide, are now rising about 55 times faster than they did even during the most recent cycle of glacial melting.

Methane, Englander says, is the wild card. It's the most effective of the greenhouse gases, meaning it traps more heat than any other. And there is beaucoup methane locked up in the permafrost—billions of tons—now melting. Aided by unprecedented levels of carbon dioxide, it could cause a runaway heat effect—something that has never happened before. This, in turn, could cause the Earth's water level to rise. Fast. Check your elevation.

But for the moment, 'global warming' or 'global climate change' is just a hypothesis that seems a lot more alarming in the summertime than in the winter. For all we know, the effect of human activity on the world's climate will be salutary. In any event, though similar in some respects, climate change is not an example of hormegeddon, as described in this book, because it doesn't spring from central planning.

Sachs would say that is a problem. Central planning, he believes, is the solution. The authorities may still forestall a catastrophe, he claims, if they will only act! Whether global warming will cause a disaster or not, I can't say. But I can make a bet with fair odds: if a sweeping, centrally planned program is put in place to prevent global warming, it will almost certainly lead to a disaster of its own.

Failure of the Internet

Back at the end of the '90s, there were people who thought the Internet changed everything. With so much information at everyone's fingertips, they thought they saw a brave new world coming. We would all have access to the information we needed to increase productivity and add wealth. No one would be poor again. All they would have to do is to go on the Internet to find out how to produce, how to make money, how to get rich. And it wouldn't require more energy; it would actually save energy because the Internet offered digital 'information' that increased efficiency and reduced the need for physical inputs—like energy. This seemed to present a way to jump the barrier posed by declining marginal utility. No further investment of energy was needed. So, no declining returns. No negative returns. No hormegeddon.

In fact, information—unless it is exactly what you need, exactly when you need it—is no benefit. To the contrary, it has negative value. It's cheap. It distracts you. It must be sorted out. Applied. And stored. It's wisdom that is dear, not information. And you don't get much wisdom on the Internet. Instead, you have to pay for it, with hard work and bitter experience.

Information is like manure. A little, at the right time, is a good thing. Pile up too much and it stinks. The Internet, for all its information shoveling power, seems to add little to our wealth.

Even *The New York Times* says so:

> For a time, the Labor Department's productivity figures appeared to support the idea of an Internet-based productivity miracle. Between 1996 and 2000, output per hour in the non-farm business sector—the standard measure of labor productivity—grew at an annual rate of 2.75 per cent, well above the 1.5 per cent rate that was seen between 1973 and 1996. The difference between 1.5 per cent annual productivity growth and 2.75 per cent

growth is enormous. With 2.75 per cent growth (assuming higher productivity leads to higher wages) it takes about twenty-six years for living standards to double. With 1.5 per cent growth, it takes a lot longer—forty-eight years—for living standards to double.

[But...] since the start of 2005, productivity growth has fallen all the way back to the levels seen before the Web was commercialized, and before smart phones were invented. [...] In 2011, output per hour rose by a mere 0.6 per cent, according to the latest update from the Labor Department, and last year there was more of the same: an increase of just 0.7 per cent. In the last quarter of 2012, output per hour actually fell, at an annual rate of 1.9 per cent.

...if the sluggish rates of productivity growth we've seen over the past two years were to persist into the indefinite future, it would take more than a hundred years for output-per-person and living standards to double.

How about that? The Internet. A time waster, like television. Not a wealth booster, like the internal combustion engine.

Fifty years ago, the stuff of our lives was not so different from the stuff we have today. We had tractors on the farm. We had chainsaws. Willis Carrier invented the first air conditioning system in 1902. Commercial airline traffic began 100 years ago, in 1914, with service between Tampa and St. Petersburg. The turbo jet engine was patented in 1930. My family got its first TV in 1958. The quantity of programming was limited, but the quality was arguably higher than it is now. In 1959 I was fascinated and delighted by TV; today I am bored by it.

Look around. The stuff of our lives today is better, but only marginally. In the late '60s, I drove across the US in a 1953 Chevy pickup. I drove about 55 miles per hour...with the windows down. I bought the truck for $200 and had to park it on a hill to get it started. Apart from that, it was reliable and perfectly agreeable. Now, I can drive my F-150 at about 70 miles an hour with the windows rolled up and the air-conditioning on. That's progress, but it's incremental progress, not quantum leap progress; not like the progress of the early 20th century. Over half a century, automobile speeds increased about 15 mph. Divide the 15 mph gain by 50 years. The rate of "progress" is negligible. It's not the kind of progress that makes you rich. And that speed increase is on some highways. The average speed on California's freeways is actually lower today than it was 50 years ago.

The Internet was more or less fully built out in the US in the year 2000. All of a sudden, knowledge from all over the world—and from all of history—was available. Information could be accessed and questions could be answered at the speed of light. People could collaborate on a global scale, across borders and time zones, innovating, creating, critiquing, and elaborating new ideas of breathtaking scope.

In the 1990s, many people believed that electronic hyperactivity would eliminate the "speed limits" on growth. Analysts advised investors that they could pay almost an infinite price for start-up Internet companies. Growth would be fast. And it would not require capital inputs, they said. The old rules, including the rule of declining marginal utility, weren't supposed to apply.

Certainly, there are many Mercedes 500 automobiles on California highways that owe their existence to the Internet. Many entrepreneurs, software developers and app creators have gotten very rich. But, as we have seen, the Internet does not seem to have led to a general uptick in prosperity. GDP minus government spending was $9.314 trillion in 2001. Ten years later it had risen to only $9.721. At that rate, it would take 167 years for the GDP to double. By comparison, GDP doubled twice between 1929 and 1988.

Over the last 20 years, the top 10% of earners are the only ones to have added to their wealth. Everyone else is even...or worse. At the bottom, among the lowest quarter of the population, people are substantially poorer now than they were 20 years ago. What went wrong? Why didn't the Internet make us richer? Instead of hopping over the rule of declining marginal utility, the Internet seemed to run smack into it right away.

The Financial Times had the answer; the internet wasted energy. According to the *FT* report, the world spends 300 million minutes a day on a single computer game: Angry Birds. Millions more are spent looking at videos of puppies or kittens. People spend 700 billion minutes per month on Facebook. The typical user spends 15 hours and 33 minutes on the site each month. Viewers spends 2.9 billion hours per month on YouTube. You get the idea. Humanity is wasting over 2.9 billion hours a month.

DECLINING MARGINAL UTILITY FURTHER ILLUSTRATED

"Parlez-vous francais?" You can learn that much French in about five minutes. If you knew no French before, this represents an infinite increase. In about five more minutes you can learn "Je m'appelle Todd" an increase of about 100% on what you knew before. Thereafter, the rate of return declines. By the time you are laboring over the past conditional form of the subjunctive mood or the archaic simple past form—used only in literature or formal writing—you will find progress hard to come by, with hours of additional time and energy needed just to make the smallest contribution to your useful lexicon.

Initial investments of energy in anything tend to produce more results than later inputs. In your first week, you learn quite a lot. Each successive week brings fewer new words. When you have become 'fluent,' whole months can go by without learning a single new word or verb form. Of course, you can persist. You can spend all your time memorizing expressions of the ancient Luberon local dialect and verb forms that haven't been used since the time of Molière. Keep it up and your friends and family will probably think you've gone too far, that you've gone a little funny in the head.

Progress comes in fits and starts. You may have to put in a certain amount of energy before you get any payoff at all. If you are breaking into a liquor store, for example, it takes a while to jimmy open the door and cut the alarm cables. Then, you can grab a few bottles and get away before the cops arrive.

In that sense, the input/output curve can be more of a stair-step pattern than a simple humpback curve. Still, when you show up at that same liquor store for the fifth time in a month, only to find that the owner has not since replaced his stock of Rebel Yell, the payoff isn't quite the same. Or imagine that you were building a bridge. You would have enormous inputs of energy over a long time while you were in the construction phase. Then, the payoff would come in a dramatic ribbon-cutting ceremony with a flat rate of return for many years. Your return on investment curve would be a single giant step.

We tend to think that fossil fuel is an exception to the general pattern. The more the merrier. The US is now blessed with an abundance of oil and natural gas. Experts tell us that it guarantees an economic boom, a renaissance of manufacturing in the US, and prosperity for one and all. But, is it so? Off hand, we don't recall that cheap energy did much for the people of Iraq, Venezuela or Russia. You might even think they had 'too much' energy for their own good. But let's keep an open mind.

THE HISTORY OF ENERGY AND PROGRESS

A long time ago, human progress was only measurable in terms of human population. Prosperity then was a matter of calories. The more food available, the more people survived and the more the human population grew. During these many years progress was scarce. One year was, we imagine, very similar to the year before. People had access only to as many calories as they could hunt and gather. And once an area was fully exploited, there was little more that could be done. The available calorie supply was limited. One group could only prosper and grow at the expense of another group. For the human race as a whole, substantial or even noticeable progress was not possible.

But when progress came, it came like growth to a teenager. We count five major growth spurts in the 200,000 years before the birth of Christ:

1. The use of fire.

2. The development of projectile weapons—slings, bows and arrows.

3. The agricultural revolution—domesticated animals and sedentary agriculture.

4. The *(actual)* discovery of America.

In each case, humans benefitted from an increase in available calories. When they learned how to use fire, for example, they were able to bring in new calories from several sources. First, the calories locked in wood and animal oils were released, providing direct heat. Second, this heat allowed primitive man to range more widely and remain longer in cold areas of the planet. Third, it also permitted him to cook certain otherwise inedible foods such as rice, beans, grains, and potatoes.

Each major innovation makes more energy available. Domesticating cattle allowed humans to tap the energy from grasses—previously unavailable to them. Sedentary agriculture concentrated edible plants in a given area, not only increasing the number of available calories but also reducing the calorie output needed to get them.

The discovery of America illustrates the episodic nature of this phenomenon. The first settlers probably came from Siberia…and when they got to the Americas what they found was a lot of very low hanging fruit. Here were two huge continents—many times bigger than all of Europe—and they had never been hunted by man, never been foraged by man, never even been walked upon by a two-legged primate.

Which is to say there was plenty of fauna and flora that were not prepared for them. The giant sloth for example. It doesn't exist any more. Why it doesn't exist, I don't know, but experts think it was hunted to extinction by early settlers. The sloth hangs from branches and spends most of its time sleeping. It must have been a very powerful animal with deadly long claws. But when a human came along with a spear, or a bow and arrow, the giant sloth was, shall we say, dead meat.

The giant sloth was easy game. It could be hunted without much exertion. In terms of calories spent to calories gained, the return on investment from hunting the giant sloth was to early man in the Americas what the Internet was to Google. It was an environment that made growth easy and fast.

This new source of calories resulted in a population explosion. Within the space of a millennium or two there were bipeds everywhere. From the Arctic to Tierra del Fuego.

And by the time Christopher Columbus came along and re-discovered America, there were millions of humans in the New World. That's progress. That's real growth. And that's what you get when you have low hanging fruit available to you.

But what happened when the Giant Sloth had been hunted to extinction? There was still plenty of game and plant life in America. But it's not as easy to hunt a grizzly bear, as it is a sloth. Deer are fast. Fish are slippery. At first, the pickins were easy. Later, not so much. Once you've picked all the low-hanging fruit, you've got to go higher up; you've got to expend more energy and take more risks. The result is less of a return for your effort. You have reached the declining marginal utility of your efforts to gain more calories. That's what always happens. And we presume it happened in the New World just like it happened in the Old. After a big spurt of growth, growth rates leveled off, until the next innovation or discovery came along.

When Christopher Columbus rediscovered America, he found that the native-born Americans had already taken the really low hanging fruit. But that was okay—a lot had happened in the intervening years. In effect, Columbus—and those who came after him—showed up with ladders! They had gunpowder. And horses. And wheels. And iron. Innovations that had taken thousands of years to develop in the Old World were put to work in a matter of decades in the new one. Settlers were able to harvest fruit that was not available to previous inhabitants. They were able to enjoy another huge spurt of growth that began around the beginning of the reign of Elizabeth I in England.

The new Americans settled the East Coast of North and South America and, again, plundered the easy sources of energy. They stripped off the forests and put the plow to the earth, before gradually working their way toward the west coast and filling in everything in between with farms and towns and people. The population boomed because the settlers were able to use evolving technologies to take advantage of the readily available energy.

During the latter half of the 19th century, the US grew rapidly again. That boom continued, more or less without interruption, until about the Jimmy Carter administration (growth rates have tended to come down since Richard Nixon took office). Today's rates of GDP growth—averaged out over a decade—are only half what they were before the decline began. Investor and author, James Davidson, describes the slowdown:

> ...over the longest time scale, from 1889 to 2009, annual average real US GDP growth was 3.4%. However, during

the 70-year span, 1939–2009, annual average GDP growth actually perked up to 3.6%.

Superficially, that sounds encouraging. But look more closely. Most of the good news in the real growth was in the immediate post-depression period. The 70-year average rate of growth greatly exceeds more recent averages. The simple fact is that economic growth in the US has been steadily declining.

Over 60 years, it averages 3.3%.

Over 50 years it averages 3.1%.

Over 40 years, it averaged 2.8%.

Over 30 years, the average rate of growth dipped to 2.7%.

Over 20 years it sagged further to 2.5%.

Since the turn of the millennium, the real growth rate of the US economy has sagged even further. The 10-year rate (1999–2009) is 1.9%.

The five-year average annual growth rate is just 0.9%.

And over the last three-years US real GDP hasn't grown at all.

A quarter or two—even a year or two—of slow growth would be nothing to be concerned about. But a trend that has lasted since the '50s may be something worth paying attention to. What caused it? What did it mean?

You can see the slowdown in growth expressed in this chart of real wages:

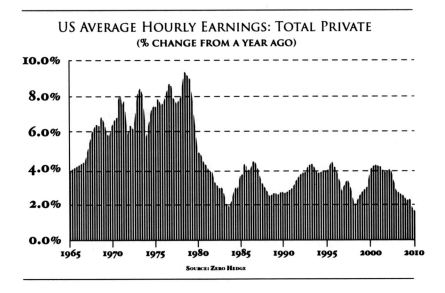

US AVERAGE HOURLY EARNINGS: TOTAL PRIVATE
(% CHANGE FROM A YEAR AGO)

SOURCE: ZERO HEDGE

In the 1970s, a typical worker could put in an 8-hour day, drive home in his Pontiac Bonneville, watch Bonanza on TV, and earn more per hour, in real, inflation-adjusted terms, than the fellow today who drives a Prius and comes home to open his Facebook page and see how many likes he has.

Real, hourly wage gains in the US peaked out in the '70s. They've never recovered. The simplest explanation is that American working people were competing with cheaper labor overseas. Foreigners were catching up.

Science fiction writers a century earlier had predicted that by the year 2000 we'd all be flying around in our individual flying cars, that we'd only have to work a few hours per week, that wars would be a thing of the past, that we'd be freer, happier, healthier, and richer than people back then could imagine.

Conditions were ripe: with many more scientists than ever before—more patents, more Ph.Ds, more engineering labs, more research facilities, more brains at work everywhere—progress should have sped up.

(We could wonder about whether progress itself is subject to declining marginal utility. Do you get to the point where you have too much progress? Do you ever have so much progress that you are actually going backwards? Those questions will have to wait...)

THE RAW MATERIALS OF PROGRESS

What do you need for material progress? Capital. Brains. Freedom. Motivation. Labor. Raw materials. Capital was more abundant over the last four decades than ever before. If you had a new idea—even a bad idea, like Webvan.com...or a crooked idea like Bernie Madoff's fund management—you could raise billions of dollars for it. Capital was cheap and easy. Money was no obstacle. No new invention or innovation should have died for lack of an infusion of investment capital.

Nor should it have failed for lack of educated, experienced workers. America was attracting the best and the brightest from all over the world. Plus, it had its own workforce, which was already the most educated workforce ever.

It also had a workforce that was easily motivated. By money. Presumably, any good innovation should make a profit, and the profit should attract workers, managers, entrepreneurs and investors who would be willing to walk over their grandmothers to take advantage of it.

In addition to the most robust capital markets and the most capable workforce, the prospective entrepreneur also had the largest, most spendthrift consumer market in world history. The US alone had more than 250 million avid consumers (now more than 300 million).

Not only were these people earning more money than any people ever had, they were also the first people in history to ever have a credit card with no limit. The change in the US monetary system, fully effective on August 15, 1971, meant that Americans could spend as much as they wanted…or almost. I'll return to this point later. For right now, let's just remember that anyone who wanted to make stuff had plenty of willing and able consumers to sell it to. The best capital markets, the best consumer markets, the best, most modern design and production capabilities. Progress never had it so good.

So how was it possible that both wage and GDP growth rates went down? What caused such a huge disappointment?

Nobody knows. But I'll take two guesses. First: the declining marginal utility of energy. Second: the post-'71 credit-based money system. I will leave the second guess for the next chapter. In the meantime, let's look a little closer at the first.

THE DECLINING MARGINAL UTILITY OF ENERGY

Available, useful, effective energy is always in limited supply. All human progress comes as a result of using it effectively. There are only so many hours in the day, only so many neurons to do their work, and only so many tons of coal in the earth's crust. You either use them well…or you don't. In a sense, everything we are talking about in this book can be explained by the declining marginal utility of energy. Not that energy itself is in any way less useful as it becomes more abundant, but that each incremental unit—*as used*—produces less real output. At the extreme of hormegeddon, in fact, additional inputs of energy—like a runaway train traveling at higher and higher speeds—destroys wealth, rather than adding to it.

In short, energy is wealth. It takes energy to turn clay into bricks and to lay them up into an apartment building. The apartment building is real wealth. But that wealth—the product of so much energy—can also be reduced to a pile of dust. Energy is the key variable in the equation. It all depends on what you do with it.

In the hundreds of thousands of years before man was fully human, he had no more energy available to him than other animals. He ate what he could gather or grab. His brain developed, allowing him to use tools and weapons and to undertake collective projects, such as hunting, war, irrigation, public hangings, government, and so forth. But this larger brain came at a cost. Brains take energy. He needed to increase his calorie intake to pay for it. That required him to invest more energy as well as use more.

For at least 10,000 years, men wandered the plains and scrub forests of what is today Texas. But it was only in the last 100 years that humans were able to extract oil and do something with it. And only in the last ten years were they able to frack out even more oil and gas. Usable, wealth-enhancing energy is a function of the technology and cultural circumstances existing at the time.

Over many, many years people learned to use energy from a variety of sources. Some figured out how to work metal using the heat from coal or charcoal, others learned to navigate the oceans using the force of the wind to drive their boats, still others figured out how to mill flour using the power of a waterwheel, and some even developed construction cranes powered by slaves walking on a treadmill. They invented these machines to move, grind, lift and hammer things. But they lacked a convenient, flexible and reliable source of condensed energy to power them. Using the energy and technology they had, output increased very, very slowly. This gave innovations time to spread widely and distribute themselves fairly evenly. As late as the 18th century there was not much difference in the level of wealth and standard of living between a farmer in Bengal, one in China or one in Virginia.

In any of those places, you might have seen two very useful machines: cows and horses. The milk cow merrily converted grass—indigestible by humans—into milk, cheese and meat. The horse converted that grass into horsepower, which could be used for transportation, war, or farm labor. For approximately 180 generations, these humble quadrupeds gave man the leg up he needed to make himself comfortable. But the machines of the Industrial Revolution gave him the biggest boost of all. Now man could use not only the sun's current energy—as expressed in living plants and animals—but also the condensed energy from millions of years of past sunlight. He could use the world's stored-up energy to make things and move them around. You can see here what this did to the human population. It permitted a staggering increase in the number of people the world could support.

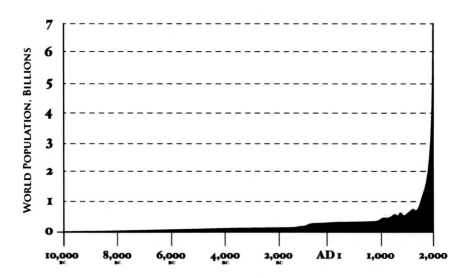

It took a while for these new fossil fuel engines to be perfected, but over the 19th and 20th centuries the results were spectacular. Nothing in human history comes even close. Now, humans could benefit from far more energy than they had in the past. You see the consumption here:

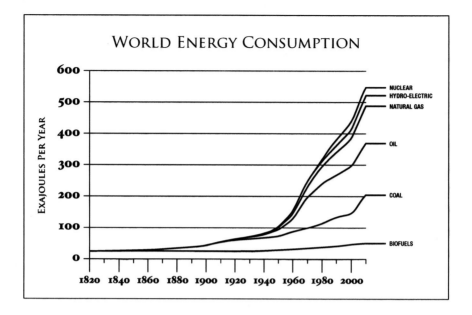

You will note also that even the small amount of 'green' energy sources shown in this chart are often only possible because of machines that use fossil fuel. Wood, for example, is harvested using tractors, chainsaws, and so forth.

This innovation is barely two centuries old. It is so new that it has yet to be fully exploited by much of the human population. Not all people had the savings, the technology, the financial system, and the property rights that would allow them to exploit energy effectively. Today, the use of energy is still extremely uneven. The average American uses 327 gigajoules of energy per year. In Vietnam the figure is only 22. In India it is only 21. Even in Brazil, it is just 44. All of these countries have plenty of room to grow simply by putting into place the innovations that have already been developed. By contrast, the rich countries seem to have reached the point where additional inputs of fossil fuel energy do not produce substantially higher levels of output. It is hard for them to put new machines into service profitably. That's why energy use is now declining in the US, Europe and Japan; it just doesn't pay. That is also why the world we see in Europe and America today is so similar to the world of 50 years ago. We had much cheaper gasoline back then. But the machines we used to turn the fuel into useful output were about the same. This is the declining marginal utility of energy, in a fuel-soaked nutshell.

I experienced all these stages of energy innovation first hand in Argentina. I bought a primitive ranch in 2006. At that time, horse-mounted gauchos drove cattle. Horse drawn plows turned the earth. Horse-powered mowers cut the hay. There was no electricity. And the only machine on the property was an old pickup truck belonging to the farm manager. It was picturesque, but inefficient and unprofitable.

When our two big workhorses died, we decided to enter the 20th century. We bought tractors. Within two years, hay and quinoa production were up five-fold. The return on investment was impressive. We had converted the stored up energy of the sun to current output.

What now? We can buy newer tractors. But a newer tractor is not noticeably more productive than an old one. While the price and availability of energy has barely changed, the returns on future investment in new energy-using machinery will be marginal, at best. The years of fastest growth are already behind us. Magnify this experience over a whole economy.

This discussion might be inconsequential; except, the future of the United States of America, Europe, Japan and the entire developed world economy hangs on it. Without substantial growth, the leading countries of the western world will all go broke. They need economic growth in order to make good on the financial obligations they incurred by making promises based on 20th century growth rates. But, if we have reached the point of declining marginal utility with energy, the growth rates of the 21st century may be substantially lower than anyone has speculated. And then we're in real trouble.

In a broad sense, you could say that all civilizations collapse because they "run out of energy." But not necessarily oil, wood or coal. Civilizations—like families, businesses, and clubs—depend on the energy of their constituent parts. If those members have the energy to meet their challenges, the organization will thrive. If not, it will decay. The more aggressive they are in using their energy, the faster it gives out. Soon, based on the circumstances, "more" turns into "too much."

One of the most important, and generally overlooked, patterns of civilization is that as a society ages, it becomes less dynamic and productive; it runs out of energy. This can be explained in many ways: in Tainter's terms, in Mancur Olson's terms, in our zombie terms (which we will get to). However you explain it, the consequence is the same. The very thing governments try so hard to prevent arrives: the future. The old is creatively destroyed. The new takes over.

Where is the exception? Not in the history books. Every organization comes and then goes. Every one prospers and grows when it uses its energy effectively. Then, when its energy is wasted, dispersed and exhausted, it declines.

Energy can never be separated from life and wealth itself. An abundance of it is a good thing; but only when it is put to good purposes. When a society is headed to hormegeddon—in any number of ways—being flush with energy merely increases its speed, so it is going faster when it runs into a ditch.

Chapter 7
THE ZOMBIE APOCALYPSE

*"Where your treasure is there
your heart will also be."*

—LUKE 12:33 & 34

Amer[A]merica's income tax was set up with thirty words in the 16th amendment. Now it runs to almost 4 million words, with one substantial change every week. In 2012, it cost Americans more than 6.1 billion hours—$168 million—to comply with the paperwork requirements.

Who benefits? Zombies in suits.

How much of the world's trouble is caused by guys with hammers or wrenches in their hands? How many bakers cause depressions? How many masons are mass-murderers? How many steelworkers or cabinetmakers or deliverymen cause mass starvation?

The common workingman may be a bumbler and a fool, but he is rarely responsible for anyone's troubles but his own.

The guy who causes real trouble is the fellow in a suit. Many of the smartest people in the nation give up honest careers in mechanics, metallurgy and upholstery to put on suits. That is, they go to law school. Some cause trouble—such as lawyers for the SEC. Some shysters get rich—such as tort lawyers who make their money with trumped-up class action suits. Others protect honest people from the attacks of the shysters and regulators. And a few actually help people beat DUI raps, dump their spouses and commit other acts of wanton humanity.

Together, the good lawyers, the bad lawyers, and the ugly suits absorb a substantial portion of the nation's resources...and contribute not a penny to its wealth.

In the final days of 2012, the suits went to war with each other over the nation's finances. The government was running out of money. It was an opportunity to add a few more pages of regulation to the books and every suit in the land knew it was not to be wasted.

At the last hour, the Senate got together and came up with a plan. That plan was a stopgap measure, everyone admitted. But it was better to fill the gap—even with folderol—than to leave it open, they said. It would allow the Feds to keep the lights on while they wrestled with the longer-term problems later—namely, the fact that the US government spends far more money than it takes in.

Inasmuch as Congress has spent too much for many years, it was hard to see how the pols would be any better at spending less in 2014 than they were in 2012. But that's just the point. They proved that, driven to the edge of the cliff, they'll always agree on ways to keep spending! The system works!

Hallelujah.

And what did Congress spend money on? It took money from productive segments of the economy—the working stiffs who actually produce goods and services that other people are willing to pay for—and gave the money to people on disability, people who make drones, and people who sit on their fat derrieres in cushy government office buildings. In other words, zombies. Nobody would willingly pay for these things, so the feds have to take the money by force, threatening jail time to anyone who resists.

But the Senate bill did not merely find a way to keep the known zombies feeding at the public trough, it also threw some meat to hidden zombies all over the country. David Malpass, former deputy assistant Treasury secretary, wrote in the *Wall Street Journal* that the legislation extends 52 tax credits for one year. That would give the zombie beneficiaries plenty of room to work on their bribes and blandishments in time for the 2013 end-of-the-year legislation. Section 206, he points out, takes care of the environmentalists. Section 312 gives a break to those running "motorsports entertainment complexes." And section 317 is intended to keep Hollywood happy.

On the letters page of the November 6, 2012 edition of the WSJ came another suggestion from the private sector. Marc L. Fleischaker is the 'Trade Counsel' for the Rubber and Plastic Footwear Manufacturers Association in Washington. Mr. Fleischaker was apparently concerned about the effect of the proposed Affordable

Footwear Act. 90% of America's footwear needs, Fleischaker reminded us, are satisfied by manufacturers working in low-wage companies in China and Vietnam.

This should have reassured the footwear worriers—we're already getting shod at the lowest prices possible. Instead, it seemed to be a source of even more anxiety. Mr. Fleischaker demanded immediate action. He wrote:

> As a nation, we do need to maintain significant tariffs on competitive imported footwear in order to somewhat balance the playing field and not lose the rest of our manufacturing base.

How do you balance the playing field by tilting it against importers? How does prohibiting free trade make shoes "affordable?" Why is it important to keep people making shoes in the US? Have cheap shoes become a strategic commodity; are we afraid of being cut off? Why is it any business of the politicians where people buy their shoes?

The zombies aren't just out to "protect" the American worker, like Fleischaker's group would have you believe. They're also out to help the non-worker. Driving through East Baltimore, I saw a billboard promoting the services of a law firm with a familiar name:

DENIED DISABILITY? Call THE FIRM. The Cochran Firm.

That's Cochran as in Johnnie Cochran, the lawyer who successfully defended O.J. Simpson. Now his firm has 30 offices around the country helping people get on disability. Apparently, he's been pretty successful at that, too. Between 2009 and 2012, the number of people on disability rose seven times faster than the number of new jobs. In one county in Alabama, 1 out of every 4 working-age adults is officially disabled. The biggest source of new claims has come from "musculoskeletal" or "mental" problems—neither of which can be verified objectively. Not that people don't feel muscle and joint pain, nor that they don't sometimes feel out of sorts. But as Winston Churchill pointed out: most of the world's work is done by people who don't feel very well and would rather not be doing it. Now, thanks to 'disability,' they don't have to do it if they don't want. They've been zombified. In 2012, labor force participation hit its lowest levels since 1979. It is estimated that a quarter of the drop was due to workers leaving the labor pool altogether in favor of the disability rolls.

I had not gone to East Baltimore for pleasure. I was going there to waste time and energy. Specifically, the state of Maryland required me to have my auto emissions checked. Practically everyone with an automobile is now forced to drive where he doesn't really want to go, wait in a line he doesn't eally want to be in, and pay $14 to have his fumes checked.

As the classic French economist Frédric Bastiat reminds us, there are always unseen consequences in addition to those that are obvious. For every 'bad' auto the test uncovers—whose emissions are unnecessarily noxious—many more good autos are forced to drive miles and miles they didn't otherwise have to drive, just to take the test. At the test station I used, there were six lines of traffic, six cars in each line, each idling its motor while waiting to move forward and prove to the government they didn't need to be there in the first place.

"It's worse than that," my secretary volunteered. "The test doesn't work on newer cars, or at least some models of them. So, you get there, they take your $14, and they just waive you through."

But emissions testing is now a part of a complex, costly economy: an entire industry devoted to activities that provide little, if any, real return. Employees are trained to do emissions testing. And lobbyists work hard to keep the whole thing going, whether it really makes any sense or not. And so, a part of the nation's energy—time, money, fuel, capital, engineering ability—is now taken up by emissions testing. As it is with filling out tax returns. Little of this shows up as government spending. It is the private sector that spends the money.

Consider the security checks in airports if you are looking for another example. Millions of people spend millions of hours per year—an immense 'investment' of energy—merely keeping people who had no intention of blowing up airplanes from doing so. This security spending even extends to trains. Taking the train from New York to Washington, for example, means running a gauntlet of gun-toting guards dressed in black—like a SWAT team on a midnight raid—holding back dogs that sniff your bags for an uneaten sandwich or an untidy bomb. Then, once aboard the Acela train, there are announcements on the electronic monitors informing you that if you "see something" you are supposed to "say something." Presumably, we all know what we're supposed to be looking for and to whom we're supposed to say something. What we don't know is how much of the nation's energy or money is consumed by keeping citizens in such a constant state of alarmed vigilance. Nor do we know if it does any good. It is a cost imposed by government, but not included in the federal budget. We don't have to concern ourselves about whether paying taxes is necessary or good, we only have to recognize that it is a substantial burden, made substantially more burdensome by the complexities of the tax code.

The Right & Wrong Kinds of Complexity

"It was unbelievable," said a colleague, encountering the complexity of modern life. "My son got arrested for having a marijuana cigarette on him. I had to go to court with him.

"First, the judge seemed to know the whole thing was a farce. She looked down at my son and the other kids who were at the same party and were all arrested along with him. She said 'you all have to realize that marijuana is against the law in the state of Maryland. Also, it is a door to more serious problems. Every addict I've had in my courtroom has started out with pot.' Then, she gave them each a $50 fine plus court costs of $57. But they each also paid about $1,500 to a lawyer, who sat with them in the courtroom but really had nothing to say.

"And this was the result of a raid on a house right off campus. The police knocked down the door and arrested almost everyone. And what did they find? Just a few marijuana cigarettes. Imagine the cost of all this...the police...the lawyers...the court...the parents. And for what?"

Joseph Tainter, in his aforementioned *Collapse of Complex Societies*, believes the decline in civilizations can be traced to problem solving. Each problem, he says, leads to a solution, which involves greater complexity. Bureaucracies, hierarchies, rules, and regulations are imposed. These things cost time, energy and resources. Eventually, the cost is too great. Complexity increases costs without increasing output. Eventually, the civilization operates at a net loss, negative returns, and then...you guessed it...hormegeddon.

Not everyone loses. There is a great transfer of wealth involved: from productive citizens to lobbyists, lawyers, accountants, bureaucrats, policemen, judges, counselors and psychologists, jailers, pundits, lobbyists, lawmakers, parole officers, social workers and thousands of others.

But a little refinement of Tainter's hypothesis is needed. There are different kinds of complexity. There is the natural complexity of the upside—with an infinite web of human and commercial relationships. And there is another form of complexity—one that is imposed by force, rather than spontaneously generated. The first form of complexity helps reduce costs; the second increases them. The first makes the system more robust—like a web of small streets in a big town. The second—like a single large highway with a tollbooth—makes the system more vulnerable. The first allows for experimentation, innovation and correction. The second cuts off innovations and forbids corrections.

Entrepreneurs flourish in the natural complexity of a dynamic economy. But planners favor complexity in its heavy-handed, directed form. Why? It is easier to understand. And easier to manipulate. It is also a rich cover in which to hide special favors and privileges. Sure, you could replace the government's revenue with a much simpler tax system, but you'd inconvenience thousands of insiders. Better to inconvenience millions of outsiders—those who don't benefit from the complexity.

Artificial, imposed complexity forces the distribution of power, status and wealth along prescriptivist lines. A dynamic economy is descriptivist. It offers no prescription for success and only a few simple rules: Thou Shalt Not Steal, for example. Prescriptivist complexity, on the other hand, brings countless new rules, forcing you to hire good lawyers and accountants to avoid running afoul of them.

Artificial complexity is what you get in a non-market system. Without a functioning market, there is no way to know what things are worth or who's valuable and who's not. Government output is not priced by an active bid-ask market. Nor are government workers hired or paid on a piecework basis. Instead, everything depends on theories, guesswork, prejudices, credentials, paperwork, and connections. As a result, resources are invested in ways that do not necessarily pay off.

Here is a simplified illustration of Tainter's idea: In the Roman Empire, agricultural output per person dropped as population increased. The problem was addressed by a policy of conquest. The Romans took resources—grain, slaves, gold—from their neighbors. But this required a large army, which was an expensive, energy-consuming enterprise. And it undermined the normal agricultural economy of Italy; free farmers couldn't compete with stolen imports and large slave-run farms. The return on investment declined and eventually went negative. The Empire collapsed. That was not necessarily a bad thing. When the decline on investments is negative, you are better off stopping the program. And archeological evidence from bones and teeth suggest that many people were actually better fed after the collapse of the empire.

As the size and complexity of society grows, the governments that are most competitive are those that draw on the most support of their subject peoples. That is why the Roman policy of conquest was so successful. They were able to turn the conquered peoples into supporters of the regime, with most of the army eventually comprised of non-Roman soldiers. The British Empire was good at this too. The empire began by subduing the Scots, who became the backbone of the British Army. Today's American army, too, depends heavily on soldiers from the southern states, who were conquered by Abraham Lincoln's armies in the 1860s.

In an early stage, a society tends to be robust and efficient—or 'simple,' in Tainter's terms. Later, additional complexity degrades returns on investment. While this complexity may be described as a form of problem solving, it is better understood as an attempt by elite groups to hold onto their wealth and power. 'Complexity' is created by people who find ways to game the system. They earn their livings without contributing to useful output (even though they may or may not be working hard). Growth rates slow as much of the society's energy is diverted to unproductive uses. In short, more and more money goes to zombies.

What are 'zombies?' Neither dead nor alive, from an economic perspective, they are people who live at the expense of others. Are you a zombie? Here's how to tell: ask yourself, in the absence of the government, would people voluntarily pay you to do what you do? If not, you're probably a zombie.

THE ZOMBIES OF HURRICANE SANDY

The wake of Hurricane Sandy in October of 2012 provided some illustration of the insidious and largely unrecognized increase in complexity and associated costs. The hurricane blew through the

Northeast. It pushed water up over the shore and into the houses of hundreds of thousands of people.

Well, BFD. What do you expect when you build houses only a few feet above sea level? You're going to get soaked from time to time. You should be prepared to clean up, rebuild, and get on with your life at the greatest speed and lowest cost possible.

But as the winds died down, residents of New Jersey, New York, and Connecticut ran into zombies. First, they could not just repair their homes. They needed permission. Most were advised that they needed to rip out everything, lest mold set in (which, as an amateur builder, I doubt was good advice). A Long Islander reported his experience in the *Wall Street Journal*, January 15, 2013:

> Before you could get a building permit, however you had to be approved by the Zoning Authority. And Zoning— citing FEMA regulations would force you to bring the house "up to code." Which in many cases meant elevating the house by several feet. Now, elevating your house if very expensive and time consuming—not because of the actual raising, which just takes a day or two, but because of the required permits.

You need engineers, architects, and lawyers. Not to actually do the work, but just to get you through the permit process in order to *then* do the work according to any number of municipal, county, state and federal regulations. This takes time, and money too. Months after the hurricane, thousands of houses were still empty and idle, waiting for official approval for work to begin.

For money, you could turn to FEMA. But good luck. Zombies like paper—a lot of it. God help you if you don't have your papers in order.

Meanwhile, over in New Jersey, the Army Corps of Engineers was running into other zombies. It was supposed to give out a contract to clean up the shore area. The price of the work would exceed $25 million, so according to another bit of complexity, the work would have to be done according to a PLA, or project labor agreement. This would force the contractors to use union labor, scaring away three out of four of New Jersey's contractors (who are not unionized) and raising the cost by about 30%, according to a report from the New Jersey Department of Labor and Workforce Development.

ZOMBIE REGS

In the US today, nobody knows how much of the economy's energy is sapped by this kind of "complexity." But it must be a lot. Every business now has its own overseers and regulators. Every business and household spends time and money complying with complex regulations—many of which did not exist a few years ago.

Google "Dodd-Frank" and you get 5,460,000 hits. Each one is an attempt to understand, influence, implement or comment on this legislation. And most of this activity occurs in the private sector of the economy, where it is recorded as positive increments to the GDP! But it is a huge diversion of resources, taking them away from what might otherwise be useful and productive activity.

An article in the Fall 2012 issue of Cato Institute's *Regulation* magazine shows the cost of the "10 Top Regulations Affecting Small Businesses." These are:

1. Energy Conservation Standards

2. Affordable Care Act Menu Labels

3. Transportation's Hours of Service Rule

4. Affordable Care Act Vending Machine Labels

5. NLRB's Union Notification Standards

6. Education's Gainful Employment Rule

7. EPA's Fracking Regulations

8. Dodd-Frank Regulation Z

9. Affordable Care Act Physician Fee Schedule

10. Dodd-Frank Regulation E

Together these cost small businesses $3.5 billion annually, according to the study. And they add 28.7 million hours of paperwork.

As another measure of how much time and energy is wasted, data from the Mercatus and Weidenbaum centers show that budgets for the main federal regulatory agencies multiplied 14 times between 1960 and 2007, in constant dollars. The payoff from all this extra investment is hard to measure; most likely it is starkly negative.

Again, we don't have to decide whether Dodd-Frank or emissions testing or airport screening is good or bad, necessary or unnecessary, we only have to recognize that much of our energy is now spent on things that reduce output. Is it worth it? The presumption is that regulation is beneficial for someone. But perhaps it is just a way to transfer wealth and power from productive people to zombies.

THE 4 STEP PROCESS OF ZOMBIFICATION:

1. All (or almost all) people who aren't saints or mental defectives want wealth, power and status.

2. They want to get it in the easiest way possible.

3. The easiest way to get wealth is to steal it, which is why all groups turn to the government, the only institution that gets to steal lawfully.

4. Over time, more and more groups find ways to use the power of the state for their own ends. Government—not productive activity—becomes the source of wealth, power, and status.

ZOMBIE HYPOCRISY

Before Mary Jo White was proposed to take the helm of the SEC, she was already nestled tightly into the industry she was meant to oversee. What the industry wants, of course, is protection from its customers—and its potential competitors—which is just what Ms. White was prepared to give. For 10 years prior to her appointment she worked for the securities industry. She and her husband were lawyers at New York's top law firms—Debevoise & Plimpton and Cravath, Swaine & Moore. They represented a number of large publicly held companies on various accounting and regulatory issues—the very rules and regulations she now enforces.

And here's a shocker. While head of Homeland Security, Michael Chertoff favored having Homeland Security's Transportation Safety Agency [TSA] install the hated nude-body scanners in US airports. Chertoff, a dual US-Israeli citizen, now works for the company that manufactures these nude-body scanners!

But Mr. Chertoff's double-dealing was dealt a blow—probably in the form of more double dealing by zombie rivals. In early 2013, it was announced that the "much hated" scanners would be removed. Not because they were ineffective—by whatever standard you can imagine—but because they had been unable to meet a deadline to come up with a 'generic' image, rather than the dirty pictures that got people riled up.

In some cases, when the zombies descend, whole new industries are created. More often, industries that used to provide value for money are corrupted. Each seems to make a devil's deal with government, whereby it gets to use the police power of the state for its own ends.

All mature economies drift towards unproductive activity like old elephants heading for the burial ground. Either they don't know what happens there. Or they feel compelled to go in that direction anyway. How does it happen? Why does it happen? Why do people permit it to happen?

In a stable society, over time people find ways to get little privileges, special favors, and elevated status. They connive to land government contracts, food stamps, special deals of all sorts. Not all of these people are lazy. Not all are dishonest. But they are all beneficiaries of a corrosive system.

One person approves the quality of your meat. Another makes sure you have put enough steel in your concrete. Another has the job of patting down your grandmother before she boards an airplane to make sure she is not packing heat. Still another advises the government on gender issues.

As more money flows through the pipes and conduits set up by the functionaries, more people get in line at the spigot. Instead of trying to provide a real product or real service—by doing honest business with their co-citizens—they go to where the money drips. One faucet gushes with jobs paying more than the private sector. Others offer free food, subsidized lodging, or medical care at someone else's expense.

"Morality is what used to pay," said the American economist, Mancur Olson. He meant that habits and values are formed by circumstances. What works becomes what is 'good.'

What used to work was hard effort, education, and saving money. The 'heartland' was where Americans made things…and prospered. Now, the money is made by people who never break a sweat. The route to success detours from the Heartland towards Washington and New York. What pays off now? Speculation, knowing somebody in power, or getting a special break from the feds.

And now, mothers want their sons and daughters to take their positions in 'the system,' to join the ranks of the bureaucrats, anglers and accredited professionals, to have an edge, to be in an insider, rather than an outsider. They know how hard it is to get ahead without an "in." The weight of taxes and regulations is just too heavy.

THE FRENCH WORD FOR 'ZOMBIE' IS *RENTIER*

Of course, this phenomenon—zombification—applies to private organizations and businesses as well as the government. As a business ages, it typically changes from a dynamic, outward-looking group to a stodgy, bureaucratic organization focused on holding onto power and status at all cost. Instead of looking ahead, it begins to look backward, at itself...just like the government.

The big difference between government and private organizations is that only the government has the legal right to use violence to get what it wants. When private organizations get infested by unproductive zombies, they go broke or get taken over by more dynamic organizations. Government generally continues favoring the zombies...until the whole country goes broke.

"That's what happened in France," a French friend explained. "What you are describing is what happened in France before the French Revolution. The monarchy had been in power for a long time. And different groups—mainly the aristocracy and the clergy—had taken advantage of it. Powerful groups or important individuals found a way to profit from the system. This was usually in the form of a stream of income from doing something that didn't need to be done.

"They would, for example, give someone a monopoly on the importation of tobacco. Or salt. Or silk. Often, the person would buy the privilege from the government.

"Some people had the right to collect taxes. And there were tolls on the roads. All sorts of things. It was fairly easy to give someone a little privilege. You give someone the right to collect money from people going up and down the river, for example. Most people don't know anything about it. It doesn't affect them. And even the people on the river, each one individually may not pay much.

"But the fellow collecting the rent had a good deal. And so the guy downriver wanted the same deal. And the guy up-river. And, as you say, over time, the river is full of people collecting tolls. We call them 'rents.' And the guy who collects them, the guy you call a 'zombie', we would call a 'rentier.'

"Of course, it's easier to give someone a rent than it is to take one away. So the number of rents grew and eventually became so high that the whole economy of France was gummed up by them. You'd take a load of potatoes from the country to sell in the city and you might have to pay off four or five different rentiers.

"You might describe these rents as friction in the system. The more the rents increased, the more the friction in the system increased. It got so bad that the economy barely worked at all. And back then it was an agricultural economy. All it took was a couple bad summers—in the 1780s—and people were on the verge of starvation. Things simmered for years and boiled up in 1787.

"A group of ragged, starving people gathered in front of the royal palace in Paris. You know the story. Marie Antoinette supposedly asked what the problem was. She was informed that the people were protesting because they didn't have any bread to eat. She is said to have replied:

"'Then, let them eat cake.' I'm not sure she ever said that. But it was the kind of remark that people remembered, whether it was true or not. Then, the revolution began, and a lot of the rentiers lost their rents and their heads."

THE ZOMBIE BANKING INDUSTRY

There was a time when banks were more or less honest businesses. Bankers took deposits and made loans. The banker himself was responsible for the losses. If the bank went down, so did he. More than one banker, ruined by losses, committed suicide rather than face the shame of his own mistakes.

But now big bankers are shielded from the harsh light of legal liability by corporate veils and federal umbrellas. They can still make money—more than ever. But the game has changed. Now they are practically public utilities—like Amtrak or the Post Office. Here's the deal: the feds keep incompetent bankers in business, and the bankers help the feds transfer money from the productive sectors to the zombies. Big banks are no longer private sector enterprises. They provide a quasi-public service. In return, they are protected from their own gross errors.

What public service?

Former French President Nicholas Sarkozy spelled it out for the bankers in 2011: the ECB would give them 489 billion euros (and call it a loan); they should use the money to buy government bonds (and call it an investment).

This cozy arrangement suited the bankers. They made profits, while the real risk of loss was borne by others—taxpayers, bondholders, and savers. So, now we have another major industry—one that was responsible for 40% of all US corporate profits in 2007—that sups with the devil. And major capital allocation decisions, involving billions or even trillions of dollars, are no longer made by independent, profit-seeking investors. Instead, they are made by favor-seeking zombies.

THE LURE OF ZOMBIFICATION

Occasionally, when I've had too much to drink, I lull myself to sleep with the notion that maybe the zombies can be brought under control before the nation is ruined by them. Then, I sober up. And make sure my passport is up to date.

You've seen my view of government. The Pauls who run it will take as much from the Peters as they can get away with. This will make more people want to leave the Peters and join the Pauls. Gradually, more and more people become insiders. And gradually fewer and fewer people are left behind who are still rowing the boat. The zombies multiply. They vote. The system is "locked in" towards war, revolution or bankruptcy.

Let's explore this further by looking at why zombification is so hard to resist. A healthy society with a dynamic economy supports few parasites. It creates wealth rather than dissipates it. Power, money and status are gained in the quirky manner of an unscripted improvisation rather than conferred by elite planners.

This kind of free economy has few real friends. Even those who call themselves friends say nasty things about it when its back is turned. Believers and supporters are so few that they could all probably be rounded up and gunned down in an afternoon. A free economy is too chancy—too unforgiving—and too uncontrollable to nurture lifelong friendships. No wonder so few people are fond of it. It is mischievous and willful, hard to get along with, and disloyal. It is even more likely to ruin its own supporters than its enemies. The zombies look out for each other, with safety nets and sweetheart deals. Like a zoo; the animals get fed regularly. A healthy economy, on the other hand, is a jungle. It is a world of sharp teeth and claw-your-way-to-the-top competition. When one competitor goes down; the others feed on it like jackals on a fallen gazelle. In the jungle, life evolves towards an uncertain future. In a zoo, the past is carefully preserved.

The zombies know how to get ahead. They go to the right schools. They follow directions. They make the right connections and say the right things. Bingo, they are soon on the board of some big corporation, waiting for their next stint at the IMF.

A healthy economy, on the other hand, offers no sure route to success. You can be smart, work hard, and go to the best schools. There is still no guarantee that you will succeed. It is all "luck and pluck"— a scramble through a wilderness with no maps and no experienced guides. And don't expect to 'win' by being the strongest, fastest, or smartest. As it says in Ecclesiastes, it doesn't quite work that way. The race goeth not always to the swift. Time and chance play a big role.

Nor, once you've succeeded, is there any sure way to maintain your position. Wealth has no fidelity, neither to any one person, group, or family. It goes where it wants. It is fickle and unreliable. Once you have made a lot of money, the same wheel of fortune that brought it to you can take it away from you. And the wheel never stops turning.

In the US in its early days, wealth and power were lost as quickly as they were gained. Declaration of Independence signer James Wilson was put in prison for non-payment while serving as Associate Justice of the US Supreme Court. There too, in the Walnut Street Debtor's Prison, in Washington, DC, he might have encountered his old friend Robert Morris, also a signer of the Declaration of Independence. Morris was once one of the richest men in the colonies and was once described as "the most powerful man in America." From 1781 to 1784, he acted as the new nation's secretary of the treasury, as its "Superintendent of Finance." But he was ruined in the Panic of 1796, bankrupted, and sent to debtor's prison.

Another illustrious veteran of debtor's prison was Henry "Light-Horse Harry" Lee, father of Robert E. Lee. He was a hero of the Revolutionary War, but nevertheless busted and sent to prison in 1808. He used his time there to write his "Memoirs of the War."

THE RICH LOVE ZOMBIFICATION

The rich tend to hate a dynamic economy even more than the poor. According to the concept of declining marginal utility, the pain of losing a dollar is greater than the pleasure of making an additional one (because each additional dollar's utility is less than the preceding one). So, when it comes to money, fear is a stronger emotion than greed. And since the rich have more to lose, they have developed a keener interest in avoiding losses than in being permitted to earn more wealth.

No sooner have the rich earned their money than they set about strangling the system that made it possible. They set up tests and hurdles designed to keep the hoi polloi off their tennis courts and out of their businesses. They use every means possible to separate themselves from the masses—language, education, dress, customs, geography. They tend to speak differently, sometimes even using a completely different language. Probably the most recent and best known example comes from Britain, where the upper classes still speak a heavily Latinized version of English, called "RP" for "received pronunciation," while the lower classes speak a more Germanic, more archaic version. A thousand years earlier, the upper classes actually spoke a different language all together—French. And a thousand years before that, they spoke Latin.

Education is a common means of helping the rich hold onto their status. Special schools typically cater only to the upper classes, teach the right accents and attitudes, and help young people make the sort of connections that will keep them, and their money, away from other people. That's why Barack Obama may talk about the 'middle class' and 'fairness' and 'equality.' But he sends his girls to an elite private school—Sidwell Friends—just like Al Gore, Bill Clinton, Joe Biden, Richard Nixon, the list goes on.

These barriers are rarely hermetic, however. They usually allow a few particularly bright people from the lower orders to enter into the moneyed classes. This has three beneficial effects. It nourishes the gene pool of the rich. It provides them with the top talent they need to stay rich. And it draws in ambitious and able young people who might otherwise compete against them.

Of course, the rich—especially if they are a coherent cultural group—tend to live together, socialize together, and do business together. These things, too, help to keep money "in the family" and out of the hands of strangers.

The right culture, tradition, habit and education can be helpful at producing real wealth as well as preserving it. The poor benefit, as do the rich. But the rich rarely stop at honest means of protecting their wealth and status. They also avail themselves of the police power of the state to block competitors and prevent losses. Typically, laws, edicts, and rules are announced to regulate everything from the professions people must practice to the clothes they wear. "Serfs" were shackled to their farms and masters; their station in life was set by law as well as by custom. Sumptuary laws forbade new money from imitating the fine dress of old money. Licensing requirements, tariffs, and regulations are used to make it more difficult to enter into a profitable trade or business, thereby protecting those who are already established in those businesses.

Taxes, too, tend to work for the benefit of the rich. In pre-revolutionary France, the aristocracy and the clergy were exempt from taxes. Even today, most taxes are impositions on getting rich, not on being rich. Governments tax income, not wealth. France is an exception with a wealth tax. But it is a relatively modest one. The top marginal rate on income, 71%, which comes with additional "social charges," is 32 times more.

Warren Buffett claimed that he paid a lower tax rate than his secretary. That was because his taxes were paid at rates levied on people who were already rich—capital gains and dividends—rather than income. The poor secretary had to pay taxes on the fruits of her own labors. Warren paid taxes on the fruits of his money.

Does this mean the rich like government? Yes, of course they do. They use it to try to slow down innovation and stymie change. As explained in the previous chapter, government's primary mission is also the goal of older, successful people everywhere: to stop the clock.

The state is a rich man's best friend. The rich return the friendship, in cash. As PIMCO founder Bill Gross reported in January of 2010, what is amazing is not that politicians can be bought, but that they can be bought so cheaply. He wrote that "public records show that combined labor, insurance, big pharma and related corporate interests spent just under $500 million last year on healthcare lobbying (not much of which went to politicians) for what is likely to be a $50–100 billion annual return." Meanwhile, the employees and political action committee of aircraft maker Northrop invested only half a million dollars in the 2012 election campaigns of key members of the House Armed Services Committee. They gave its chairman $113,000 in the period 2009–2012 and set a team of 26 lobbyists to work. The payoff? The $2.5 billion Global Blackhawk drone program, which the Air Force itself wanted to stop.

GREASY PALMS & REVOLVING DOORS

The defining characteristic of a zombified system is the way it hands out its rewards. In an honest economy, people do their best. They work hard. Or not. They take their chances. Some prevail because they are productive. Others are just lucky. The chips fall where they may.

But as the system is taken over by zombies, the chips fall where they are told to fall. Rather than to honest and efficient producers, the rewards go to those who curry favors.

Elizabeth Fowler knows how it works. She labored at the left hand of senator Max Baucus, drafting the collection of crimes and punishments that came to be known as 'Obamacare.' Senator Baucus admitted that he had better things to do than actually read it. He didn't have to. His chief health policy counsel, the aforementioned Madam Fowler, knew what was in it. As a former top lobbyist for Wellpoint, America's largest health insurance provider, she had put the plum in the pudding herself.

"If you drew an organization chart of major players in the Senate health care negotiations," wrote *Politico* at the time, "Fowler would be chief operating officer."

Fowler had already been through the revolving door more than once or twice. She worked for Baucus before joining Wellpoint…and after. When she came back to Baucus she replaced Michelle Easton, another Wellpoint lobbyist, who helped guide the senator on health policy while Ms. Fowler was on the Wellpoint payroll.

Then, after the legislation was passed, the White House turned to the clever lobbyist to implement it. After all, the sugar spot in the legislation was the provision requiring people to buy products from companies such as Wellpoint, whether they wanted to or not.[5] As America's new Special Assistant to the President for Healthcare and Economic Policy at the National Economic Council, her job was to make sure Wellpoint got a good return on its investment.

And then, in December 2012, *whoosh!*, she went back through the revolving door. Type in "Elizabeth Fowler" and "revolving door" and you will get the whole story. The 'architect of Obamacare,' say the papers, left the White House to go to the honey-pot at Johnson & Johnson.

What will she do there? Will she test the adult diapers? Will she take out the trash or write advertising jingles? No, she is up to her old tricks, in a 'senior position' at their 'government affairs and policy group.'

You go girl!

Wellpoint was not the only winner in the health care sector in 2012. The *New York Times* reports:

> WASHINGTON—Just two weeks after pleading guilty in
> a major federal fraud case, Amgen, the world's largest
> biotechnology firm, scored a largely unnoticed coup on

---

[5] This is not the first time this sort of special privilege has been granted in the USA. The ethanol industry got it coming and going, too. Tax credits subsidized farmers for growing corn and then federal mandates required fuel companies to buy it.

Capitol Hill: Lawmakers inserted a paragraph into the "fiscal cliff" bill that did not mention the company by name but strongly favored one of its drugs.

The special favor was buried in Section 632. It involved a kidney dialysis drug—Sensipar—that was spared from cost-cutting restrictions for an additional two years. This was the fruit of efforts by 74 Amgen lobbyists. It is expected to cost the Medicare system up to $500 million.

And so the gears of the zombie machine grind away. Congressional staff members slip favors to private sector companies. Then, the companies return the favors, giving staff members cushy jobs. One of the chief Amgen lobbyists, for example, had been an employee of the same senator—Max Baucus, head of the Senate Finance Committee. Jeff Forbes was the senator's chief of staff. Amgen has given the politicians $5 million since 2007, with $68,000 to Baucus.

But poor Elekta AB. The Swedish maker of radiation tools got stabbed in the back in the same last-minute legislation. That's the way zombieism works too; the rewards go to people who are best able to pervert the political process. Elekta was at a disadvantage. As a foreign company, it couldn't give money to the politicians. Varian, its competitor, could. Varian put 18 lobbyists on the case and managed to get Elekta's payments cut in half.

THE CANTILLON EFFECT

In 2012, a Berkeley economist calculated that "the 1%"—the richest people in the country—had captured 93% of all of the income gains since the "recovery" began in 2009. "Is that all?" commented a rich friend. "We'll do better next year."

Meanwhile, one of the richest of the rich, Gina Rinehart, offered the 99% some advice: "stop drinking, stop smoking and work harder."

It was not only a convenient myth, it was also a useful one. Earning money the old-fashioned, honest way is still your best bet...unless you've got the government in your pocket.

In economics, the phenomenon is known as the "Cantillon Effect."

Richard Cantillon was an associate of John Law—the world's first fully modern central banker. Cantillon noticed that Law's new paper money—backed by shares in the Mississippi Company—didn't reach everyone at the same rate. The insiders—the rich and the well connected—got the paper first. They competed for goods and services with it as though it were as good as the old money.

But by the time it reached the laboring classes, this new money had been greatly discounted—to the point, eventually, where it was worthless.[6]

A version of the Cantillon Effect was observed in Soviet gulags and German concentration camps. Victims reported that those close to the kitchen were more likely to survive. The food often ran out before it reached those who worked in the fields and forests.

As the society evolves from jungle to zoo all eyes turn to the zookeeper. He is the one with the soup!

If they are poor, people implore the government to 'tax the rich' and give the money to the poor. If they are rich, they want the government to protect their wealth and status—with every means available to them. Democratically-elected governments generally do both. They support the poor with loud attacks on the rich and a trickle of cash. Vote for vote, the poor can generally be bought much more cheaply than the rich. As for the rich, their support is more subtle and underhanded. There are tax credits and loopholes for anyone who can afford

---

[6] Cantillon was a beneficiary of this phenomenon. He speculated in Law's Mississippi Company shares. Then, foreseeing disaster, he sold out at the top. This so enraged the buyers who were ruined that they plotted to murder him. Cantillon may have staged his own death to escape them.

them; there are greasy contracts for the insiders and plenty of jobs for the well-credentialed blowhards.

The rich complain about the poor. The poor complain about the rich. Both complain about the government. And everybody hates an honest, dynamic market economy.

But over time, the giveaways, bribes, regulations, intercessions and meddling on the part of the government, and on behalf of the special interests of which it is composed, have a big effect on the economy. They add costly "complexity." They also depress output. The more the government interferes with market signals and market-based capital allocation, the less able the economy is to produce real wealth. More and more resources are purloined by the insiders. Paperwork, lawyers, administration, regulation, taxes take a toll. So does misallocation of capital investment to huge, unproductive industries such as education, health, finance and defense (and make no mistake, these are not "services," they are industries). There is also a shift of wealth generally from those who earn it to those to whom it is redistributed; from capital formation to consumption.

A dynamic economy requires capital. You have to save money before you can invest it. Zombieism, on the other hand, is all about getting and consuming. Gradually the economy becomes paralyzed and parasitic; nearly everyone gets poorer. And often, the state—along with the mobs that support it—becomes desperate for more money.

WHERE THE ZOMBIES ARE

By early 2011, America's housing slump had wiped out 8 years of price increases.

Bloomberg was on the story:

> Home prices in 20 US cities dropped in March to the lowest level since 2003, showing housing remains mired in a slump almost two years into the economic recovery.

The S&P/Case-Shiller index of property values in 20 cities fell 3.6 percent from March 2010, the biggest year-over-year decline since November 2009, the group said today in New York. At 138.16, the gauge was the weakest since March 2003.

Nineteen of the 20 cities in the index showed a year-over-year decline, led by a 10 percent slump in Minneapolis. The exception was Washington, where values climbed 4.3 percent.

Did you notice? Alone among major metropolitan centers, Washington, DC alone posted real estate gains.

How was that possible? Almost all GDP growth in the 10 years before 2012 came from increases in government spending. And the majority of household income growth since the beginning of the crisis in '07 came from government transfer payments. What does that mean in plain English? Washington is transferring wealth from the rest of the nation to itself. *Reuters* had the story:

In the town that launched the War on Poverty 48 years ago, the poor are getting poorer despite the government's help. And the rich are getting richer because of it.

The top 5 percent of households in Washington, D.C., made more than $500,000 on average last year, while the bottom 20 percent earned less than $9,500—a ratio of 54 to 1.

DC's wealth gap is the biggest in the country. And while the District only represents 2% of the US population, it gets 15% of all government procurement spending, according to Stephen S. Fuller, director of George Mason University's Center for Regional Analysis.

In 2010 and 2011, I saw this first hand. I lived among the zombies, in Bethesda, Maryland. I watched them coming and going. I learned their zombie language and studied their zombie ways. From a distance, they look like normal people. But up close, you see that they are imposters. Only their lowest-ranking members do any real work—picking up garbage or teaching kindergarten. As you move up the zombie hierarchy you find managers with no real responsibility and intellectuals with no real ideas.

Almost any profession or career can be a nest for a zombie; an auto mechanic, who rips off his customers by packaging useless emissions testing with even more useless services like replacing rear differential fluid, could be called a zombie. He may consume more than he produces. More often, zombies are found in charitable organizations and large bureaucracies. There, in corner offices as well as broom closets, careers pass and no one notices the lack of real output.

Washington is the zombies' favored habitat. There, they are born and bred. Government transfer payments create whole armies of them. Government bailouts turn useful industries into zombies. Government employment turns millions of otherwise reasonably honest and reasonably productive people into leeches. A guy who might have been a decent gardener, for example, becomes an SEC lawyer or a Homeland Security guard. A woman who might have been a nice waitress becomes head of the FDA. George W. Bush, for example, would have probably made a great gas station attendant. What a missed opportunity.

When Ronald Reagan first entered the White House only 30% of US households were supported by government benefits. Then came the Morning in America years—which were supposedly a lurch to more free-market policies. And then came the Bush years, the Clinton years, the Bush II years, and now the Obama years. Year after year, the number of zombies goes up. And now we find that nearly half of all households have a hand in the government cookie jar. *The Wall Street Journal* reported near the end of 2011:

> Families were more dependent on government programs than ever last year.
>
> Nearly half, 48.5%, of the population lived in a household that received some type of government benefit in the first quarter of 2010, according to Census data. Those numbers have risen since the middle of the recession when 44.4% lived [in] households receiving benefits in the third quarter of 2008.

That was an all-time record for our fair land. Meanwhile, the number of taxpayers took a nosedive. That year, the Tax Policy Center estimated 46.4% of households paid no federal income tax.

Republican presidential hopeful Mitt Romney latched onto the 48% figure. Too many people weren't paying their fair share, he said. Wrong move, Mitt. The freeloaders vote. And in the event, they voted en masse for his opponent. There are now so many zombies that the mathematics of democracy have made putting a stop to this trend impossible.

The state of America's entitlement epidemic was outlined for us by Nicholas Eberstadt in the January 25, 2013 *Wall Street Journal.* In the half a century since 1960, he tells us, government transfers through its various entitlement programs rose from 6% of personal income to 18%. The total cost of those things now comes to over $7,400 per person in the country, or about $2.3 trillion annually.

Some people claim that this huge increase can be explained by an expansion of Social Security as the nation aged. Eberstadt counter-claims that only about 10% of the increase is really the consequence of an aging population.

Between January of 2009 and June of 2013, for every person added to the workforce 10 have dropped out. In March, 2013 alone, 663,000 people left the labor market, bringing the number of non-working adult Americans to a record 89,967,000. This reduced the average time spent on work-related activities to less than four hours per day—or about half as much time spent working as spent sleeping.

The first four years of the Obama Administration were magical. Not since the Franklin Roosevelt administration had so many weird and wondrous things happened in such a short period of time. In addition to a plague of disability, the Feds also brought a plague of debt. For every dollar the feds raised in taxes, they spent around $1.58. Where did the extra 58 cents come from? It was borrowed. But the debt went far beyond the official budget figures. Much of it was in the form of future obligations that did not show up in the US deficit number. For example, had the US government been forced to report numbers on a GAAP (Generally Accepted Accounting Principles) basis, it would have shown a deficit for 2012 of $6.9 trillion—or about $3 dollars of deficit for every dollar of tax receipts. Tax rates would have had to go to 50% of GDP—an impossible level—to balance the budget. This borrowing was on such a colossal scale it threatened the entire society with financial destruction. Why was it necessary?

The Feds said they were borrowing to 'stimulate the economy.' The US government borrowed $5 trillion between '08–'12. But despite this huge additional debt, there was little pick up in the real economy. Why? Because the money went to parasites—the banks, Wall Street, the regulators, the halt, the lame, the retired and the sick. The Feds were feeding zombies.

THE WORLD'S BIGGEST ZOMBIE

The Pentagon is the world's biggest spender. It uses more gasoline. More steel. More food. More of just about everything than any other organization on the planet. The military budget was $685 billion in

2012. But that was just the beginning of it. Hundreds of billions more were spent to support intervention efforts all over the globe—including foreign aid, trade missions, embassies, spooks, and other meddlers. Altogether, we have seen estimates as high as $1.2 trillion per year as the cost of maintaining the US imperial agenda. This makes the 'security industry' in America the world's biggest zombie. It consumes on a gargantuan scale. But what is the real value of its output?

The 'War on Terror' began in 2001 and continues, with no end in sight. Every year, we were told, the US had delivered crippling blows to al-Qaida. Yet the devilish terrorists refused to die. Here's *Wired*'s Spencer Ackerman, reporting on a Senate hearing in May 2013:

> Asked at a Senate hearing today how long the war on terrorism will last, Michael Sheehan, the assistant secretary of defense for special operations and low-intensity conflict, answered, *"At least 10 to 20 years."* …A spokeswoman, Army Col. Anne Edgecomb, clarified that Sheehan meant the conflict is likely to last 10 to 20 more years from today—atop the 12 years that the conflict has already lasted.

It is hard to resist the conclusion that this war has no purpose other than its own eternal perpetuation. This war is not a means to any end but rather is the end in itself. Not only is it the end itself, but it is also its own fuel: it is precisely this endless war—justified in the name of stopping the threat of terrorism—that is the single greatest cause of that threat.

Dwight Eisenhower would have recognized the point. He was a career military man. He knew how susceptible the defense industry was to zombification. He saw with his own eyes during WWII the effects of the stretched and twisted feedback loop of war and defense. In his farewell address, he warned:

"In the councils of government, we must guard against the acquisition of unwarranted influence, whether sought or unsought, by the military-industrial complex. The potential for the disastrous rise of misplaced power exists and will persist."

Then, in 1961, the US faced a real, belligerent foreign enemy. The Soviet Union was an aggressive imperial power that had recently defeated Nazi Germany. Many thought its centrally planned economy would permit it to overtake the US in terms of wealth as well as military power.

But today, in real terms, the US spends more than twice as much as it did when Ike gave his speech. How come we spend so much today? Is the world really a more dangerous place? The Soviet Union renounced communism in 1989. It admitted that its system was a failure. It also admitted that it could not compete with the US militarily or economically.

China made the same sort of admission nearly a decade earlier. Without giving up its lip service to communist political ideology, it conceded that collectivism as an economic system was a mistake. "To get rich is glorious," Deng Xiaoping is credited with saying, making nonsense of the whole Marxist creed.

But as the external threats disappeared, the defense industry moved to defend itself. US theorists developed reasons for actually spending more, not less, on defense. Then, on a September day in 2001, the defense industry hit the jackpot. The terrorist attacks allowed the defense industry to put the nation on a war footing, shifting substantially more of the nation's wealth towards the "military industrial complex" even without a real war. We have seen estimates that Pentagon and domestic policing contracts now account for 40% of all US manufacturing.[7] Billions and billions more were spent, as if the nation's survival were at stake. The only thing really at stake was the continued prosperity of the military establishment.

---

[7]   Honest, market-based contracting has moved to China!

Here's how it works: money from the federal government is handed out to military employees and contractors, who then recycle some of it back into the political process. Campaign funds, lobbying, pimping by retired generals and admirals—the money gets around. A general, for example, might insist that the Pentagon needs a new weapons system. Then, in retirement, he might find that he is a valuable consultant to the company that makes it. He will likely earn far more as a consultant than from his military pension. Likewise, a congressional flunkey might help push through a new anti-terrorist computer system and then find his services in demand in the electronic industry, where he is regarded as a key "political expert."

In 2010, the defense industry employed more than 1,000 lobbyists, more than enough to strong-arm every member of Congress twice over. It spent $144 million on lobbying activity and contributed $22.6 million to political candidates in the last election cycle. These efforts pay off.

The *Washington Post* describes just how much:

> The commanders who lead the nation's military services and those who oversee troops around the world enjoy an array of perquisites befitting a billionaire, including executive jets, palatial homes, drivers, security guards and aides to carry their bags, press their uniforms and track their schedules in 10-minute increments. Their food is prepared by gourmet chefs. If they want music with their dinner parties, their staff can summon a string quartet or a choir.

> The elite regional commanders who preside over large swaths of the planet don't have to settle for Gulfstream V jets. They each have a C-40, the military equivalent of a Boeing 737, some of which are configured with beds.

Even after they retire, the zombie generals keep feeding on the productive sector. Nearly 3 out of 4 retiring three- and four-star generals and admirals "took jobs with defense contractors or consultants," reported the *Boston Globe* in 2010.

As the military industry degenerates, its mission slowly and stealthily creeps from protecting its host to using threats against the public to shift power and money to itself. "If you see something, say something," it warns. Say something to whom? To the security zombies. *Ch-ching!*

The military is so focused on its own perks and benefits, so larded with overly-sophisticated (expensive) weapons, so dominated by lumbering, incompetent, self-serving bureaucrats, so top-heavy with senior officers who are rarely tested and never fired, that it can no longer do its job. The 'defense' budget shifts along with the rest of the organization—from real military spending to various forms of padding and luxury for security industry insiders. Pensions and healthcare costs, for example, are soaring. In just 10 years—between 2000 to 2010—the Pentagon's personnel costs doubled, from about $70 billion to over $150 billion.

In short, it becomes an army of zombies, not of fighting men. These zombies make the decisions about how the Pentagon spends its money. Naturally, they shift resources from genuine defense to zombie defense.

THE (ZOMBIE) WAR ON TERROR EXPLAINED

Since the war on terror began, I have been inspected by the Department of Homeland Security an estimated 487 times. Each time involved delay and expense. The qualifier 'unnecessary' seems, well, unnecessary. Not a single time did I have any intention of blowing up an airplane.

This is obviously the sort of 'complexity' Tainter was talking about. It is also the sort of zombie activity I am talking about. The expense of it is recorded on the federal government's books as a debit for 'security.' On the books of the millions of harmless travelers who were subjected to fondling, probing, x-rays or naked imaging, it was recorded only as a nuisance. How was it recorded on the terrorists' books? We don't know. For all we know they may have been blowing up planes left and right without it.

Amid the TSA agents patting down wheelchair-bound grandmothers and looking for bombs in briefcases are thousands who match airplane tickets with photo IDs at the rate of about one every 30 seconds. In an 8-hour workday an agent might examine nearly a 1,000 of them. That's 5,000 in a week; a quarter million per year. Yet, in all of that complexity, he is unlikely to discover a single threat to the nation or its airborne commerce. A few phony driver's licenses, perhaps. Not much more. As far as we know, not a single attempt at homicide by airplane has ever been foiled by a TSA checking driver's licenses. We have not been able to discover the suicide rate for TSA agents, but whatever it is, it is a tribute to the human imagination that it is not higher. Somehow, they are able to persuade themselves that their work is meaningful, even necessary.

All of this is to say, the War on Terror is not a real war. It is a zombie war. Real soldiers fight real enemies. They risk their lives in real battles over objectives thought to be of life or death importance. To a real soldier, the War on Terror is an embarrassment. It is like shooting a circus bear. He finds it phony and disgraceful.

Despite provocations that would have led Mother Teresa to pick up a machine gun, serious enemies have been remarkably scarce. Probably, because they don't exist. We are encouraged to imagine that they are hiding behind every stop sign, plotting their next attack because 'they hate our freedoms.' More likely, the few amateur terrorists who manage to find time and funding (perhaps from one of America's anti-terror black-ops groups) are driven by a desire for revenge against heavy-handed US policies in the Mideast. At least, that is what the terrorists who have lived long enough to express an opinion have said.

So now we see the elegant mischief of the War on Terror and the crucial role zombies play in the coming disaster. With no real enemy, the war on terror cannot be won or lost. But the harder it's fought, the more enemies it creates (there you have it: hormegeddon in 10 words). This reinforces support for the war, diverting more resources to the zombies. Then, as the number, power and wealth of the zombies grows, support for zombie policies increases further. Correction becomes almost impossible.

ADDING IT ALL UP

How many zombies does the US now support?

Cindy Williams, of MIT's Security Studies Program, figures that the US now devotes about 6.2% of its GDP to "defense" and related activities, including international affairs, homeland security, veterans' affairs, and intelligence. She was not trying to figure out how much the nation could spend effectively on real defense, only on what it could afford. That, she calculates, is between 2.1% and 3.4% of GDP.

If this is true, we could say that the difference between what it can afford and what it spends is about 3% of GDP—either wasted, unnecessary, or unaffordable. There being no way to measure what portion of security spending is earmarked for zombies, we will take Ms. Williams' figure as a proxy. That's about $450 billion worth of zombie spending right there.

As to health care, we can assume that the standard of health care is acceptable in those countries where people live much the way Americans live (only longer). In those countries—mostly in Europe—people spend about half as much as they do in the US, giving us an overspending of about $2,500 per person—$750 billion total—or about 5% of GDP.

The US currently spends about 6% of GDP on education. Education expenditures are twice what they were, in real terms, 40 years ago when US students got the same results they get now. This suggests that half that figure is wasted. That's another $450 billion.

As for finance, again it is impossible to measure how much of it is worthwhile and how much is just money-shuffling and debt mongering. But let's take a guess anyway. In 1940, the financial industry accounted for just 2% of the economy. By 1960, it was about 3%. Today, it is 8% or 9%. Before the big run-up in debt began—in 1980—the financial industry probably averaged about 4% of GDP. The extra 4% is arguably wasted or, worse, merely transferred from the wealth-producing parts of Main Street to the wealth-collecting parts of Wall Street. Four percent of GDP is another $600 billion, give or take.

Adding it up, more poetically than scientifically, zombies in health, education and security may be costing the nation $1.65 trillion—almost exactly the amount of the 2011 deficit and $500 billion more than the 2012 deficit. In other words, if just *this* squandering were stopped, the US budget would be comfortably in balance.

Add the waste in the financial industry, and you are up to $2.25 trillion—or 15% of GDP. That is just the beginning. There is also the cost of compliance and the economic distortions caused by regulations, taxes, mal-investment and so forth.

A few zombies here and there probably never hurt anyone. They may even provide a public benefit of some sort. Like a deformed, blind beggar on the steps of the cathedral, he may remind passersby how lucky they are. But the point of diminishing returns is passed quickly. Then, once it goes negative with the exponential increase of zombies in every corner of the private and public sectors, it goes *really* negative. And before you know it, you're barricaded in an abandoned building with two rounds left, one of which you're saving for yourself. This is not a movie, this is hormegeddon.

Chapter 8
HEALTHCARE
(AKA *ZOMBIE MEDICINE*)

"First, do no harm."

—HIPPOCRATES

AFTER EATING HOT PEPPERS, a 40-year-old woman experienced burning chest pain. One time. While exercising. Looking for relief, she went to see her family doctor. He was fairly sure she wasn't in grave danger. She just had a case of serious heartburn. But to be safe, he sent her to the emergency room. The hospital admitted her as a patient immediately. Everyone wanted to be sure that nothing was overlooked. The ER doctor sent her on to a cardiologist. This stay-at-home mom was perfectly healthy. She never wanted to go to the hospital at all. She just wanted some relief from her pain.

At this point, three doctors had seen her. None of them thought she was having a heart attack. It was a very unlikely possibility. But, it still remained a possibility. A small possibility, no matter how unlikely. Hearts fail from time to time, even in 'healthy' people.

Each doctor, in turn, wanted to play it safe. Why take chances? Every doctor in the country has been menaced with a malpractice suit. Trial juries are not experts in medicine, or statistics. They probably don't know about declining marginal utility. As for The Downside, they've never heard of it. In a courtroom, long after the fact, they would only see a poor soccer mom victim. A person who "didn't get treated properly." So the poor woman got her heart exam, her EKG, and her stress test. She got probed. She got zapped. She got analyzed and scrutinized. She also got a perforated artery, which killed her.

She got an abundance of excellent healthcare services. Right up until she died.

Unfortunate incidents like hers are classified as iatrogenesis. They are the "unintended negative consequences" that arise in the ordinary delivery of care. Health care is undoubtedly a good thing. Few people imagine that you could have too much of it.

In an informal email exchange, a doctor explained how too much health care came to be:

You come to see me with a headache that is new in nature.

I find that there is no underlying cause in your history and perform a careful physical examination, which includes a thorough neurological exam (checking for the correct functioning of all your incoming and outgoing nerve systems). This physical exam takes less than five minutes and say it is totally normal, as it is most of the time.

At that point I have several options:

1. I can reassure you and give you an aspirin
2. I can get a CT Scan (Three dimensional Xray of your head)
3. I can get an MRI (Magnetic Resonance Imaging, much more sensitive)
4. I can do a sophisticated PET scan (Positron Emission tomography)
5. I can do a sleep study (you sleep all night in a clinic, with a technician watching you while an electroencephalogram is obtained)
6. I can refer you to a Board Certified Neurologic Specialist

Each one of my actions has a cost involved; clearly the aspirin is the least expensive one.

Now here is where it gets very interesting: "Most of the time" an Aspirin is more than adequate therapeutic behavior for this scenario. By most of the time, I mean 99.9% of the time. However, let's say you have a newly formed brain aneurism, which is a small artery in your brain that has weakened and it is ballooning out and ready to explode. The physical exam will be normal, but if I do a CT with contrast or an MRI, I can find it, refer you to brain surgery and remove it before it explodes.

Suppose I did give you the aspirin, and then your aneurism explodes and as a result you die or become paralyzed for the rest of your life. You or your widow would now sue me for malpractice.

In the USA, the outcome is decided by a jury made up of very concerning "average" folks. Experts are brought in on both sides, and of course, I am covered by expensive malpractice insurance, whereas you have left a widow and five young children whose lives I have devastated by not having been more aggressive. No problem, my insurance kicks in and pays the huge damage (in the millions). However, my insurance premia go up, not just for me, but for all other internists, the history goes into my lifetime record, and I have difficulties in getting hospital privileges, etc.

Question: What do you think I would do in a case like this?

Answer: I probably refer you to the Neurologist.

The "laying of the hands'" rule says that as soon as the specialist sees you, I am off the hook!

Mistakes will happen, of course. But they are presumed to be infrequent, like airplane crashes. And like accidents in air transportation, they are presumed to decline as more time and money is spent. But is it so?

Accidents can be reduced by purposeful planning. But hormegeddon is no accident. It is the result of careful planning. LOTS of careful planning.

Every year, studies estimate the number of unintended deaths from healthcare "accidents" in the United States. Here is a recent set of estimates:

- 7,000 due to medication mistakes in hospitals
- 12,000 from unnecessary surgeries
- 20,000 due to other hospital errors
- 80,000 from infections acquired while in hospitals
- 106,000 from the negative effects of prescribed drugs

That's up to 225,000 unintended deaths, each year. Statistically, you're at least 2,000 times more likely to be killed by your doctor than by a terrorist. Even automobile accidents cause only about one-seventh as many victims. In a broad review of medical records and death certificates over a 30-year period, published in the *Journal of General Internal Medicine*, researchers reported that out of 62 million deaths, almost a quarter-million deaths were coded as having *"occurred in a hospital setting due to medication errors."*

Why so many casualties? Because the human body is a complex, natural thing. It was shaped by millions of years of trial and error, mutation, adaptation, and genetic selection. Like a society or an economy, it is more likely to be damaged by heavy-handed intervention than improved by it. Nobody knows for certain, but medical practitioners were probably a net negative to human health from the beginning of time until the 20th century. (Life expectancy in the Paleolithic period is estimated at only about 33 years. By the beginning of the 20th century, it had fallen to only about 31 years.)

Also, medicine is not a pure science. It is a mixture of science, art and hocus pocus. A surprising study done by Ted Kaptchuk at Harvard showed that patients reported improvement when give a placebo— even when they knew it was a placebo. This result was reinforced and amplified in a further study. One group of patients was given sham acupuncture treatments (with retractable needles, the skin was never punctured). Another group got the same bogus treatment but with much more personal attention from the doctor. The group that got most 'care' from the doctor reported the most relief.

The early doctors realized that medicine was not rocket science. They urged caution and modesty on the profession, with the ancient warning, included in the Hippocratic Oath: *primum non nocere* (first do no harm). Whether the profession is a net negative today, I don't know. But that it does a great deal of harm is undeniable.

A 2003 research article entitled "Death by Medicine" documented how the American medical system became the leading cause of death and injury in the United States. It did more harm than good, said the authors. Then, a follow up article in 2010, published in the *New England Journal of Medicine*, found that one quarter of all people admitted to hospitals were injured or killed after being admitted. An organization called "HealthGrades" provided more detail. It found "the incidence rate of medical harm occurring is estimated to be **over 40,000 each and EVERY day** according to the Institute for Healthcare Improvement." Another study, by the Office of Inspector General for the Department of Health and Human Services, found that one in seven Medicare patients who were admitted to the hospital were harmed by the system and nearly half of the harmful events were preventable. These "mistakes" carried a price tag of more than $3.8 billion per year.

One major source of harm is hospital-acquired infections that cause sepsis and pneumonia, leading to 48,000 deaths annually. One study found that one in nine hospital patients were infected. Some of these infections are of a particularly nasty sort—super bugs that were created by the health care industry itself (more on that later).

While thousands of people are victims of mistaken drug prescriptions, an estimated 450,000 people each year suffer adverse reactions to drugs that were correctly prescribed. Why? Too much medicine. There were 3.68 billion prescriptions filled in the US in 2009; that's 12 for every man, woman and child in the country. The combination, often prescribed by different doctors for different ailments, can be lethal. Of Medicare patients, 89% take prescription drugs regularly. Nearly half are on five or more different prescription medicines. More than half take drugs prescribed by different doctors.

DRUGS GONE WILD

In the beginning of modern healthcare, drugs were simple. And very effective. The German company Bayer learned to isolate and manufacture Aspirin in 1897. It was good for headaches and sprains and general pain relief. It was cheap, effective, and its use spread widely. The very same compound is still marketed today.

The same story might be told for antibiotics. When first introduced, they were inexpensive, effective, and saved literally millions of lives from what would have been damaging and even fatal infections. If one drug was good, then surely more would be better, right? So began the multi-decade proliferation of research, development and release of thousands of medications.

Some worked better than others. But almost all had one strange thing in common: With the solitary exception of antibiotics that kill micro-organisms, drugs don't actually cure any disease. What they do is suppress symptoms. So while they can deliver comfort and relief to the patient, they often do nothing to eliminate the underlying cause of the condition.

Which means for many conditions, the customer will have to keep taking the prescribed drug…forever. This has become the dominant form of medical practice in all advanced countries. Manage the case. Contain the condition. But never promise or provide a cure. Patients learned to ask for a pill to solve their problem, and doctors provided the pills as desired.

Since direct-to-consumer ads have been allowed, prescriptions for drugs that are not advertised have risen by 5.1%. Prescriptions for drugs with consumer advertising have risen by 34.2% over the same period—or about six times faster than the population. How could drug use increase so much? People were taking multiple drugs. One drug for blood pressure. One for cholesterol. Another one for the side effects, another one to counter the negative interactions...and on and on. More than 30 million Americans are currently taking five or more prescription drugs. In just the last ten years, the percentage of seniors taking five or more medications has risen from 22% to 37% This phenomenon has come to be known in the healthcare industry as "polypharmacy".

CBS News did a profile of one such drug addict:

> Fifty-two-year-old Lenette Martin takes so much medicine, she's lost count.
>
> "Regularly, I take 11, maybe 12," she said.
>
> It's 12, plus four over-the-counter. With each added drug, the risk of side effects increases. For example, Prilosec, which lowers stomach acid, can weaken the effect of the blood thinner Plavix.

The report goes on to expose how seniors feeling the supposed side effects of old age (fatigue and memory loss, for example) may in fact be experiencing the side effects of their prescription drugs instead.

Dr. Barbara Spivak, a prominent internist in Massachusetts, laments the drug status of one of her patients:

> I have a patient who has 18 different problems…and 25 different medicines. If you look at one of the most common reasons why people get sick, it's because of confusion about their pills.

But drugs aren't just for old people.

The *New York Times* reports that "Even among children under 12, more than 22 percent were using at least one prescription drug… and so were almost 30 percent of teenagers."

Today, just the top two American pharmaceutical companies generate well over $100 billion a year in revenue. Meanwhile, on a worldwide scale, Big Pharma is now a $1 trillion industry.

We are not concerned with who is to blame. It is the phenomenon that interests us, not the culprit. Both regulators and regulated have grown fat and sassy. From a one-man laboratory operating out of the Patent Office in 1848 drug regulation has grown into a federal workforce of over 14,000 today.[8] When the FDA was created in 1930, it oversaw a small industry; today it connives with a big one. As always, the regulators and the regulated enjoy a symbiotic relationship, happily conspiring one with the other against the public interest.

US spending for prescription drugs more than doubled over the first decade of the 2000's in inflation adjusted dollars. Americans spent $234 billion on medications in 2008, up from $104 billion in 1999.

Both patients and doctors presumably believe these drugs have been scientifically proven to be relatively safe and effective. Often

---

[8] Lewis Caleb Black began analyzing agricultural chemicals at the Patent Office in 1848. Widespread drug regulation began in 1906 with the passage of the Pure Food and Drugs Act. The FDA as we know it was created in 1930.

they are neither. There is a special field of medical research, called meta-research, in which analysts study the reliability of other health research. One of the leading figures in meta-research is a Greek professor, formerly of Johns Hopkins University and the National Institute of Health, named John Ioannides. He and a small team of mathematicians, statisticians, chemists and biologists examine the claims, methods and conclusions of medical and drug tests. What they find is that 90% of it is flawed.

The tests are rigged, sometimes intentionally, sometimes not, to prove what the drug companies want to prove. The researchers are motivated to come up with positive conclusions. And the methods used often do not measure up to any scientific standard whatsoever. For example, a test may administer a drug to a group of people suffering from an ailment. Then, three months later, the people taking the drug will be asked if they 'feel better.' If they respond 'yes' the conclusion may be that the drug provided relief from the ailment. Whether it did or not, is still completely unknown. If they don't die of a disease, most people feel better after three months, simply because they have gotten used to the pain or discomfort, whatever it was. In the well-known placebo effect, about a third of patients feel better almost no matter what you give them. The researcher might just as well conclude that the drug was a failure as a success; because there is no proven connection between it and the 'feel better' findings. Nor is there any real evidence that the cause of the discomfort had been in any way addressed. But there is no glory, no money, and no future in 'no' findings. Drug companies don't want them. The organizations that give our research grants don't want them. The medical journals don't want them. The doctors are not interested in them. And the patients don't want to hear it. So, the whole research industry is biased towards positive results.

Most drug testing is focused on a narrow and specific reaction. There is often no proper consideration of collateral damage. You might just as well cut off a man's leg with a rusty penknife and ask him if he still has a headache. But interfering with the delicate and subtle workings of a living organism can have unexpected consequences. 'Too much' in the health care area goes up in an asymptotic curve. A little bit too much produces a little bit of harm. A little bit more causes much more harm. If you take three drugs, and then add three more, you do not double your risk of adverse reaction, you triple it. The downside of taking drugs is irrefutable. The more you take, the more they are likely to hurt you. But what is the upside? No one knows.

YOU ARE WHAT THEY TELL YOU TO EAT

Even before we get to the return on investment from healthcare spending, we should spend a minute or two on how the need for so much healthcare arose in the first place.

In the second half of the 20th century, nutritionists, doctors and food company executives found an opportunity for collusion. This is an example of a disaster within a disaster. First, they had a theory: people should eat something other than what they liked and other than what millions of years of adaptation had prepared them for. The theory, based on claptrap science, was that natural animal fats are bad for you. Specifically, the makers of Crisco, developed the notion that their product—a combination of cottonseed oil, bleach, and other ghastly ingredients—was "a healthier alternative to animal fats." This theory was later proven to be totally bogus.

"Procter & Gamble's claims about Crisco touching the lives of every American proved eerily prescient," wrote Dr. Drew Ramsey and Tyler Graham. "The substance (like many of its imitators) was 50 percent trans fat, and it wasn't until the 1990s that its health risks were understood. It is estimated that for every two percent increase in consumption of trans fat (still found in many processed and fast foods) the risk of heart disease increases by 23 percent."

Then, came the central planners. Senator, and one-time presidential candidate, George McGovern headed up the Senate Subcommittee on Nutrition and Human Needs, whose goal became to convince Americans that they should eat more Crisco and less butter. This also became the mantra of a whole generation of government regulators and their crony capitalists in the packaged food industry. Trans fats were cheaper and easier to make, ship, store, and sell than normal fats. Sales rose. Margins expanded. Much like the drug companies, these fast food companies had more money to spend on 'research,' advertising and lobbying than did their competitors in the old-fashioned agricultural sector.

Pre-packaged food companies made money. Madison Avenue was pleased to help with the marketing. Magazines and TV stations enjoyed the ad revenue. Everyone benefited. Except people who actually ate the stuff. Consumers got fat. And diabetic. And their hearts failed. Obesity, diabetes and heart disease were scarcely observed before the 1950s. Soon after, they became endemic. There was only one person out of 150 who was considered obese in 1900. By 2012, one out of three had become a lard-ass. Doctors rarely saw adult onset diabetes before 1950. Now, 32% of the Medicare budget is spent on it. Heart disease, too, was so uncommon that cardiologists were a rarity in 1950. Now, there are 25,901 of them, and the medical industry considers this a *shortage*.

Sick people need 'healthcare.'

In this sense, albeit only part of the story, the entire healthcare industry became a zombie enterprise. It exists largely because of a huge public policy 'mistake.' Instead of better health for the American people, the alimentary policies of the US government, in cahoots with the packaged food industry and the healthcare establishment, created a nation of sick people, who then needed more 'services' from the people who had made them sick in the first place.

Doctors, researchers and scientists who understood the error were effectively silenced. Though they offered their critiques, there was no interest in publishing them widely nor in changing public policy. For example, Dr. William Castelli, one of the directors of the landmark Framingham study, rocked the boat in 1992, writing in the *Archives of Internal Medicine*:

> We found that the people who ate the most cholesterol, ate the most saturated fat, ate the most calories weighed the least and were the most physically active.

In other words, those who did the opposite of what the government and the healthcare industry advised were actually the healthiest!

But by then the negative feedback loop had been clogged by too much money. The contradictory findings were never fully digested and never fully disclosed to the American people. Instead, the "big fat lie" was allowed to persist. Millions of people's lives were darkened, but the insiders in the healthcare/government/packaged food industries basked in the warm light of fraudulent fortune. Dietary Guidelines, published in 2010 and in effect until 2015, continue to tell Americans to "consume more of certain foods and nutrients such as…fat-free and low-fat dairy products…[and]…fewer foods with saturated [animal] fats."

MONEY BADLY SPENT

The typical American spends twice as much for health care as anybody else. Is he twice as sick? Or does he get half as much for his money? Professionals estimate that 20% or more of total modern health care spending goes directly to various forms of waste. Over-treatment, lack of care coordination, failures in care delivery, administrative overhead, fraud, abuse—it adds up to $500–$850 billion a year. The majority of those dollars are attributable to inappropriate treatments and unnecessary testing.

Approximately half of all health care is applied to overhead, insurance, paperwork, legal claims and so forth. The typical doctor, for example, is believed to spend 2.5 hours per day on forms and paperwork. You'd think the nation's health would be better served if the doctor spent that time with patients. But perhaps not. It could be that the paperwork requirements actually spare patients from what Nassim Taleb calls naïve intervention and prolongs their lives.

Or, if you counted as waste the spending that does not seem to prolong life (to be detailed later), the total in the US would be as much as $6,700 per person, or more than $2 trillion per year.

At best, this 'waste' merely reduces the return on investment. But waste is not necessarily a bad thing. You'd expect a robust health system to be untidy. You'd expect it to experiment. And you'd expect that many of those experiments would fail, resulting in what appears as wastage.

But let's look at the overall results. As of 2000, of the 191 countries studied, The World Health Organization ranked the U.S. health care system as highest in cost. The percentage of GDP that the US spends yearly on healthcare has risen from 5.2% in 1960 to 15.2% in 2008. Costs have gone up at almost double the rate of income growth. And yet the US has a higher infant mortality rate than the majority of the world's industrialized nations. Its current life expectancy rate is ranked 42nd in the world. That places it a bit after Chile (35th) and Cuba (37th). Its overall performance ranking is only slightly better (37th) and at 72nd, the country's standing when it comes to overall level of health is objectively abysmal.

"Health is the most important thing," old people say to each other. If that is true, it seems completely logical to spend more and more money on it. A person ought to be able to spend his money as he pleases. If it is health that pleases him—or even the illusion of it, like the illusion of riches offered by a casino—he ought to be able to spend his money on it.

This suggests that health is beyond the reach of our analysis. People spend as much as they want. They get more or less what they pay for, aside from the occasional hospital mishap. But that ignores the critical role of central planning in the healthcare industry. It also ignores the character of hormegeddon. It is more wily, cunning, and perverse than you imagine. It works like this: you spend more and more on healthcare, and then you die.

Over the course of the twentieth century, the US made astounding gains in public health. In 1900, America was still largely an agrarian country. There were a few large industrial cities. Over the course of the next 70 years, life expectancy rose by 30 years. At least 25 of those extra years are probably the result of improvements that have little to do with doctors or the healthcare industry. Instead, they came primarily from one cause: we flushed the bugs down the drain. Basic efforts in public sanitation and personal hygiene brought killers like typhoid, tuberculosis and cholera under control. Hot and cold, clean running water and cheap and better food are probably responsible for most of the gain in life expectancy.

Mass vaccinations seem to have played a minor role in eliminating smallpox and polio. Infectious diseases like measles, rubella, tetanus, diphtheria, and the flu, which had previously killed or injured millions were also reduced. But most of the gains came before the vaccinations were introduced. Some people claim that the vaccinations themselves cause problems. Some believe they increase the likelihood of autism, for example. Others believe that these diseases are not so bad. The human body is similar to the human character, they say; it needs adversity in order to grow strong.

Most of the gain in life expectancy actually came before the pain of higher costs even started. In other words, the connection between health spending and health results is largely coincidental. Both things happened. But one did not cause the other.

In the 1970s, two epidemiologists at Harvard University, John B. and Sonja M. McKinlay, released their research into the question about whether medicine had any real effect on the falling mortality rate:[9]

> In general medical measures (both chemotherapeutic and prophylactic) appear to have contributed little to the overall decline in mortality in the US since 1900—having in many instances been introduced decades after a marked decline had already set in and having no detectable influence in many instances. More specifically, with reference to those five conditions (influenza, diphtheria, pneumonia, whooping cough and poliomyelitis) for which the decline in mortality appears substantial after the intervention, and on the unlikely assumption that all of this decline is attributable to the intervention, it is estimated that at most 3.5% of the total decline in mortality could be ascribed to the medical measures for the diseases considered here.

In terms of return on investment (ROI), the rate of return on health care spending began to fall early in the 20th century. By the 1980s, the real rate of return was approaching zero. Meanwhile, the cost of medical intervention in the US, per person, is about twice as much as it is for any other country. Singapore, for example, has a higher life expectancy than the US, but spends only about a quarter

---

[9] *The Questionable Contribution of Medical Measures to the Decline of Mortality in the Twentieth Century* by John B and Sonja M Kinlay was first published in *The Milbank Memorial Fund Quarterly. Health and Society,* Vol. 55, No.3. (Summer 1977), pp. 405–428.

as much. Cuba spends less than 5% as much as the US and gets about the same result (in terms of life expectancy).

As we can see on the following chart, more than twenty countries have far better ROI from their health spending.

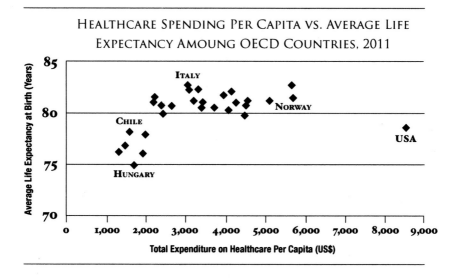

HEALTHCARE SPENDING PER CAPITA VS. AVERAGE LIFE EXPECTANCY AMOUNG OECD COUNTRIES, 2011

Still, what's the harm in spending more besides the waste of resources, you're probably asking? Well let's see.

DO NO MORE HARM THAN GOOD

One area in which medical intervention historically has almost always done more harm than good is maternity care. The introduction of antibiotics and neonatal education are credited with reducing infant mortality by 90%. The mortality rate for delivering mothers has been cut by 99%. But it's probably worth pausing here to wonder why it was so high in the first place.

It would be a strange world in which giving birth were often fatal to the mother. It is the sort of thing natural selection probably would have culled out of the race a long time ago. Yet, as recently as the late 1800s, as many as one in three women died in childbirth. More interesting is the fact that the wealthier the woman, the more likely she was to die. And a wealthy woman who had her child in a hospital was practically dead on arrival.

The reason for this is well known and well documented. It is the classic case of iatrogenic morbidity. In 1773, puerperal fever first appeared in a lying-in ward of the Royal Infirmary of Edinburgh. Women who went there to have their babies died. Those who stayed at home did not. Doctors guessed that there was a contagious disease on the loose in the hospital. But they didn't realize that they were the cause of it.

Doctors continued to deliver babies with unwashed hands for the next 100 years.

Dr. Ignaz Semmelweis discovered the reason for the deaths in the 1850s. He urged his colleagues to wash their hand before delivering babies. When doctors paid attention, the rate of maternal death plummeted. At first, however, doctors resisted, refusing to believe that they could be the cause of so many unnecessary deaths. Dr. Semmelweis was ostracized and reviled. He went mad, was sent to an insane asylum, and died—according to some reports—of puerperal fever.

China had its own health revolution in the 1950s. When Chairman Mao took over, the rural Chinese had essentially no access to healthcare. Infectious diseases were prevalent. Infant mortality was high. Life expectancy for the peasants in remote areas was low. So he started vaccinating them. And instead of resulting in the deaths of millions, like most of his other plans, Mao's healthcare initiative seemed to get it right.

Seeing the success of the rural vaccination program, Mao had another idea. In an ambitious effort to bring "health to the masses," the Barefoot Doctors program was created.

China had a long tradition of rural, village-based natural healers known as "barefoot doctors." Historically, they were the only practitioners available to millions of rural peasants. The barefoot doctors used traditional herbs, acupuncture, and rudimentary first-aid to treat people. But they had none of the modern weapons used to fight infectious diseases.

The new idea was to use the barefoot doctors to bring simple and effective aspects of modern medicine to the people. Beginning in 1965, tens of thousands of promising candidates were trained in rudimentary modern medicine and emergency care. They were then deployed to the rural villages. The emphasis of the approach was to provide basic care: prevention, hygiene, immunization, emergency care and sanitation. They were given a few modern drugs, most importantly, antibiotics.

The trainees got less than a year of education on average. No college. No med school. No advanced training of any sort. The whole system was deliberately conceived to be simple, cheap, practical and fast.

By 1975, at least 1.5 million barefoot doctors had been trained and sent out. By 1980, China had achieved over 90% coverage of the rural communities. Huge strides in health were made across the board. The World Health Organization recognized China's dramatic improvement in all the key areas. Infant mortality, infectious diseases, life expectancy—all showed tremendous gains. For the average rural peasant, his overall health skyrocketed. And the cost had been minimal.

We see the same sort of payoff from cheap, rudimentary health care improvements in Cuba. Even when controlled and planned by an over-bearing, know-it-all government, these minimal investments seem to reduce infectious disease and increase life expectancy.

At least, that's one way of looking at it. There are others. One is that the numbers coming from the Cuban government are fictitious, in which case we know absolutely nothing about the return on investment from Cuban healthcare spending. Another is that Cubans' health and life-expectancy have actually benefitted from their own government's incompetence. By failing to intervene effectively, the Cuban medical industry may have done people a favor.

Cuba was always a relatively healthy place. In 1950, before the communist takeover, it had health indices not far from those of the US and Canada. Much of the countryside reported little access to modern medicine. But that didn't seem to matter. Life expectancy at birth was 63 years in 1955, compared to 69 years in the US.

In 1959, Fidel Castro brought central planning to Cuba's health care system. According to the constitution, every Cuban had a right to free health care services. The trouble was, the government had no way of fulfilling its promise. Doctors fled the country en masse following Castro's invasion and military victory. That didn't seem to matter much either. If you believe the numbers, life expectancy rose to 65 years by 1965.

Between 1960 and 1990, life expectancy continued to climb despite piddly spending by the Cuban government. Then, even the piddly amounts declined. The support given by the Soviet Union came to an end. Not only did the availability of medicines decline, so did the availability of food. After 1990, the Cuban people found themselves on starvation rations. Instead of too much, Cubans were faced with what most considered too little: too little medicine, too few calories. Not enough money to support hospitals and clinics.

"The famine in Cuba during the Special Period was caused by political and economic factors similar to the ones that caused a famine in North Korea in the mid-1990s," explained a paper by the Canadian Medical Association. "Both countries were run by authoritarian regimes that denied ordinary people the food to which they were entitled when the public food distribution collapsed; priority was given to the elite classes and the military."

It wasn't until 1993 that the Cuban government lightened up and allowed donations of food, medicines and money from the United States. In the meantime, people suffered. Or did they?

A 2007 report by *The Guardian* indicated that famine during this "special period" had actually forced a healthier lifestyle—less food and more exercise—on Cubans:

> The collapse of the Soviet Union and its subsidies to the island ushered in a decade of severe food and fuel shortages that compelled people to slash their calorie intake and to travel on foot or bicycle.
>
> As waistlines contracted along with the economy there was a steep fall in deaths linked to being overweight, according to a study published last week in the American Journal of Epidemiology. Between 1997 and 2002 deaths caused by diabetes declined by 51%, coronary heart disease mortality dropped 35% and stroke mortality by 20%.

And what was the result? Again, if you believe the numbers, life expectancy just kept going up. From 65 years in 1965, the average person could expect to live to 74 by 1990. And today, life expectancy in Cuba is 78 years.

Nothing is proven. But it is a fair bet that when it comes to healthcare, the marginal utility of further investment begins to decline very quickly. Cuban healthcare costs about $300 per person. Even if the statistics lie a little, the story they are telling is probably more or less correct. You get about the same result whether you spend $300 or $7,000+. And you might get an even better result if you throw in a famine and some bicycles.

But that doesn't tell us much about hormegeddon. Americans may get nothing from the extra $6,700 per person they spend, but what's the harm?

SPECIALISTS

According to the American Academy of Family Physicians, over the past decade 90% of medical school graduates in the US have chosen to enter niche sub-specialties. Med students today want to do things like orthopedic surgery, radiology and dermatology much more than enter family practice. Only a slim 10% of graduates are now choosing primary care.

This is a multi-decade trend. At this point, only 38% of Americans even have a primary care doctor. When something serious is wrong with them, most people want to see a specialist.

Surely specialists are superior doctors. They have more schooling; more must be better, right? Certainly their skills are valuable in some defined situations. They can be very effective in acute and emergency cases. Cases where intervention is desperately necessary. They are good at certain surgeries. And specialization brought some strong advances. In cardiology, for example. But interestingly, most of the progress comes in the earliest phase. When a developing specialty comes on the broader scene, it can have a positive impact initially. But those gains tend to flatten out over time. They tend to stay flat, in spite of any additional investment of resources.

A study done at Dartmouth looked at cardiac care as provided from 1986 to 2002. While costs rose steadily throughout the period, survival rates for the patients leveled off. They have basically stagnated, with no improvement, since 1996. And yet the expenditures for specialized cardiac care continue to rise.

Why? A successful specialist can make $500,000 or more a year. Often that's with working 20 or so hours a week. A family doctor will earn an average of $120,000, working more than 60 hours a week. Even an average-earning specialist makes at least twice as much as the average general practitioner. This financial differential has resulted in the exact situation you might expect: approximately 70%

of American doctors are specialists. Only 30% (and shrinking) are primary care providers.

It may be a shame that people continue to throw every dime they can at an increasingly ineffective medical industry. But then, it is also perfectly reasonable. It is reasonable for drug companies to want to make a profit. It is reasonable for doctors to want to increase their incomes. It is reasonable for regulators to want to help the industry they are paid to look out for…and to help their own careers too. It is reasonable for patients to want to get as much as they can for as little as they can. And that is when the disaster arrives.

THIRD PARTY PAYERS

In the US, only $1 out of every $10 in health care spending comes directly from the patient. The other $9 comes from insurance companies, group healthcare plans and the US government. You'd expect a bit of distortion in such a system. He who calls the tune only pays the piper 10 cents on the dollar? It would not be surprising to find that his musical selections are a little on the rich side.

The Rand Corporation conducted a study back in the '70s. The idea was to discover how "free" medical care affected people's health and longevity. One group (involving thousands of participants) was given health care 100% free. Another had to make co-payments. As might be expected, the free group consumed 25% to 30% more healthcare services. Were these people healthier? Not in any way that the researchers could detect.

Specialist doctors merely rise to the challenge, meeting the demand for more medical intervention from people who don't have to pay for it. It is as if a third party picked up 90% of the tab for dinner every night—there would be many more bottles of Chateaux Petrus imbibed, whether the diners liked it or not. We can see this phenomenon more clearly by imagining a system in which we paid only 10% of the cost of our vacations. If we take the family to a state park for a weekend of camping, the total cost may be $300, of which we pay $30. Or, we may fly the family, first class, to Italy for a Roman holiday at a cost of $20,000. This would cost us more—$2,000 rather than $30. If we go to the state park we save $1,970. But the cheaper alternative means we forego $18,000 worth of consumer enjoyment. Even if we don't like linguini we'd be inclined to get on the plane. You can then imagine that more and more of the travel industry would shift toward offering these high-end vacations. Most likely, the state park would be empty.

That dynamic is not at work in any other kind of marketplace. When we enter a grocery store, we don't buy everything we can possibly eat. Nor in a clothing store do we purchase everything that we could possibly wear.

But that is essentially what is happening in the healthcare market. Because they don't pay the real costs, consumers and doctors spend wildly. There is an incentive to order up every test and service and drug imaginable, with no financial downside to either patient or doctor.

You'd get more or less the same results if employers and the government paid for interior decoration. In a low mood, you might call in a decorator.

"Do you think my house needs a little up-dating," you might ask.

The decorator—who is paid only by giving a positive response—is likely to find some areas that need improvement. There is no incentive—neither professional, nor financial—for the decorator to reply:

"Hey…what's the matter with it? Looks okay to me."

Nor do doctors have any reason to give a patient a common sense reply:

"Lose some weight. Get a little exercise. Stop being such a complainer."

Without this 'third party' payment system, the system would probably correct itself quickly. Instead, it lurches towards a real hormegeddon.

The system not only steers doctors away from general practice; it financially incentivizes them to specialize. As it does so, patients get progressively less of one thing that is known to be effective: cheap, simple, infrequent primary care.

Studies show that (under certain conditions) adding one primary care physician per 10,000 in population—around a 20% increase— brings a 6% decrease in deaths from all causes. That's almost 35 lives saved per 100,000 people. Infant mortality also drops substantially.

Nonetheless, the supply of GP's continues to drop. And as a result, so does the public's access to them. When people can't easily get in to see a primary care doctor, they tend to react in ways that reduce their life expectancy. For example, many of them go to the hospital emergency room. Not only is the single most expensive place a patient can get medical care, it is also likely to be the most dangerous. Just ask the 40-year-old woman who went to the ER with hot peppers and exercise-induced heartburn. Or perhaps more accurately, ask her next of kin.

MORE TESTS

As we explained in the previous chapter on zombies and their coming hormegeddon-flavored apocalypse, resources invested in a non-performing sector bring forth their own demand. If the government undertakes to build unnecessary bridges, it would create an industry of unnecessary bridge builders that would soon have its own lobbyists in Congress, clamoring for more unnecessary bridges. Local districts would compete for the next unnecessary bridge, since it would bring opportunities for jobs, contracts, and various benefits, privileges and giveaways. Soon, the nation with "too many" bridges has a hard time turning down another one. Bridges are not usually lethal, but a society that spends all of its economic surplus building bridges—like the ancient Egyptians and their pyramids—may soon lack bread. And when it lacks bread for too long, well, that is an unnecessary bridge too far. In that sense, a downside of wasting money on health care is obvious and inescapable. Resources spent on healthcare, but which produce no improvement in health, make the society poorer.

"He's undergoing tests," is a common answer to a question about a relative's health status. The test, it is hoped, will reveal something, like a murderer's home address. Then, the doctors can send a SWAT team. Trouble is, the SWAT team in this case only carries napalm.

Specialists order exponentially more testing, imaging and other diagnostic procedures than GP's. Let's look at an example from cardiology:

One exotic test, called Radionuclide myocardial perfusion imaging (RMPI), is used to evaluate arterial disease in the heart. Over a fourteen-year period ending in 2002, the use of this test by radiologists increased at a very modest 2% rate. However, among cardiologists, the rate of RMPI testing increased by 78%. The vast majority of that increase took place in cardiologists' own private offices. Why would that be?

In their own offices, they were not simply ordering more of the tests from outside providers. They were conducting them on their own equipment. And then evaluating the results as well. By bringing the testing in house, they now collected more of the spending. In the past, they may have referred the heart patient out to the local hospital for the test. Or ordered it from an independent facility. But this would allow someone else to reap the reward. It would be like sending a restaurant patron out to a bar to get a glass of wine. The in-house tests, on the other hand, were like having a liquor license in a town of dipsomaniacs, all with unlimited bar tabs. Naturally, the rate of testing soared. And not just for heart patients. The same thing can be seen across all the specialties: urology, oncology, ENT, OB-GYN, and so forth.

The trend toward the use of specialists doesn't only lead to increased testing. The more specialist care is involved, the less any one doctor understands the big picture of a given patient's case. That leads to redundant testing and services. Not to mention errors, miscommunication and accidents. Those situations lead to complications and corrective care. Which generates more fees for the providers, hospitals and suppliers. And so costs grow significantly. As do the 'mistakes.'

I hesitate when I write "mistake," "accident" or "mishap." I put the words in quotations, as if I didn't really believe it. Why? They certainly aren't intentional. And yet, they are foreseeable and preventable. They are foreseeable in a purely mathematical sense. The more times you do something that is inherently dangerous, the more often something will go wrong.

As mentioned above, the payer is not the same person who gets the treatment. But neither is the person prescribing the treatment the same person who has to take it and suffer the complications. The doctor will be protected and well paid if he prescribes unnecessary tests, medications and treatments 'just to be on the safe side.' The patient will suffer the effects of negative utility.

On more than one occasion, I have been confronted with these tests personally. Each time a PSA or a colonoscopy was suggested, I told the doctor that the study results found no positive correlation between the tests and life expectancy. Each time, the answer was the same.

"Yes, the tests have a lot of flaws. But what if you were one of the people who were saved by the tests?"

The doctors had not seemed to grasp the symmetry of statistics. In order for the net gain to come out at zero, there has to be one person who was killed for every person who was saved. I would be just as likely to be the victim as the survivor.

We've seen that improvements to hygiene, living conditions and diet are probably responsible for the big increases in life expectancy in the 20th century. We've also seen that infectious diseases were brought under control long before the medical industry began to develop cures and antidotes for them. Since then, the amount of resources devoted to health care has increased hugely, with no apparent connection between the amount of investment and the return. We've also seen that incidence of many modern diseases—ailments that barely existed before the 20th century, such as diabetes, asthma, heart disease, chronic fatigue syndrome and certain types of cancer—has greatly increased, probably thanks to central planning and government activism.

Interventions are, logically, more dangerous to healthy people than to very sick people. A man who is on the verge of death has little to lose. A healthy young person has a lot. As the population becomes healthier, generally, the risk of a negative payoff from heavy-handed health care interventions increases. What we don't know is whether today's healthy living conditions would have added even more to our life expectancies, had not the medical industry intervened.

SUPERBUGS

One of modern science's great victories, if you look at the history, is antibiotics. Dangerous bacterial infections can now be controlled, saving millions of lives. Initial efforts were relatively cheap and yielded great results. That success encouraged the widespread adoption of the antibiotic treatment approach. These new wonder drugs were deployed worldwide. It was a scary time if you happened to be a germ. Antibiotics could swiftly kill your entire family. But they never wiped out 100% of the bacteria. And of course the bacteria that did survive were the hardiest of the bunch. Those were the ones most naturally resistant to the drug used against them.

Nietzsche's comment "that which doesn't kill you makes you stronger," applies better to a group than to an individual. Antibiotics make humans weak and bacteria strong. They protect the most feeble and least well-adapted people in the human population while they cull out the weakest of the bacteria.

Over multiple generations, those hardiest survivors in the germ world evolved. Their DNA reacted to the antibiotics that were being used against them. After untold generations of germ replication, but just a few human years, drug resistant bugs emerged. Then, of course, they proliferated. The antibiotics were now found to be ineffective against these bugs. This unfortunate development spread through most infections that were treated with antibiotics: pneumonia, tuberculosis, venereal diseases, and skin infections. New drugs were developed to fight the superbugs; these killed more of the bugs but, again, strengthened the bug population by allowing only the most resistant to reproduce.

So the drug regimens were changed again. Over several decades, the bugs that still existed had been exposed to multiple and different antibiotic treatments. They seemed to become more resistant each time. New antibiotics became ineffective more quickly. And thus were born the Superbugs. In spite of pharmacology's best efforts, new strains of bacteria emerged that were immune to every known drug treatment available. Patients were being lost to infections that would have been easily treated a few years earlier. At the same time, those superbugs found their ideal environment to thrive. They were most prevalent in a place where antibiotics and antibacterial surface treatments are used every day: the hospital.

One superbug that's caused a lot of problems is known as "MRSA." Methicillin-resistant *Staphylococcus aureus* is a drug-resistant staph bacterium. You may know MRSA by its popular name: "Flesh-eating bacteria."

MRSA infection starts gently, almost innocently. But it can progress substantially from the initial symptoms within just a day or two. If it's still on the upswing after three days, the MRSA can get a stronger hold on human tissues. Eventually, if not stopped early, it can become very resistant to treatment. At first MRSA will show up as small red bumps. The infected person often writes them off as pimples, spider bites, or boils. The victim may develop a fever and sometimes rashes.

Within just a few days, the bumps rapidly grow larger and more painful. Eventually they break open into deep, pus-filled and extremely painful boils. They begin to consume skin and muscle and connective tissues. They can burrow into bones.

Many of us are carrying around MRSA, harmlessly latent in our nasal passages. In healthy people, it doesn't advance. In the worst cases, MRSA spreads into vital organs. Or the whole body can become infected, leading to sepsis or toxic shock syndrome.

Methecillin went into widespread use in 1959. By 1961, MRSA infections were showing up in Britain. Through the 1960's, MRSA spread and outbreaks popped up across Europe and then Australia. The superbug would not be stopped. By 1968, it made its way to the US, where Boston City hospital experienced an outbreak. The rate of infections climbed steadily. By the '70s, MRSA was recognized as endemic. It had become a part of the typical hospital's everyday environment. In 1974, 2% of all hospital-acquired *S. aureus* bacterial infections were from the aggressive MRSA. By 1995, it was 22%. By 1997, half of all hospital bacterial infections were coming from MRSA.

And then it all got much worse.

On April 24, 2012, Chinese scientists discovered a new, rapidly emerging *Staphylococcus aureus* gene, called sasX that appeared to aid the bacteria in colonizing tissues in your body, increasing the potential of lethal infection. Up until then, the sasX gene was considered to be extremely rare. But after analyzing samples of *S. aureus* from three hospitals, researchers found that from 2003 to 2011, the presence of sasX had nearly doubled, jumping from 21% to 39%.

And if you didn't already have enough to worry about, the CDC counts seventeen more diseases and pathogens (not counting MRSA) that have evolved antimicrobial resistance. These include anthrax, strep throat, the flu, typhoid fever, and, most alarming of all, the erstwhile docile STD known across college campuses as "the clap," or gonorrhea.

Today, 99,000 people die each year in the United States from hospital-acquired infections. For them, hormegeddon is not a theory. It's a matter of life and death. What can be done? More new drugs to fight the bugs that are resistant to the old drugs? New money to fix the problems caused by the old money? That's what propelled us into this flesh-eating hormegeddon in the first place.

As in any sweep to the downside, there is a powerful downdraft that keeps you going in the wrong direction. Pharmaceutical companies make money on new products, not on withdrawing old ones. Each new generation of antibiotic means a new, patentable and very profitable product to market. Everyone gets what he wants. Patients, doctors, pharmacists and the corporate drug makers.

And as health care grows more important, more costly, and more ubiquitous, so does the downdraft grow more powerful. Every year there are more and more patients coming in for un-needed testing and ineffective treatments. Every year, there are more elective and often unnecessary surgeries. Combine these increasingly greater numbers of unnecessary hospital patients with the development of drug-resistant superbugs and you have a nice formula for spreading the unstoppable deadly bugs far and wide.

The solution to this problem is the same one Napoleon faced at the Berezina River. "Turn back," said the voice of reason. "Go ahead," said the mischievous gods.

The zombified health industry has little incentive to turn around. There's no money in de-escalating the bug war. Instead, the money is in coming up with super-antibiotics to fight the super-bugs. It's a biological arms race of both the highest and smallest orders.

Reports a zombie doctor, Josh Bloom, in the May 31, 2013 *Wall Street Journal*: 'Enterobacteriaceae , or CRE, has emerged that could create a scenario to rival the most terrifying of science-fiction movies…It makes [MRSA] seem like a hangnail."

Dr. Bloom, however, seems more pleased than alarmed. Why? In the article we learn that, for the first time ever, the US government is giving $200 million to GlaxoSmithKline to help the company "search for new antibiotics." Dr. Bloom applauds this measure as though it were the only thing standing between the human race and extinction.

But who is Dr. Bloom? It says at the bottom of the article he is on the staff of a non-profit group, "American Council on Science and Health." The group will not disclose its source of funding. But let's take a wild guess—GlaxoSmithKline?

CANCER

In 1971, US President Richard Nixon signed the National Cancer Act. He issued a strong proclamation to inspire scientists to find a "cure" for the dreaded disease. Since that day 42 years ago, the US federal government and various non-profit groups have raised and spent more than $2 trillion in the effort to find the ever elusive "cure" for cancer.

How's the campaign going?

First, 144,000 plant extracts were examined, looking for a cure. Not a single one emerged as an approved anti-cancer drug. Second, the number of Americans diagnosed with cancer each year more than tripled, with 1.6 million new cases in 2013 (not including non-melanoma skin cancers) and nearly 600,000 deaths. That is nearly an 80% increase since 1971.

Evaluating the effectiveness of cancer treatments, especially chemotherapy, is difficult business.

First, the disease known as "cancer" doesn't actually exist. It's a category used to denote a few hundred different types of disease in which cells divide irregularly; among them carcinoma, sarcoma, leukemia, lymphoma, myeloma, and various central nervous cancers. Just because a treatment seems to work with one type doesn't mean it will work with another. And just because chemo cured Bob's lung cancer doesn't mean it will cure yours. Steve Jobs understood this, which is why he convened some of the best geneticists in the world to sequence his specific cancer and his entire genome, then design a protocol specific to both. Unfortunately, he understood this too late.

Ask a doctor about chemo's effectiveness. The response will be, "it depends." Caught early on, some cancers respond to it…sometimes. Caught too late, and chemo is not effective at all. For instance, it will not cure advanced lung or colon cancers. Yet, patients still ask for the chemo, many believing that they've got a chance at survival. A recent study found that 81% of chemo recipients with advanced colon cancer misunderstood the purpose of their treatment: they thought the doctors were trying to cure them. In fact chemo in those cases is only used to delay death for a few weeks or months at best.

Popular cancer treatments function largely on the napalm principle: if the enemy is hiding in the jungle, set the jungle on fire. To be sure, it can be occasionally quite effective. Once in a while you hit a commie or two and maybe even an entire camp if you're lucky. The trouble is that you end up with a lot of collateral damage and little else to work with.

The nebulous nature of cancer treatments is further compounded by the severity of their side effects, which often include nausea, diarrhea, fatigue, kidney damage, memory loss, internal bleeding, and, sadly, a second type of cancer.

Meanwhile, doctors are still spraying napalm.

There's a silver lining, of course. Profits from chemo and other cancer therapies are hitting $35 billion a year. According to the *Journal of the American Medical Association*, up to 75% of the typical oncologist's earnings come from the selling of chemotherapy drugs in their practice. With a very healthy markup. It's no coincidence that the American Cancer Society is one of the biggest not-for-profits in the country. Its CEO, John R. Seffrin made over $2 million in 2010 alone.

As usual, it would appear that there are forces other than just medical judgment at work in these situations.

DIABETES

Along with cancer, obesity is probably the biggest medical problem facing the developed countries. Nearly half of all Americans are considered to be too fat. In the decade from 1993 to 2003, the number of people considered overweight grew 70%. Those classified as fully obese grew by 12%. Professionals estimate that obese adults generate annual medical costs 36% higher than normal people.

The obesity epidemic is fueling the explosion of people with type-2 diabetes and pre-diabetes. The cost to treat them is more than $113 billion a year. The way things are going, that number will expand with their waistlines, through $200 billion by 2020.

Why so expensive? Why not just tell them to lay off the desserts? Because, the system has a bias towards money-spinning. That is, it is skewed towards drugs and surgery.

IN A WRINGER

For decades women were told that getting an annual mammogram was the best way to monitor their status for breast cancer. Many women got mammograms even more frequently.

Multiple millions of mammograms were performed. Clearly, some cancer cases were caught early. But the percentage of women who had malignant breast cancer was very low out of the total population. Women were now getting regular and ever-increasing doses of radiation to their breasts. It seems that breast tissue is particularly inclined to genetic damage from radiation. Soon after this new mammogram emphasis began, breast cancer rates started their alarming rise.

Studies suggested that the radiation from the mammograms caused new cases of breast cancer. Since the widespread introduction of mammography screening, the rate of one type of breast cancer called DCIS has increased by 328%. It is suspected that at least two hundred percent of this increase is due to the radiation exposure from mammography.

Surely the healthcare system learned a lesson, changed course, modified its recommendations? The American Cancer Society along with the American College of Radiologists still insists on pursuing large-scale mammography screening programs for breast cancer. That includes for younger women, who are most at risk for radiation damage. The push continues even though the National Cancer Institute and other knowledgeable experts now agree that those exams are more likely to cause additional cancers than to detect existing ones.

DEATH AND THE DOWNSIDE

Never is the outcome of a health procedure more certain than when a person has entered the final stage of a terminal condition. Life itself is a terminal condition. Investing to beat death is a losing proposition. You might reasonably assume that in those cases, spending would wind down. This is a war that cannot be won; why waste ammunition?

But the health care field marshals don't surrender; they order a full frontal attack! Spending increases hugely in the final weeks of life. Even though everyone involved is absolutely sure how the battle will turn out.

The US federal government estimates that 70% of US health-care expenditures are spent on the elderly. Eighty percent of those dollars are spent in the last month of the patient's life. Much of that final effort goes for desperate life-sustaining "heroic measures."

What's the return on investment? Nobody seems to care, because none of them are fronting the cash. Doctors don't seem to mind—another test, another dollar. Hospitals don't mind—a bed filled is a pocket filled. Suppliers of all the medications and equipment don't mind—there's plenty more where that came from. And the families can feel better too; knowing that "everything possible" was done for their loved one. Dollars are lined up like doughboys and ordered to go 'over the top.' No surprise; they end up dead. Wasted. Gone forever.

It's difficult to convey in the abstract how absurd this routine practice has become. Let's look at a real example.

Lisa Krieger is a reporter for the *Mercury News* in California. Her elderly father's health was rapidly deteriorating. He entered the hospital in serious condition. The man had lived a simple and frugal life. Knowing his health was not good, he had the foresight to give specific instructions—an advanced directive—that no extraordinary measures should be taken to keep him alive, if he was near the end.

He had the advantage of being cared for in an excellent hospital at Stanford University. In the ten days of his stay there, he continued to swiftly decline. Lisa struggled with each decision on what measures should be taken to extend his frail life. He got the absolute best of care. The bill for those services over the final ten days of his life? $323,658. This for a man, as valuable as any of us, but a man that was certain to die very soon regardless of what was or wasn't done for him.

Can you say the system was truly serving the patient? Was it acting in his best interests? Or its own?

Hope springs eternal, as they say. There are new cancer drugs coming out all the time. Many of them are wildly expensive. Bristol Myers Squibb has one called Yervoy. It's targeted at malignant melanoma, a very aggressive and often fatal cancer. Yervoy does have some promising benefits. Some patients using it—a small minority—do live years beyond typical life expectancy. But on average, the benefit of using this new chemotherapy is 3.6 months of additional life. Those four months of extra life come at a cost of $120,000. Per patient.

Even if the patient is only a customer for four months, that's not a bad revenue model. Especially if you're also selling the drug to the huge majority of patients who get no benefit from it. What the heck? They won't complain. Assume 10% of patients benefit. That brings the cost of the 3.6 months of extra life to $1.2 million, or roughly $10,000 a day. Worth it? Sure, as long as it's someone else's money.

HEAL THYSELF?

You might object: isn't the US a free economy? Why doesn't competition create more efficient, safer, and more effective health alternatives? Why don't entrepreneurs step up to the plate and offer a better product? Why doesn't someone start a "Pretty Good Health Care 4 Less" franchise? Imagine how it might work. You walk in. You don't see a doctor. You see a nice, sympathetic person with a computer who has been trained for six months on how to use it. It is like an Apple store with private booths. Your 'health technician' listens attentively. He gives you an exam. He asks questions. He reviews your symptoms. He feeds the data into a computer, perhaps one outfitted with some sort of open-source programming. The computer is programmed to draw upon the entire world's medical experience and give you an answer. Or, to pass, and tell you to go see a real doctor.

Most people do not have strange ailments. They have the problems that most people have. Those are the common ailments that a person with modest training could recognize and treat with simple procedures and cheap generic drugs. Aided by electronic tools and perhaps a few good doctors in India, connected by Skype, you could probably get as good advice in that private booth as you could get at any hospital anywhere in the country. Maybe better.

And before you react in horror at the idea of patients not dealing with licensed doctors, consider the fact that one of my children—who has a chronic skin condition—routinely goes to a top dermatologist's office in New York, and has yet to see an actual doctor. Instead he goes in and sits with a "physician's assistant" who types his ailments into a computer and prescribes medications that my son is now so familiar with, he could pick them off a shelf in the pharmacy and forego the fee he pays to the dermatologist he never sees. Still, the medical establishment would never allow that. Nor would it allow the physician's assistant to go into business for himself and undercut his useless boss. And at the end of the day, who cares? Insurance ends up paying. What a great racket!

If the PA were allowed to open his own business, you might pay about as much as you would pay to have your muffler changed. Cash or credit card. No paperwork. No insurance forms. No re-imbursement plans. You would also agree not to sue anyone.

In and out. No muss. No fuss. Nothing fancy about it. If you had a brain tumor you would probably go elsewhere. But for a benign rash, it would be the place to go.

Soon, there would be competing nationwide chains giving customers a choice and a range of prices and services that would accommodate each income bracket. Employers would pay a modest fee to enroll their employees. If the employee wanted to spend more, he could enroll in a more traditional program.

Why won't that work? Were you born yesterday? It's against the law! The feds reward their protected industries with almost boundless wealth. Zombies lining up a smorgasbord for other zombies. And then, to make matters worse, they punish challengers. You can't practice medicine without a license. And you would still have to pay for the Feds' health programs, without getting anything out of them. Even though your clients had specifically agreed not to sue, you'd be pursued by every shyster lawyer in the country.

Health care is a protected industry. It's a zombie industry, which cushions life for the people who profit from it while making it very hard for competitors. Why can't a patient agree not to sue in return for lower medical costs? Where have you been? Tort lawyers, those who bring these sorts of cases…and advertise on billboards in poor neighborhoods…are among the biggest campaign contributors to the political system. They, along with doctors, pharmaceutical companies, hospitals, and insurance companies, all support lobbyists. All have an interest in keeping the industry alive—as it is. None wants to see an upstart bring a disruptive technology to the zombie world of healthcare. None wants to give up his edge, his subsidy, or his privileges. None wants a free market in the biggest, most lucrative industry in the country.

Health care is little different from anything else. It quickly reaches the point where the marginal utility of further inputs goes down. Then it just keeps going. All the elements of a major downside catastrophe are in place. Central planning. Heavy government involvement. Zombies. Public information is overbought; individual private experience is oversold. And the feedback loop is twisted. People who pay the costs and suffer the "accidents" are not the same people who run the system. Self-correcting becomes self-reinforcing. Too much becomes even more. The system continues to absorb resources and cause more and more unnecessary deaths. Healthcare is hormegeddon, incarnate.

Chapter 9
DEBT

"The modern theory of perpetuation of debt has drenched the earth with blood and crushed its inhabitants under burdens ever accumulating..."

—THOMAS JEFFERSON

I N THE PERIOD BETWEEN 2008–2013, the major economies of the world were busily proving that the problem of 'too much' could not be solved by 'more.' Less was the right answer. But by then, the disaster-bound public policy of MORE could not be stopped. The whole economy had been transformed by it and had come to depend on it. Without it, without more, zombie industries—health, education, defense, finance, social welfare—all were doomed.

After the crisis of '08–'09, the economies of the US, Europe and Japan tried to recover. But they were like an alcoholic trying to recapture the magic of his first drink. Debt no longer excited them as it once did, however. So instead, they continued to borrow, but without the excitement of the old days.

We know why. Debt had long passed the point of declining marginal utility. Now, credit was directed to zombie industries, with negative rates of return. Debt had become a drag on the whole system. Too much debt threatened Europe's periphery. In America, it stabbed at heartland cities—with Detroit the first to declare bankruptcy in the summer of 2013. And as for consumers, it weighed them all down.

Debt prevented them all from moving forward. The resources that they needed had been claimed by the past. Capital had already been committed. It was needed to complete a transaction, the first part of which took place when the debt itself was contracted. The second will be concluded in the future, when the debt is paid, or otherwise excreted from the financial system.

When you owe money, it is often for things that no longer exist. Hamburgers eaten a month ago. Clothes that went out of style last summer. Ski vacations taken in last winter's snow. The pleasure may be long gone, but the discomfort of paying still lies ahead. With this burden of the past on your shoulders, you find it hard to move into the future. You shuffle along like a slave, forced to pay for yesterday's spending with tomorrow's work. If you owe an amount equal to your annual revenue, for example, at an interest rate of 5%, you will have to devote more than one working day in 20 just to pay the interest on the debt. I say "more than" because you have to pay the interest with post-tax money. At a tax rate of 50% (just to keep the math easy…and not far from the facts) you reduce the present and future enjoyment of your work by 10%.

With total debt in the US at about 350% of GDP, at 5% interest, forgetting taxes and other complications, Americans must work nearly one day per week just to pay for past consumption. Even serfs in the Dark Ages only had to work one day in ten for their lords and masters.

"Too much" comes readily to the lips. But at the lowest interest rates since WWII, few people noticed. At an interest rate of zero, debt is light as a feather…until the bill comes due; then it hangs with the dead weight of an albatross.

MONEY, MONEY, MONEY

But let us begin this excursion, not by visiting debt itself, but the stuff in which it is measured—money. I quote an article that appeared on Thomson Reuters' *Alpha Now* website, chosen more or less at random in the summer of 2013:

> To the extent that central bankers around the world are able to use forward guidance to influence market expectations of their own future policy rate, then of course they retain some control over the shape of their own yield curve. Nevertheless, what lies beyond their control is the size of the risk premium that drives a wedge between the average expected future policy rate and the yield on government debt.

The comment is not indecipherable. Nor is it meaningless. But what meaning it has depends on a complex amalgamation of ideas, theories and abstractions. The typical reader is baffled. Without a background in finance or economics, he suspects it is gobbledygook. He is mostly right.

The general subject of the comment is something we all know about: money. It's something we all understand. Or think we do. But this is a particular kind of money: credit-based money. It's a kind of money that is seen, since the Bronze Age, only episodically, and always with regrets.

David Graeber is an anthropologist. In his very clever book, *Debt: The First 5,000 Years,* he sets out to explore his subject from a new perspective—without the familiar clichés of an economist or speculator. Like so many academics, he often takes himself far too seriously. More than once he makes the biggest mistake you can make in historical analysis: *post hoc, ergo propter hoc.* Just because A happened after B, it doesn't mean B caused A. Often, neither A nor B actually happened at all. They are just artifacts of popular myth, best regarded as entertainment; not to be taken seriously. And some of what he writes is breathtakingly silly. For example, he writes that "politics...is the art of persuasion; the political is that dimension of social life in which things really do become true if enough people believe them." What is he thinking? Politics is the very opposite of persuasion. Markets require persuasion; politics requires force. In markets, you can't really force people to buy or invest or lend or exchange. Mao was right; politics is a matter of pointing a gun at someone and forcing him to do what you want. As for the reality of shared fantasy, I hardly know where to begin. If only we could know precisely when everyone comes to believe something that isn't true, we could make a fortune taking the other side of the bet.

Still, I thank Mr. Graeber for helping to reveal the nature of money.

Many things can be regarded as "money.' But they can be fit into two broad categories: one is credit-based, the other is bullion-based. The fundamental difference between the two is that with credit-based money you have to read the sort of comment you find in Alpha Now, above, and try to figure out what the hell they're talking about. With bullion based money, you don't.

In a small community, modern, bullion-backed money is not necessary. The exchange of goods and services takes place as part of the cultural, social, religious and political life of the community. Markets as we know them, based on simple, rational calculations, do not exist.

People in tribal settings give gifts. They pay for brides. They trade favors. They practice a form of proto-communitarianism—each providing what he can, others taking what they need, infinitely nuanced by the particular beliefs and prejudices of the people involved. To the extent they keep score, individuals remember who owes what to whom and weave complex webs of credit that stretch over many generations, involving family relationships, social status, and much, much more. This form of credit-based money still held on in small towns in Europe, Graeber says, at least until the Enlightenment. Merchants gave out their products on credit, trusting reputation, honor and community relationships to get something in return. In 16th and 17th century England, according to Craig Muldrew, credit-based money was still in use. A "reckoning" was held every six months, in which debts and credits were settled out.

Credit was the first "money."

But although this form of money—endlessly elaborated over thousands of years—is suited to small groups, it won't work for large ones. Small groups are different from big ones. Big groups can also organize themselves and solve problems, but not in the same way. The evolutionary adaptations that make humans suited to problem solving in small communities cause them to make a mess of problem solving on a large scale. Their small-scale instincts are inappropriate. As I explained earlier in this book, our brains are evolved for the scale of Paleolithic communities. At the first sign of danger, for example, a young man may be programmed to protect his family at all costs. This may be necessary for the survival of the group. But the same instinct, magnified onto a nation of 300 million people and informed by a self-interested military industrial complex may lead to less than optimum results.

In the same way, the credit money system of small communities is inappropriate and dangerous for large-scale, modern economies. A stockbroker in New York walks around in shoes made in Italy; surely he has a debt to the cobbler. Should he send him a stock tip? Should he offer to trade his portfolio for free? Should he offer him his wife? And what about the mason in Queens who built his chimney? Or the assembly line worker in Malaysia who put together his iPad? It would be impossible for him to maintain a recollection of all the obligations he owes these people, even if he knew who they were.

What can he do? He needs a different kind of money.

A headline from the *Financial Times*:

> Geithner joins after-dinner top table with $400,000 for three speeches.

Without modern money, Geithner's speech might bring him two goats and one chicken. Instead, today, his payoff for bailing out the banks with other people's money is more of other people's money. From the banks, of course. Deutsche Bank alone gave him $200,000, according to the FT. Blackstone and Warburg Pincus each ponied up as much as $100,000 more. You can't accuse the bankers of ingratitude. Geithner gave the bankers trillions—in cash and guarantees. He helped them to earn extravagant fees, commissions and bonuses when the going was good. Then, when their reckless wagers blew up and the going turned bad, he and the Fed dug them out of the rubble and forced the public to pay the losses.

None of this would have been possible without a specific kind of money.

DIFFERENT KINDS OF MONEY

Money expresses a relationship between people. A man with 'money' has a claim on the time and possessions of other men. He can buy a house from his neighbor. He can buy an hour of his neighbor's time. Not so long ago, he could even buy his neighbor's sister or daughter (then, as now, it paid to live in a good neighborhood)!

A man without money has no claim; he has only a need. He must give up his time, his house, or his daughter to the satisfaction of other men to service that need. A man with debt is in an even more inferior position. He has negative money; he has an obligation to give up something to others, but has not yet done so. He is, in effect, a slave to others. "The man who has made himself responsible for interest he cannot pay has accepted voluntary slavery for life," said St. Basil.

Ancient credit obligations, kept by collective memory, stretched over many generations. Often they involved transactions of a subtle or ambiguous nature; far too nuanced to be recorded in a dry, modern 'due to, due from' ledger. A man borrowed one neighbor's bow and another's arrow. He shot a deer. He owed one cut of meat to the one whose arrow he used and a better cut to the one who lent him a bow. If he had been unable to deliver, the debt could be carried forward, perhaps to the next generation, with interest, to be paid in choice intestinal parts.

When trade, agriculture, and war brought people together in greater numbers, the credit-based money system broke down. Who could keep track of so many details? Besides, soldiers had to be paid in something other than contingent credit commitments. They wanted something they could carry. Women and loot worked for a while. But as armies grew larger, and became more stationary, the Sabine women and the ready supplies of portables were quickly exhausted. The authorities needed another way to keep their soldiers in the field.

So did merchants need other ways of settling accounts. In a small tribe, everyone could run an open tab almost indefinitely. One man gives another a chicken. He gets a cow in return. He still has an obligation.

The open tab system doesn't work in a large, extended community. Buyers and sellers might not be from the same family or the same tribe. They might not speak the same language. They might not worship the same gods. They need a way to handle transactions with total strangers. That's when 'money' enters the picture.

At its dawn, money was a true revolution in convenience. Instead of running an open tab forever, people were able to conclude their deals on the spot. You no longer had to worry about whether your counter-party was solvent. Or whether you could remember his cousin's name. Or whether his daughter was pretty. Instead he gave you a chicken. You gave him a little piece of metal. The deal was final.

As Aristotle pointed out, anything could be designated as 'money.' Anthropologists have found all sorts of money—including shells, beads, feathers and stones. In the Virginia colony, tobacco was once designated as legal tender. But Aristotle missed the distinction between a centrally-planned currency and one that arose spontaneously. In pre-civilized tribes a leader might be able force the group to recognize a certain thing as money. So might he declare that everyone should wear a yellow flower in his hair. In the contemporary world, almost every detail of life is subject to this kind of activist rule-making. Today's money is too. But while a government can declare anything it wants money, it cannot guarantee the price at which the money will trade. The Zimbabwe dollar, for example, was the official currency of Zimbabwe...until it became completely worthless. Then, it ceased to be money, no matter what the authorities said.[10]

As the scale of the community and the distance (in space, culture, language and so forth) of its component parts increases so does the need to discover simple, universal rules rather than make up particular

---

[10] Zimbabwe has since banned the use of a national currency.

ones. So too does the need to discover real money. Just because the authorities say something is so, that doesn't make it so. In other words, money is only a social convention and/or the result of governmental edict up to a point. Then, it is something else. Some philosophers, Al-Ghazali for example, believed that gold is a God-given currency, with no purpose other than as a natural form of money:

> A thing can only be exactly linked to other things if it has no particular special form or feature of its own—for example, a mirror that has no color can reflect all colors. The same is the case with money—it has no purpose of its own, but serves as a medium for the purpose of exchanging goods.

Of course, no one knows what the value of a gold coin actually is. In terms of what you can buy with it, it changes all the time. Markets do not know what things are worth. They do not set values. They only discover them. And were humans to suddenly discover that they no longer want this kind of money, the value would surely fall. Because, while gold has some limited ornamental and industrial uses, it is as money that it is most valuable. But it scarcely matters that prices change. You may look in the mirror and never see exactly the same thing twice either. Still, you know what it is you're looking at.

The introduction of bullion-based money made possible further division of labor. It made trade and commerce easier. It quickly spread throughout the civilized world. By the time of Roman Empire, a person in Rome could buy a carpet made by a person in Persia with the same coin as a person in Carthage could buy a Gallic slave.

Despite being perhaps the most resilient and effective money in the history of civilization, gold eventually met its match—officially speaking—on the 15th of August, 1971 when President Richard Nixon announced that dollars were no longer convertible to precious metal at a fixed rate. For the first time ever, the world's leading brand of money did not even pretend to be backed by anything other than good faith and good judgment of US public employees. Instead, the US would revert to what was essentially primitive, credit-based money. People were to take the new dollars and count on the full faith and credit of the US government to make sure they were valuable. If they had any doubt about it they could review the US accounts. They could examine all the many credit arrangements that stood behind the dollar and decide for themselves what it was worth. And good luck to them!

The system was described by economists as new and experimental. It was widely thought to be an improvement. But it is really something quite old. As we have seen, credit-based money pre-dates bullion money by thousands of years. And, not coincidentally, institutional larceny has been around—episodically—for almost as long.

FIAT MONEY, PEREAT MUNDUS

Bankers are only human. Under pressure, they, like everyone else, tend to take the easy way out. In the *History of Financial Disasters,* a huge tome published by Pickering & Chatto of London, we find the story of a late 18th century French currency called the assignat.

Andrew Dickson White sets the stage:

"It began to be especially noted," he observed, "that men who had never shown any ability to make or increase fortunes for themselves abounded in brilliant plans for increasing the fortune of the country at large."

At the time, the French believed they needed big armies and big budgets to defend their glorious revolution. Much like today's "War on Terrorism" or the "Financial Crisis," the French faced problems largely of their own making. And then, like today's politicians eyeing "the 1%," the French looked for a new source of revenue. They found it in the lands of the church. They proposed to create a new 'rent'—assigning the right to the income from church property to others. That was to be the backing to their new currency: the 'assignat.'

> "Amidst so many extraordinary things, paper-money undoubtedly holds the first rank," wrote Louis-Sébastien Mercier. "It was created by necessity, as we throw a wooden bridge over a foaming flood; and as we must pass over the trembling bridge, we pass with our eyes shut."

It even seemed to work. For a time. But Francois d'Ivernois had a darker view of it:

> "It was by this terrible round of confiscations, dilapidations of public wealth, executions and emissions of new paper that the credit of the assignats was supported for more than a year, and the Republic was actually enabled to provision her fourteen armies at a cheaper rate, though with paper money, than the Allies [France's enemies] could with their specie. To produce this political miracle, cost Robespierre nothing more than a declaration that half the property of France was to change it owners by violent means."

The priests put up little fight. They were said to be in league with the English, and maybe with the devil himself. They had few friends and no protectors. The revolutionary government, ruthless and unfettered, set out to destroy them. For this work, the guillotine cranked night and day until it was deemed to be too slow. Then the activists found other means. In Bordeaux, for example, hundreds of priests and nuns were chained together and thrown into the river.

The printing presses kept pace with the guillotine. In 1791, they emitted 561 million livres' worth of assignats. That amount rose to

1,420 million in 1792, approximately doubling each year until 1796, when more than 30,000 million livres were printed.

What result would you expect from such vigorous money-printing? Was more better? According to the volume theory of money, prices should go up, which is exactly what happened. In 1791, 100 livres (in assignats) bought 91 gold livres. The following year, the same number of assignats bought only 72 gold livres. Thereafter, the purchasing power of the assignat continued to decline, to 51 gold livres in 1793, 40 in 1794, 18 in 1795 and less than one half of a single gold livre in 1796.

Finally, on the 19th of February 1796, "all the apparatus and machinery for printing [assignats] was solemnly destroyed and burnt."

At the beginning of the 19th century, gold was restored as the foundation for France's money system. The country had learned a valuable lesson.

Bullion money restricted the total quantity of money to the amount of bullion available. It also restricted the amount of credit, since loans had to be settled in bullion. And since the quantity of bullion could not be readily increased, the purchasing power of bullion money tended to be stable over long periods of time. Prices in 1910 were little different from those in 1810. As Roy Jastrow demonstrated in "The Golden Constant," you could buy about as much with an ounce of gold in 1560 as you could four hundred years later.

DON'T TRUST THE GOVERNMINT

Early on, governments took control of the new bullion money. They imprinted it with emperors' faces. And then, they tried to use it to cheat people. "Give me control of a nation's money and I care not who makes its laws," said Mayer Rothschild, who saw the possibilities.

In England, there was a practice of trying to raise or lower the value of money by 'crying up' or 'crying down' the currency. More typically, they made the coins a little smaller or replaced precious metals with base metals. Naturally, the value of the 'de-based' currency went down. The gold aureus, for example, was minted in the reign of Julius Caesar, with 8 grams of pure gold. Three centuries later, it was replaced by the 4.5 gram solidus. The denarius, Rome's silver coin, shrank even faster. In Augustine Rome it represented a day's wage for the typical laborer. For centuries, it had been fixed at a weight of 4.5 grams of silver. But by the end of the second century AD the silver content had been reduced to just 70% of its weight. By 350 AD there was almost no silver left in it; it was worthless.

Sir Isaac Newton, Warden of the English Mint, was determined to do better:

> "The use and end of the public stamp is only to be a guard and voucher of the quality of silver which men contract for; and the injury done to the public faith, in this point, is that which in clipping and false coining heightens the robbery into treason..."

Modern paper money was a later innovation. It worked well—as long as the paper was backed by gold at a fixed rate. But it offered more opportunities for cheating. Un-backed by gold, it has the same problems as any primitive credit-based monetary system.

1. The tab remains open. You get assignats. Or shares in the Mississippi Company. Or dollars. But they are just debt, backed by more debt. They are promises. They are speculations on how well the managers of these enterprises will do. You never know for sure what they are worth until the end...when they are worth nothing.

2. The total amount of 'money' in circulation is open-ended. The money supply must be limited. Because the amount of

real goods and services it buys is limited. If it isn't limited it is just a matter of time before there will be a lot more 'money' than there are goods and services.

3. The value of the 'money' is subject to manipulation. You can't manipulate bullion—or, at least, you can't do so easily or for very long. It is what it is. You have it or you don't. But the value of money—confected out of shares in a company, or income from church property, or based on Federal Reserve policies—is subject to tomfoolery and chicanery.

The French experience with credit-backed money was fresh in the minds of the people who formed the US. In the Constitution itself we find their attempt to avoid a similar disaster. Credit-backed money is specifically prohibited. The states (which had the power then to mint their own money) were not to "make any thing but gold and silver coin legal tender in payment of debts." The founders had seen what happened to France's 'funny money' schemes. Since the invention of bullion based money, governments had often been tempted to go back to credit systems. Why? They offered more opportunities for cheating. The government issued pieces of paper—IOUs—and declared it 'money.' Usually, these hybrid systems began with some collateral backing up the paper. Issuers typically had gold in their vaults and agreed to exchange the paper for metal at a fixed rate. Holders of the paper money were told that it was 'good as gold.'

In some cases, people believed the IOUs were better than gold. When John Law began modern central banking in France, he backed his paper money with shares in a profit-seeking business—the Mississippi Company. You could take his scrip and imagine that it would grow in value along with the profits of the company. Trouble was, the Mississippi Company never made any profit. It was a failure…and a fraud. Great prospectus. Few real investments. When people realized, they wanted to get rid of their paper money as soon as possible. The system collapsed in 1720 and John Law fled France.

As we have seen, later in the 18th century, the French tried again. The assignat system blew up in 1796. Napoleon Bonaparte, on the scene at the time, declared that "while I live I will never resort to irredeemable paper money." He realized that a credit system cannot last in the modern world. Because, as the volume of credits rise, the creditworthiness of the issuers declines. The more they owe the less able they are to pay. The more dollars they provide, the less each additional dollar is worth.

James Madison, in the Federalist Papers, described paper money as an "improper or wicked project." And in his 1819 *Dartmouth College v. Woodward* decision, Chief Justice John Marshall explained that credit-backed paper money had "weakened the confidence of man in man and embarrassed all transactions between individuals by dispensing with a faithful performance of engagements."

Congress resorted to paper money—greenbacks—during the US War Between the States. Five hundred million paper dollars were issued. This led to higher prices, which pleased debtors. They had borrowed in dear money; they repaid in cheap greenbacks. Prices in the North rose 75% from 1860 to 1865.

After the war, the Greenbacks went away, but the desire for cheap money continued. Farming was the largest sector of the economy in the 19th century. Typically, farmers borrowed to expand their farms during booms, when prices were high. Then, in the correction, they cursed the bankers who had lent them money and railed against the gold standard.

William Jennings Bryan took up their cause late in the century. The rural proletariat had gone bust in farm crash of the 1880s and now found itself so deep in debt it was willing to take up with a fool like Bryan, who—like a quack promising a baldness cure—offered relief. The roads choked up with dust when Bryan came to a cow town in the Midwest. There, he ranted and raved against all that the farm-folk detested.

"You shall not crucify mankind on a cross of gold," he roared, to the approving hallelujahs of the yokels. The speech had a ring to it. It was a rhetorical flourish with great power. Remembered and repeated, it is still almost as readily recognized as the Lord's Prayer. But it was empty, nothing more than bombast and fraud. Jesus was crucified on a cross of wood. Since then, millions have been crucified financially by paper money (a wood product).

What Bryan had against gold was the same thing that all paper money pushers—including modern central bankers—have against it. Gold is uncooperative. It is stiff-necked. You borrow it and you have to pay it back. The lender expects to get his money back in real money.

Prices from 1800 to 1913, when America's central bank was founded, were more or less stable. New discoveries of gold in South Africa, California and Australia had increased the money supply significantly. But increases in output kept pace. In the 100 years since, when paper money was the stuff most often issued by the US Treasury, prices have gone up about 1,000%. No point in trying to be too precise about it. Instead, I'll give you a single example. A postage stamp was 3 cents in 1950. Now, it's 42 cents.

Bryan got his way after all. Nobody in America suffers from an honest currency. Nobody pays back as much as he has borrowed. Nobody is crucified on a cross of gold. Even contracts with 'CPI adjustment' clauses fail to make the lender whole—the feds have seen to that too; more than once they have reformed the way they calculate the 'inflation rate,' each time getting a lower number.

If 'money' is to be a reliable store of value, the quantity of it cannot be allowed to expand too fast. Gold is the top bullion brand because it is expensive and difficult to mine. The quantity of aboveground gold grows at about the same rate as the quantity of goods and services for which it can be exchanged.

Credit based money, on the other hand, is very hard to restrain. In the US, total credit has risen from 150% of GDP before 1971 to over 350% today. Compared to GDP, the 'monetary base'—assets held by the US Federal Reserve—grew 100 times as fast in the period, 2009–2013.

What is this 'money' really worth? You say you have a US T-bond that matures in 2020? You say it will fund your retirement? The Fed will give you 'guidance.' Speculators will make their bets. And economists, in the employ of the US government, will tell you that they aim to make your 2014-era dollar worth precisely 98% of your 2013-era dollar. No more, no less.

Imagine that the Argentines have promised to make a payment on a US dollar bond in 2015. That obligation could be part of a sophisticated derivative instrument—which is one of the key assets of Hedge Fund A, which borrowed the money to buy the derivative from Bank B. Now, Hedge Fund A's debt to Bank B is a critical part of Bank B's capital. What happens if the Argentines don't pay?

As we will see, everything is more or less okay as long as you are on the downward side of the yield curve. Lower interest rates make it possible to greatly increase the total amount of debt a society can carry. As rates go lower the weight of debt goes down. At zero interest rate, for example, the burden of an infinite amount of debt is zero.

KISS OF DEBT

Like energy, the marginal utility of debt depends on what you use it for. It may be fairly high when you are using it to build a business or a bridge. Those are things that could "pay you back."

A good debt-financed investment brings forth a revenue stream—a result that justifies and pays for the investment. With a little luck, the investor recovers enough money to pay back the loan—with interest—and ends up with a little bit extra.

But the marginal utility of debt declines sharply when you begin to use it for everyday spending. There is no future revenue stream from Social Security payments, fighter jets, the latest fashions, or other consumer items. The money is quickly spent. Used up. Consumed. It is no more.

Keep up this borrowing and spending, and at some point you will be unable to continue. The weight of the past will be too heavy. Your legs will buckle and your back will break.

Thomas Jefferson was very familiar with debt. By all accounts, he was a bit of deadbeat. At the time, there were no bankruptcy protection laws. If you did not pay your debts, your creditors hounded you. They could take everything from you. Jefferson had such a reputation that his creditors were perhaps awed by it, or sympathetic. They did not push him too hard. Otherwise, he might have been ruined. Or even put in prison for non-payment of debt.

Throughout history, excessive debt has been a great danger with serious consequences for the unwary. There were heavy penalties for not satisfying your debts. Hammurabi felt the need to spell it out. His code specified: "If any one fail to meet a claim for debt, and sell himself, his wife, his son, and daughter for money or give them away to forced labor: they shall work for three years in the house of the man who bought them, or the proprietor, and in the fourth year they shall be set free."

Similarly, in Ancient Greece the debtor could be taken into 'debt bondage.' He was made a slave, in other words. So many people became enslaved in this way that in about 600 BC the "lawgiver" Solon banned the practice with a law called the 'seisachtheia,' which allowed the debt slaves to return to their farms as free men. The debt was not erased, however, and the debtor was still at risk of becoming his creditor's slave if he failed to respect the new credit terms.

The Romans were less forgiving. A creditor could execute insolvent debtors. Even by ancient standards, this was considered harsh.

The penalty for failure to pay debts in Europe during the Middle Ages was prison. There, conditions were appalling, as you might imagine. Typically, the debtor's family had to continue providing food and clothing. If the prisoner had no family support, he would starve. In prison, of course, he had little means to repay the debt, which commonly brought the story to a miserable conclusion.

Going broke was also an abominable disgrace. It was a blemish on a family escutcheon, telling the world that a member of the family—often the head of it—had let down his friends and associates. Read the novels of Thackeray and James; you will find young women of good society who are unmarriageable because their fathers defaulted on their financial obligations. Non-payment of debt sullied the whole family—for generations. To avoid this stain, uncles, cousins and others would come together to discharge the debtor's obligation.

The penalties of excess debt also figured heavily in commercial relations—especially in the banking industry. Until the creation of the Federal Reserve System in 1913, and the later Depression-Era reforms that allowed banks to operate behind a corporate shield, bank owners were personally responsible for their bank's losses. There was no federal deposit insurance and no banking cartel that could come up with new money when it was needed. Money was real—expressed as a unit of gold. Losing it meant real losses. Failed banks went into receivership. The receiver would tally up the losses and send a bill to the owners. Each paid his share of the losses or he would be judged insolvent too.

As you can imagine, bankers were a lot more prudent back then. So were borrowers. Both shared a keen interest in not over-doing it. Because both were directly exposed to penalties if anything went wrong. There was a direct connection between the debtor and his suffering, whether or not he operated behind the big brass doors of a bank or the flimsy wooden door of a tenement apartment.

PAPER MONEY CAUSES PROBLEMS

Gold-backed currency served the 19th century well. But it was a victim of the Great War in the 20th. The costs of the war forced all major participants—save the United States of America—off the gold standard. Bullion-based money had been severely injured, but it survived and licked its wounds for the next half-century. Finally, the Nixon administration stabbed it in the back, removing gold from the system entirely in 1971. The new, elastic currency—with no connection to gold—would be more cooperative.

It took a few years to adapt to the new credit-based money, but it wasn't long before the US economy began to like it. The sharp upward bend in the debt/GDP curve came ten years later.

People want money, power, and status. And they want to get it in the easiest way possible. Theft is easier than industry, at least when you have a gun in your hand. And paper money is easier than real money, when you have a printing press. It offers an easy way to transfer wealth from the people who earn it to the people who control the money.

The American economy was radically transformed—just in the way you'd expect. Fewer and fewer people found they could get ahead the old fashioned way—by working hard, saving their money, and investing it in productive enterprises. Instead, manufacturing (i.e. making money by making things) declined while finance (making money by helping people go further into debt) increased. You could see the change for yourself simply by visiting places where money ends up: Aspen, Colorado, Palm Beach, Florida, and most important, Greenwich, Connecticut. By the year 2000, the mansions still owned by people who had made their fortunes in manufacturing and commerce had become 'old money.' The 'new money' mansions were owned by hedge fund managers, bankers, and stockbrokers.

This trend has been so well documented, we can dispense with more facts and figures on it. The important thing from our point of view is to understand that the economy of the post-'80 period was very different than the economy of the previous period. Growth no longer came from greater productivity and higher wages and earnings. It came from an expansion of debt. People spent money they didn't have. And it was this debt that merchants put in their bank accounts and used to pay their suppliers. Gradually, the whole society became saturated with the stuff—wealth that didn't really exist. Accordingly, the typical American family was no better off in 2013 than it had been in 1950, despite dwelling in the most fertile ground for material progress in human history. Hourly earnings increased until the early '70s—peaking out almost exactly when the new credit-based money was put into service. Since then, the average American has made little or no progress; many people have actually slipped backward.

According to the official numbers, one dollar when I was born (after WWII) was worth about $10 today. But the official numbers are fishy, as we have seen. So, let's look at a couple big-ticket items. An average house in 1950 sold for only about $8,000. Today, (after a big sell-off following the sub-prime mortgage debacle of 2008) the typical house sells for about $150,000. On that basis, keeping up with your number one cost—housing—would require 15 times as much money as it did in 1950.

Do people earn 15 times as much? Not quite. After the war, a typical family had a single wage-earner with a salary of about $250 a month, or $3,000 a year. The minimum wage was 75 cents an hour, or about $120 a month. On an average wage, a man was able to support a family and buy a new car every three or four years. A new car—an Oldsmobile 'Rocket 8' for instance—was priced at around $1,500, or about half a year's wages.

Income numbers are (as usual) a little spongy, but by my calculation (multiplying the median hourly wage times the number of hours worked) a typical man earns only about $30,000 per year. That is only 10 times as much, in nominal terms, as in 1950. This gives him much less real purchasing power than he had 6 decades ago. Without even beginning to calculate the effects of higher taxes, healthcare and education expenses, we can see that he has to devote at least a whole year's wages to buying a new family car—twice as much as in 1950. As for the house, that's 5 years' wages, or twice as much as it was in the '50s.

As you can see, the real wages of the typical man have actually gone down for the last 60 years. A wage slave has only his time to offer. In terms of his time, his most important acquisitions are much more expensive today than they were in 1950.

How did American workers survive with lower real wages and higher living costs? First, they began to work longer hours. Wives went to work. Husbands worked a second job. Now, Americans work more hours than any other group. Second, and most important, from our point of view, they began to borrow. Aided, induced, and bamboozled by the feds' EZ-credit policies, they went deep into debt to keep up with their own standards of living.

Almost everyone misunderstands why the rich got richer and the poor got poorer. They think deregulation allowed capitalists to take more money away from the proletariat. Or, they believe the rich suddenly became greedier. But why would the character of the greedy rich suddenly degrade? And we note that the total volume of regulation actually increased during the whole period under review. Just look at the tax code or SEC rules; there are far more rules than there were in 1950.

Something else was happening to the middle classes, something subtler and more insidious: The feds were clipping their coins.

THE ROLE OF CENTRAL PLANNING

Not all of this debt expansion was the direct result of central planning. Much of it came unbidden, as the unintended consequence of central planning. The planners created a world in which debt could expand far more than in the past and in which the negative feedback loop from debt was pinched shut.

Prior to 1971, foreign nations could exchange their dollars for gold at a fixed rate. If Americans spent too much on overseas purchases (notably, imports from China), the Chinese would soon have a large stock of dollars that they had received in payment for their goods. These would be presented at the 'gold window' at the US Treasury;

the Treasury would take in their dollars and give the Chinese gold in exchange. As gold was the foundation of the money supply, the outflow represented a shrinkage of the base on which the whole system operated. The supply of credit shrank too, thereby reducing the desire and ability of Americans to continue spending. The system self-corrected.

But after 1971, the gold window at the Treasury Department was nailed shut. Henceforth, foreign nations took their dollars…and kept them. Dollars, not gold, became the cornerstone of the world financial system. Credit markets no longer depended on real savings. This new credit-backed paper money—was infinitely expandable. And the rates at which it expanded depended on the rates at which money could be borrowed. These rates were not under the direct control of the central planners at the Fed and the Treasury department, but almost. The Fed set the rate at which member banks borrowed from it. Other rates tended to follow. Not surprisingly, the central planners were more likely to favor low rates (which encouraged borrowing and spending) than high rates. And not surprisingly, total debt levels soared.

Ben Bernanke misread the signs completely. He called it the era of "Great Moderation." But the stability he saw was a mirage. EZ-money functioned like a liquor store that made home deliveries; it kept the alcoholics from appearing in public. Debtors stayed at home and found it almost impossible to sober up. No matter how they mismanaged their affairs, someone would lend them more money. It's easy to chase the debt dragon when the dragon comes to you.

By 2007, the private sector could take no more. Wisely, it began rapidly shedding debt. Since then, the aim and efforts of the Feds have been to reverse and annul the private sector's good judgment. 'Recovery' is what the authorities say they want. But a real recovery can't be bought with more borrowed money. Friedrich Hayek explained why in 1933:

> To combat depression by a forced credit expansion is to attempt to cure the evil by the very means which brought

it about; because we are suffering from a misdirection of production, we want to create further misdirection—a procedure which can only lead to a much more severe crisis as soon as the credit expansion comes to an end.

Too much is too much. Once the rate of return on credit sank below zero further investments merely produced more losses. Low lending rates were not creating new wealth, they were increasing the value of existing wealth while actually reducing the resources available for growth and development.

HEADED TO HORMEGEDDON

Debt can be denied. It can be delayed. But it can't be disappeared.
Cullen Roche in *Pragmatic Capitalism*, July 2013:

> Okay…a lot of government debt. But that also means the private sector has a lot of savings (by accounting identity, the government's debt is the non-government's saving). I know people seem to have an aversion to government debt, but debt alone is not an ingredient for disaster. After all, our entire monetary system is credit based. One person's liabilities are someone else's assets. That's just double entry bookkeeping.

Unfortunately, double-entry bookkeeping doesn't tell you whether the debt is good or bad. The fact that one person owes a lot of money does not mean that he's ever going to pay. The books always balance out to zero—debits on the left, credits on the right. But the credits may be worthless, while the debt will still be owed. It will go away too, eventually, but how? That is the disaster we are talking about.

John Maynard Keynes, the leading economist of the 20th century, was a debt denier, too. He rejected the evolved wisdom of thrift. He claimed that saving was no virtue and referred to "conventional wisdom" as a criticism. Now, his unconventional thinking has become the conventional wisdom of much of the economics profession and most of the world's central banks and Treasury departments.

Keynes' thoughts were 'out of the box.' Debt, thought to be a bad thing for thousands of years, was turned into a good thing. How did that happen? What was he thinking? Let us begin by having a look into the box from which Mr. Keynes emerged.

In Keynes' box was a lot of history. It tells us that debt may be a good thing in small doses. It allows debtors to do things they couldn't otherwise do. If those things are rewarding enough, the debtor can pay back his debt or at least enjoy the satisfaction of defaulting on it. But debt soon follows the familiar pattern. A little grows into a lot. The marginal productivity of debt declines and then goes negative.

In the private sector, too much debt is a common thing. But it is a problem that is quickly remedied. Creditors cut their debtors off. In some communities, bill collectors send polite notices. In others, they send men with baseball bats. This feedback loop produces a rapid change of direction.

But public debt is another thing. It is a shift of resources from the future to the present. We live in modern democracies. The present votes. The future doesn't.

You can already see how the feedback loop is severed. The people who will suffer the debt are not those who make the decision to incur it. Present politicians, voters and parasites get the benefits. The costs are pushed onto others, often those who haven't even been born yet.

You can also see how easily 'too much public debt' fills out our framework for hormegeddon. It is inspired by theory, not by experience. It is a monster created by central planning. The plan's proponents are not personally injured by its failures; on the contrary, they tend to benefit. And it creates a large and growing class of zombie supporters who block corrections that might help those who don't exist…yet.

As to the declining marginal utility of debt, there is little question. Both experience and intuition tell us that the more you borrow the less good you'll get from it. But let us imagine that we have to prove the point. We shoulder the burden of proof simply by showing the US national accounts from 1950 to 2007. A simple chart makes the argument clearly. As debt increases, output increases less and less rapidly. Each additional unit of debt yields less additional wealth, in other words. In the '50s and '60s, it took only about a $1.50 to produce an extra dollar's worth of output. Half a century later, the economy borrowed $5 or more for every incremental dollar of GDP.

That's declining marginal utility of debt, illustrated:

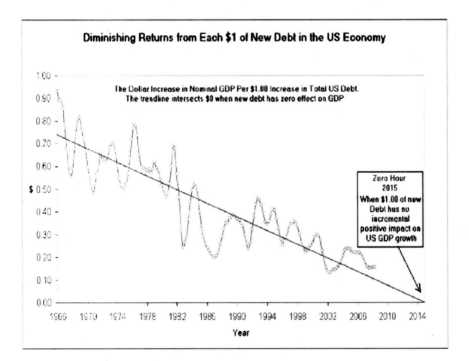

SOURCE: FEDERAL RESERVE FLOW OF FUNDS, U.S. BUREAU OF ECONOMIC ANALYSIS

Nor is it hard to see why this is so. You borrow money and apply it to the most productive uses—where the payoff is most immediate and most rewarding. Then, as you borrow more money, you turn to more marginal projects, those you are less sure will be fruitful. Eventually, you reach projects that do not pay off at all—such as the dot.com start-ups of the late '90s and the expansion of housing and malls in the bubble period of the mid-'00s. Money is invested in projects that are worth less than the resources that went into them. Real wealth is destroyed. Only debt remains.

The US public, generally, is wary of debt. It reached its limit in 2007, when the weakest link in the debt chain—subprime mortgage debt—broke. Since then, five million people have had their houses repossessed. Their mistakes were corrected. They are older and wiser as a result.

But, public debt continues to increase. And the fact there are few visible bad consequences to America's growing public debt is widely celebrated. In the words of France's great post-war economist, Jacques Rueff, the US enjoys "deficits without tears." Thanks to the willingness of people all over the world to take in dollar credits and hold them dear as if they were worth something, they are in fact worth something. And they will continue to be worth every penny as much… until they aren't anymore.

You can see from the chart above that the current explosion of debt began in the early 1980s, approximately coincidental to the first Reagan administration. Seeing the handwriting on the wall, I gathered a small group of children together—including my own son, 7 years old at the time—and sued the US government on their behalf. We argued that selling 30-year bonds by the US government amounted to a kind of debt slavery; a ball and chain which young people would have to drag around all their lives, without ever getting to vote on it. Their own tax money will not be used to pay their government's expenses. Instead, the money has already been spent, by their parents' government on projects that seemed like good ideas to their parents at the time.

The courts threw the children's case out. And their parents' generation went ahead and borrowed more money—public and private—than any generation ever had. Curiously, government bonds also rose in price during the entire borrowing spree. For the 33 years from 1980 to 2013, the general direction of bond yields (the inverse of bond prices) was down. Long-dated T-bonds yielded 15% in 1981. Since then, US government debt went from $1 trillion to $16 trillion. But the price of bonds went up, so that by mid- 2013, long-dated Treasury bonds yielded only about 3.5%.

At first, this would seem to contradict everything we know about markets and our 'too much' hypothesis. More appears to be better. The more debt the US government issued, the more investors, lenders and savers seemed to like it. According to the principle of declining marginal utility, you'd expect just the opposite. You'd expect investors' desires for US debt would have been substantially satiated long ago and that every additional increment would be less highly prized than the one that preceded it. But just because something hasn't happened yet doesn't mean it will never happen. As this is written, it looks like the trend towards higher bond prices peaked out in May of 2013.

Meanwhile, the accumulation of debt is accelerating. It took 64 years for the feds to build up $1 trillion in debt (achieved in 1981). Now, that much is added every 14 months. And over the five years from 2008–2013, the total spent worldwide—100% debt financed—to bring about an economic recovery was estimated between $7 trillion and $12 trillion.

The official tally from George W. Bush's 8 years in office revealed $800 billion of debt added…per year. Barack Obama's first term saw a $1.2 trillion annual increase. More by half. Federal debt grew more than twice as fast as tax receipts for the last ten years and 4–5 times as fast as the economy itself during Obama's first term.

When you look at the debt in GAAP-basis accounting terms—as any publicly traded corporation would be required to do—including unfunded liabilities as well as cash in and out the door, the velocity of the debt build-up is breathtaking. Instead of a deficit of about $1 trillion for 2012 you find one of $7 trillion. And instead of a national debt of $16 trillion, as widely reported, you have total debt and unfunded financial obligations of $238 trillion (figure cited by Professor Niall Ferguson)—making it the biggest bubble in history. And instead of growing 4–5 times as fast as GDP, this real debt is growing 20 times as fast.

But that is how a real disaster works. Uncorrected, it runs smooth and fast—unstoppable—until it finally meets its immoveable object.

ADDICTED TO DEBT

Alarmists love the drug addict analogy. Like any analogy, it has its limitations and its dangers. But there is one element of it that has been widely ignored. As anyone who has ever had a serious drug addiction knows, you don't just stop being addicted. You have to go all the way with it, until you hit the wall. You do not 'recover' spontaneously or voluntarily. First, you need to live through your own personal hormegeddon. Addicts call it 'rock bottom.'

But the feds try to stretch the addiction out as long as possible. Why? Because running a rehab clinic can be a good business, especially if the patients never recover. Patients are never allowed to hit bottom. They never get better. And the quacks keep transferring more and more wealth and power to themselves and their friends.

In financial matters it is hard to get a full downside experience without a central bank to manage it. The US had a financial panic in 1907. In a panic—or a 'debt crisis'—lending rates go way up, fast. Short-term, callable loans carried an interest rate of as much as 80% in the panic of '07. At that price, only the strongest financial institutions survive. I mentioned this crisis earlier. Back then, we still had a bullion-backed dollar. The Federal Reserve had not yet been created. Without central planning, it came and went in a few short months during the autumn of 1907.

Then, a major depression hit in 1920. Industrial production was slammed with a 30% drop. Auto production went down 60%. The Dow Jones Industrial Average dropped in half. And consumer prices fell 15%. But again, it provoked no countercyclical response from the authorities. Just the opposite. The Fed raised rates twice during the crisis. The US government offered no response at all. Bankers, speculators, investors, businessmen and householders were left to suffer the fates they deserved. And lo and behold, the depression was over by 1921 and full employment had returned by 1923.

I will not bother to draw the comparison to the panic of 2008. It is obvious enough. Instead of being tossed out, those who made mistakes in the 21st century were generally rewarded with bonuses and the lowest borrowing rates in history. Instead of dying natural deaths, obsolete and imprudent businesses were kept alive. They became expensive zombies—supported by zero interest rates, guarantees and Quantitative Easing. Instead of liquidating bad debt, the authorities added to it. And instead of allowing bankers to learn from bitter experience, they protected them from their own errors with the biggest printing presses in the history of the world.

The first quantitative easing program in the US began in November of 2008. Then, it was viewed as an emergency measure to 'stabilize' the system. The private sector continued to de-leverage. Unemployment stayed high. A second round of easing followed to relieve investors' fears and otherwise grease the skids a bit more. The "Twist" emerged in September 2011, in which the Fed sold short-term securities and bought longer-term holdings. The idea was to lower long term lending rates—which are critical to the housing industry as well as to major capital investments. It was about this point that the European Central Bank joined the action with its own Long-Term Refinancing Operations.

The next phase of the adventure began in the summer of 2012. ECB president Mario Draghi said he would do "whatever it takes" to save the euro. The danger of a default greatly reduced, European bond yields fell.

QE III came to the US in September of 2012. The Fed extended its purchases of mortgage-backed and US debt securities to $85 billion per month. Not only that, it said it would continue printing money (buying assets with money created specifically for that purpose) until the unemployment rate fell below 6.5% or as long as inflation remained below 2.5%.

GOVERNMENT DEBT IS SELF-REINFORCING

Reducing credit is to economists of the early 21st century what breast-feeding once was to the pediatricians of the 20th. It may be natural, but it is a bugaboo. They think it's unhealthy. Retrograde. They believe they need to stop it. Of course, you come to believe what you need to believe when you need to believe it. And by the 21st century, economists running central banks and the government needed to believe that they could fix a heavily indebted economy by further increasing debt. Debt was all they had.

Governments borrowed money just to spend it. They said it would 'stimulate' the economy. Central banks lowered interest rates below the rate of consumer price inflation so that the private sector would be encouraged to borrow more too. No one worried about paying it back. As near as anyone can tell, it is 'free' money.

Everybody knows there is something fishy about getting something for nothing. But everybody also knows he doesn't want it to end. Like St. Augustine, he intends to stop, but not right away.

And always and everywhere, debt leads to trouble. Too much debt caused France to default on its sovereign debt eight times. Spain defaulted six times before 1800 and then another seven times later.

Between hyperinflation, defaults, and banking debacles spread over two centuries, Latin America scammed US banks out of billions.

In the '80s, Nicholas Brady tried to rescue New York bankers with his U.S.-backed "Brady bonds." Readers can guess what happened next. Within a few years, seven of the 17 countries that had undertaken a Brady-type restructuring had as much or more debt than they had before. By 2003, four members of the Brady bunch had once again defaulted and by 2008, Ecuador had defaulted twice.

Even non-existent countries go broke. In 1822, "General Sir" Gregor MacGregor issued bonds from a fictitious country he called Poyais, whose capital city, Saint Joseph, was described by the offering prospectus as having "broad boulevards, colonnaded buildings, and a splendid domed cathedral." The bonds sold at lower yields than those of Chile. But it didn't matter whether the country was real or imagined. All of them defaulted.

HOW IT WILL END

Nobody ever intends a public policy disaster. Still, disasters happen. Credit-based money in the modern world comes with a fuse attached. No credit-based money has ever survived an entire credit cycle. This will be no exception.

The fuse is lit when interest rates begin rising. As of this writing, it appears that rates began to go up in May of 2013, after falling for 33 years. As they go up, debt becomes denser and more volatile. Even a small spark can set it off.

The feds will have only two familiar choices. More or less. Less will mean depression, possibly riots and looting. More will mean hyperinflation and even more catastrophe. They will choose the latter. Because the time to choose the former has past. As we have seen, there are too many zombies to turn around now. All have a keen interest in seeing the credit-bubble expand even further. We are on course for hormegeddon. We will go all the way...until we hit bottom.

What will a blow-up look like? First, let us look at South America for a recent example.

Nowhere more than in Argentina has the introduction of the printing press to Latin America been such an obviously regrettable decision. In the 1990s, no one trusted the credit-based money of Argentina. They had seen what had happened to it. So, the Carlos Menem government vowed to keep the peso strong by pegging it to another credit-based money of uncertain value—the dollar. This removed the currency risk, supposedly, encouraging lenders to buy Argentine peso-denominated debt and making it possible for the Argentines to borrow huge amounts of money.

The government—riddled with corruption and waste—continued to spend more than it could afford. I remember visiting Mr. Menem in the late '90s. "Are you going to hold fast to the dollar-peg?" we wanted to know.

"Yes, of course," was the answer. "Without it, the Argentine economy will collapse."

No, was the fact of the matter. And by 2002, the Argentine economy had collapsed.

The dollar went one way. The peso went another. Banks were closed. And when they reopened, savers found that their dollars had been transformed, like wine into water, into pesos worth only a third as much. Many people were bankrupted. Retirement plans were destroyed. Thousands of formerly middle-class people were reduced to scavenging through trash, looking for something to eat...or sell.

But debt was reduced. And after a few years, Argentina bounced back—more or less. It is now shambling along as it always did, burdened by corruption and incompetence, and once again in danger of financial collapse.

Argentina is a success story, really.

Here's another recent example: Zimbabwe began running large, chronic deficits and financing them with printing press money about the same time as America began her own big debt run-up, in the early 1980s. Ian Smith had been driven from power. Robert Mugabe took over, promising a new beginning.

Mugabe's government enjoyed favorable press for decades. Rhodesia was yesterday. Zimbabwe was tomorrow. So was a downside disaster. The new government ran deficits for decades before anyone fully realized what a jam the country had gotten itself into.

In the 1990s, the Mugabe government began taking land away from white owners and giving it to its supporters. Alas, his cronies lacked the capital or the skill to farm. Production fell. And so did the government's revenues. But the ruling Zanu-PF party did not correct its policies. It doubled down. Then tripled down. It printed money to pay its bills.

The additional cash, along with falling output and widespread distrust of the government, led to hyperinflation. Food production fell in half. Manufacturing dropped by about 80%. So did employment. Life expectancy fell too.

But it was in prices that Zimbabwe really broke records.

In 2001, the monthly inflation rate hit 200%. After that, the sky was the limit. In February 2008 the monthly rate was said to be 164,900.3%. Nice touch. Putting on the '.3.' It made it almost look scientific. As if it were something that could be accurately measured, or even controlled. Then, five months later, consumer price inflation in Zimbabwe was clocked at 231.2 million percent. Finally, in September, the IMF saw prices rising faster than the speed of light—at an estimated 489,000,000,000%.

By then, the statisticians were only amusing themselves. The numbers meant nothing other than that Zimbabwe had blown itself up.

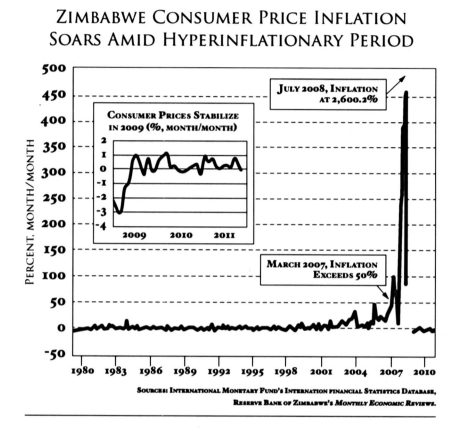

ZIMBABWE CONSUMER PRICE INFLATION
SOARS AMID HYPERINFLATIONARY PERIOD

CONSUMER PRICES STABILIZE
IN 2009 (%, MONTH/MONTH)

JULY 2008, INFLATION
AT 2,600.2%

MARCH 2007, INFLATION
EXCEEDS 50%

PERCENT, MONTH/MONTH

SOURCES: INTERNATIONAL MONETARY FUND'S INTERNATION FINANCIAL STATISTICS DATABASE,
RESERVE BANK OF ZIMBABWE'S MONTHLY ECONOMIC REVIEWS.

Life in Zimbabwe became harder and harder as inflation rates
rose. It was called an 'hour economy,' as prices changed every hour.
You would take a bus into town at one price. By the time you went
home, the fare had risen ten times, or 100 times.

In one of the many currency reforms engineered by central banker
Gideon Gono, a $10 billion Zimbabwe bill was turned into a single
Zimbabwe dollar. The *Economic Times* newspaper noted on June 13,
2008 that "a loaf of bread now costs what 12 new cars did a decade
ago," and "a small pack of locally produced coffee beans costs just

short of 1 billion Zimbabwe dollars. A decade ago, that sum would have bought 60 new cars."

People learned to live with rapidly increasing prices, quickly ciphering prices, adding zeros as necessary. But there was no way for business to keep up. Orders for basic foodstuffs could not be honored. The price of bread went from $1Zim to $10Zim to $1,000Zim to $10 billion Zim. Then, bread vanished from the shelves altogether as bakers could no longer buy flour or afford to sell bread at the allowable price.

The problem was aggravated by government price controls. In Zimbabwe, as is always the case when government imposes artificially low prices, products disappeared from the shelves.

Services collapsed. Police, fire, schools, hospitals—all lacked basic supplies. Then, they had no one to do the work. Public employees walked off the job. By the time their money reached them, it was worthless. Janet Koech writes:

> Hyperinflation and economic troubles were so profound that by 2008, they wiped out the wealth of citizens and set the country back more than a half century. In 1954, the average GDP per capita for Southern Rhodesia was US$151 per year (based on constant 2005 U.S.-dollar purchasing power-parity rates). In 2008, that average declined to US$136, eliminating gains over the preceding 53 years...

You couldn't measure the increase in consumer prices because there were no consumer prices to measure. If the price of a single cup of coffee had to be paid in 1 Zim dollar bills, there were not enough forests in the world to provide the paper currency.

Finally, the Zimbabwe currency was thrown out all together. And then, after the dust settled, Gideon Gono, chief of the Bank of Zimbabwe, was asked why he did such a thing. He didn't have a choice, he said. The government had bills to pays. Debts. Operating costs. It needed money. He produced it.

Besides, he pointed out that there was no qualitative difference between what he did in Africa and the quantitative easing programs in America, Europe and Japan.

He is right. And the results will probably be similar too.

Argentina and Zimbabwe put together have a GDP equal to approximately 3% of the US. So, on that basis alone the coming hormegeddon will be about 30 times as big. In a credit based money system, everything depends on the good faith and good credit of your counterparty. Today, everyone's number one counterparty is the US government. Its bills, notes, and bonds are the foundation of the world's money system.

A blow-up in the US money will be felt around the globe. It will probably be the biggest public policy disaster of our lifetimes. What exactly will happen, and when it will happen, we will have to wait to find out. But it will be bad, that much is certain. We will hit rock bottom.

Chapter 10
CIVILIZATION AND ITS MISCREANTS

"The veneer of civilization is very thin."

—MARGARET THATCHER

W E HAVE COME TO THE END of our argument. You may rehearse it as follows: Hormegeddon happens. There is no way to avoid it. It is a feature of human life. Like infectious disease. War. And taxes.

It is part of a life cycle. From virtue to corruption, from growth to decay, from birth to death...life goes on. The world is not linear. It is round. You start in one spot, keep going long enough, and you end up back where you began.

We have looked at this phenomenon, or bits of it, in previous chapters. One phase gives way to the next, inevitably and ineluctably. There is no improving on it. And no avoiding it.

Or, is there?

Hormegeddon is a modern phenomenon. It is only possible since the advent of civilization. Without civilization, there are no masses. Without the masses, there are no mass movements, no mass delusions, no mass revolts and no mass epidemics. All mass phenomena function in a similar way to the behavior of disease. Passing from one person to another in large groups, infectious bacteria multiply and mutate. Those killed by antibiotics and natural anti-bodies die off. Those not killed continue adapting and evolving.

Without frequent contact with the enemy, the target grows soft and vulnerable. Over time, the more successful people become at protecting themselves—by avoiding the invasions of deadly bacteria—the more susceptible they become to the next mutant invader. As defenses weaken, the risk/reward ratio—for the potential invader—improves. The more successful he has been at resisting invasion, the more irresistible the target becomes.

This insight puts us in an extremely cynical and pessimistic frame of mind. Progress of any kind in collective human life seems impossible. The more civilized people become, the more they are tempted to barbarism. Imagine, for example, a community so civilized that there are no locks on the liquor cabinets and merchants leave their goods, unguarded on the sidewalks, while policemen take their mid-afternoon naps. Who could resist the urge to larceny?

It is true that cooperation builds trust, and high levels of trust bring benefits to a society, lowering transaction costs while encouraging specialization and trade. But this only increases the rewards to the non-cooperating rule-breaker. As the risk/reward ratio goes higher cheating becomes more attractive.

Imagine a town in the Dark Ages, surrounded by strong stone walls. Such a town could become wealthy by trade and commerce—cooperative activities that yield a profit, which could be accumulated. The stone walls, manned by skilled soldiers, would hold off enemies. The better the defenses, the longer the town's merchants and producers could carry on their trades without being molested. And the more wealth they could accumulate. But this growth would cause the potential attacker to redo his math. The cost of attack—weapons, mercenary soldiers, outfitting, supplying, and so forth—might stay the same. But the reward would increase, promising a better return on investment.

At the same time, the town, having not been attacked in decades, would become complacent. It might ignore its defenses and neglect to pay its own soldiers. 'Why bear the cost of protection when it is clearly unnecessary,' the city fathers would ask of one another? This, of course, would lower the cost of a hostile takeover...and further tempt the potential parasitic invader.

In the modern, developed world, we see this temptation to parasitism in much less threatening forms—free medical care for seniors, disability payments to obese people, government agencies pretending to 'do good' and so forth. We see it in less benign forms also—drones, spying, loss of habeas corpus, foreign wars, etc.

We see the cycle of civilization in the bond market too. The rising trust and cooperation of advancing civilization produces net positive returns...and falling interest yields. This is not just speculation. According to Sidney Homer and Richard's Sylla's "History of Interest Rates," in the 14th and 15th century interest rates averaged from 10% to 25% in the Spanish Netherlands and from 15% to 20% in France. As civilization advanced, interest rates fell—in the United States in the 20th century, to an average of about 3% to 4%.

But this grand progress, lowering interest yields over centuries, was not a straight-line affair. It was cyclical. Each time rates fell "too low," too much money was lent to too many marginal borrowers. The civilized rule is simple: when you borrow money you must repay it. But households over-extended themselves. Lenders overlooked the weakness in their borrowers' balance sheets. Borrowers tended to overstate their financial solidity. Entrepreneurs overreached. Merchants oversold. Defaults increased. And the real rate of return declined as trust gave way to fear (of losing money). High cooperation = high temptation. At the margin, where all the important things in life take place, lax lending standards lead borrowers to take out loans they can't pay back. The desire to gain privileges, status, and income streams overwhelms the respect for the cooperative protocols that brought the positive returns in the first place. New 'values' appear that seem to justify departure from the original rules. Self-reliance, forbearance, and independence, for example, are replaced by fairness, security, and universal health care. However, you will notice a clear distinction between the old values and the new ones. They reflect a change in attitude, from risk taking to risk avoidance, from wealth building to wealth preservation, and from laissez-faire to centralized control. They may also be expressed as different kinds of rights. The former are rights to do something for yourself. The latter are rights to force someone else to do something for you. The former require cooperation. The latter need only fear and then violence.

Without civilized cooperation, hormegeddon wouldn't be possible. Collective enterprises on such a grand scale need the wealth and organization of civilized societies. Such societies become civilized because they eschew the short-term benefits of violence in favor of the longer-term benefits of cooperation. Their success begets failure, trust begets aggressive parasitism, and we see a return to violence. Under the strain of policing and enforcing the new rights, the return on investment falls. Then, the zombie elite becomes ruthless in its efforts to protect its gains.

Government is the key player in this process. As we have seen, government is always and everywhere a reactionary institution, favoring the interests of the (voting, contributing, backstabbing) past and present over the (unborn, unknown, helpless and harmless) future. But in the downdraft of hormegeddon, government becomes a real monster.

But this discussion requires a clear understanding of 'civilization.'

THE FIRST 200,000 YEARS

Understanding that we are painting not with a broad brush, but with a spray rig as big as a fire hose, I propose a simple way to conceive of civilization. Readers will recognize that it is not necessarily what any particular civilization is at any particular moment, but rather what it ought to be all the time.

Forget the ancient Greeks, with their prejudice against peoples who didn't speak their language. Supposedly, that is how we get the word, 'barbarians.' To the ancient Greeks, the non-Greek speakers seemed to speak gibberish—bar, bar, bar, bar, bar, bar. Forget Aristotle, who thought than anyone who lived outside of a city-state's walls must be "a beast or a god." Forget also the religious interpretations, in which people who worshipped other gods were 'savages' or, worse, 'heathen.' And put aside prejudices based on culture, race, aesthetics, technology, politics or other bugaboos.

Instead, let us simply divide the human experience into two big periods. The first was 'mean, brutish and short,' to use the pithy phrasing of Thomas Hobbes. The second, in which we are living today, is basically a civilized world with frequent relapses into barbarity. What's the difference? Just one and only one thing makes sense of it: the role of violence.

The word "civilization" was first introduced by a French historian less than 300 years ago. Since then there has been much argument about what it actually means. We enter the fray gingerly, but sure of ourselves. It only makes sense on our terms, and no others: a civilized community is fundamentally peaceful; a barbaric one is not.

"Three times have Italians saved civilization from barbarians," said Benito Mussolini. The most recent time, was in WWII, when the Bolsheviks menaced all we hold dear. At least, Benito thought so. And he believed it right up to the moment he stopped believing anything. That is the moment in April 1945 when partisans found him in a German armored car, headed north, in costume.

Mussolini—the defender of western civilization—was dressed as a soldier in the Wehrmacht. Too bad for him that one of the partisans recognized him. And too bad for him that his German custodians put up no fight to save him. Instead, they turned him over. And soon he was hanging from a lamp post in a public square, upside down, along with his mistress, Claretta Petacci. Typical of both the enemies of civilization and its defenders, his executioners made no distinction between a real enemy and his paramour. As if poor Claretta was guilty of anything more than being in love with the wrong man at the wrong time. Navy SEALs made the same judgment in their reported assassination of Osama bin Laden. They killed an unarmed woman on the scene; what was her crime? In an even more ambitious plan to safeguard civilization, called the Desert Campaign, troops of General Juan Manuel de Rosas, in 19th century Argentina, took up the energetic slaughter of every native tribe in the pampas. Once they were virtually annihilated, the natives posed no further threat to civilization.

But what kind of civilization is this, where you kill people who get in your way? How was it any different from the barbarism of the pre-civilized era?

What happened in all those many thousands of years before 'civilization' first appeared in Egypt, Mesopotamia, India, and China? We don't really know. We weren't there. But let's take a guess. In the very old days, survival itself was no sure thing. And survival, for humans, depended on cooperation (as well as other things like luck and skill). But never far from cooperation is competition. The male animal in a predator species (with eyes in front, rather than on the side) establishes a relationship of power between himself and other males. This is a competitive relationship that bears on his rank in the group and his access to females or, sometimes, to food. The females have their hierarchy too—connected but not identical to those of the males with whom they mate.

This phenomenon has been observed among primitive tribes as well as among other primate species. Among langur monkeys, for example, a single male will chase off other males and establish himself as master of a whole harem of females. He lives among them and his offspring as a sultan or a king. But what do the other males do? They wait for a chance to replace him.

Howard Bloom, in *The Lucifer Principle,* describes what happens:

> In the jungle nearby roams a gang of postpubertal hooligans who have left home permanently to hang with toughs their own age. Their newly spurting sexual hormones have triggered the growth of horniness, muscle, and a cocky aggression. Periodically, the gang of youthful thugs advances on the territory where the well-established elder sits in the midst of his large family. The hoodlums try to get his attention. They mock and challenge the patriarch. He sometimes sits aloof, refusing to dignify

their taunts with a response. On other occasions, he ambles over to the periphery of the harm, then rears up and puts on a display of outrage that chases the young turns away. But from time to time, the massed delinquents continue their challenge, starting a fight that can be brutal indeed. If they are lucky, the upstarts trounce their dignified superior thoroughly, chasing him away from his comfortable home.

What happens next? They kill his offspring—every one they can catch, anyway—and then mate with the females themselves.

At least there is a pay-off.

Similarly, Jane Goodall observed primates in the Gombe Stream national wildlife preserve in Tanzania over a 45-year period. Many people thought she had evidence that violence against one's own species was limited to humans and was probably a feature of civilization itself. Chimpanzees appeared to be so peaceful, except for the fact that they killed and ate other monkeys. She wrote a book, *In the Shadow of Man*, which greatly flattered the gentleness and human-like qualities of the chimps. Scarcely had the book been released when she found that chimpanzees were more human than she thought. The troop she was watching had become too large to remain on its home territory. There were fights. Then, a group split away from the main body and established itself in a new territory not far away.

At first, all went well. But then, the males of the original group attacked the males in the breakaway group. They killed them all, along with one elderly female, and took over the new territory and its fertile females.

Since Ms. Goodall's observations, wars among chimpanzee and gorilla groups have been extensively documented. Meanwhile, their human cousins look on with noses upturned, and handguns cocked.

Years ago, I read an account by one of the early explorers in Canada. He described a summer visit to a tribe in the far north of the country. For no apparent reason, the men de-camped and began a trip, carrying their supplies and weapons. The explorer accompanied them, without knowing the purpose of the expedition. For six weeks, they continued to the north, crossing hundreds of miles of wilderness. Finally, they arrived at an Eskimo village on the edge of a vast lake. They immediately attacked the village, killing everyone—men, women and children. Then, they returned home.

One of the most thoroughly observed tribes of barbarians are the Yanomami of the Amazon. They were called the "fierce people" by Napoleon Chagnon, who studied them for years. They enjoyed cruelty, he said, especially beating their wives. The spouses were complicit, he added. They wore their scars like wedding rings and complained that their husbands did not care for them if they were not beaten regularly. Needless to say, they are not terribly popular with their neighbors.

The advent of civilization changed human behavior…but not immediately, and not completely. The event from early Roman history known as the 'rape of the Sabine women,' was remarkably similar to a Yanomani raid, but with more cunning and planning involved. According to Livy, the early Roman settlement on the banks of the Tiber River had a shortage of women. And Rome's Sabine neighbors refused to share their women. This led to a ruse. A group of Sabines were invited to a party, a celebration of Neptune Equester. On a signal from a leader, the Romans pulled out their swords, struck the Sabine men and captured the women. Livy says the women were not violated, but simply allowed to take Roman husbands. Nevertheless, the Sabines did not seem to grasp what a great privilege marrying Romans was and the abduction led to a full-scale war. That's when Rome discovered its calling. Within a few short years, Rome was at war with the Caeninenses and then with the Antemnates and then with the Crustumini and then with the Sabines again.

The difference between Rome's wars and America's wars, however, was that Rome's wars paid—at least, at first. They got something out of them. America's do not. This is a point we have already made, but to which we will return one final time before we are finished.

THE COMPETITIVE IMPULSE

Our lifestyles and social arrangements have greatly changed since the Paleolithic period. As far as we know, our minds and bodies have not. We have more or less the same brains with more or less the same instincts and impulses.

We can describe our competitive urge today in the following way: everybody wants to get ahead—by accumulating more money, more power, or more status than his neighbors. Why would he want these things? Most likely, at some primitive level, he believes it will help him to procreate.

For most of our time on Earth we lived so near to the edge of survival, there was little surplus available to support other distractions such as art or government. There is some archeological evidence that old people—those too infirm or disabled to take care of themselves—were taken care of by others. But given the probable realities of economic life, there was likely a sharp limit on charitable activity and the amount of resources allocated to supporting unproductive people.

Until about 10,000 years ago, there were no musical instruments, no writing of any sort, and no sophisticated tools. There were no schools. No jobs. No careers. No money. No sporting events.

How then did men compete? How did they show each other who was boss? How did they keep score? Who got the girl? Again, we don't know, but until fairly recently, only one possibility stands out—by violence. Primitive men competed by hunting…and fighting. A man could only gain an advantage by killing something, just like all other predators in the animal kingdom. All takeovers were hostile. And the only portable, measurable wealth was women. Among the

Yanomami, for example, the best killers have the most wives…and the most children. The Yanomami word for marriage, by the way, means 'dragging something away.'

Which makes sense. In some sense, life's sole purpose is perpetuation. Men fought and died for the right to reproduce. The race itself may have only survived thanks to a persistent selection preference for fit, aggressive males. Who knows? Humans are infinitely complex and adaptable. But the status of the able killer has rarely been challenged. Even in the time of the Roman Empire, a successful general came back to Rome and was awarded a "triumph." He paraded through the streets, while admiring crowds cheered, his enemy chief in chains behind him, waiting to be strangled. But the very highest honor a Roman general could receive was only awarded twice in all of Roman history. It is an award you can only get by killing an opposing general in personal combat.

Pre-history is *terra incognita*. We don't know what really happened. But don't bother to tell us that primitive peoples were 'more civilized than Wall Street's predatory bankers, or that they respected nature and the environment.' Rousseau's idea of the 'noble savage' was a fantasy. Margaret Mead described the governing protocol among pre-civilized tribes as follows: A person of your own tribe is a "full human being," someone you will cooperate with. Someone from another tribe is a subhuman, someone you should try to kill.

Over such a long period of pre-history, with so many different peoples in so many different locations, with little communication between them, we can imagine an almost infinite variety of customs and organizational patterns. But it is very hard to imagine any in which violence was not a central part of life. These were hunter/gatherers. Gathering took energy. The net return on energy invested was low. Humans needed a more concentrated source of calories to support their large brains. They had to kill. And for many, if not most, killing was not just a matter of survival, but the only way for social advancement.

With some important exceptions, there were probably few opportunities to get ahead in the pre-historic and ancient world, except by violence. You had to take someone else's property. His food. His land. His women. His life. Wealth was not created, it was discovered...or taken from someone else. That is, of course, the plot for almost all the 'history' we know of up until fairly modern times. Skirmishes, raids, ambushes, border wars—fighting was not exceptional, it was common. Individually and collectively. As soon as a group was powerful or desperate enough, it pushed into the territory of another group, taking whatever it could.

A truly primitive man could not hope to create much wealth. What could he invent? There was so little old technology in use there was almost no room for new technology. No wheels. No power. No electronics or mechanics. No metalworking. No stonemasonry. No architecture. What about success in business or investment? Forget it; capitalism hadn't evolved yet. Art? Music? A higher SAT score? More money in the bank?

Today, we have many different ways to gain power, status and wealth. You can invent a killer app! Or you set up a hedge fund. Or, you write a best-selling novel. You can compete by trying to achieve something important.

Or, you can run for Congress. That is not merely a cheap joke. Politics is more closely akin to the violent competition of the Paleolithic era than to the cooperation of modern capitalism. Running for public office, you are competing to replace someone else's finger on the gun with your own; hopefully crushing your opponent so thoroughly that you *kill* his political career. This is not a win-win situation and every voter knows it. As a member of Congress you will not add to the world's wealth. All you can do is move it, from one person to another. Paul can only win if Peter loses.

Between the carrot of cooperation and the stick of force, government goes for the stick. Every law, every edict, every regulation and pettifogging directive comes with penalties attached. Even most "incentives" government offer are really not incentives at all; they are offers *not* to punish. A tax credit, for example, spares some of your money from the taxman, if you agree to do as the government suggests.

Today, we channel our competitive urges into many different activities. Some people drive expensive cars. Some build mega-mansions. We have team sports—including American football, where one team acts as though it were trying to kill the other. But it is in business, careers and investment that people find competition most rewarding. Traders on Wall Street talk about 'ripping the faces off' their rivals. Entrepreneurs read Sun Tzu and Clausewitz for hints on how to win their next campaign! And now, thanks to modern capitalism, you can get wealthy without taking anything away from others. Wealth is no longer a zero-sum game. The supply of hunting land and women may be limited, but the amount of modern wealth a person can create today is, as far as we know, almost infinite. The world's wealth can be increased by hard work, saving, innovation and investment. People who succeed at capitalism gain wealth, and in America, they gain status. They make themselves richer…and other people too. Arguably, for men, wealth makes women available, too.

SLAVERY

"Behind every great fortune is a crime," said Balzac. Before the age of capitalism that was largely true. So, what lay behind the fortune with which Anthony van Sallee used to buy up much of Long Island, New York, in the 17th century: larceny, murder or slavery? All of the above. This ancestor to some of America's richest families—including the Vanderbilts and the Whitneys—was, in the language of Baltimore's street life, "one mean motherf*****."

What did he do? Where was he from? The name gives us a clue…

The 'van' part is Dutch. Like most of New York's early settlers, he carried a 'van' meaning 'of' or 'from' to tell us that he was from

Sallee. But where is that? Ah. Check the map. You will find no Sallee anywhere near Amsterdam or Liege. In fact, it is not to be found anywhere in Europe. Instead, it is a city in North Africa. On what was known as the Barbary Coast, the center of the white slave trade.

What follows is a discussion of involuntary servitude, capitalism and how to explain it to a hundred or so drunken Irishmen crammed into the back of an Irish bar. It comes from a trip to Kilkenny, Ireland, in November 2013, where I attended an unusual conference on economics. Described as "Davos without the hookers," it was not much like Davos in any way.

First, Kilkenny has little in common with Davos. The former is a tiny, quaint medieval Irish town. The latter is a chic resort in the Swiss Alps.

Second, the focus of the discussion was not on how to improve the world, but on how to give the limping Irish economy a boost.

Third, the local conference organizer—David McWilliams—did not invite Janet Yellen or Paul Krugman. Instead, he invited me, which I took for a sign of desperation. Or else, there is something wrong with him. As a precaution, I avoided the tap water.

Luckily, there is a pub on every corner in Kilkenny and two or three just down the street. A man in need of another pint has only to haul himself a few steps in any direction. But even a few steps was too much for a couple of the girls we ran into on Saturday night. They were dressed in the latest fashion for fat girls—tight white dresses cut off just below the crotch—and awkwardly balanced on high platform shoes ('arse-lifters' in the vernacular). It is hard enough to walk on stilts when you are sober. After three hours in Cleere's tavern, it is practically impossible. Coming out onto the street, they had scarcely gone three steps before they began listing dangerously. One caught a light-post and steadied herself. The other, no public utility within reach, sank to the street. There she lay, on the cobblestones, as we stepped over her.

We had just come from a discussion with economists. Every economist knows that people always act in their own rational self-interest. Since we couldn't figure out any way a girl could benefit from laying in the middle of the rainy street, in a party dress hiked up to the very edge of decency, we had to conclude that the girl could not exist. That is what happens when you talk economics; you lose touch with reality.

Inside Cleere's the discussion had been on the nature of capitalism. The question we were meant to address was: how could it be kept on the 'straight and narrow?' But the crowd had already been drinking for hours before we began. We had raised a pint too, leaning on the bar and talking with other economists. It was hopeless from the beginning. No two people had the same idea about what capitalism actually was. And our opponent was well prepared with intoxicating gas.

"These dreamers...these idealists...imagine a perfect world of cooperation, invention, and freedom," he began, pointing in our direction. "But it doesn't work that way. In practice, they get a world where money talks...and it tells us all what to do. They preached deregulation...and brought about the worse financial crisis since the Great Depression. They're always complaining about the government, but if it were not for the government this crisis would have turned into another Great Depression. Without the government, we'd all be completely unprotected against these greedy, rapacious rich people. Besides, they would be nothing without the government. The government provides the infrastructure. It provides a system of laws and justice that makes it possible for them to earn their fortunes. Government is the source of major innovations too. It wasn't the free market, for example, that developed the Internet; it was the government. Private companies were offered the opportunity to develop it themselves. They refused. Because they couldn't figure out how to make a profit on it.

"So I say, stop bellyaching about the government...stop pretending that the free market can solve all our problems...and sit down and figure out how we can get these banksters off our backs…and make this mixed system, of capitalism with some measure of state control, work better."

This opening salvo drew a warm applause. He had scored a direct hit a-midship. He had the audience on his side. We hadn't said a word and we were already taking on water.

We charged our guns, making notes on the back of an envelope. We prepared to fire back. But our opponent had also laid a thick screen of smoke over the whole area. So many misconceptions, so many false targets…so little time.

He imagined that 'capitalism' has something to do with the system of crony banks, managed economies, and zombie regulators…

…that these regulators protect average people…rather than the industries they regulate…

…that de-regulation is what caused the crisis of '08…

…that you can't have law without having government. (what legislature wrote the 10 Commandments, for Pete's sake?)

…that the government is the source of all substantial innovation. (Good God, he thinks Al Gore invented the Internet!)

We tacked hard to the right. We aimed our cannon. There was no point in asking for quarter or seeking safe harbor somewhere in the middle. This was going to be a blast fest. Better to aim high and hit hard.

"Look, let's start in the beginning. There are only two ways to get what you want in this life. You take it by force and violence. Or you get it peacefully by making, trading, and cooperating with others.

"That's true of material wealth. It's true of stuff. It's true of power and status. And it's as true of sex. You can get it by negotiation…or you can get it by brute force.

"So, let's try to agree on the basics. Wouldn't you all agree that we're better off generally if we stick with consensual, peaceful, cooperative ways to get what we want in life?"

The audience was silent.

"Okay...well, you're all hopeless. Girls, don't let a stranger walk you home in this town!

"Seriously, I'm not saying that there aren't plenty of cads and gigolos in what we call the 'free market.' But a cad is not the same as a rapist. And a private company is not like the government, which always has a gun to your head.

"That is, of course, why people like government so much. No persuasion necessary. No seduction involved. You don't have to buy dinner and a few drinks.

"Plus, it's the oldest and surest way to get what you want. Humans have been around for about 200,000 years. And for the first 190,000 years, not to mention the millions of years that came before, force was about the only game in town. The supply of animals—and more importantly, women—was limited. It was a zero sum game. If you wanted to get ahead, you had to be prepared to take something away from someone else. Otherwise, it was likely that someone would take something away from you.

"And look at it from the woman's point of view. You were going to live to be 40 years old if you were lucky. You were going to have a few children, of whom few would live to adulthood. Who would you want to be the father of those children, someone who was capable of defending you and your children, or someone who would be killed or pushed aside?

"Note also, that when a new man took over...he would likely kill any infant children you had so that you would be ready to bear his child as soon as possible.

"We are programmed by millions of years of evolution to use force and violence to get what we want. But it's not the only way.

"Today, people compete for wealth, status and power. And they don't mind using violence to get it."

We interrupt the debate scene at Cleere's pub to wander down to the coast, to the little tourist town of Baltimore, Ireland. It is a tiny and mostly forgotten relic today, but what a story it has to tell; one of the most remarkable stories in Christendom. For it was the only town in Britain, Scotland or Ireland that was ever attacked by Moors. Why? They wanted more.

Man did not transform himself from a barbarian to a civilized person overnight. Nor did he leave his most primitive instincts behind when he moved to the city. There were transitional issues. And the new wealth, new institutions, new organizations and new technologies made it possible for him to be barbaric on a larger scale.

Slavery, as we imagine it, was probably unusual before 10,000 BC. A hunter/gatherer tribe had no use for another mouth to feed. And it was too easy for the slave to slip away. In that sense, at least, pre-historic man had a hint of nobility about him. But the advent of 'civilization' turned slavery into a paying proposition. Slaves could work the meanest jobs in antiquity—tilling fields, digging irrigation systems, building pyramids and rowing boats. Before the development of steam engines (and later internal combustion engines) slaves, horses and oxen provided the power. They could labor on roads and houses. They could build fortifications, too, protecting their masters from becoming slaves themselves.

Mass slavery was a transitional phenomenon. It arose with civilization. It disappeared with mechanization. It flourished in a civilized, market-based economy, but it depended on the use of pre-civilized violence. It required a society with domesticated animals and farming, sedentary communities, and government—but the society couldn't be so civilized that it eschewed involuntary servitude.

In supposedly civilized communities, slavery was not only financially rewarding, it was socially popular. Owning slaves was not only acceptable, it was a mark of superior status. The more slaves, the higher the rank of the owner. Aristotle took it for a fact of life: "For ruling and being ruled are not only necessary, they are also beneficial, and some things are distinguished right from birth, some suited to rule and others to being ruled". Slaveholding was so much a part of life that even Christ, who preached 'Love Thy Neighbor,' didn't bother to condemn it. And the US Constitution, which was a blueprint for the most civilized political system yet designed, nevertheless tolerated slavery.

But slavery was an appalling shock to poor Joane Broadbrook. She awoke early on the morning of June 20, 1631, to discover her roof was on fire and troops of the Turkish Ottoman Empire were breaking down her door. 'Heavy with child,' she must have thought it was a nightmare. But it was a nightmare that wouldn't stop, even if she pinched herself. A notorious Barbary Coast pirate named Morat Rais had organized a slaving expedition, with a crew of desperados, backed by 230 regular Turkish troops and the Janissaries, in their bright red tunics and curved yatagan sabres.

Mr. Rais was Dutch, aka Jan Jensen. He had been a slave too. But in the open meritocracy of the Barbary Coast slave trade, he had risen through the ranks to become an admiral of the fleet. Now, he made Sallee, on the Moroccan coast, his base.

Who could know that by taking Jan Jensen a slave you would be laying the foundation for one of America's most notable families? One notable member of which was none other than Richard Whitney. He served ten years on the Board of Governors for the New York Stock Exchange, seven years as Treasurer of the New York Yacht Club, and three years as an inmate at Sing Sing Correctional Facility.

Back in 1631, on that day in June, Mr. Rais and his band of adventurers were in the middle of what could be described as an entrepreneurial venture. The project had been financed, equipped and staffed by trained professionals, months before. Mr. Rais's ship had left port in Algiers to a tumultuous send-off, much like cutting the ribbon on a new factory. The raw material—107 residents of the town of Baltimore on the South coast of Ireland—had been taken in. They were now being processed: first by driving them into the hold of their vessels, then by shipping them back to the retail market in Algiers, and finally by putting them up for sale.

The slave market in Algiers was a 'free market,' in some respects. Much like an auction of used farm equipment, prospective buyers were allowed careful inspection. The men were poked and prodded, potential buyers wanted to see how they might hold up. And they were asked questions: What had they done? What skills did they have? How hard had they worked? The unlucky ones had the calluses and muscles of field hands. They were sent to the galleys and to the quarries, where they were usually worked to death after a few years, although we know there were many exceptions.

The lucky ones had marketable skills—such as gunsmithing—and were spared the oars and the sledges. Instead, they were brought into a complex, sophisticated, and highly nuanced system of slavery, which was also curiously 'free' in its own way.

Most of the captives from Baltimore were women and children. It was the women that got the closer inspection. Bidders were allowed to feel for themselves the firmness of a woman's breasts and determine whether or not she was still a virgin. Each buyer formed in his own mind the right value of the merchandise and then, in an outcry auction, a price was established. We don't know if the price thus established was 'perfect' in the sense that today's economists use the term. But it was the best they could do under the circumstances.

In the early 17th century, business was good, and it was protected and regulated by the government. The white slavers roamed as far as Iceland bringing back the valuable fair-skinned women. And business was often mixed with perverse pleasure. On one particular venture to Iceland in 1627, Morat Rais and his troops went wild, murdering, mutilating and raping hundreds of innocent islanders—men, women and children. They were there on business. But they didn't seem interested in maximizing profits. Half the population was wasted before it was even loaded up for shipping. What kind of business was this?

Documents from the period show the going rate for women was between $86 and $357. An extraordinarily beautiful woman, however, could bring more. Men, generally, sold for less.

Pirates like Morat Rais were bringing hundreds of new slaves to the market. Demand had a hard time keeping up. The Sultan already had about 1,000 wives and concubines in his Topkapi harem. What could he do with another one?

Also, you have to adjust these prices to the modern world. At the time, a clergyman might work all year for $100. So, we can imagine that a pretty young woman, in today's terms, would have fetched about as much as a cheap house or an expensive car.

Back in the bar...

"I can't believe you compared government employees to rapists?" One of the attendees at the Kilkenny economics hoedown got on our case. "That's ridiculous. They're there to protect people. What about policemen? Firemen? Not to mention, the people who saved the economy from another depression?"

"Well...stick with us a minute," we enjoined. "We're just trying to understand the real nature of government regulation. Is it something to which you can 'just say NO!'? Or is it something where you're gonna get...(I hesitated a moment. The sentence I was about to complete required the f-word. The audience would understand it. But I'm not an f-word kind of guy.)...where you're gonna get screwed, whether you like it or not?"

The Irish women bought on the slave market were usually taken into harems, either as concubines or servants. There, they were protected by guards, eunuchs, regulators and ultimately, by the Ottoman Turk Army. That is, they were regulated and protected by the government. But what kind of protection was it? Could they just say NO?

Concubines were not even asked. They had been bought for the pleasure of their owners. As far as we know from first hand accounts, they didn't have to be forced to submit. They went along with the program, like travelers in a TSA line or taxpayers enduring an audit. When the feds tell you bend over, your choices aren't Yes or NO, they are "How far" and "How long." That is very different from a market economy, where you might be compelled by necessity or by desire, but not by naked force.

Surrounded by silks and sunshine of Algiers, the Baltimore women might have looked on the bright side. Rather than a lifetime of sex-slavery (in which they may never be called to active duty), they might have thought they got a reprieve from the prison of hard work and the relentless cold, dark and damp of Ireland.

Besides, getting to share the pasha's bed was an honor. If it brought children, the children might inherit his money and his position; their mother might become ruler of the harem itself. Many European women made what must have been happy marriages in the Islamic system. Many became rich and powerful themselves. Many felt their new masters treated them better than their husbands back home. And when, 14 years later, a warship from Britain arrived in Algiers and negotiated the Baltimore slaves' release, only two women—out of an original 34—wanted to go back.

For men, if you weren't sold off into hard labor, slavery in North Africa could be similarly supple. Slaves could practice their own religions. They spoke their own languages. They were free to operate their own businesses. They could make money. They could learn skills and fill important roles in almost all industries. Some became slavers themselves—like Jan Jensen, who became Morat Rais, whose son Anthony, used the family name Van Salee and moved to New York. With the profits of the white slave trade he was able to buy a substantial part of what is today Brooklyn.

Some slaves became traders and financiers, buying and selling goods from all over the Mediterranean. At least one amassed a fortune, while still a slave. Some got away, like Miguel de Cervantes and Captain John Smith, of the Virginia colony. Others didn't want to get away.

Algiers was an advanced economy with a standard of living—for people who weren't slaves and even for many who were—considerably higher than in London or Paris. Part of the reason for its prosperity was probably the freedom it allowed its slaves.

Slavery came with many contradictions. In North Africa as well as North America it prospered in what were otherwise successful market economies. And in both places, it was reinforced, regulated and subsidized by the government. Poor whites in Alabama paid (modest) taxes to help support the government, whose main challenge was to control their unpaid competitors in the slave-based industries. Few poor whites probably realized it, but they were victims of involuntary servitude too—forced to subsidize the slaveholders, by paying some of the costs of policing their involuntary labor. Likewise, on the Barbary Coast a vast and confusing web of levies, fees, commissions and taxes were used to maintain the garrisons that kept slaves from escaping.

Do we have to spell it out? In every industry, in every epoch, the regulators and the regulated—the parasite and the host—share the same goal: to connive against the public interest, using the police power of government for their own benefit. Good? Bad? Who can say? But we can tell whether it is civilized or barbaric. Here's the simple test: can you 'just say no' to it?

Government was complicit in the slave trade at every level. How slaves were to be marketed, employed, and disposed of was typically codified by the legislature and enforced by the police. Runaways were captured at taxpayer expense. Punishments were established by government employees and often administered by them. Most important, government bore much of the cost of policing slavery.

But today, slavery has been abolished in most of the world. We still have wage slaves, and tax slaves, but chattel slavery has largely disappeared. Not because Abraham Lincoln and the abolitionists of the mid-19th century thought it was a bad idea. It disappeared because—even with the subsidies of the government—the rate of return fell to the point where it was no longer profitable. This is the big difference between civilization and barbarism. It is the one thing that distinguishes the two: in barbaric communities, violence pays... in civilized ones, it rarely does.

In Maryland, for example, slavery was fast disappearing before the US War Between the States. Already, the cost of maintaining and policing slavery was rising steeply while the returns from slave output declined. Slaves in Maryland found it fairly easy to run off—like Frederick Douglass, who took a train to Wilmington, Delaware. Slaves were often freed, simply because it was cheaper to hire them than to support them. This trend was visible throughout most of the world, from which—with the big exception of the United States—slavery disappeared without a fight. Today it is hard to imagine slavery functioning anywhere, except in the most backward economies.

Progress has been made. It is not an eternal cycle of cooperation, followed by violence, after all. Over time, cooperation increases.

Why is that? It is because cooperation pays. By contrast, violence pays badly. You might be able to whip a group of field hands to keep them on the job, but their output would be minimal. Only at the most rote tasks is slave labor a practical alternative. In modern industries, it is not competitive. Imagine slaves elaborating a marketing strategy. Imagine slaves driving trucks or even greeting customers at WalMart. Imagine slaves in the accounting department. Imagine slaves in Hollywood, rewriting scripts. Imagine them in the pharmaceutical industry, conducting double-blind tests. Imagine them with chainsaws clearing power lines. Compared to free workers, with stock options and healthcare plans, equipped with the latest machinery and trained to use it, slaves can't compete.

Several inconclusive experiments have been conducted on the issue. As we have seen, Germany ran much of its industry on slave labor during WWII. The Soviet Union operated a quasi-slave economy for decades. The Japanese used the forced labor of their prisoners of war on various projects. In the modern world, slave labor does not seem to be productive, except in these emergency or ideologically driven contexts; and even then "productive" is a relative term. Napoleon tried to re-introduce slavery to French possessions in order to use forced labor on sugar plantations. This effort failed so miserably that France not only abandoned the whole project, it sold Louisiana to the United States.

THE POSSIBLE DISAPPEARANCE OF GOVERNMENT

This makes us wonder about government itself. Is it transitional too? Will it disappear, like slavery, when the rate of return goes starkly negative?

The comparison between slavery and government is hard to miss. In both cases, you can't 'just say no,' to your masters. Fundamentally, government, like slavery, is based on violence. Even in historic times, whole peoples were enslaved, typically by an invading government. That of course is the familiar Old Testament story of the Jews. They were conquered and enslaved at least twice—once in Egypt for 400 years and again in Babylon after Judah was conquered in 586 BC.

It is a story that played out almost everywhere, over and over. The Incas conquered many different tribes in the South American highlands. Each tribe then became a vassal, its people required to perform extended periods of labor for the conqueror. And in the very recent example of the German invasions of both Eastern and Western Europe in the '40s, the subject populations were again required to do forced labor for the German "war machine." The 'raffles' in France were much less murderous than the mass deportations from Poland and the Soviet Union, but the idea was the same. Slave labor was a component part of the new system of government. And today, the most enlightened nations often require a period of military servitude from their young men.

Tax slavery seems more benign. Much like the silken cords of the harem, the chains can be so light that the slaves would prefer to leave them on. Indeed, many readers may believe, along with Oliver Wendell Holmes, that "taxes are what we pay for civilized society." But that only makes us wonder about Holmes' other opinions.

Curiously, tax rates have risen over the last century. When Oliver Wendell Holmes was on the bench, the top income tax rate was around 2.5%. Then, in 1895, income taxes were declared unconstitutional. It wasn't until 1913, and the passage of the 16th amendment, that federal income taxes made a comeback. Then, the top rate was 7%, with the average rate near 2%. The top rate applied only to incomes of $500,000 or more—roughly equivalent to a billion dollars today.

Now, in 2013, the top rate is 39.6%, with a number of surcharges and special calculations, along with much higher state and local taxes too. In California, all taxes included, a high-income couple will pay nearly 60% of their annual earnings in taxes. If taxes were the price of civilization, either Americans are getting a lot more civilization or a lot less for their money.

Why the big growth in taxes? The explanation is simple. Government is fundamentally a vestige of barbarism; it is an armed parasite. As the economy has grown richer, the leech has swollen.

But there's more to the story. The nature of government has changed, too. With the major exception of the throwback regimes of the 20th century—Maoist China, the Soviet Union, and Hitlerian Germany—governments have come to resemble large, coercive insurance schemes with very lax financial standards. European governments now tax their citizens only to return most of the money to them in the form of various social welfare programs. US tax receipts, including social security and mandatory add-ons, are largely recycled back to the voters too. And the percentage of total government spending, represented by these non-discretionary 'transfer' payments, is increasing.

Not surprisingly, as more of their own and other peoples' money is given back to them, the more the voters support a high tax regime. But there is an obvious limitation: you can't say no. And if you can't say no, the program will suffer the typical problems of any primitive, violence-based project. That is, it will be a losing proposition, headed to hormegeddon.

Taxes are not the same as voluntary contributions or willing, civilized and consensual payments for services rendered. They are, like all of government's activities, carried out at the point of a gun. This tends to greatly reduce the rate of return, partly because—as with all forms of slavery—there are the costs of policing and the costs of the 'complexity' of the system itself. Tax returns can involve hundreds of pages of documents. The cost of this has been mentioned earlier. More important, the interests of the 'customer' are never quite foremost in the service provider's mind. Government services are designed and operated by zombies who look out for themselves. Being human, over time they find more and more ways to transfer the transfer payments to themselves.

Competitive private companies can always operate more efficiently and effectively than the government. Not because they are smarter or more virtuous. They simply have the proper incentives: the profit motive on the upside and the risk of bankruptcy and job loss on the down side. In the aggregate, the private providers—operating in the win-win world of modern, civilized business—will be able to return far more of the taxpayers' money to them in insurance, retirement and healthcare benefits. The only thing they can't do is the uncivilized part—that is, they can't take money by force from its rightful owners.

BEYOND GOOD AND EVIL

Readers will be quick to make the leap: civilization is good, barbarism is evil. But there is no reason to think so. Civilization—a culture of cooperation rather than violence—was an adaptation that took place over millennia. It is not because barbarism is evil that people turned away from it. On the contrary, it is because it is unprofitable.

Recalling Mancur Olson's dictum again, "virtue is what used to pay." The virtue of cooperation is that it pays. As a consequence, we think it is good. And as far as we know, cooperation is set to become even more virtuous, as it appears to pay off better and better.

People did not suddenly awake to a civilized dawn. Instead, they gradually felt their way through the periods of relative darkness, including a total eclipse from time to time. So don't bother to tell us that the Germans were supposed to be civilized…yet they exterminated millions at Auschwitz…or that Americans are sending drones to kill people they've never met and thus the notion of 'civilization' is a lie.[11] Even the most civilized peoples do uncivilized things. And most peoples, no matter how civilized they have become, still maintain some archaic, barbaric habits and institutions.

As civilization became more complex, we refined our rules for cooperation. You can see this progress on exhibit in the Bible. The Old Testament is full of war, and many rules for how people are to get along with one another. In the New Testament, Jesus proposes only one rule, which leaves little place for making war: do unto others as you would have them do unto you.

This—and the other innovations that came along with civilization—gave the civilized man a big advantage. Using the tools of civilization—cooperation, consent, money, markets, trade, commerce—he could advance technically and materially. Then, he was in a position to practically exterminate his more backward competitors!

Civilization gives the civilized man not just a sense of his own superiority, but also the tools to kill on a larger scale. That is the history of the conquest of Africa, Australia and the Americas. As we pointed out earlier, it also was a large part of Hitler's justification for invading

---

[11] No matter how much a Black Friday shopping trip may indicate otherwise…

Eastern Europe. "Hey," he said, or words to that effect, "you Americans invaded Kansas!" Both invasions—of the Great Plains by white settlers and of the Eurasian steppes by the Nazis—were successful because both invaders enjoyed an edge in civilized arts—including the art of doing something that was inherently very uncivilized, making war.

And so, the world still turns. As soon as people draw deeply from the well of civilization's many benefits they are ready to act like barbarians again. You might even say that one of the chief benefits of civilization is that it allows you to act like a beast and get away with it. This is completely in line with our earlier discovery: the more people cooperate, the more they are tempted to break the rules. Killing people is clearly breaking the rules of civilization. But how can you resist when you have a machine gun and your enemy has a bow and arrow?

In the event, civilized man all-too-often found he could resist everything but temptation. And as it happened, he was tempted to kill, to steal, and to enslave. He gave up slavery when it no longer paid. But he has not yet given up killing people, or using the force of government to seize power, wealth and status from his fellow civilized man.

Slavery looked eternal at the time of Christ. It wasn't. Two thousand years later, it was gone. Government now appears to be a permanent feature of life too. Maybe it is. Maybe it isn't. But if it turns out that government is merely a transitional nuisance rather than a permanent one, hormegeddon may disappear too. Without the police power of the state, hormegeddon is much less of a sure thing. If we are right—that a more sophisticated economy depends more and more on cooperation rather than force—it may become clearer that the violence of the state is not a necessary evil, but an unnecessary one.

But what about civilization? Could it be? Is civilization itself subject to our hormegeddon rule: a little of it is great; too much is disastrous? Civilized commerce increases wealth. As the benefits of wealth increase, there are fewer people whose livelihoods are not linked to it and fewer left to resist it. The pay-off appears benign and positive, but so did the payoff from all hormegeddic debacles in their early stages.

As civilization increases, the stakes rise with it. The 'human load' on planetary resources increases, possibly making the whole human enterprise more fragile and more vulnerable. Complexity increases. Armed by civilization, man is already capable of destroying himself. He has provided a fat target for infectious microbial adversaries and then culled out the weakest of them with his civilized medicines. His riches allow him to waste time and money on a scale that pre-civilized man would have thought fantastic, all while keeping want and adversity at bay...at least until the wall gives way. Will it be a new bug? A computer virus? A war? Global warming? Global *cooling*? Bankruptcy? Misallocation of resources and financial breakdown? Or just a giant space rock that renders central planning not just useless, but laughably pointless?

We'll have to wait to find out.

THIS IS NOT THE END...

Dear Hormegeddon Reader,

Hi, my name's Will Bonner. I hope you enjoyed my father's book and I hope it's given you new insights into how the world truly operates.

I hope most of all, you can use the ideas you've just read to improve your life and the life of your loved ones.

But please, don't stop here...

You see, although this is the end of Hormegeddon, my dad writes and publishes a brand new article five days a week in his online newsletter, *Diary of a Rogue Economist.*

Diary of a Rogue Economist is 100% FREE.

In fact, it's "better than free" because when you subscribe you'll also get access to 3 valuable special reports my dad has written that go beyond ideas within this book.

There is no catch and no obligation. When I say "free," I mean it.

All I ask is you don't share the below link with anyone else. It's for Hormegeddon readers only.

Fair?

Then subscribe to *Diary of a Rogue Economist* and claim your 3 free special reports here...

www.BonnerAndPartners.com/freegift

Sincerely,

Will Bonner,
Publisher, Bonner & Partners

CPSIA information can be obtained
at www.ICGtesting.com
Printed in the USA
FFOW03n0659290518
46678521-49111FF